DEFENDING THE AMERICAN WAY OF LIFE

OTHER TITLES IN THIS SERIES

New York Sports: Glamour and Grit in the Empire City

LA Sports: Play, Games, and Community in the City of Angels

Making March Madness: The Early Years of the NCAA, NIT, and College Basketball Championships, 1922–1951

San Francisco Bay Area Sports: Golden Gate Athletics, Recreation, and Community

Separate Games: African American Sport behind the Walls of Segregation

Baltimore Sports: Stories from Charm City

Philly Sports: Teams, Games, and Athletes from Rocky's Town

DC Sports: The Nation's Capital at Play

Frank Merriwell and the Fiction of All-American Boyhood

Democratic Sports: Men's and Women's College Athletics

Sport and the Law: Historical and Cultural Intersections

Beyond C. L. R. James: Shifting Boundaries of Race and Ethnicity in Sports

A Spectacular Leap: Black Women Athletes in Twentieth-Century America

Hoop Crazy: The Lives of Clair Bee and Chip Hilton

DEFENDING THE AMERICAN WAY OF LIFE

SPORT, CULTURE, AND THE COLD WAR

Edited by Toby C. Rider and Kevin B. Witherspoon

THE UNIVERSITY OF ARKANSAS PRESS

FAYETTEVILLE | 2018

ISBN: 978-1-68226-077-7 (cloth)
ISBN: 978-1-68226-076-0 (paper)
eISBN: 978-1-61075-652-5

22 21 20 19 18 5 4 3 2 1

Designer: April Leidig

Library of Congress Cataloging-in-Publication Data
Names: Rider, Toby C., editor. | Witherspoon, Kevin B., editor.
Title: Defending the American way of life : sport, culture, and the Cold War/ edited by Toby C. Rider and Kevin B. Witherspoon.
Description: Fayetteville : University of Arkansas Press, 2018. | Series: Sport, culture, and society | Includes bibliographical references and index.
Identifiers: LCCN 2018010578| ISBN 9781682260777 (cloth : alk. paper) | ISBN 9781682260760 (pbk. : alk. paper) | ISBN 9781610756525 (eISBN)
Subjects: LCSH: Nationalism and sports—United States—History—20th century. | Sports—Social aspects—United States—History—20th century. | Sports—Political aspects—United States—History—20th century. | Sports—United States—History—20th century. | Olympics—Political aspects—United States—History—20th century.
Classification: LCC GV706.34 .D43 2018 | DDC 306.4/83—dc23
LC record available at https://lccn.loc.gov/2018010578

Contents

Series Editor's Preface

Sport is an extraordinarily important phenomenon that pervades the lives of many people and has an enormous impact on society in many ways. At its most fundamental level, sport has the power to bring people great joy and satisfy their competitive urges while allowing them to form bonds and a sense of community with others from diverse backgrounds and interests and various walks of life. Sport also makes clear, especially at the highest levels of competition, the lengths to which people will go to achieve victory. It is also closely connected to business, education, politics, economics, religion, law, family, and other societal institutions. Moreover, sport is partly about identity development and how individuals and groups, irrespective of race, gender, ethnicity or socioeconomic class, have sought to elevate their status and realize material success and social mobility.

The Sport, Culture, and Society series seeks to promote a greater understanding of these many other issues. Recognizing the powerful influence of sport and its ability to change people's lives in significant and important ways, the series focuses on topics ranging from urbanization and community development to biographies and intercollegiate athletics. It includes monographs and anthologies that are characterized by excellent scholarship, are accessible to a wide audience, and are interesting and thoughtful in design and interpretations. The authors and editors represent a variety of disciplinary areas and use different methodological approaches. The series also includes works by individuals at various stages of their careers, both scholars of outstanding talent just beginning to make their mark on the field and more experienced scholars.

Defending the American Way of Life: Sport, Culture, and the Cold War furnishes much-needed insights into the role of sport and how it was used during one of the most tumultuous periods in history. As the editors Toby C. Rider and Kevin B. Witherspoon make clear, recently the number of scholarly works on various aspects of Cold War sport have increased. This volume is the latest within that genre. Themselves experts on the topic, Rider and Witherspoon have assembled an excellent cast of writers who add immeasurably to our understanding of sport during the Cold War period through essays ranging on topics from Mal Whitfield and sport and foreign policy during the 1960s to sex testing and Cold War sport and Gerald Ford and the President's Commission on Olympic Sport. An overriding theme of the volume is the firm belief in the United States in the power of sport to break down barriers and bring diverse people together through friendly athletic competition, irrespective of differing political ideologies and cultural beliefs. This was true even though many in the United States found communist ideology abhorrent and were deeply troubled by the sports programs it fostered and clung to so tenaciously.

David K. Wiggins

Acknowledgments

The study of Cold War sport in American society has come a long way in the past decade. When the two of us first met at the 2009 conference for the North American Society for Sport History, we were some of the few academic scholars presenting on the topic. Naturally enough, we were paired together in the same session and we each greatly appreciated the fact we had come across somebody else doing very similar work. We returned to the same conference every year and were increasingly struck by the steady rise in Cold War–themed papers presented at each gathering, all of it fascinating and exciting. Before long, we decided that it was time to give some of this new research a mutual home. The end result is *Defending the American Way of Life*. We hope readers enjoy studying these essays as much we did editing them.

First things first: we would like to thank all of the stellar authors that contributed to this collection. Each one has been gracious, kind, and patient. Moreover, a book like this would be impossible to produce without the archivists who lent each writer valuable guidance and assisted in locating various photographs and artwork. We also owe a debt of gratitude to David Wiggins and the wonderful staff at the University of Arkansas Press. They have been incredibly supportive and enthusiastic about the project ever since we pitched to them. Kevin adds a special thanks to the Lander University Foundation, which provided funding for several research trips associated with his work. Finally, we would like to express our gratitude to our families, the vessels that keep us afloat. Thank you to Shannon, Gus, Milly, and Sam and to Jacky, Lexi, and Andrew.

DEFENDING THE AMERICAN WAY OF LIFE

INTRODUCTION

Sport and American Cold War Culture

BY TOBY C. RIDER AND KEVIN B. WITHERSPOON

The English novelist George Orwell is credited with first using the term "Cold War." It appeared in his article "You and the Atomic Bomb," published in 1945, just two months after the United States dropped a pair of nuclear explosives on Japan and ended World War II. Orwell, as usual, was being prophetic. He wondered how political relations would evolve between countries that possessed this destructive nuclear technology—at the time, the Soviet Union was feverishly seeking its own. "We may be heading not for general breakdown but for an epoch as horribly stable as the slave empires of antiquity," Orwell wrote. He feared "the kind of world-view, the kind of beliefs, and the social structure that would probably prevail in a state which was at once *unconquerable* and in a permanent state of 'cold war' with its neighbors." It may, he speculated, "put an end to large-scale wars," but only at the "cost of prolonging indefinitely '*a peace that is no peace.*'"[1]

Before long, it had happened. The Allied victory in World War II could not have been secured without the manpower and resources of the United States and the Soviet Union. Once the war reached its conclusion, the already fragile cord that tied the nations together stretched to its limit, then snapped. Almost immediately the two superpowers turned from fighting a hot war against a common foe and began to fight a cold war instead.[2] "Not since Rome and Carthage had there been such a polarization of power on this earth," US undersecretary of state Dean Acheson famously stated in February 1947. "Moreover, the two great powers were divided by an unbridgeable ideological chasm. For us, democracy and individual liberty were basic; for them, dictatorship and absolute conformity."[3] Both nations sought to dominate global affairs—to expand their political, economic, and cultural reach—but the threat of nuclear annihilation ensured that they never stood toe to toe on the battlefield.

For Americans who experienced this unconventional struggle, writes historian Kenneth Osgood, the Cold War "was not a unique state of peaceful competition, but a war waged by other means." The United States, he explains, vied with the Soviet Union to secure the allegiance of foreign audiences and nations, be they hostile or not, in the realm of ideas rather than just in terms of armaments. The superpowers "channeled" their efforts into winning an ideological war through the mobilization of culture. This is why the Cold War was "all-embracing" and all consuming. As Osgood asserts, "Virtually every aspect of the American way of life—from political organizations and philosophical ideas, to cultural products and scientific achievements, to economic practices and social relationships—was exposed to scrutiny in this total contest for the hearts and minds of the world's peoples."[4]

In many respects, the Cold War had a profound influence on the structure, traditions, and philosophy that defined America's sporting culture. Indeed, the arena of modern sport provided an ideal space for the two opposing superpowers to compete. "During a military or nuclear stalemate such as the world is now experiencing," remarked US attorney general Robert F. Kennedy in 1964, "athletics can become an increasingly important factor in international relations."[5] Medals and victories, tallied up and assessed, could help demonstrate national strength and ideological superiority. Athletes from both the East and the West became symbols of a political system, of a way of life. The Soviet athlete, trained and funded by the state, purportedly represented the collective and selfless essence of communism; the American athlete, taught and developed by voluntary clubs, businesses, organizations, or a college, supposedly exemplified the virtues of private enterprise and liberal democracy.[6]

History tells us, though, that this type of rivalry was not necessarily a unique feature of the Cold War. Ever since international competitions emerged at the end of the nineteenth century, nations have sought national repute on the field of play. America was no different.[7] But after 1945, the primacy of performance and the symbolic capital of victories escalated to new heights. The miraculous improvements of the Soviet Union and its East European client states in international sport, particularly in the 1950s and thereafter, quickly compelled Americans to reconsider the established mores of their sporting culture. A series of losses to the Soviets in high-profile events such as the Olympic Games were, many thought, a tremendous blow to US prestige and a mighty propaganda coup for the communists.[8]

The cultural war had also become an athletic one, forcing US citizens to rethink the foundational ideas of their national sporting culture. Similar questions had been asked before, but they had never been taken so seriously. The US public increasingly began to debate and reconsider how they organized sport and trained athletes, whether or not the government should fund the development of elite performers, if American women should be provided more resources and technical support, how to overcome the issues of racial inequity that were frowned upon by foreign observers, if amateur traditions should be jettisoned in order to defeat the Soviets in international competition, and if performance enhancing drugs were a necessary evil. The public discourse on many of these issues was far from uniform and often bitterly divided; potential solutions were sometimes met with staunch opposition or deep concern. Some Americans openly worried that beating the Soviets might ultimately mean trying to emulate them.[9]

The anxiety over outcomes reveals a great deal about the scope of the Cold War. While it can be easy to view the conflict through a bipolar lens—that is, as a battle between two antagonistic states—it was a truly global encounter.[10] For this reason, the need to defend the American way of life extended into the realm of statecraft and foreign policy. After all, the security of the United States—not to mention its economic vitality—depended on a world amenable to the free flow of capital and access to key natural resources. Many reasoned that a planet consumed by communism could mean an end to the American way of life once and for all.[11] To further guard against what some politicians viewed as an impending national disaster, the US government took steps to secure American influence in international sport and block another avenue of communist incursions.

These steps included a range of overseas activities that can be labeled public diplomacy or propaganda, what scholars like to call a form of "soft power" that states deploy to shape or attract the "preferences of others."[12] The decision of US president Jimmy Carter to punish the Soviet Union for invading Afghanistan by blocking America's participation in the 1980 Moscow Olympics is infamous and well documented.[13] Recently declassified documents have revealed other actions. Whether it was using athletes as diplomatic ambassadors, looking to manipulate the actions of the International Olympic Committee, or attempting to disseminate images of American society to global audiences, the government was operating in a manner that was unique to the Cold War. Never before had the White House been so concerned with sport and its relevance to foreign policy and never before had it so blatantly used sport to this end. While government officials might downplay the political component of their work, the motivation for this unprecedented campaign was to protect America's sporting values and to ease the way for US foreign policy.[14]

In large part, the US government was able to wage its sporting war against communism because of the cooperative network it built with the American public. For example, running the overseas sports tour program required the voluntarily support of athletes and US sports organizations.[15] However, these components of the US sports establishment and the American public they represented found themselves in a difficult moral conundrum. They had been raised to believe in the value of sport as a force for peace and friendly competition, not to mention all that was good about the American way of life. They hoped that athletics could break down barriers between the East and West and lead to a better world. Yet at the same time, they displayed a strong antipathy to communist ideology and the sports system it produced.

The proper role and higher meaning of sport was further complicated by the often-virulent anticommunism of the era, best exemplified by the political witch-hunts Senator Joseph McCarthy conducted in the early 1950s.[16] This anticommunist consensus and its sporting component also bled into American popular culture. Newspapers, magazines, novels, television shows, and movies provided dark and negative accounts of communist sport and described American athletes and America's sporting pastimes as emblematic of free and democratic processes. The hit Hollywood film *Rocky IV* (1985), captured the contrast between "good" and "bad" as well as any cultural product of the Cold War. It told the story of how the American boxer Rocky Balboa lifted tree trunks and ran in waist-deep snow to train for a fight against the steroid-taking machine-produced Soviet competitor, Ivan Drago. Rocky prevailed, of course. This was a comforting and reassuring end, a tale Americans wanted to hear.[17] The fact that it blurred the lines between truth and reality was easily overlooked or even completely dismissed.

This Cold War lingered on until the collapse of the Soviet Union in 1991, dominating international affairs and leaving an indelible mark on US society. As this book demonstrates, America's sporting culture was not impervious to what Orwell had called "a peace that is no peace." For Americans who believed that sports represented a positive expression of their national power and principles, the Cold War demanded a renewed commitment to guarding those beliefs, a commitment that was, in many ways, a defense of the American way of life. Yet this effort sometimes resulted in outcomes that contradicted or led to change in the values Americans were trying to defend. Often, moreover, solutions were reached not through revolutionary change, but through negotiation as the United States strove to sustain what it perceived to be as both athletic and moral superiority over the Communist Bloc. In the end, as this book contends, America could claim neither.

The essays that follow are intended to provide readers with a broad understanding of American sporting culture during the Cold War, in particular the many and varied ways sport was used to defend the American way of life. They consider a wide range of sporting outlets, from the global mega-event of the Olympics to modest exhibition track exchanges and basketball games. Some focus on the American home front and how the pressures of the Cold War shaped domestic affairs while others address American athletic interests abroad. They discuss sporting concerns from the perspective of America's highest officials—several essays address how various American presidents used sport to wage the Cold War—and its humblest citizens. Some of the essays present groundbreaking new research drawn from previously untapped archival sources while others provide fresh assessments of high-profile and much-debated topics.

In the opening section, readers are introduced to Cold War sport in the abstract: sport as a cultural phenomenon, a subject for writers and film-makers, and a propaganda tool for the US State Department. As Toby Rider observes, sport took its place alongside other forms of culture, such as dance, music, literature, the visual arts, and film, as contested terrain between the superpowers. Rider explores how US policymakers, in part by celebrating American athletic success and the wholesome, egalitarian quality of its athletes and teams, propagated a message of freedom, progress, and happiness to global audiences. In contrast, Dennis Gildea reveals how American football was an object of mixed cultural interpretation in the United States. While many Americans celebrated the hard, rugged, and patriotic elements of the "All-American" pastime, others critiqued a sport that robbed many citizens of their health, their dignity, and even their lives. In particular, Gildea explains that Millard Lampell's novel *The Hero* offered a scathing indictment of the abuses in college football at the height of the Cold War, an approach so controversial it landed Lampell on the blacklist.

Section Two wrestles with one of the fundamental challenges American sports officials confronted during the Cold War: how to achieve and maintain athletic superiority without adopting the methods of its rivals. Put another way, were American claims that athletes on the other side of the Iron Curtain cheated while US athletes were morally pure grounded in fact? In the view of John Gleaves and Matthew Llewellyn, the answer is simply no. American athletes used many of the same methods athletes in the USSR and the Eastern Bloc used, including doping. And yet after decades of finger-pointing across the ideological divide, the myth persists that Cold War doping was driven by the clandestine practices of nefarious and vast state-controlled athletic programs behind the Iron Curtain. According to Nevada Cooke and Robert Barney, the United States was more successful in resisting the urge to mimic its Soviet rivals on another controversial front: state-controlled athletics. Throughout the 1960s and 1970s, many American officials called for greater governmental control of US sport, but Presidents Richard Nixon and Gerald Ford rejected such proposals. In the end, Cooke and Barney contend, the Amateur Sports Act of 1978 was a compromise solution: a federal intervention that aimed to improve America's performance by restructuring, not taking over, the nation's private sporting edifice.

America's struggle to uphold its traditional gender norms is the theme of Section Three. Lindsay Parks Pieper argues that conflicting views of appropriate women's roles in society seemed to favor female Soviet athletes over Americans. While the Soviet state invested in women's sports in order to win medals and state prestige, notes Pieper, in the United States, female athletes confronted intense pressure to appear domesticated, graceful, and feminine. American sports officials, frustrated at the growing supremacy of Soviet female athletes, eventually resorted to claims that those athletes were not "female" at all, leading to a humiliating process of sex testing in the mid-1960s. All female athletes suffered as a result. In a case study of women's basketball between the United States and the USSR, Kevin Witherspoon confirms many of Pieper's arguments. He demonstrates that US players were ridiculed in the American media for their physical strength and "manly" attributes. Unable to beat the Soviets on the court and unwilling to subvert traditional gender norms in the interest of athletic success, American officials opted to simply discontinue the contests in 1968. Katelyn Aguilar looks at masculinity, the other end of the gender spectrum, in her analysis of Ronald Reagan and his policies. Assuming the presidency during a time of crisis and following the ineffectual Jimmy Carter in the White House, Reagan strove to fashion an image of himself as a tough, uncompromising Cold War warrior. In doing so, Reagan frequently called upon memories of his days as a football star and a football legend on screen (he played the Gipper in the 1940 film *Knute Rockne, All-American*). Reagan's connection with football, argues Aguilar, helped him craft a public persona that was perfectly suited to the heated, confrontational atmosphere of the late Cold War years.

If gender issues presented difficulties for US officials who were attempting to promote the American way of life, the issue of race, the subject of Section Four, may have been even more vexing. As the United States suffered the convulsions of the Civil Rights Movement and stories of lynchings, battered protestors, and painfully slow change made headlines around the world, the US government attempted to demonstrate that democracy in the nation was legitimate and that blacks genuinely enjoyed equal opportunities. Kevin Witherspoon shows how American officials viewed Mal Whitfield, one of America's best black track stars in the late 1940s and early 1950s, as an outstanding example of black success in the United States. So successful were his visits abroad, notes Witherspoon, that he ultimately made diplomacy his career. Over time, however, Whitfield grew frustrated by the ponderous pace and limited nature of change in his country. He became a supporter of the Black Power movement and an advocate of racially motivated Olympic boycotts in 1964 and 1968. Cat Ariail argues that Wilma Rudolph's inspiring personal story, athletic excellence, and racial identity made her a nearly perfect choice for the US government's overseas sports tour program. However, Ariail demonstrates that while Rudolph promoted an image of equality abroad at the behest of the State Department, she confronted the dual discrimination of racism and sexism at home. Arthur Ashe, for a time the top-ranked tennis player in the world, became an important advocate for racial justice in the United States and abroad. As Damion Thomas explains, early in Ashe's career, the tennis star carried controversial views against the deeply entrenched racial system of apartheid in South Africa, advocating contact and interaction with South Africans instead of the cultural boycott many African Americans supported. When Ashe was finally allowed to visit South Africa personally in 1973, he met fierce opposition from black South Africans, who felt that his presence provided white leadership with a false example of racial sensitivity and actually damaged their cause. Eventually, Ashe himself accepted this premise and changed his view, supporting the cultural boycott.

The final section of the book focuses on the endeavors of the US government to manipulate, or at the least harness, the highly prestigious and globally popular Olympic movement. As all three authors in this section of the book make clear, long-held perceptions that diplomats and cultural strategists in Washington remained aloof from Olympic affairs are no longer tenable. Heather Dichter reveals definitive proof that the US State Department worked in tandem with high-ranking American Olympic officials in an attempt to control the deeply politicized issue of the International Olympic Committee's recognition of West Germany. Both Dichter and Thomas Hunt used newly available declassified documents to construct their analysis. Hunt uncovers a number of government activities related to sport during the Lyndon B. Johnson administration, including extravagant designs to impress the world with live satellite television coverage of the 1964 Tokyo

Summer Games and creating an elaborate cultural exhibit at the 1968 Summer Games in Mexico. As Hunt notes, however, US officials often agonized over the extent to which they could use the Olympics and what could be done without appearing to be interfering with a festival that espoused the rhetoric of peace. Yet perhaps President Ronald Reagan faced the greatest Cold War Olympic conundrum in the leadup to the 1984 Summer Olympics in Los Angeles. Reagan first had to handle a series of difficult requests from the visiting Soviet team and then the eventual challenge of a Soviet boycott. For Brad Congelio, the president handled this complicated period by staying true to his beliefs in laissez-faire economic policy and in the need to ensure the success of a Los Angeles Olympics that represented Reagan's own commitment to the private sector.

In the concluding chapter, Mark Dyreson offers a perspective on American sport in the post–Cold War era. In particular, he examines the evaporation of the superpower rivalry between the United States and USSR after the collapse of the Soviet Union and other communist states in Eastern Europe. Dyreson observes that public memory in the United States still associates and connects Cold War history with sporting encounters such as high-profile protests, mass boycotts, or the Hollywood-style story of the "Miracle on Ice" at Lake Placid in 1980. Although, as Dyreson contends, the post–Cold War years have not hailed a new rival to replace the former Soviet Union, the Olympics—and international sport in general—remain a powerful vehicle for narratives about American national identity and exceptionalism.

Although these essays cover an impressive breadth of subject matter, this text is not intended as a comprehensive account of sport in the Cold War era. Our hope is that readers and researchers will find their curiosity piqued by topics not fully addressed here and by the many questions that remain unanswered. Building on the material in the pages that follow, other scholars will surely discover further stories to tell, adding detail and nuance to the picture. The endlessly rich and complex story of American sport in the Cold War will likely not be told for years to come.

I

The War of Words

Presenting and Contesting America through Sports

—1—

Projecting America

Sport and Early US Cold War Propaganda, 1947–1960

BY TOBY C. RIDER

In early Cold War America, Soviet sport, like all aspects of Soviet life, became the object of intense and bitter scrutiny. "The leaders of Soviet Russia have always considered sports to be a matter of primary importance to the state," wrote John N. Washburn in a 1956 article published in *Foreign Affairs*. "They have stated that there can be no 'sport for sport's sake.'" Rather, he noted, sport "is alleged to have been placed at the service of the masses, to have increased their cultural growth and their well-being, and to have developed their spiritual and physical capabilities." Although the domestic successes of this strategy were worrying enough for Washburn, he was equally keen to highlight that the Soviet Union was intent on demonstrating the superiority of its cultural and political life beyond the Iron Curtain. By turning athletics into a "tool" of propaganda, he argued, the Soviet regime was trying to create the impression that the noble aims of its sports model were representative of the virtuous goals of the Soviet state.[1]

While many Americans echoed these fears and were quick to express them, the message of communist propaganda did not elude the political establishment in Washington. Long before Washburn's story went to press, the US government's official propaganda program had already begun to speak to international audiences about the Soviet sports system and the merits of the American alternative. In countless written descriptions and visual presentations sent overseas to the "free world," the US information apparatus used America's sporting culture to project the vitality and merits of the American way of life and the nation's earnest commitment to liberty, democracy, and international peace.[2] The sports theme was merely one of many in a broad US propaganda strategy that evolved after 1945 as the White House strove to counter the threat of communist expansionism in the destabilized conditions of the postwar world.[3] Through materials distributed in a global propaganda network, writes historian Laura Belmonte, "US policymakers propagated a carefully constructed narrative of progress, freedom, and happiness" in American society. "They not only 'imagined' an American 'community' but also presented their vision to the world in hopes of persuading foreign peoples to reject communism and adopt democratic capitalism."[4]

This chapter serves to reinforce our understanding of the pliable nature of sport in the conduct of foreign policy and statecraft.[5] This phenomenon perhaps peaked during the Cold War, when the two superpowers consistently molded sport to suit a particular ideological doctrine. The Soviet Union (and its communist allies) claimed that sport had been integral to the formation of the socialist state and a culture that solved the inequities of capitalism. Just as vehemently, the United States claimed that sport had played a significant part in the development and maintenance of its republic and the democratic principles that guided it. Both the United States and the Soviet Union competed in many of the same events, under the same set of rules, and yet sport symbolized totally different things to the two nations. Depending on who was competing or describing the events, sport could be viewed as both profoundly "good" and despicably "bad," played the "right" way, or the "wrong" way. Both Soviet and American propaganda experts believed that if overseas audiences could understand how their nation played sports they could understand the nation itself, or at least a better version of it.

Sport, Propaganda, and the Cold War

These propaganda campaigns reveal much about the peculiarities of the Cold War. In order to avoid the devastating consequences of a direct military and nuclear confrontation, the United States and the Soviet Union fought to gain a preponderance of power in global affairs through mobilizing and exploiting ideas and culture. Each country invested a huge amount of resources in propaganda. At the onset of the Cold War, however, the United States was poorly equipped for such a battle. Even though the United States had created a sprawling propaganda machinery during World War II, it had largely dismantled that machinery after the defeat of the Third Reich. But in response to the desperate realities of the fractured postwar world, the waxing power of the Soviet Union across Europe, and the sheer effectiveness of communist propaganda, the United States began to reassemble its information network. In 1948, Congress eventually gave the overseas propaganda program permanent legislative authority (the Smith-Mundt Act), and endorsed the use of print, film, radio, cultural exchange, and exhibitions to "promote the better understanding of the United States among the peoples of the world and to strengthen cooperative international relations."[6]

As the Cold War intensified, the information apparatus continued to grow. In 1950, the Harry S. Truman administration launched a massive Campaign of Truth to address and counter the claims of Soviet propaganda. A year later, the head of the program, Edward Barrett, announced that the results of the US information effort were "encouraging." He proudly stated that the United States had over 160 information centers around the world; the government's radio station, the Voice of America, broadcast the national "message" in forty-six languages; approximately 400 million people watched the program's films; and the government had arranged for more foreign citizens to visit "this country to see us first hand than ever before."[7] When Dwight D. Eisenhower took office in 1953, propaganda became even more enmeshed in the conduct of America foreign policy. The new president was a firm believer in the power of the "p-factor," and under his leadership, the propaganda program was taken out of the State Department, where it was originally housed, and placed under the aegis of the United States Information Agency (USIA).[8]

The officers who staffed the propaganda program soon recognized that sport had become enveloped in the Cold War contest for hearts and minds. Throughout the late 1940s and into the 1950s, streams of reports from American diplomats overseas documented the increasing number of Soviet athletes competing in various international events and embarking upon cultural exchanges. State Department officials also noted that Soviet propaganda saluted the achievements of communist athletes, celebrated their victories, and praised their contribution to global good will.[9] At the same time, the Kremlin alleged that sport in America "poisoned" the minds of youths, fed the tyrannical capitalist system, distracted workers from their class struggle, indoctrinated the population to believe in the "superiority of the Anglo-Saxon race," and furthered the pursuit of America's ruthless militaristic and imperialistic agenda.[10] "Both at home and abroad, the Soviets have been promoting the idea that only under their system can sports attain perfection and embrace the masses of the population," explained a USIA intelligence analysis in 1955.[11]

Responding to all facets of this Soviet challenge proved difficult. Some members of Congress called for a federal intervention to fund American athletes, especially at the Olympics. But such an intervention would have been a historical first. The entire structure and administration of American sports was independent from state control, and the US government, not to mention the American public, was reluctant to alter this arrangement in any considerable way. A unilateral effort to emulate the Soviet approach to sport was therefore totally impractical and fundamentally against national tradition.[12] Instead, the White House directed its energy and resources into other endeavors. An overt aspect of this strategy, guided by the State Department, involved organizing overseas tours for American athletes and teams to act as cultural ambassadors in carefully selected destinations. Yet this tactic, which Eisenhower turned into a regular sports tour program in 1954 as part of the President's Emergency Fund, only worked because of the approval of US sports authorities, most notably the Amateur Athletic Union and the United States Olympic Committee.[13]

Somewhat more secretly, however, the intelligence establishment funded exiled Eastern European sports groups and helped them facilitate the defection of Soviet-bloc athletes to the "free world." This clandestine approach enabled the United States to embark on a more aggressive form of political warfare, but it also had to accept the unpredictability of working with ostensibly "private" groups embittered by the fact their homeland had been "stolen" from them.[14]

The production and distribution of propaganda was not hampered by many of these practical restrictions. The USIA could go about its work without asking for permission from US sports officials or having to worry about the distinction between state and private spheres. American propagandists could write a story or produce a cartoon with relative freedom. To some degree, the government was finally in control of the national sporting culture and could use it, within reason, as it wished. Officials soon realized that this medium could be successfully exploited because it had such immense range. In numerous planning papers, propaganda experts discussed the universal appeal of sports, particularly to the "man-on-the-street," the "worker," and the world's youth.[15] They recognized that sports topics easily stirred interest on a global scale and allowed the United States to communicate with audiences abroad in a shared language and culture. People may become tired or disenchanted with diplomats and leaders, but they still read the sports pages, cheer for their team, or play in their leisure time.

While stories about America's sporting culture were present in US propaganda at the outbreak of the Cold War, they became a staple subject as the Soviet "sports offensive" gathered momentum. By 1952, the government's overseas information bulletin contained a regular column titled "Sports

World," and in 1954 the USIA established a monthly "feature packet" on sports that was full of cartoons, glossy photographs, articles, and carefully selected reprints from American newspapers and magazines. These materials—along with books, pamphlets, and films—were sent to US information centers, embassies, and public affairs officers around the world for distribution overtly and covertly in local and national media outlets. The programming of the Voice of America also included live sports coverage and stories that were translated into dozens of languages to an estimated audience in the hundreds of millions.

Sport, Community, and the Common Good

If this was the method, then what was the message? Although US propaganda had a defensive tone and attempted to refute communist accusations about the role of sport in America, there was more to the story than this. The content of US materials sought to present America as a land of sports that were far more vibrant and diverse than the physical culture experienced under communism.[16] Some of the central themes of this approach were, in many ways, a repetition of ideas that had gathered a growing chorus of followers in the final decades of the nineteenth century, a narrative that claimed for sport a pivotal role in the reproduction of American social, cultural, economic, and political life. According to this view, sports and robust forms of leisure taught the US public the value of competition and endeavor, that those who strive and struggle will be rewarded no matter who they are or where they are from, that fair play and social justice were important, and that communities are built by people and not the government. Therefore, if sport was played the correct way and for the right reasons, it was a force for good.[17]

During the early Cold War years, image sculptors in the US government dusted off this well-worn script, only this time the story was directed to people abroad. A prominent component of this message portrayed sport as positive social force that was constantly unifying and enriching the lives of citizens from coast to coast as they indulged in a mutually shared passion for physical activity. The US information program produced a slew of stories suggesting that on any given day people across the country willingly participated in a range of sporting activities such as hunting, hiking, fishing, swimming, sailing, boating, cycling, auto racing, tennis, football, ice skating, skiing, basketball, and volleyball. The USIA carried stories on Eisenhower's partiality for golf and included pictures of the president dressed in athletic attire, swinging a club.[18]

Recognizing that people in the United States played sports that were unfamiliar to overseas audiences, propaganda experts embraced the need to explain the customs and culture of uniquely American games in an approachable and sincere manner. "A 'fever' peculiar to the United States will reach its highest peak across the nation the first week of October," said one State Department *Air Bulletin* article in 1947. "It's called 'baseball fever' and it becomes most prevalent during the 'World Series' played by the champion teams of the two best baseball leagues in the country."[19] In another romantic treatise on the game, a story declared: "Baseball is, indeed, America's 'national pastime'!"[20] As eager as policymakers were to show that the United States had a distinctive sporting culture, they also emphasized that Americans enjoyed games that were popular in other countries. A movie titled *Foreign Sports in the United States*, for instance, demonstrated that visitors to the country should not be surprised to see traditional Irish hurling or find organizations linked to the Czechoslovakian Sokol movement.[21] Striking an even more global chord, another *Air Bulletin* story charted the "mounting" interest in soccer in America and the game's ability to stimulate "international understanding and goodwill."[22]

At the same time, though, US propagandists were cautious not to overemphasize the national interest in professional sports, fearing that it would reinforce perceptions overseas that "money and prowess" were "inseparable in the American mind."[23] Information experts thus paid homage to the voluntary aspects of US sports and praised their place in forging a morally and physically sound community. In order to show that the United States was a nation of people who celebrated the common good, propaganda materials stressed the care given to athletes, the safety-oriented practices of sports organizations, that sports helped in the recovery of injured serviceman, and that sports opportunities were available for people with disabilities. One USIA story told how the *Chicago Tribune* sponsored a charity boxing competition between fighters from Europe and America to raise money for "poor, sick, and crippled" children. This philanthropic initiative, noted the USIA, demonstrated "US concern for unfortunate people."[24]

These examples of civic engagement also exemplified the limited role of government in the everyday lives of American people. With this in mind, propaganda strategists continually tried to contrast the state-dominated model that prevailed under communism with the citizen-led teams, leagues, and competitions that flourished in the United States.[25] They acknowledged that while the White House initiated national fitness campaigns and offered encouragement to national teams, it left the administration and funding of sports to private individuals and organizations. In a series of stories, US propaganda took great care to explain that the United States Olympic Committee was "self-governing" and raised money by soliciting voluntary donations from the American public.[26] This divide between state and private spheres supposedly demonstrated that sport in America was free from the type of nefarious political intrigue that inevitably stemmed from excessive government control. America was a land of freedom, information experts claimed, and its sporting culture reflected this fact.

In a more general sense, propaganda experts endeavored to depict US athletes as ordinary human beings in a way that overseas audiences could relate to.[27] The USIA thus published many stories about the hardworking, happy, diligent, humble, and well-mannered people who represented the Stars and Stripes. These profiles clearly countered communist claims that American athletes were "rough, dirty-fighting, gangster-like competitors," and they also addressed communist accusations that America was a "cultural wasteland."[28] The USIA explained that male and female athletes had various hobbies, interests, and cultural talents and that they enjoyed oil painting, drawing, writing, singing, listening to music, or playing a range of instruments.[29] And unlike communist athletes, they were also able to express their religious freedom. Several articles on the "Vaulting Vicar," Rev. Bob Richards, celebrated his commitment to preaching, and another story on Florence Chadwick's swim across the English Channel underlined the "spiritual inspiration that guided her."[30]

Democracy and the Level Playing Field

The theme of social equality was a central feature of the information program's portrayal of American society. Under a system built upon the ideas of liberal democracy, so the narrative went, anyone could progress through hard work and honest fortitude; anyone could become a paragon of "People's Capitalism."[31] And because the United States continually sought to level the social and economic playing field, pursuing the American dream became ever more viable with each passing year. Propaganda experts conveyed this theme through descriptions of sport in the United States. According to the information program, sports that were traditionally regarded as pastimes for the social elite were opening up to all Americans. "The sport of sailing, for many years a diversion of the wealthy, is now enjoyed by an estimated 200,000 average-income persons in the United States," a *USA Life Bulletin* article proclaimed.[32] Elsewhere, the USIA trumpeted that the United States had more than 5,000 golf courses, all of which were becoming the "nuclei of community recreation." Golf "can be played by everyone," claimed the USIA in one story. "The game now is enjoyed by people in virtually every walk of life."[33]

Just as significantly, US propaganda declared, sport created conditions that mirrored the spirit of a true democracy. The meteoric rise of an athlete from obscurity to national renown was indicative of the economic and political conditions that thrived in a free society. USIA employees loved the movie *The Bob Mathias Story*, for instance. One government official described it as "an almost perfect portrayal of the best phase of American life—a small town boy with his family, his sweetheart, his career, his interest in sports—all building up to his two time triumph as one of the outstanding athletes in the history of the Olympics. . . . If it hasn't got the American values we want on screen, then we have got to start looking for a new set of values to publicize."[34] But propaganda experts also liked the "rags to riches" plotline of the American dream. The career of "Jersey Joe" Walcott, who became the world heavyweight champion at the age of 37, fit nicely into this category. "Achievement of dramatic and unexpected success is not uncommon in American life," an article in *USA Life Bulletin* stated in 1951. "And when an American gains such success, the people as a whole seldom fail to feel excitement and delight."[35]

The story of Walcott was doubly effective. As an African American, his success and popularity helped directly counter one of the most powerful and persistent themes of communist propaganda: racial discrimination in the United States. This was an issue that undermined the notion of a true democracy, and the Soviets did not need to look far for examples to prove it. As a result, propagandists attempted to deflect attention from racial segregation in US society by portraying a gradual process of integration and change.[36] To "expose the deceit of Communist claims," the USIA applied the same strategy in its sports output by preparing stories to "show that all Americans, regardless of race, color, or creed, have an equal opportunity to win recognition for their particular skills or abilities."[37] A long feature on the "dozen or more" black athletes playing major league baseball noted that they were "leaving an indelible record of accomplishment" on the national pastime. According to the USIA, "exciting" performers such as "Satchel" Paige, Willie Mays, and Don Newcombe were cheered in ball parks around the country and were "but a few" of the players "who promise to continue performing outstanding feats in the game America accepts as its most democratic athletic institution."[38] This racial narrative alleged that progress continued beyond the athletic field. Numerous cartoons and articles indicated that black athletes enjoyed watching movies and playing golf, owned nice cars, had high incomes, and

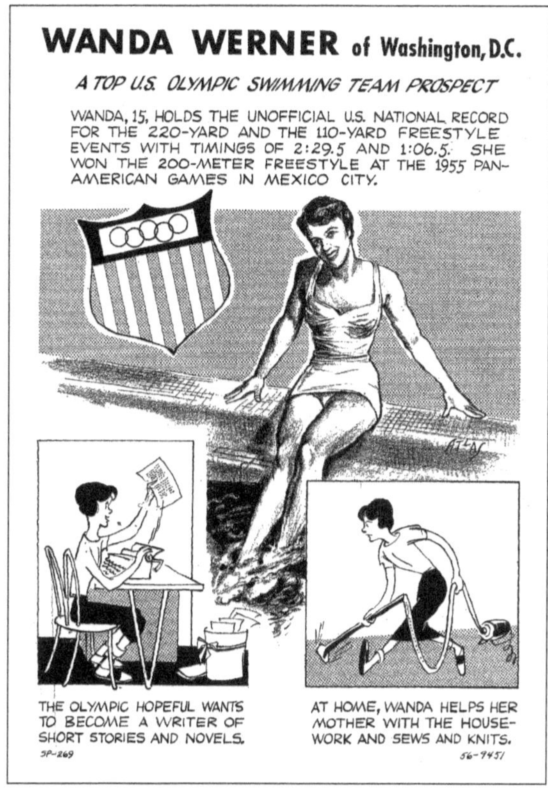

A United States Information Agency cartoon of the swimmer Wanda Werner. *Courtesy of the National Archives and Records Administration.*

planned to start a business or go to college once they retired from competition. According to US propaganda, sport was in the vanguard of ending racial inequality in America.

Information strategists were equally judicious in their portrayal of female American athletes. Glossing over the fact that women were often marginalized figures in American sports, US propaganda answered communist accusations that American women were "slovenly, ugly, and silly."[39] A feature on figure skater Carol Heiss noted the sixteen-year-old's "determination to win," her quest for improvement, and her "desire to excel." In between training sessions that started before 6 a.m., the profile continued, Heiss was "busy" with school, took ballet lessons, and displayed a maturity beyond her years. The "pretty" young prodigy, one of the leading contenders for gold at the 1956 Winter Olympics, combined her exceptional determination with "natural grace," poise, and "dexterity" on the ice. Many other profiles sought to portray American women as wholesome, feminine, domesticated, and productive.[40] Cartoons were filled with illustrations explaining that female athletes enjoyed doing housework and cooking, liked to sew and knit, hoped to marry and raise a family, and aspired to attend college or find a job.

International Sport, Goodwill, and the Spirit of Fair Play

Although sport was undoubtedly used to construct a positive image of life in the United States, US propaganda explained that American citizens were noble participants in the far larger community of international sport. This community, the information program highlighted, brought people together in friendly nonpolitical contests that promoted peace and understanding between nations. A host of features described the mutual transfer of ideas that occurred when foreign athletes, coaches, and physical educators visited the United States and praised the Americans who traveled abroad to share their expertise about skills, techniques, and training methods. These overseas excursions, many of which the State Department organized as part of its cultural exchange program, provided just the sort of copy information experts craved. Pictures and articles of Americans on missions abroad were proof of a nation committed to fostering amity and goodwill.

The story of Sam Fox coaching the Turkish national basketball team was typical. In a highly productive yearlong stay, Fox wrote two books on the fundamentals of the game in Turkish, conducted clinics for referees, organized various tournaments, and was awarded a Medal of Honor from the governor of Istanbul. So beloved had Fox become in Turkey, gushed the USIA, that when he announced his intention to leave, "school children signed petitions begging him" to stay. As for Fox, he believed that sports taught "cooperation, courtesy, discipline and democracy."[41]

The USIA also orchestrated a publicity blitz for prominent American athletes involved in the Eisenhower administration's cultural exchange program. In addition to covering the tours in features and photos sent to information posts around the world, the State Department provided USIA field officers with "voluminous biographical data" and promotional items to plug the trips.[42] Working through contacts in the locales the athletes visited, USIA officers supplied press releases to local newspaper and radio outlets, accompanied athletes as they moved from location to location, and organized meet-and-greets for journalists to attend.[43] In the majority of instances, information officials waxed lyrical about the propaganda impact of these cultural exchanges. "In many places around the world," a State Department official reasoned, "people hold a false image of American youth as gum chewing, smart-aleck, 'decadent' weaklings—an image gained in some cases through communist-inspired misinformation, in other cases the result of lack of understanding." Then, the official added, "along comes a Bob Mathias, a Bill Miller, or a Bob Richards—and in one flash that image is shattered."[44]

For the USIA, American athletes on tours were effective representatives of their country because they understood and preached the core moral values of sport. This, in itself, served as a powerful metaphor. In life, as in sport, US propaganda enumerated, Americans played the "right" way and deified the importance of sportsmanship, fair play, and abiding by the rules of competition.[45] A range of articles underscored that winning was certainly not the only thing; how one competed was just as important as the outcome itself.[46] As one US sports official said in the *USA Life Bulletin*, "We want American boys and girls to win and will do everything legitimately possible to that end, but we believe the most important thing is how they win."[47]

While it highlighted the virtuous conduct of American athletes in various events and competitions, the information program was particularly keen to demonstrate that the United States was an upstanding affiliate of the Olympic movement. The Olympics were a priority focus for the information program from the moment the Soviet Union was elected as a member nation of the International Olympic Committee in 1951. Propaganda strategists acknowledged that the games were a globally admired festival driven by a compelling, even if largely mythical, mission to make the world a better place through "friendly" athletic competition. This philosophical bedrock of the event, commonly referred to as Olympism, resonated deeply with US information experts. They recognized that by telling overseas audiences that the American public upheld and revered Olympic principles, they would be insinuating that the United States was also committed to the same essential goals.[48]

In the leadup to the Winter and Summer Olympics, the information program filled its overseas output with a range of material expounding on the virtues of Olympism. Around the time of the 1956 Melbourne games, the USIA used copies of the book former US Olympian John V. Grombach had written, *Olympic Cavalcade of Sports*, as a "presentation item" for media representatives and visitors at the Olympic city. The USIA determined that the book, "a straight forward objective account" of the festival's past, was "effective in countering" Soviet attempts to link athletic victories to the "superiority of socialism" because it emphasized "the true spirit of the Olympic events, i.e. a healthy athletic competition without" any relation to politics. For the 1960 Rome games, the USIA purchased 5,000 copies of the updated tome to be handed out at no cost in information posts worldwide.[49] Even if America might lose to its adversary on the track, propaganda experts tried to claim the moral high ground by deemphasizing the symbolic value of the games as a measuring stick for national strength.[50]

Presenting the Communist Sports System

While the main thrust of the US propaganda offensive aimed to counter Soviet "lies" about America's athletic culture, it also sought to tell overseas audiences the "truth" about sport under communist rule. Articulating this message involved dismantling and exposing what government experts believed to be the blatant fallacies of Soviet propaganda. "In other words," a State Department official elaborated in 1951, "sports in the slave world are conceived primarily as a tool of propaganda, an instrument of national policy, a means of strengthening the party line of Soviet superiority and of further indoctrinating Communists."[51] Conveying this message became even more crucial throughout the 1950s as Soviet athletes began to significantly improve their performances at the Olympic Games and other notable international competitions. Concerned by the "climate of opinion" these Soviet results might create, US information experts determined that Soviet victories could at least be discredited if people understood how these victories were achieved.[52]

Many of these attacks on the Soviet sports system were delivered, quite deliberately, in an "unattributed" manner. This approach, a form of "gray" propaganda designed to hide government involvement, left audiences unaware of who was levying the attack and, in theory, freed the United States from accusations of injecting politics into sport.[53] One such item, a pamphlet titled *Sport*, was distributed by US officials at a Berlin sports exhibition in 1951. During the gathering, more than 70,000 copies of the pamphlet, specifically tailored to "interest the large numbers of youth" expected to attend the event from the Soviet zone, were handed to Germans from the east and west sections of the city. Small enough to "conceal" for those wishing to hide it from communist authorities, the contents of the diminutive publication contrasted the "theme of the Western concept of sport as a means of developing the individual" with the "Communist perversion of sport as a means of capturing the youth for political purposes."[54]

The myth and reality of Soviet sports was treated in even greater detail in another publication, *Sport behind the Iron Curtain*. The booklet, which the British government produced and the USIA circulated to information officers worldwide for unattributed use, systematically responded to a number of claims repeated in Soviet propaganda. But above all else, it dismissed any possibility that sport under communism was in the service of the people. "Games are supposed to be played for their own sake," the pamphlet read, "but, however enthusiastic the Soviet public may be about its sports, the growth of sport in the Soviet Union and the participation of Soviet teams at international meetings is not the result of a spontaneous popular movement, but of a Soviet Government decision." The pamphlet insisted that the reason the state funded athletes to train and compete was not to achieve world peace or generate goodwill. "The prestige the Soviet Government hopes to create is one that implies a general feeling of Soviet superiority, and also suggests in a particular way the advantages of Soviet Communism," the booklet asserted.[55]

Many of the information program's stories about sport under communism were based on accounts from Eastern European refugees living in the West. Fueled by a desire to end communist rule in their homeland, refugees told negative stories about the goals of communist sport and about restrictive aspects of life in Eastern Europe. In one scathing attack that was broadcast on the Voice of America, a Hungarian émigré named Jozsef Halmay said that communist states were solely focused on developing athletes for the sake of propaganda. Halmay, an Olympic canoeist who defected in 1954, also charged that athletes were locked in their hotel rooms during international competitions and locked in buses when they traveled to events. "I knew I was being used as a tool. It is questionable how long I could have stood the pace." The refugee continued, "[The communists] were driving me the way a bad jockey drives his horse. They gave me shots—vitamin B and also ten cubic centimeter sugar shots. In addition to being harmful, this was very painful."[56] US propaganda depicted the Eastern European people as victims, imprisoned by a ruthless and repressive dictatorship.

However, many of the information program's stories about refugees were also scripted to include a happy ending. The USIA frequently highlighted that emigres were now living safely and contentedly in the "free world," a claim that clearly illustrated the difference between life in the East and life in the West. Numerous features revealed the happiness and fulfillment refugees from Soviet Bloc countries were experiencing as residents of the United States, not to mention the warm welcome they received. An article on Jan Miecznikowski, a Polish distance runner, told how he defected after a track meet in Berne, Switzerland, in 1954; subsequently entered Germany; and from there waited patiently for the "chance to go to America." A year later, Miecznikowski arrived in the United States and soon enrolled at the University of Houston to study diesel engineering. Jan, the USIA article noted, "is looking forward to the opportunity of representing the United States in international meets once he becomes an American citizen."[57]

Conclusion: The Limits of US Propaganda

Judging or gauging the effectiveness of the US propaganda campaign in the early Cold War years is fraught with difficulties. Did the wide spectrum of materials sent to audiences throughout the "free world" actually change perceptions? Did it really alter the "climate of opinion" on sports in the United States or the communist countries? In many ways, forming an understanding of how the United States was able to influence the thoughts of the public is an immensely challenging, if not impossible, task. The USIA did not produce any large-scale or detailed audience analysis of its sport-related materials and investigating the impact of news stories on a country-by-country basis is beyond the scope of this work.[58] Perhaps someday such a study, or studies, will be done. Nonetheless, the available documents reveal the limits of US propaganda. Some of the issues were predictable. As propaganda experts discovered, particular sports or competitions were not popular in certain countries and therefore aroused very little curiosity. "Temperatures of [a] hundred degrees generally melt[s] interest [in] winter sports," was the response from a US official in Pakistan after the 1956 Winter Olympics.[59]

Other problems were far more substantial. Unsurprisingly, constructing and presenting America's sporting culture was not necessarily straightforward. Sports, of course, are riddled with contradictions, but sometimes the message was simply lost in translation depending on where it was sent. Take America's amateur traditions, for instance. Initially, US propagandists believed that highlighting the professionalism of Soviet athletes in amateur events such as the Olympic Games could be effectively juxtaposed with the integrity of American amateurs. Indeed, this was a common theme of American propaganda for the 1952 Olympic festivals. But soon thereafter, propaganda experts increasingly judged that the amateur question was not as clear cut as they had originally imagined. After all, American athletes from the military received full pay while they trained, college athletes accepted scholarships, and even athletes employed by private businesses were still given some "concessions" while they trained or competed. These issues seriously compromised the notion that athletes on America's Olympic team were truly uncompensated for their efforts.[60] Additionally, intelligence gathered from overseas confirmed that many people were unsure exactly what amateurism was and struggled to tell the difference between American and Soviet methods. Surveys even indicated that some nations preferred a state-directed athletic system.[61] In the end, the USIA downplayed the amateur theme in its feature packets to avoid accusations of hypocrisy and sour grapes.

Another, and perhaps bigger, problem for US propagandists was the symbolic power of international sports competitions. A 1960 review of US information strategy judged that "Soviet victories in international sporting competition do have propaganda value, particularly with younger people in many countries and with those not ordinarily concerned with international political issues." Therefore, "Free World efforts to remove factors of national prestige and ideological significance from international athletic competition are not likely to succeed in the foreseeable future."[62] Policymakers came to realize that no matter how much they promoted the merits of the US system and denigrated the flaws of the Soviet model, the outcome of a sporting event carried a message that was hard to control. Words, they lamented, could not trump deeds.

Despite that reality, some of the most influential figures in the early Cold War information programs showed a distinct appreciation for the role of sports in shaping public opinion. They understood that sports were a common link between people across the globe, a cultural phenomenon that attracted billions of fans and participants. Through this shared medium, they tried to convey a picture of American life. The image they chose to project was a repetition of ideas Americans had championed in the final decades of the nineteenth century. They portrayed an America where sport brought people together, formed communities and mutual understanding, spread democracy and social freedoms, and shaped the "right" kind of citizens. Sports were good, they argued, and America was a land of sports.

—2—

Millard Lampell

From Football to the Blacklist

BY DENNIS GILDEA

Maybe, as he maintained later, the remark was spontaneous, something that quite naturally occurred to him in the moment, something he felt compelled to share. Or maybe it was calculated, a bit of stagecraft that would surely draw a startled reaction from the audience, a gathering of what one newspaper account referred to as "celebrities" decked out in formal attire.[1] Regardless, as Millard Lampell stood at the dais at the Americana Hotel in Manhattan clutching the 1966 Emmy Award he had just received for writing the television play *Eagle in a Cage,* he looked out at a group that represented the power elite of the entertainment industry, not to mention television cameras covering the ceremony live for a national audience. He started his thank-you address, paused, and out it came: "Everyone here ought to know I was blacklisted for 10 years."[2]

Val Adams, who was covering the event for the *New York Times,* wrote: "Most of those accepting awards responded in the manner that viewers of such ceremonies have come to expect. But Millard Lampell, an author cited for 'Eagle in a Cage,' a drama on N.B.C.'s Hallmark Hall of Fame, surprised the audience" with his comment.[3] Lampell's statement was hardly confessional; rather, it was a piece of information he felt the audience at the Americana and Americans in general should know. At a news conference after the ceremony, a reporter asked Lampell why he had made the remark. "I had to stop and consider, and a line of the philosopher Santayana's swam into my mind, 'Those who cannot remember the past are condemned to repeat it.'"[4]

Given the complex and often confounding events of his life, Lampell's abrupt departure from the norm in his Emmy acceptance speech is understandable. He most certainly remembered the difficult events of his personal history, a narrative that paralleled the nation's history in the post–World War II period when the Federal Bureau of Investigation (FBI) and many in Congress launched relentless hunts for communists in America. Lampell was identified as a communist in *Red Channels: The Report of Communist Influence in Radio and Television* that came out in the final months of 1950, and in 1952 he was subpoenaed to appear before the Senate Committee on Internal Security, where for the first time he learned "some clues to the nature of the charges against me."[5] At the time he was listed in *Red Channels*, Lampell had been a prolific and successful professional writer for eight years. "I had published poems, songs and short stories, written a novel and adapted it as a motion picture.... Then, quietly, mysteriously and almost overnight, the job offers stopped coming."[6]

To rely on the cliché that throughout his life he moved to the beat of a different drummer would be to engage in a whopping understatement. In his 1997 obituary, the *New York Times* described him as "a screenwriter, novelist and songwriter."[7] To that list the writer could have added: writer of radio and television plays, journalist, aviation machine gunner in World War II, founder of the pioneering folk singing group the Almanac Singers, expert on Appalachian folk culture, supporter in 1947 of the blacklisted Hollywood Ten, and high school and college football star. Lampell went to West Virginia University (WVU) from 1936 to 1940 on a football scholarship.

This essay offers a brief recounting of Lampell's life leading to his blacklisting in the 1950s and a close textual analysis of Lampell's 1949 football novel, *The Hero*, a work that he and Sidney Buchman turned into a film, *Saturday's Hero*, that was released in 1951. Conforming to the strictures of Hollywood's Production Code, the film has a different and—no surprise—rosier boy-gets-girl ending than the novel has.[8] About *The Hero*, cultural historian Ronald D. Cohen argues that "drawing upon [Lampell's] experiences, the story revolves around a working-class football player from New Jersey who is injured while in college in the South and discovers the dark side of competitive sports.... It includes little of Lampell's politics."[9] On the contrary, I argue that the novel is similar to John R. Tunis's 1928 piece published in *Harper's*, "The Great God Football," a critique of commercialism and academic abuses in college football. In addition, Tunis's *All-American* (1942) was a novel for young readers that examined the racism rampant in football.[10] Francis Wallace contributed another voice in mainstream media that consistently advocated reform in college football. Wallace, a sportswriter for daily newspapers and a frequent

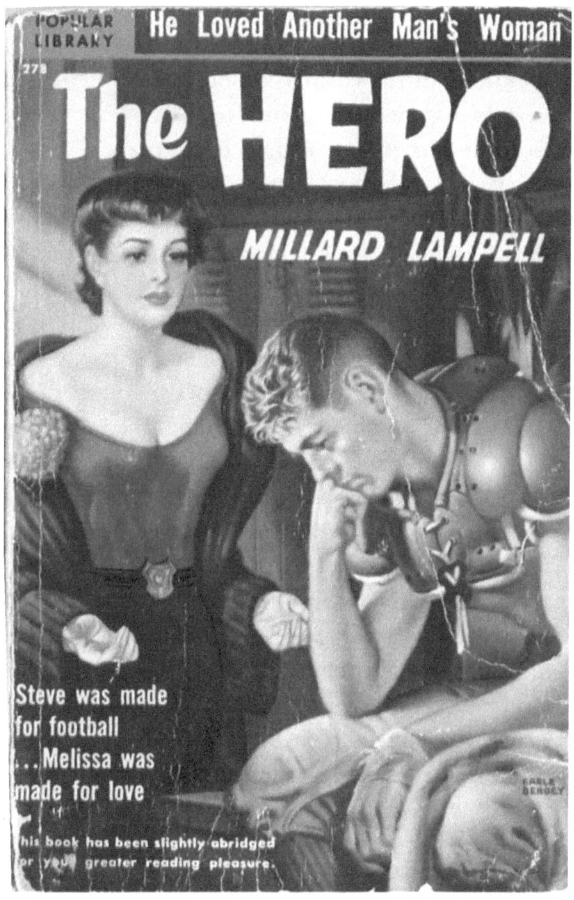

The cover of Millard Lampell's book *The Hero.*

contributor of fiction and nonfiction to major weekly and monthly magazines, railed against the hypocrisy of allegedly amateur college football.[11] A short piece of fiction, "The Pigskin Heart," by Joel Reeve, was published in *Collier's* in 1947. Reeve's story depicts a fictional college football coach as a tyrannical figure who abused his players.[12]

Because Lampell's work was an especially compelling narrative and possibly because it was based on his own disillusionment with football, *The Hero* is more insightful and more powerful than the other pieces dealing with the necessity of reforming college football. *The Hero* goes beyond the realm of the athletic department to reveal explicitly, perhaps for the first time in American literature, the connection between sports and politics, especially how ambitious politicians use football stars to enhance their political agenda.[13] In making a direct correlation between football and American politics in *The Hero*, Lampell can be understood as a forerunner to Dave Meggyesy, who wrote *Out of Their League* in 1970, a book that narrates his counterculture struggle with coach Floyd "Ben" Schwartzwalder at Syracuse University and later the owners and commissioner of the National Football League (NFL). Both Lampell and Meggyesy were at least somewhat radicalized by their experiences in big-time football and by their education. More so than Meggyesy, though, Lampell's life and work reflect what he called his "humanistic socialism," a philosophy that at times flirted with the ideology of the Communist Party of the United States of America (CPUSA).

Legendary West Point coach Earl Blaik maintained that football is "the game most like war." He added, "It is also the game most like life, for it teaches young men that work, sacrifice, courage, perseverance, and selflessness are the prices you have to pay to achieve anything worthwhile."[14] Blaik's assessment of the multiple benefits football engendered in young men was not new. In the first decade of the twentieth century, Theodore Roosevelt urged Americans to pursue the "strenuous life," and pioneering football coach Walter Camp of Yale detailed what he called the "manly" qualities that football produced, namely, temperance, patience, self-denial, and self-control.[15] For Blaik and many other influential Americans in the early years of the Cold War, the values they found inherent in football served as an antithesis to the perceived Soviet threat to the American way of life. Historian Kurt Edward Kemper writes that in the postwar period, football was cloaked "in the rhetoric of national defense and the cult of toughness."[16] Sports journalists in the postwar period turned frequently to the role football played in building physical and mental toughness.[17] Proponents were confident that football taught the importance of teamwork and that teamwork was American democracy in action, a recurrent theme in the popular short fiction, magazine profiles of athletes, and biopic films produced in the time period.[18]

While most cinematic, journalistic, and literary works conformed to the popular theme of defending football as the athletic manifestation of the preferred American way of life, Lampell's *The Hero* grabbed both the game and the prevailing political philosophy by the throat and squeezed the life out of them. Even the film version of the novel, *Saturday's Hero*, ran counter to the belief that football represented the best in American culture. Michael Oriard describes *Saturday's Hero* as "the one genuinely critical postwar football film."[19] Lampell wrote the screenplay with some contributions from Buchman. *New York Times* film reviewer Bosley Crowther did not attempt to suppress his glee with the film's attack on a sacrosanct American institution. "Hooting with fiendish derision at all the good old rah-rah college attitudes so often expressly ennobled in certain items from Hollywood, Millard Lampell and Sidney Buchman have ripped out a sulphurous script which makes college football look more vicious than organized mugging and the white slave trade."[20] The film had its premier showing in early September 1951, just a few weeks after the news broke of the West Point cribbing scandal that led to the dismissal of the majority of coach Blaik's football players.[21] How the film "will please the people who run the college football leagues—or, for that matter, the ones who run the colleges—is something we wouldn't like to say," Crowther wrote.[22] Praise by Crowther and other film critics notwithstanding, *Saturday's Hero* was not a box-office success. Because the film was "an exposé of an All-American sport" at the height of the Cold War, it incurred the wrath of "several loosely based anti-Communist groups" that picketed theaters showing the movie.[23]

A Rebel with Numerous Causes

Lampell was born in 1919 in Paterson, New Jersey, the son of Jewish immigrants. His father owned a ladies' hat store in New York City and most likely was surprised when his only son developed into a football star at Eastside High School in Paterson, the alma mater of Larry Doby, who graduated four years after Lampell.[24] West Virginia University recruited Lampell, and in the fall of 1936, he was on the freshman team in Morgantown.[25]

Early in his varsity career, Lampell suffered an injury serious enough to end his football playing days. He roomed with a football teammate who came from a small coal-mining town in West Virginia. Visits to his roommate's hometown proved to be an epiphany for the young man from suburban New York City as he saw the deplorable working and living conditions the coal miners endured. He also saw firsthand and heard tales of battles between the rank and file of the United Mineworkers and the coal company bosses. His visits to the West Virginia coalfields contributed to his lifelong commitment to exposing and fighting social injustice.[26]

During his senior year at WVU, Lampell's political activism increased. He refused to participate in mandatory military training and university administrators suspended him. Lampell, however, could write, and when an essay he submitted to an ROTC contest won the top prize, the administrators relented and allowed him to graduate.[27] Ironically, even as he was writing the essay that would win the ROTC prize, he was also writing what became his first national publication, a piece that ran in the August 12, 1940, issue of *The*

New Republic under the title "Is There a Fuhrer in the House?" In the essay, Lampell (publishing under the pen name Mike Landon) cautioned against what he perceived to be a growing fascist movement in the United States, one of the leaders of which was "Joe McWilliams, fuhrer of the American Destiny Party," who calls himself the "anti-Jewish candidate for Congress." Lampell concluded his essay with these lines: "This year the fascists are making their first widespread bid for seats in Congress. It is important for the voters to be able to spot these men, know their records and know what they stand for."[28]

Two months later, *The New Republic* published another of his essays, this time under the name Mill Lampell. In "Not So Free Election," Lampell attacked American fascism again, this time drawing on his experiences in West Virginia. The American Legion had saturated the state with pamphlets listing the names of citizens who had signed election petitions supporting the CPUSA. "In Fayette County, two coal-company employees whose names appeared on the list were fired," Lampell wrote. "Coal miners who signed petitions were evicted from company houses.... One way that fascism comes is by an almost imperceptible system of limitations on public liberty, an accumulation of suppressions."[29] A decade later, he would be victimized by those who possessed the same tendency to suppress individual liberty.

By the time the magazine pieces were published, Lampell had taken his WVU diploma and moved to New York City. Another interest sparked by his visits to the Appalachian region was his fascination with rural folk music. In the fall of 1940, Lampell met Lee Hays, who came from Little Rock, Arkansas, and who attended Commonwealth College, an Arkansas institution with a deserved reputation as a radical labor college. Hays had spent his time in Arkansas "preaching in local churches, collecting songs, writing plays, and absorbing the native radicalism of his colleagues."[30] Of his meeting with Hays, Lampell wrote: "We explored the Bowery, prowling past the battered ten-cents-a-night flophouses, the seedy one-arm joints offering a chipped china bowl of soup and a side of bread for fifteen cents. By nightfall, we had become enduring friends."[31]

Lampell and Hays soon teamed with Pete Seeger to form the Almanac Singers, a group that eventually and occasionally included Woody Guthrie, Bess Lomax, Leadbelly, and Burl Ives, among other musicians. The Almanacs "specialized in pro-labor union, racial equality, and antiwar songs."[32] In that regard, they were representative of what cultural historian Michael Denning labels the "cultural front," an expression of beliefs in the betterment of conditions for the working class born in the Popular Front's leftist struggle against fascism. The cultural front was the manifestation of those beliefs in popular works of art. Denning contends that the cultural front was "the result of the encounter between a powerful democratic social movement—the Popular Front—and the modern cultural apparatuses of mass entertainment and education."[33] This designation fits the ideals and musical creations of the Almanac Singers, and it is a designation behind which many conservative Americans "spied a hammer and sickle."[34]

Lee Hays came up with the idea of naming the group the Almanac Singers because while visiting homes throughout the rural south, he noticed that the families typically owned just two books, the *Bible* and the *Farmer's Almanac*. "The Bible helps them to the next world and the almanac helps them through this world," Hays noted.[35] The mission of the folk-singing group was to improve the lot of the downtrodden in this world.

About his involvement with the Almanac Singers, Lampell wrote:

> We were all children of the Depression, who had seen bone-aching poverty, bummed freights across country, shared gunny-sack blankets with the dispossessed and disinherited. We had learned our songs from gaunt, unemployed Carolina cotton weavers and evicted Dust Bowl drifters. . . . We were against hunger, war and silicosis [a lung disease coal miners contracted from dust in the mines], against bankers, landlords, politicians and Dixie deputy sheriffs. We were for the working stiff, the underdog, and the outcast, and these were the passions we poured into our songs.[36]

Lampell did not exaggerate. The group toured the country, more often than not "performing at union meetings and left-wing benefits for Spanish refugees, striking Kentucky coal miners, and starving Alabama sharecroppers."[37]

A "Slick and Sassy Lyricist"

Lampell performed with the Almanacs, but he was never a lead singer. Rather, as Bess Lomax characterized him, he was "a slick and sassy lyricist (by far the quickest and cleverest of us all in that department, young and handsome with a long train of girlfriends)." Throughout the group's relatively short career (they disbanded in 1942), the former football player was "completely reliable and dedicated to the cause" of fighting social injustice.[38]

Among the lyrics Lampell wrote or wrote in collaboration with other members of the Almanacs were songs that may be identified as labor-union anthems, antiwar songs, and songs that supported the role of the Allies in World War II. Lampell, Hays, and Pete Seeger collaborated to write a "Song for Bridges," an homage to Harry Bridges, the San Francisco union leader. The song was featured in an album called *Talking Union*.

Let me tell you of a sailor, Harry Bridges is his name
An honest union leader who the bosses tried to frame.[39]

"Get Thee Behind Me, Satan" recognizes and warns against lures of the flesh and financial bribes that capitalists used to try to dissuade and distract labor from forming unions.

Boss comes up with a five dollar bill
Says, "Get you some whiskey, boy, and drink your fill."

The first day of the military draft before the United States became involved in the war was October 16, 1940, a date that Lampell referred to in his "Ballad of October 16th"; the song was included in the album *Songs for John Doe*. Lampell's lyrics make clear that it would most likely be the poor young men who get drafted while the captains of industry applaud from the plush safety of their corporate offices.

When my poor old mother died, I was sitting by her side
A-promising to war I'd never go.
But now I'm wearing khaki jeans and eating army beans
And I'm told J. P. Morgan loves me so.

The opening line of the chorus is: "Why[,] nothing can be wrong if it makes our country strong." Lampell's and the group's isolationist position and resistance to the draft may well be attributed to the CPUSA's support of the Molotov-Ribbentrop nonaggression pact of 1939. In June 1941, Hitler violated the agreement when his army invaded the Soviet Union.[40] That invasion and the Japanese attack on Pearl Harbor in December 1941 convinced Lampell to change his tune about the war. Lampell, Guthrie, and Seeger combined to write "Round and Round Hitler's Grave," a song that was part of an album of prowar tunes they produced in January 1942 titled *Dear Mr. President*. Lampell wrote most of the lyrics

Now I wished I had a bushel
Wished I had a peck
Wished I had old Hitler
With a rope around his neck.

The Almanacs performed "Round and Round Hitler's Grave" and other songs from the album on February 14, 1942, during Norman Corwin's nationally broadcast radio show *This Is War*.[41] The *Daily Worker*, a publication of the

CPUSA, treated the Almanacs most favorably. An article in the newspaper referred to Lampell as "the dark one with the energetic shoulders, who wrote the song," a reference to "Round and Round Hitler's Grave."[42]

In a story that reviewed the *This Is War* broadcast, a mainstream New York City newspaper depicted the Almanacs as communists who should not have been allowed to perform on the show. The story ran under the headline "Commie Singers Try to Infiltrate Radio."[43] The incessant red-baiting took a toll on the individuals in the group, and the growing pressure led to their decision to disband. Following the dissolution of the Almanac Singers, Lampell worked as a writer before enlisting on June 8, 1943, in the United States Army Air Corps. Like one of the football-playing characters he created for *The Hero*, he saw action as a machine gunner on a B-24 bomber over Italy, achieving the rank of sergeant. He also wrote scripts for the AAF Radio Network. "I wrote, produced, and directed official Air Force radio programs on all the networks," Lampell said in 1952 when he testified before the Senate Committee on Internal Security. "These shows were transcribed for distribution to Army hospitals and were also transcribed for use by the Treasury Department. . . . [They were] distributed to stations to help sell war bonds."[44] However, the committee and the moguls of the entertainment industry were unimpressed with this background; they opted to pay more attention to his work with and for labor unions and the rural poor as justification for his blacklisting.

Conservative members of Congress had no difficulty justifying their decades-long search for communists in the entertainment industry. Lampell was still playing football for WVU in 1938 when Martin Dies, a Democratic senator from Texas, chaired the Committee to Investigate Un-American Activities, a committee that in 1946 had morphed into the House Un-American Activities Committee (HUAC). One of the targets of the committee was the Federal Theater Project, which owed its existence to the New Deal of Franklin D. Roosevelt. According to committee member J. Parnell Thomas, the plays produced by the project amounted to little more than "sheer propaganda for Communism."[45] The Dies committee became something of a national laughingstock when it listed ten-year-old star Shirley Temple among the film figures who offered support for a French communist newspaper *Ce Soir*.[46] World War II came along to force an end to the work of the Dies committee, but the war was no sooner over when HUAC resumed its investigations into communist influence in the entertainment industry, the State Department, and academia.

When the war ended and Lampell was released from the army, he leaped enthusiastically into writing full time. He reworked his interviews with veterans into a radio play titled *The Long Way Home*; it was published in book form in 1947.[47] In August of that year, he went to Hollywood, ostensibly to write a screenplay based on *The Long Way Home*, but the film was never shot. Around this time he became a member of the Writer's Guild and the screenwriters' union. After the Hollywood Ten received subpoenas to appear before HUAC, he became a vice-president of the Committee for the First Amendment. The celebrated Hollywood Ten, seven of whom were screenwriters, were part of a group of nineteen film-industry figures HUAC subpoenaed as suspected communists. Nine were not called to testify, and the ten who did testify refused to cooperate with the committee and eventually served prison time. All were effectively blacklisted.[48] The Committee for the First Amendment was a short lived and ultimately ineffective attempt to support and defend not just the Hollywood Ten but all people working in the film industry who believed they had a constitutional right to freely choose and support a political ideology they believed in.[49]

As early as 1946, the FBI began to investigate Lampell and compile a file on his connection with the CPUSA and his sympathy for "subversive organizations." Among the agency's findings was that in 1946 Lampell had sponsored the Congress on Civil Rights in Detroit and that he chaired the Veterans Against Discrimination of Civil Rights Congress of New York, a group that included among its goals the abolishment of HUAC. The investigation concluded that Lampell was a "Communist Party member of long standing."[50] Especially in the United States, fear and hatred of communists were rampant in the early nuclear age. *American Magazine*, for example, published what amounted to a "how to" story under the headline "Can You Spot a Communist?" One of the most popular television series of the period was *I Led 3 Lives*, a televised sequel to an earlier radio drama, *I Was a Communist for the FBI.* Both productions were based on the true stories of FBI agents who infiltrated the CPUSA, Matt Cvetic in the case of the radio show and Herb Philbrick in the television series.[51] The federal government, enflamed by what Lampell called "belligerent patriotism [and] the growing government impatience with any dissent from official policy," had its eye on the former football player, and it was just a matter of time until he was subpoenaed and blacklisted. In 1950, he was named along with 150 others in *Red Channels*, a publication produced by former FBI agents. In 1952, Senator Pat McCarran, a Nevada Democrat and the chair of the Senate Committee on Internal Security, made public the results of an investigation that stated that a "band of pro-Communists" had assumed control of the Radio Writers Guild. Lampell's name appeared in the report and in subsequent newspaper stories about the investigation.[52] A talented and decorated writer, Lampell suddenly could not find a job. A television producer told him, "Pal, you're dead. I submitted your name for a show, and they told me I couldn't touch you with a barge pole."[53]

Recruiting the Football Star: Groundwork for *The Hero*

Before the blacklist made Lampell a pariah in the entertainment industry, his football novel was published. As is the case with many fiction writers, Lampell used, reimagined, and likely magnified experiences from his own life. For the opening pages of *The Hero*, he calls upon his memories of being a young athlete wooed by college football recruiters. He describes the reaction of his protagonist, Steve Novak, the son of a blue-collar Polish immigrant, as recruiters from the fictional Jackson University in Virginia visit his house.

> Upstairs in the shabby living room with the overstuffed furniture and the colored picture of St. Theresa, the men were waiting. Two of them. They rose as Steve came in: a tall, gray-haired man in an expensive, well-tailored business suit, and a bulky redhead dressed like a college boy in a tweed jacket, gray flannels, and bow tie. The gray-haired man came forward, putting out his hand. "You're Steve Novak, I expect. How do you do? My name is Belfrage. I wrote you." His voice was soft, a delicate, perfect voice.[54]

Everything about Belfrage's pitch for Jackson University strikes Novak as perfect. From the start of the novel, Lampell suggests the unmistakable gap between the social classes—the "working stiff" and the corporate-culture gentleman. If he were more experienced and worldly wise, Novak would have been humming the lyrics of "Get Thee Behind Me, Satan" during Belfrage's recruiting spiel, but he is neither experienced nor worldly wise. That would come later. At this point, the high school senior thinks of Jackson as an aristocratic school, a college populated, as the recruiter assures him, by "boys from the finest old families."[55] Novak's family, which includes his widowed father, Poppa, and his older brother, Joey, an embittered veteran of the Pacific front in World War II, is far removed from the nation's "finest old families." Novak, however, is determined to leave behind the squalor of his New Jersey mill town and move into the ranks of aristocratic gentlemen. Football will be the vehicle he would ride to his conception of the American good life, the "golden world," he calls it, a world of the football hero and a world that impressionable young Novak conjures from the mass media, from "a thousand movies and magazine stories, second-rate novels and photographs in the advertisements."[56]

Lampell's Jackson University is fictional, of course. In the reality of the college football world of 1949, Jackson can likely be read as a version of the University of Virginia. "We've had a President of the United States, and a few Cabinet members. Four Supreme Court Justices," Belfrage tells Novak. "It's one of the oldest colleges in the country—founded before the Revolution."[57] Like Jackson University, the University of Virginia was southern, it fancied itself as aristocratic, and at the time, it was unscrupulously determined to move into the ranks of big-time, profitable football programs. In 1948, the National Collegiate Athletic Association (NCAA) began to flex its regulatory muscle when it adopted the Sanity Code, an attempt to curtail the practice of giving grants-in-aid to athletes based solely on their athletic talent rather than on financial need. In 1950, the NCAA tried to oust from its membership what came to be known as the "Seven Sinners," universities that refused to abide by the recommendations of the Sanity Code. The vote to oust them failed, but one of the "Seven Sinners" was the University of Virginia.[58]

Novak accepts Jackson's offer, one that calls for him to be financially sponsored by a football booster. "We call them 'benefactors,'" Belfrage explains. "Certain well-to-do alumni will adopt a boy. Pay his tuition, room, meals, books, that sort of thing. Not just a cold business proposition. More like father and son."[59] Cultural historian Michael Oriard notes: "This was the arrangement by which stars such as Frankie Sinkwich and Charlie Trippi emigrated from Pennsylvania coal country to the University of Georgia and other southern institutions in the 1940s."[60] Novak's benefactor is T. C. McCabe, a man so wealthy he has a town named after him, a man so powerful that he and his wealth are the real rulers of Jackson University. Novak does not meet him until he arrives on campus, "serene and magnificent." Novak comes from White Falls, New Jersey, where "the seasons come without poetry," ushered in "on the stale wind across the Jersey marshes."[61] White Falls is "a shabby town cut off from the heroic traditions of the nation."[62] Jackson University, in contrast, is awash in poetry and heroism—southern poetry and southern heroism. The chapel is adorned with "torn Confederate battle flags, the framed letters signed by Jefferson Davis and Jeb Stuart."

> To Steve it seemed that here in Virginia, in the foothills of the Blue Ridge Mountains, was the real America. This was the country of history-book tales, of the songs he had learned in grammar school: "Oh, beautiful for spacious skies, for amber waves of grain." This was an America Steve

> had never known, only dreamed about, only caught sight of in the pages of books, dimly silvered with history. Now he would be part of it.[63]

Or so he believes. Hopes. But of course it is all an illusion.

Football Heroes and Real Heroes

Not surprisingly, the word "hero" recurs frequently throughout the novel, and just as Lampell forges a deliberate contrast between social classes, he creates a contrast between types of heroes that runs throughout the narrative. The first reference to a "hero" occurs when Novak imagines what his life at Jackson might be like, a daydream that comes not from anything real but from the "voice of Warner Brothers and the *Saturday Evening Post*." Novak projects himself into his mass-mediated notion of the "portrait of the hero as a young man lounging in a Buick advertisement, athletic, tailored, confident, the American legend. For Steve Novak, football was part of the legend."[64] Football, Novak believes, is "clean and beautiful, its ritual somehow comforting, the clipped green field far removed from the dirt of the world."[65] And, as he prefers to believe, football at gentlemanly Jackson would be far removed from the mill-town dirt of White Falls.

As the recruiters begin their sales pitch in the Novak living room, Steve notices with "a prick of embarrassment and annoyance that Poppa's Polish newspaper lay open on the table."[66] Poppa, Jan Novak, is the first representative of a different kind of hero in the novel. Poppa's brand of heroism bears no similarity to anything that might appear in American mass media. Rather, he became a "minor hero" for his militant role in the "great silk strike of 1913."

> He had marched on the picket line, shouting songs at the top of his powerful voice; he had been one of those chosen to take part in the massive public meeting staged by John Reed in Madison Square Garden. And on the sunny morning when the police approached carrying children's baseball bats, Poppa had been in the front ranks. He had been badly beaten, and herded off to jail with a bleeding face. Those were perhaps the only days when Poppa felt completely accepted among men, and he bloomed.[67]

In a clever bit of literary irony, Lampell makes clear that when Steve suffers a career-ending football injury, he is most definitely not accepted among Jackson men.

As the novel progresses, another working-class hero emerges: Steve's older brother, Joey. Like the World War II veterans Lampell interviewed for *The*

Long Way Home, Joey experiences difficulty with assimilating himself in the life of postwar America. He is unemployed and his prospects seem dim compared with those of his football-hero brother. "My little brother's gonna be an educated man," he says derisively. "An educated snotnose. That's the way it goes. One son turns out to be an educated man, and one son turns out to be a bum."[68]

Joey, though, turns out to be anything but a bum. On one of his rare trips home from Jackson, Steve discovers that Joey has a job and that he is a union leader. "In the shop here, the company used to give hams for Christmas," he tells Steve. "A beautiful gesture. They were paying less than any place in the state, but everybody got a nice ham. When we brought in the union, we stopped that fast. We told them to put it in the pay envelope." In addition, Joey is going to night school where he is studying "electrical stuff" for work. "And politics. I've learned a few things they don't teach in that college of yours; what makes the big boys, and what breaks them."[69]

The Politics of the "Big Boy"

At Jackson, the biggest of the "big boys" is Novak's benefactor, T. C. McCabe. The self-made millionaire has a heavy hand in directing the decisions of the university's administration and the athletic administration. When he wanted football players, he paid them.[70] In fact, McCabe treats everything and everyone associated with him as property, including Novak and McCabe's niece, Melissa. Novak and Melissa become romantically involved, but Melissa knows that sustaining the relationship will be difficult, that McCabe will put an end to it, a realization that puzzles Novak. "Why? Why would he want to do that?" Because, Melissa explains, "It isn't his. It's something we did ourselves. He can't stand that."[71]

McCabe's relationship with his niece Melissa is unusual, to say the least. He calls her "Lovecat." His wife is dead and Melissa is his constant companion. If she becomes even slightly involved with a young man, McCabe disapproves, even to the point of sabotaging her engagement to a "prominent lawyer from Roanoke."[72] As Novak's and Melissa's relationship grows more intense, McCabe objects. Both Novak and Melissa, young and powerful figures who are rendered powerless, are in every significant way subservient to their "benefactor."

By the time his sophomore football season arrives, Novak is entrenched as Jackson's resident football hero. As Jackson wins games and the headlines praising Novak become more commonplace, McCabe cunningly uses Novak's stardom to further the political goals he has for his handpicked candidate for governor. At a reception on the evening following a victory over West Virginia (Lampell most likely could not resist the temptation of inserting his alma mater in the losing column), McCabe presides over a celebratory gathering that includes the governor, the university president, wealthy alumni, and the football team.

> "Gentlemen," McCabe said softly with a little gesture toward the players' table, "I give you these boys, the spirit of America. . . . Let the history books write about the generals and statesmen—the children of America will continue to fashion their heroes in the image of the athlete."[73]

No football hero is greater, McCabe asserts, than Steve Novak. McCabe announces that Novak will be the first Jackson player to wear jersey number 44, a retired number that belonged to Johnny Masters, a sports and military hero who was killed in action in World War I. Novak is called to a place of honor at the front of the room, everyone sings the alma mater, and Novak is enthralled by his moment of glory. "The singing, the pride, the feeling that he was one of them, one with the Governor and the trustees, the men of historic names and historic position—the sense that this moment would hold through the years."[74] No longer is he the son of a working-class Polish immigrant from a gritty industrial town. He is what he always believed he could be, what he feels he deserves to be, a Jackson gentleman.

Novak is also a good and industrious student who establishes a special bond with his academic adviser, Professor Megroth, who includes him in gatherings in his home with Jackson's few students of an intellectual bent. However, Novak's focus on academics changes when McCabe coerces him into going on the road with him to attend meetings of alumni and wealthy citizens of Virginia after the football season. Ostensibly the aim of the meetings is to generate enthusiasm and funds for Jackson football with Novak as the star attraction. That function, however, is secondary to McCabe's political agenda, a machination Novak does not fully comprehend until after he suffers a career-ending injury in a game against the University of Alabama. It is his sportswriting friend Eddie Abrams, who has taken a job as a public relations agent for Jackson football, who finally makes him aware of McCabe's true intentions. "McCabe's been using you, and the team, and the goddamn university to build himself a political machine! . . . He got the backing of people in this state who'd ordinarily hate his guts! He's trying to be the King-maker. He wants to ride his man into the Governor's seat."[75]

In addition to being duped, Novak allows McCabe to convince him to play in the Alabama game even though he has already been badly injured. "You're going to play because there's nothing else you can do," McCabe tells him.

"What the hell are you without football! You're nothing."[76] McCabe, Novak reasons, is right about one thing—he is not one with the aristocratic gentlemen of Jackson. He has come full circle from White Falls to Jackson and back again. In a scene analogous to the one that occurs when he is first recruited by Belfrage, Novak, now aware of the hypocrisy of McCabe and big-time football, decides to quit Jackson. "He felt a revulsion toward the place. It was a symbol now of something grotesque and embarrassing, a symbol of a ridiculous and adolescent dream, a dream that he could enter some exclusive and aristocratic world."[77]

Before he leaves, he pays a visit to Professor Megroth, and Megroth teaches him his final college lesson. He says:

> Of all the nations on earth, it seems to me that America is peculiarly a country fed on myths. . . . We've developed a whole culture designed to send young men chasing after a thousand glistening and empty goals. You too, Novak. You believe the legend. Like the rest of us, you've dreamed up your image of the Hero—the man you want to be. . . . And it is the world of amateur athletics that is particularly the realm of the Great American Myth. . . . It is the chance for success and acclaim most easily within reach. For some—boys from mill towns and coal camps—it is almost the only chance.[78]

Like work in the mills or coal mines, Megroth continues, amateur athletics is an industry built on illusion and the physical sacrifices of young men, the laborers who work for virtually nothing, sustained by impossible dreams. "You have to recognize the myth, Novak. You have to learn what is the illusion, and what is the reality. That is when you will cease being hurt, baffled, disillusioned by a place like this."[79]

In the throes of his injury and his decision to leave college, Novak receives word that Poppa has died. Still, for Novak, there is Melissa and the tantalizing prospect of getting the girl, fulfilling at least that part of his dream. Novak tells her that he is leaving Jackson for good and returning to White Falls, and Lampell dangles the possibility before his readers that Melissa will forsake McCabe and his wealth for a life with Novak in his mill town. In *Saturday's Hero,* the film version of the novel, that is what Melissa (Donna Reed) does. The film ends with her phoning Novak (John Derek) to tell him she will be joining him in White Falls.[80] To his credit, Lampell concludes his narrative with a decidedly more ambiguous—and more realistic and intelligent—ending. Alone on the familiar streets of White Falls, Novak feels he has returned to his roots, not the "golden world where all people were beautiful, where each day was triumph."[81] For the first time in his life, he knows where he is going and that what he has to do "did not depend on Melissa or on anyone else except himself."[82] Novak does not need Melissa; he does not need anything related to the American myth he was chasing. He asks Joey to get him a job in the mill while he finishes college in night school. "He grinned at Joey in the darkness. 'One bum in the family is enough.'" This line takes both of them back to their argument on the night that Belfrage made his recruitment offer. "Joey sat on the edge of the bed, rocking back and forth. 'An educated man,' he said gently. There was no irony or bitterness; his voice was proud. 'My little brother's an educated man.'"[83] This time the line rings true. Steve Novak is no longer the mythical football hero. He is exactly and finally what Joey says he is—"an educated man."

Postscript: Surviving the Blacklist and Fighting 'Forgettery'

After Lampell's novel was published and made into a film, the professional void began. "I began to have increased difficulty in getting telephone calls through to producers I had known for years." Eventually, Lampell's agent "called me in, locked her door, and announced in a tragic whisper, 'You're on the list.'"[84] Lampell's annual income dropped from five figures to $2,000. He sold his car, moved his wife and children to a cramped apartment, and "when my savings ran out, lived on small loans from friends and what I could earn from a thin trickle of odd, ill-paid assignments." Like other blacklisted writers, he used a pseudonym on television scripts and took assignments writing "industrial training films, travel shorts, doctoring Broadway plays."[85]

The blacklist, Lampell asserted, lasted longer in New York–based broadcasting than it did in Hollywood. Finally, in 1964, he wrote a play for television for which he received name credit. *No Hiding Place* told the story of "a Negro family moving into a white suburb" and the ensuing difficulties they experienced. Lampell later remarked that the televised play was "the first time my name had appeared on the home screen in more than a decade."[86]

Eagle in a Cage, the televised play for which he won an Emmy, was produced the following year. As if the blacklist decade had never happened, Lampell was back on top of the professional writing game. However, he remained wary and politically active. In 1965, Lyndon B. Johnson began to escalate American military involvement in Vietnam, a decidedly more incendiary chapter in the Cold War battle. In June of that year, Lampell was included in a White House program to celebrate the arts in America. A scene from his latest play, *Hard Travelin'*, set during the Great Depression, was staged. It was a scene in a boxcar between "a Negro escaping from a Georgia chain gang and a decent white boy who was drifting." The dramatic fragment, Howard Taubman reported in the *New York Times*, spoke eloquently of two contemporary concerns in the 1960s, "the lot of the Negro and the fight against poverty." The segment was included in the program and Lampell appeared at the showing "despite the fact that [he] had joined in picketing the White House a month ago in a protest against Vietnam policy."[87] As was the case in the years following World War II, again the nation was put at risk by "a flare-up of belligerent patriotism, signs of official impatience with dissent," as Lampell noted. Fearing that, as Carl Sandburg had once remarked, "man has a quick forgettery," Lampell continued to battle, as he always had, for causes he felt were right and just and deserved the public's attention.[88]

II

Winning the "Right" Way

Performance, Amateurism, and the American Moral Compass

3

The "Big Arms" Race

Doping and the Cold War Defense of American Exceptionalism

BY JOHN GLEAVES
AND MATTHEW P. LLEWELLYN

On February 28, 2017, American swimmer Michael Phelps testified before a US House of Representatives subcommittee tasked with investigating the ongoing Russian doping scandal. "I don't believe," stated Phelps, the most decorated athlete in Olympic history, "that I've stood up at an international competition and the rest of the field has been clean."[1] This claim should probably have raised a few eyebrows and perhaps even some follow-up questions. For example, "How did you manage to beat so many drug cheats en route to winning twenty-three gold medals?" Or, "How many more medals do you think you would have won against a drug-free field?" Instead, a foot race for a photo opportunity with the storied Olympian took priority for most people in the room.

The hearing itself was largely a farce. Yet with allegations of covert Russian doping set against the investigations into Russian president Vladimir Putin's political interference in the 2016 US presidential election—not to mention growing concerns about Russian geopolitical interests in general—Washington officials found themselves in one of those moments where history seemed to be repeating. Given this repetition, examining how Americans responded to rumors of Soviet doping during the Cold War offers some guidance to contemporary audiences and further reveals how sport acted as a tool for manufacturing national identity.

In popular memory, the use of pharmacological substances among elite athletes to enhance sporting performances remains intimately tied to the Cold War. Casting their gaze behind the former Iron Curtain, western journalists regularly refer to doping cases involving athletes from both the Soviet Union and German Democratic Republic (GDR) when writing about twenty-first-century doping scandals. Historical works and documentaries also pay considerable attention to doping during this period.[2] Public recollections of Cold War sport often evoke images of steroid-enhanced Eastern Bloc athletes topping medal podiums and secret state-run laboratories where communist sport scientists work into the night preparing the next round of wonder drugs that will fuel their athletes' illicit propaganda victories. Revelations in the 1990s and 2000s about systematic doping practices in the GDR, which occurred from the 1960s to the 1980s, further ensconced images of the "nefarious" communists in collective memory.[3]

Collective memory, however, is often unreliable. It reinforces popular narratives while selectively forgetting or misremembering the *who*, the *what*, and the *when*. This is especially true when the public remembers the morally fraught history of athletes using performance-enhancing substances. This added layer of illicit drug use compounds the typical "'good guys' versus the 'bad guys'" historical narrative. In the end, it becomes easy for the public to imagine the other team as cheaters capable of secret doping regimes and the home team as morally superior athletes competing purely on grit and talent.

The haziness of collective memory is not the only challenge for historians investigating doping. Numerous methodological challenges and choices require careful thought. First, the concept of doping is problematic because it changes based on context. For example, many scholars wish to limit the definition of doping to the use of banned performance-enhancing substances, but this ignores the fact that previous generations used the term before any bans were introduced.[4] Similarly, many referred to the practice of blood transfusions in the context of elite sport as "blood doping" before the International Olympic Committee (IOC) became the first sporting organization to ban it in 1985.[5] Second, historians studying doping are working with a practice whose moral evaluation has fluctuated greatly from tacit approval to scandalous condemnation.[6] This makes issues of presentism—when scholars read present views into past events—an even greater challenge, as contemporary moral views of doping practices can seem to contrast starkly with the permissibility or ambiguity expressed by earlier generations. As this chapter will show, changing views of the morality of doping influenced how people remembered the past. Retired athletes speaking in the 1980s about their use of performance-enhancing substances during the 1960s do not speak as openly and enthusiastically as they did two decades earlier, when they (and the public) did not consider the practice unethical.

The most important challenge for historians researching doping is separating fact from fiction. Doping practices often occurred in secret. This makes verifying claims rather difficult. However, rumors and innuendo about secret doping practices grabbed headlines, particularly during the Cold War. Thus, media reports often provide historians with the best insight into past doping practices. As will become apparent, however, these reports present their own challenges. Occasionally, the media reported rumors that turned out to be true. The flood of Stasi files that emerged following the reunification of Germany in 1990 both confirmed the suspicions about doped GDR athletes and demonstrated an even greater level of state-supported doping than was previously assumed. Other times, corroboration of rumors proves difficult or illusive. Despite myriad allegations by western journalists and athletes, historians have yet to uncover substantial evidence that indicates systematic doping within the Soviet Union. Historian Jenifer Parks, a leading expert on the Soviet sport system, acknowledges that in stark contrast to the abundance of material that reveals the clandestine GDR doping program, evidence of a comparable state-funded Soviet doping infrastructure is unavailable.[7]

The unavailability of documents confirming the practice is important, but what does it mean? On the one hand, the absence of evidence requires historians to exercise caution about accepting claims that doping was widespread among athletes in the Soviet Union. As will be clear, the claims of Soviet doping emerged through rumors reported by western media at a time when Soviet athletes began challenging western hegemony within international sport. Still, most historians remain doubtful that the doping rumors are complete fabrication. The overwhelming evidence from the Stasi files on GDR doping and research into doping in the Federal Republic of West Germany and the United States indicates the Soviet Union likely engaged in some form of doping similar to other communist and capitalist nations in this period.[8] It is most likely that doping fueled a "big arms" race on both sides of the Iron Curtain as international sport became another proxy battleground in the Cold War.

Sport behind the Iron Curtain

In the decades before World War II, the Soviet Union rarely participated in international sport. Illustrating Stalin's distaste for the West, the Soviets refused to affiliate with international sports federations and in most instances boycotted direct competition with bourgeois states.[9] Instead, the Soviets participated in mass (*Massovost*) physical activities, pageants, and military parades designed to promote national defense, social integration, and the health, hygiene, and nutrition of the communist worker.[10] The postwar geographical restructuring of the world's political and economic balance, however, pulled the Soviet Union slowly out of diplomatic isolation and toward participation in elite international sport as part of a cultural and ideological battle for the "hearts and minds" of the world.[11]

Sport provided the most global, symbolic platform for Cold War rivals seeking to demonstrate the superiority of their respective ways of life. Unable to compete with the capitalist West in the economic arena, the Soviets embraced international sport as a political forum for defeating their ideological opponents.[12] Soviet sport was a completely government-run enterprise. All Soviet sport facilities and clubs came under the absolute control of the state, which lavishly funded and methodically devised methods for discovering, nurturing, and harnessing sports talent.[13] Soviet athletes were transformed into "ambassadors for socialism" tasked with the responsibility of bringing international prestige to the Soviet Union.[14] Soviet athletes received sinecures for fictitious work in the armed services or state industries. Many were also state-supported full-time students (and would remain so throughout their entire athletic careers) and attended one of forty-two elite performance sports boarding schools. Under Stalin's regime (and beyond), winning was absolutely necessary to justify participation in international competitions. Defeat threatened the entire propaganda message, and Soviet officials left no stone unturned in pursuit of victory.[15] In this context, it is not difficult to imagine (despite the absence of definitive proof) that clandestine doping programs also were a key ingredient in the Soviets' recipe for attaining international sporting success.

The 1952 Summer Olympic Games in Helsinki marked the first meeting between athletes from the rival Cold War states. The participation of the Soviet Union alongside the United States raised the political propaganda stakes to a feverish pitch. The Soviets mobilized for success on an unprecedented scale. Internal memorandums reveal that Politburo officials authorized ministries and departments to release all Olympic athletes from work and school with elevated pay for the six months leading up to the games.[16] Despite implementing an elaborate, scientific system replete with pioneering training methods and professional practices, the Soviets finished narrowly behind their ideological rivals, the United States, in the final medal standings. Stalin's desire to translate Olympic gold medals into a propaganda victory had to wait.

Defeat failed to halt the Soviet sport and propaganda machine. The success of the Soviet team at the 1956 Melbourne games revealed the extent of its state-funded sport apparatus. The Soviets also succeeded in fostering a collective socialist identity through elite sport. Soviet officials welcomed officials from neighboring communist countries intent on reproducing its effective sporting structures and scientific fitness programs and in promoting state amateurism through army and security forces clubs, elite boarding schools, and other institutions.[17] The GDR, perhaps more than the other Eastern Bloc satellites, best adapted the communist model of systematic state-run amateur sport, which transformed the small state into a global sporting powerhouse.[18] The world eventually learned decades later that the GDR had extended its Soviet-style sport administration to include a state-sponsored doping program, "State Plan 14.25," in which an estimated 10,000 athletes received performance-enhancing drugs.[19]

In the 1950s, however, any doping practices in the Soviet Union occurred behind the Iron Curtain and away from the suspicions eyes of western journalists and sporting officials. Although the IOC banned doping in 1938, the rule was subsumed under larger reforms of its amateurism code.[20] Violations of amateurism, not doping, often provoked sensational headlines and minor scandals in sport throughout the 1950s and 1960s. Accusations of communist—and, more specifically, Soviet—doping that appeared in the western media during this period stand out for their rarity. As early as the 1952 Helsinki Olympic Games, rumors of "secret" Soviet doping practices surfaced after the USSR challenged the United States for dominance in weightlifting events. "I don't know what it was. . . . It was a drug, or a stimulant or something," recounted Dietrich Wortmann, chair of the US Amateur Athletic Union Weightlifting Committee. "Before each lift a bottle of the stuff would be put under the competitor's nose and he'd take a deep whiff," Wortmann detailed, "then his eyes would become glassy and he'd start lifting like a maniac."[21] American weightlifting coach and physical culturalist Bob Hoffman went further, claiming, "I know they're taking that hormone stuff to increase their strength."[22]

Accusations of Soviet doping emerged again in the weeks before the 1960 Rome Olympic Games, when a British journalist questioned Nikolai Romanov, chair of the All-Union Soviet Sports Committee, about "feeding pep pills to athletes" and asked whether Romanov "suspected that there had been doping of athletes at meets." Well versed in the art of political brinkmanship, Romanov, a high-level Communist Party bureaucrat, denied knowledge of any doping. "The Soviet Union refused to dope its athletes because it was harmful to them and shortened their careers," he reassured the journalist.[23]

Soviet weightlifter Yury Vlasov (center) winning the gold medal in the heavyweight division at the 1960 Summer Olympic Games in Rome. Vlasov defeated Americans James Bradford (left) and Norbert Schemansky (right). *Source: Wikimedia Commons.*

Reports of the drug-related death of Danish cyclist Knud Enemark Jensen at the Rome Olympic Games three weeks later further diverted attention away from Soviet athletes.[24]

Sport in the Capitalist West

The communists were not alone in pursuing pharmacological support for athletic success. The United States also used—in varying degrees and through alternative, often surreptitious channels—government resources, scientific knowledge, and pharmacological substances to boost sporting performances. The interference of the state in sporting affairs conflicted with the traditional US dictum that sport should be run by private, voluntary associations comprised of mostly unpaid individuals. The United States prided itself on the fact that all Olympic campaigns were financed by private donations rather than the largesse of its government and that its athletes were amateurs in the purest sense of the term.

Peeling back the layers of convenient mythology reveals an alternate reality. The United States pioneered the "science of sport."[25] Through training manuals, physical education periodicals, laboratory studies of physiology and diet, and film analysis of technique, various types of professionals helped US athletes become world leaders.[26] The groundbreaking advancements of the human physiology laboratories of Harvard, Yale, and the University of Chicago helped solidify the United States' claims to international sporting dominance.[27] In the competitive US collegiate environment, professional coaches established and promoted a comprehensive scientific basis for improving sporting performance. College coaches actively recruited talented athletes and rewarded their sporting performances by financing (to varying degrees) their studies and living expenses.[28]

The United States' application of science to sport intensified significantly amid the growing political importance of sport in Cold War cultural diplomacy. Many in the West feared that their programs had not kept pace with Soviet Bloc advances in sport science.[29] Citing concerns that "Eastern European countries had developed sophisticated sports medicine programs," the USOC created a panel of experts in 1976 to explore "areas considered taboo," including nutritional, pharmacological, and medical approaches to training and "extensive research into the effects of anabolic steroids and blood-doping on performance."[30] The United States also pursued private ventures outside the orbit of bureaucratic and governmental influence. The American running shoe company Nike established a pseudo-professional running club named Athletics West to signify both its geographic roots in Oregon and its political ideology.[31] Athletics West provided resources for postcollegiate US athletes that included training facilities, living quarters, and monthly stipends, and access to coaches, massage therapists, exercise physiologists, sport psychologists, and even illicit anabolic steroids, corticosteroids, and blood transfusions.[32]

Contrary to the popular narrative, the performance of US athletes also came under government scrutiny. Alarmed by the emergence of the Soviet sport system, US politicians took to the floor of Congress before the 1956 Olympic Games to support subsidies for future Olympic teams. This proposal, a direct affront to the private-voluntary model that had funded previous US Olympic campaigns, spoke to the political conditions of Cold War competition. Although the proposal to subsidize US Olympic athletes failed to win congressional approval, the government began launching secret programs to expose the professional and corrupt practices of communist sport.[33]

Over time, the growing failure of the United States to defeat the Soviet Union and its communist allies at the Olympics pushed the US government to become increasingly involved in US sport. The Eisenhower and Kennedy administrations took the first steps toward government intervention by creating the *President's Council on Physical Fitness and Sport* (formerly the *President's Council on Youth Fitness*) to address fears of falling standards of fitness. Sport-for-all governmental initiatives, however, failed to curb Soviet sporting advances. US vice president Gerald Ford acknowledged the growing political value of Olympic victory. "It is not enough to just compete," Ford said in a 1974 interview with *Sports Illustrated*. "Winning is very important. Maybe more important than ever."[34] The sight of Soviets atop the Olympic medal table during the 1970s eventually prompted the US government to reevaluate its role in the country's domestic preparation for the Olympic Games. In 1978, President Carter signed the *Amateur Sports Act*, which comprehensively reorganized US elite sport and awarded the USOC the lucrative commercial rights to the five-ring Olympic logo within the United States.[35]

The US public soon learned that American athletes had used many of the same scientific methods used by the Soviet Union and its Eastern Bloc satellites. In the summer of 1969, Bill Gilbert's extensively researched three-part article "Something Extra on the Ball" in *Sports Illustrated* provided readers with a picture of widespread performance-enhancing drug use in elite sport. Gilbert documented open confessions of drug use from American gold medalists such as 1956 hammer-thrower Hal Connolly, 1964 shot-putter Dallas Long, and 1968 shot-putter Randy Matson.[36] Jack Scott's 1971 *New York Times* article "It's Not How You Play the Game, but What Pill You Take" said that Bill Toomey, the US gold medalist in the 1968 Olympic Games decathlon, claimed to have used drugs. Scott also reported US weightlifter Ken Patera's assertion that "the only difference between me" and his Soviet rival Vasily Alexseyev "was that I couldn't afford his drug bill. Now I can." Patera enthused "when I hit Munich next year, I'll weigh in at about 340, maybe 350 [pounds]. Then we'll see which are better—his steroids or mine." Scott also quoted Dr. Tom Waddel, a physician and American decathlete, who claimed that "more than one third of the US track and field team was using anabolic steroids during the pre-Olympic high-altitude camp at South Lake Tahoe in 1968."[37] Four years later, one month before the 1972 Olympic Games in Munich, the *Los Angeles Times* published the claim of Pat O'Rea, the US Olympic weightlifting team physiologist, that "if every member of the US Olympic weightlifting team who took non-therapeutic drugs was disqualified, the United States would not have a team at Munich."[38]

(Re)Writing the Story

The 1972 Munich Games marked a turning point in American attitudes about doping. Though the Munich terrorist attack on September 5, 1972, consumed the media's attention, the US coverage of the Olympic Games before that event included extensive discussion of doping issues. The IOC had announced they would introduce a test for anabolic steroids at the Munich games.[39] The wonder drug had been banned, and it became harder for American audiences to accept American athletes using it. While fewer athletes offered confessions, media coverage continued to speculate about widespread drug use, the effects of the new drug tests, and Cold War rivalries.[40] Stuart Auerbach, a reporter for the *Washington Post,* wrote from the Munich Olympic Village S. public about "magic pills" known as anabolic steroids, which he explained were first introduced into the 1960 Olympic Games by Soviet athletes. Auerbach credited Dr. John Ziegler, a prominent American physician, with uncovering the source of the Soviet's strength and athletic success.[41]

Auerbach's claim—one of the earliest to directly cite the Soviet Union as the source of anabolic steroids—remains a common belief in popular perceptions of Cold War doping history. This is largely due to the media's reproduction of Ziegler's claim, which Auerbach cited, about the source of testosterone use.[42] Ziegler, the chief physician for the US weightlifting team at the 1954 World Championships in Vienna, told of how his Soviet counterpart let slip "after a few drinks" that Soviet weightlifters secretly used testosterone to build muscle. Ziegler claims to have returned to the United States and with the help of Ciba pharmaceuticals developed Dianabol in 1958, an anabolic steroid that could help American athletes compete with their Soviet counterparts.[43] Ziegler's story had everything Cold War US audiences wanted to believe: a drunk Soviet, a naïve American physician, and an honest effort to level the playing field with the communists who, after all, had moved the goalposts. However, this narrative is mostly spurious. In fact, the reproduction of Ziegler's story illustrates the pattern of revisionist mythmaking about performance-enhancing drugs that occurred in the United States during the Cold War.

Anabolic steroids, following from the synthesis of testosterone in 1935, had gained modest but sustained interest in the medical community as a means of enlarging muscles following World War II.[44] Their spread into sporting arenas in the 1950s corresponds with the Soviet Union's entrance into the Olympic movement. However, as historian Paul Dimeo points out, "the question of who first used steroids for sporting competitions has yet to be conclusively answered."[45] John Hoberman underlines the claims espoused by popular science writer Paul de Kruif about the benefits of testosterone, which first appeared in major US magazines including *Reader's Digest* and *Newsweek* as early as 1945.[46] De Kruif's 1945 book *The Male Hormone* linked the championship-winning St. Louis Cardinals and the St. Louis Browns football teams to the use of "super-charged" testosterone pills.[47] Two other examples—German physician Martin Brustmann's administration of testosterone to a German rowing team in 1952 and Danish physician Axel Mathiesen's prescription of the testicular extract Androstin to Danish rowers in 1950—are reliable examples of synthetic testosterone use in sport that predates Ziegler's claims linking the hormone to the Soviet Union.[48]

Interestingly, Ziegler's claims that linked his knowledge of anabolic steroids to the Soviets did not circulate in the US media before 1972 (and the embellished mention of "a few drinks" being involved did not appear until 1983).[49] Ziegler's story surfaced nearly two decades after the event allegedly occurred, after the IOC banned anabolic steroids and after the Soviets won the overall medal count in Munich. Others have pointed out Ziegler's loose relationship with facts.[50] But perhaps the most damage to Ziegler's story comes from John Grimek, an Olympian turned body builder, a two-time Mr. America, and a winner of the Mr. Universe contest. Grimek claimed that "by the time they met" in 1954, Ziegler was "giving testosterone injections to fellow trainees [at a gym] in Silver Springs [Maryland]."[51] Grimek insisted that by the summer of 1954, he was "experimenting with a variety of chemical substances provided by Ziegler."[52] This was all before Ziegler accompanied the US weightlifting team to the World Championships in Vienna that October. What is more, when he returned from Vienna, Ziegler expressed annoyance that the Soviet coaches suspected *him* of supplying US athletes with a secret stimulant but made no mention of testosterone use by the Soviets, who had bested the US team at the event.[53]

Although Ziegler's story is light on facts, its focus on drug-taking Soviets made it an instant classic in western reporting on doping throughout the Cold War. As Soviet athletes solidified their dominance at the Olympic Games—winning the most medals at every Summer and Winter Olympic Games from 1972 to 1980—US media revelations about its own athletes previously using performance-enhancing drugs suddenly stopped. In part, the IOC's ban on anabolic steroids in 1972 and the increasing familiarity with anti-doping rules removed much of the moral ambiguity about doping that had previously existed in media coverage. Few, for instance, could applaud US weightlifter Ken Patera's desire to measure his steroids against the Soviets when everyone knew that using them violated the rules.

The US media discourse changed direction at the precise moment when the Soviets seized control of Olympic medal tables in the 1970s. In an effort to rationalize defeat, the US media contrasted drug-fueled Soviet professionals with honest American amateurs who played in accordance with the rules and spirit of sportsmanship and fair play. Despite the wealth of claims to the contrary, Dr. Peter Riehl, the 1972 US Olympic physician, claimed that there was "very little use [of anabolic steroids]" on the US team. Riehl added that "none of the boys are on [anabolic steroids] now."[54] The Soviets, the US media howled, paid little attention to the rules of international competition. When Soviet sprinter Valeriy Borzov won both the 100-meter and 200-meter sprints at the 1972 games, columnist Jim Murray hinted in the *Los Angeles Times* that there was something more going on: "They gave Borzov the standard doping test but that ain't about to satisfy me. I want to check him for wires and valves and reset button. . . . This guy wasn't born, he was programmed." Foreshadowing the United States' desire to copy aspects of the communist state sport system, Murray concluded, "I suggest we write to the University of Kiev and find out the components of a Valeriy Borzov and turn the contract over to North Americans. I mean, if the Russians can do it, dammit we can get ours higher, right?"[55] Journalist Neil Amdur also promulgated the narrative of secret Soviet Bloc doping. He reported that "a *New York Times* inquiry into the drug situation at Munich disclosed that athletes from the Soviet Union, East Germany and several other Eastern European nations had access to large quantities of a new drug that could be taken as late as 15 minutes before a competition to stimulate performances." Amdur's article failed to mention US swimmer Rick DeMont, who inadvertently tested positive after using his asthma medicine; it focused exclusively on knowledge of communist doping practices that was emerging from behind the Iron Curtain.[56]

Excuses for Failure

The 1976 Montreal Olympic Games proved disastrous for the United States; both the Soviet Union and the GDR bested the Americans in the final medal count. The sight of successful Soviet wrestlers, GDR swimmers, Romanian gymnasts, Polish volleyball players, and Bulgarian weightlifters demonstrated the athletic prowess of the Communist Bloc nations on North American soil. The communists' dominance, many Americans rushed to say, came not only from their willingness to embrace state-sponsored "shamateurism" but also from their application of scientific practices, including the use of anabolic steroids.[57] Yet the narrative that clean US athletes lagged behind their doped Soviet counterparts conveniently overlooked the two American weightlifters, Paul Cerutti and Phillip Grippaldi, who tested positive for anabolic steroids in Montreal.[58] Behind the scenes, the USOC moved to close the gap in the "big arms" race by allocating $2 million to establish a major sports medicine program in the hope that "American athletes can start utilizing the same complex medical data that has benefited athletes in Communist-bloc countries."[59] As Dr. Irving Dardik, chair of the USOC sports medicine commission, explained: "We want to go into blood doping, steroids and all these other areas that have sprung up in athletics. Our purpose is to leave no stone unturned. We want to find out what these things mean and then develop polices to govern their use."[60]

Neither reports of US athletes using banned performance-enhancing substances nor the USOC's decision to fund sports medicine programs garnered much media coverage. Instead, the US media focused its attention on communist chicanery. The Soviets and their Eastern Bloc satellites, US audiences were repeatedly told, were the ones who transgressed the spirit of sport by funneling drugs into Olympic arenas. With a combination of Cold War intrigue and misdirection, the *New York Times* cited unnamed "West German doctors" who claimed that "steroids were secretly sanctioned years ago by the Soviet-bloc nations."[61] *Washington Post* reporter Nancy Scannell spun a similar yarn, noting the rumors "which have for years drifted out of the Soviet Union and East European satellites, particularly East Germany, of drug experiments with athletes."[62] Noting that "the Montreal Olympics were riddled with stories of athletes resorting to blood doping, steroids, air inflation, electrical stimulation of muscles and other such medically mysterious ways of improving performance," reporter Paul Attner of the *Washington Post* reassured US readers that "these stories rarely involved American athletes. Indeed, the joke was that Americans couldn't be involved because they didn't know anything about the procedures."[63] Such claims were bolstered by stories of communist athletes who failed drug tests.[64]

Within the bureaucracy of elite international sport, the issue of anti-doping increasingly reflected the Cold War divide. As historian Thomas Hunt has documented, the politicization of anti-doping among sport officials in the 1970s and 1980s played out in the enforcement of anti-doping rules.[65] For example, a 1978 vote to uphold the ban on Soviet track athletes Nadezhda Tkachenko and Yevgeniy Mironov split along ideological lines: all eight votes in favor came from representatives of western countries and all six votes in opposition came from the Eastern Bloc.[66] Soviet officials later dismissed the allegations against swimmer Viktor Kuznetsov, alleging that "'certain circles' were trying to discredit their country."[67] The Soviets dismissed claims of state-sponsored drug use in communist sport as slanderous propaganda drummed up by bourgeois states that were carefully scripted to mask the rampant drug use among western athletes.[68] US sporting officials claimed to see through Soviet maneuvering. When Soviet Yuri Titov, president of the Fédération Internationale de Gymnastique, dismissed the need for drug testing in gymnastics, US coach Roger Council implied that he did so to benefit Soviet doping. "Titov is so politically biased toward the Russians," Council thundered, "that he obviously would be aware of what was happening."[69] Capturing the zeitgeist of the decade, *Washington Post* journalist Barry Lorge wrote, "East-West polarization and mutual suspicion also has produced an athletic chemical arms race. . . . Athletes everywhere seem to be sure their competitors are using drugs, especially steroids."[70]

Closing the Gap

However, the reality was that US athletes were not the pristine purveyors of fair play that the US public wished to believe. The Olympic medal race drew athletes on both sides of the Iron Curtain into a pharmacological game of cat and mouse. As Dr. Anthony Daly, the US Olympic team orthopedist, explained in 1979, "I think a lot of athletes would like not to have to take anything, but they are convinced that their rivals are taking drugs, and that they must do so too if they're going to compete on the same level."[71] Olympic sport had reached such a high level of performance and specialization that athletes found it increasingly difficult to compete at the top level without the use of performance-enhancing substances. "I know that practically all the American Olympic team qualifiers in many events—weight events, jumping, sprints, use steroids," Gideon Ariel, head of the USOC's biomechanical research group, explained. "If you don't use them, you don't make the finals. That's the common belief."[72]

Despite the inescapable evidence, many US observers clung to convenient mythology, insisting the United States was the clean team in international sport. "We think we have everything to gain from stricter doping tests," US track and field coach Brooks Johnson proudly proclaimed at the 1983 World Championships. Within a few weeks, events in Caracas, Venezuela, would make Johnson eat those words.

The 1983 Caracas affair dispelled any naiveté about US doping.[73] At the time, *Sports Illustrated* called the Caracas affair one of "the broadest and most publicized drug scandals to hit amateur sports."[74] The 1983 Pan American Games in Caracas, Venezuela, employed German scientist Manfred Donike to oversee a sophisticated drug-testing laboratory. Many US athletes expected no drug testing and arrived at the competition still using prohibited anabolic steroids.[75] Two days into the contest, reports that eleven athletes, including eight medal winners, had tested positive for the substance convinced twelve US athletes to return home.[76] Though some of the twelve athletes cited illness, injury, or "homesickness," many interpreted their hasty withdrawal in the wake of strict doping testing as clear evidence of the athletes' guilt. In fact, US triple jumper Mike Marlow explained to reporters at the Caracas airport that his return was tied to concerns that "the tests might be too revealing."[77] Other athletes who stayed at the Pan American Games reportedly underperformed or withdrew, citing last-minute injuries so as to avoid providing a dubious sample for drug testing.[78] The farcical behavior by US athletes at the Pan American Games removed doubts that only communist athletes embraced illicit doping practices.

Making the Myth

The publicized events of 1983 intensified the narrative that US athletes used banned doping products only in order to compete with their enhanced communist adversaries. In a four-part series on anabolic steroids, the *Los Angeles Times* proffered a defense. "The irony is that athletes in the United States began taking steroids in the 1960s to compete with Iron Curtain athletes, who had begun using them in the 1950s to close the gap between them and athletes in the West." No longer able to deny the doping, many offered moral justification. "I can't compete if I stay clean," one unnamed US female athlete said. "So you wash your hands of it and try to act like it doesn't make any difference. But you know when you look at the record book that you didn't do it on your own. It's not a good feeling." Track coach Brooks Johnson, who weeks before the Caracas affair had claimed that US athletes would benefit from increased drug testing, now explained that "the feeling of guilt that athletes have when they use anabolic steroids is more predominant in the West than behind the Iron Curtain, since fairness in sports competition is essentially a British concept." Johnson added that "American athletes operate under morals of Judeo-Christian ethic. . . . But Eastern Bloc athletes have been encultured differently than Western Athletes. . . . They are told what they are doing is for the good of the state, not for personal gain."[79]

The boycott of the 1984 Los Angeles Olympic Games by the Soviet Union and fourteen of its Communist Bloc allies did not reduce US doping practices.

At the Los Angeles games, US cycling staff member Ed Burke provided controversial blood transfusions to US cyclists in the hope of securing victories on home soil.[80] News of the blood transfusions sent shock waves through the IOC and generated significant media attention. However, the media's fuss over the blood-doping scandal overshadowed the claims of US doctor Robert Kerr, who publicly admitted to having prescribed anabolic steroids to a number of medal-winning US athletes in Los Angeles. These athletes avoided detection, Kerr revealed, only because they had cycled off the drugs weeks before to their events.[81]

After the reciprocal boycotts of the Moscow games in 1980 and the Los Angeles Olympic games in 1984, the intensity of Cold War sport slowly diminished. When the two superpowers lined up against each other again at the 1988 Olympic Games in Seoul, it was Canadian sprinter Ben Johnson and not a communist athlete who made global headlines after testing positive for anabolic steroids.[82] The fallout from the Johnson scandal prompted both the United States and the Soviet Union to make public—rather sanctimonious—claims about the need for increased drug testing to effectively aid the "war on doping."[83] The two Cold War rivals even signed a memorandum of understanding to pave the way for US and Soviet drug officials to test the other country's athletes.[84]

As efforts to address the doping problem in sport mobilized, stories of past Soviet doping practices continually resurfaced in the US press. Testifying before Canada's Dubin Inquiry into Ben Johnson's 1988 positive test for anabolic steroids, Robert Kerr reinforced the myth of Communist Bloc doping programs, contending that "Soviet-backed countries" had scientists who were "doing nothing but investigating blocking agents that can be used to block the detection of anabolic steroids." He alleged that communist strength athletes used "nerve gas and strychnine," while swimmers had been "injected with 1½ liters of air into their rectum and transverse colon . . . to give better flotation capacity at the hip joint."[85] Kerr's testimony inspired the publication of further sensationalist claims. On March 24, 1989, the Associated Press reported an outlandish theory that the Soviets had converted the ship *Mikhail Sholokhov* into a secret doping laboratory while it was anchored 60 kilometers from Seoul during the 1988 Olympic Games. Citing the Soviet youth magazine *Smena*, the article alleged that the $2.5 million laboratory had been commissioned by the Kremlin to ensure that the "widespread doping" among Soviet athletes would pass undetected.[86] This story, like Ziegler's claims that the Soviets invented anabolic steroids, would become a recurring anecdote in journalistic articles about communist doping.[87]

Conclusion

Ultimately, the long-standing assumption that doping only existed on one side of the Iron Curtin or that communist athletes have full responsibility for widespread drug use in sport reflects western imaginations about their ideological foes. Indeed, the United States' entry into the "big arms" race appears to have been identical to that of their Soviet rivals. Evidence indicates that immediately following the Soviet Union's entry into the Olympic Games, the United States sought to at first defend and later to reclaim its status as the leading athletic superpower by using doping practices. US sporting officials and media scribes directed attention away from the nation's illicit behavior by castigating their communist adversaries for using banned substances. While rumors and accusations floated in the press about Eastern Bloc drug cheats, US weightlifters, track and field athletes, and cyclists, to name but a few, sought similar pharmaceutical advantages. These doping practices at times were officially sanctioned but more often involved national teams tacitly sanctioning their athletes' illicit practices to ensure American success and insulate sporting officials from the morally objectionable practice.

Yet the way the US media reported doping during the Cold War and the way Americans today remember doping suggest a different story. Many Americans today still view Cold War doping as something practiced exclusively within the Eastern Bloc among athletes whose "Otherness" and misguided ideological beliefs made them capable of committing such unscrupulous deeds. This is due in part to the post–Cold War focus on state-sponsored doping in the GDR and allegations of similar practices in the Soviet Union. In the context of sustained cultural attitudes about American superiority, few Americans wonder how US athletes could have remained so competitive without seeking the same pharmacological advantages if doping was so widespread in the communist East.

However, Americans could be asking themselves this question today in light of revelations about state-sponsored doping in Russia that emerged in 2015. Two independent investigations by the World Anti-Doping Agency, the *Pound Report* and the *McLaren Report,* concluded that evidence indicated widespread state-sponsored doping within Russian sports. In a return to Cold War propaganda, Russian president Vladimir Putin dismissed these findings as "anti-Russian politics" and characterized them as "highly politicized, probably pushed by the sinister hand of the United States."[88] And despite efforts to ban the entire Russian delegation from the 2016 Rio de Janeiro Olympic Games, few in the international sporting community appear to be looking beyond the Russian athletes for evidence of illicit doping practices. It raises the question of whether Cold War era doping narratives in the US press have influenced twenty-first-century perceptions of doping. As Russia returns to its familiar role as "the bad guys" in global politics, might it be too convenient to focus only on Russian athletes doping? If history is any indication, sporting officials ought to be especially aware of how perceptions and biases—which are potentially shaped by Cold War memories—can influence who they perceive as the "bad guys" and the "good guys." In this regard, the lessons of the "big arms race" can serve as a useful caution to those engaged in twenty-first-century efforts to address doping, politics, and elite sport.

—4—

Preserving "the American Way"

Gerald R. Ford, the President's Commission on Olympic Sports, and the Fight against State-Funded Sport in America

BY NEVADA COOKE
AND ROBERT K. BARNEY

The Amateur Sports Act significantly reorganized amateur sports in the United States. The 1978 act resolved nearly a century of conflict among the bodies that govern amateur sports that had degenerated over time into untenable working relationships that prevented America from fielding its best possible international amateur sports teams, particularly at the Olympic Games. The debate about amateur sport governance, which featured internecine distrust and a quest for power between the Amateur Athletic Union of the United States (AAU) and the National Collegiate Athletic Association (NCAA) was further exacerbated by the entrance of the Soviet Union into the Olympics in 1952. This quickly led to the erosion of the position of the United States at the top of the medal tally. In the shadow of Cold War politics, America's deteriorating performance, which climaxed in an especially poor showing at the 1972 Summer Olympics in Munich, was attributed to an administrative malfunction within amateur sport that required major change if the nation was to do well at the 1976 Summer Olympics in Montreal and beyond. The fact that the United States would be celebrating its bicentennial in the same year as the Montreal games added urgency to the mission of restoring America's status at the Olympics.

The Amateur Sports Act has been studied in the context of sports management and policymaking.[1] Historians have also examined the act against the backdrop of the Soviet threat in the Olympic medals race.[2] The fact that the Amateur Sports Act resulted in a huge windfall for the United States Olympic Committee (USOC) by virtue of exclusive rights it gave the committee to use the Olympic five-ring logo in American territory has also been studied.[3] This essay examines the conflicts that preceded the passage of the act that culminated in the passage of the Amateur Sports Act. It focuses on the events surrounding the formation of the President's Commission on Olympic Sports and its agenda of preserving "the American way."

America Loses Its Supremacy at the Olympics

When Gerald Ford Jr. took office on August 9, 1974, as the thirty-eighth president of the United States, he found himself at the center of several vexing dilemmas, not the least of which were those connected to the nation's preoccupation with the Cold War. Ford became president because Richard Nixon had resigned in the wake of the Watergate scandal. The nation was reeling in response to the revelations of Watergate and the first presidential resignation in the country's history.

The United States also faltered in international sport. The Olympic Games had been dominated from the outset of their recent history by US athletes. In the early Cold War years, however, American Olympic supremacy was severely challenged by athletes from the Soviet Union.[4] The Soviets repeated their success at the 1952 Olympics in the ensuing years, much to the consternation of Americans.

While the Olympic Games from 1952 to 1968 revealed a weakness in the US Olympic effort, the results of the 1972 Games in Munich caused considerable alarm. In Munich, the Soviets overwhelmed the Americans with fifty gold medals, an unprecedented feat. In fact, the entire Eastern Bloc performed well. Altogether, the Eastern Bloc countries finished with 94 gold medals and 266 total medals, 48 percent of the total number of gold medals and 43 percent of all medals awarded at the Olympic Games that year (see Table 2). In Munich, Eastern Bloc women's gymnasts won all but the bronze medal in team competition. Soviet and East German athletes won four of the "premier" athletics events: Soviet athletes won the men's 100- and 200-meter races, and East German athletes won the women's 100- and 200-meter race. The most embarrassing moment for the United States occurred on the basketball court. The United States, which had won the gold for basketball every year since basketball became an Olympic sport in 1936, lost to the Soviets in a game during which three seconds were put back on the clock

TABLE 1. Olympic medal performance of the United States and Eastern Bloc countries, 1952–1968

Nation	Gold	Silver	Bronze	Total
United States	187	119	112	418
Soviet Union	161	151	147	459
Soviet satellites	123	121	139	383
Total Eastern Bloc	284	272	286	842

TABLE 2. Medals awarded at the Munich Olympics in 1972

Nation	Gold	Silver	Bronze	Total
United States	33	31	30	94
Soviet Union	50	27	22	99
East Germany	20	23	23	66
Soviet satellites	24	38	39	101
Total Eastern Bloc	94	88	84	266

twice in the final moments.[5] As the *Washington Post* described it, "Russian terror mathematics stretch[ed] the one remaining second on the electric clock into a useful six."[6] In protest over what the *Los Angeles Times* characterized as "the great gold robbery," the American team unanimously voted to reject their silver medals.[7]

These poor results were coupled with a series of administrative blunders. First, Rick DeMont, a distance freestyle swimmer, was stripped of his gold medal in the 400 meter following a positive test for ephedrine. Although ephedrine was a component of prescription medication DeMont took for asthma, it was on the IOC's list of banned substances. Second, Bob Seagren, the world record holder in the pole vault, was not allowed to use the fiberglass pole he preferred. Forced to jump with an unfamiliar pole, he finished second. Third, sprinters Rey Robinson and Eddie Hart were disqualified when they failed to arrive on time for their quarter-final heat. In each instance, team administrative officials received most of the blame. Even though DeMont had properly declared his use of ephedrine on his medical disclosure forms, the USOC failed to argue his case with the IOC. It also failed to defend Seagren's right to use his preferred pole. And even though they had the updated schedule long in advance, USOC officials failed to notify the sprinters of the changed start time of their event.[8] In addition, in an attempt to get Robinson and Hart advanced to the second round of preliminary heats, USOC officials fabricated a story that the athletes had been stuck in traffic.[9]

At the close of the 1972 games, it was clear that the US Olympic team faced severe challenges. It had just been soundly defeated by the Soviet Union and the rest of the Eastern Bloc. Though US athletes dominated in the swimming events, the performances of their colleagues in many of the premier Olympic events were disappointing. The performance of the US team at the Munich games seemed to symbolize the general malaise the United States faced.

A Harris Poll conducted in early October 1972, less than a month after the closing ceremonies at the Olympics, showed that 45 percent of those surveyed were dissatisfied with the American performance in Munich and only 29 percent were satisfied.[10] Other events played a considerable role in fueling this dissatisfaction. Although the Vietnam War was slowly deescalating (a cease-fire was signed in January 1973), it remained a divisive subject among Americans. The nation's experience in Vietnam left Americans sorely in need of something to celebrate. The 1976 Olympic Games were uniquely important because they occurred in the year of the 200th anniversary of the signing of the Declaration of Independence. The period between the 1972 and 1976 Olympic Games proved to be a watershed for American amateur and international sport.

The Amateur Athletic Union and the National Collegiate Athletic Association

The battle for control of amateur athletics in the United States has a long and tumultuous history. At the heart of the problem was conflict between the National Collegiate Athletic Association and the Amateur Athletic Union of the United States. The NCAA termed the struggle between the two as "the problem that won't go away."[11] The AAU, formed in 1888, was an umbrella organization for amateur sport disciplines such as track and field athletics, wrestling, and swimming. Each individual sport was organized and administered by a national governing body.[12] The AAU's general mandate was to deal with problems of corruption, hypocrisy, and brutality in amateur sport. Most important, the AAU certified the amateur standing of athletes, which qualified them to participate in domestic, international, and Olympic competitions. The AAU's control over amateur sport was unchecked until the NCAA, which had jurisdiction over college athletics, was founded in 1906. Because college athletes competed in various domestic and international sporting competitions, many of which the AAU governed, disputes over "ownership" of athletes rapidly became an issue. When the popularity of intercollegiate sports increased, this conflict became even more intense.[13]

The conflicts between the AAU and the NCAA festered for decades. Their contentious relationship was notable for its hindrance of the American Olympic effort. The USOC, which was formed as a committee under the AAU's jurisdiction, did not receive a federal charter that allowed it to solicit tax-deductible contributions as a private, nonprofit corporation until 1950. This charter, codified under Public Law 805, also gave the USOC the authority to select the country's Olympic teams, granted it exclusive ownership of its Olympic logo symbols, and protected it from parties who might attempt to falsely represent themselves as an agent of the USOC.[14] The problem was that the majority of prospective Olympic participants were under the jurisdiction of the AAU or the NCAA.

The new status of the USOC as an independent organization after Public Law 805 failed to designate it as the sole sanctioning body for amateur eligibility. The AAU and NCAA still had the authority to revoke an athlete's amateur status. While the relationship between the AAU and NCAA was much more complicated and nuanced than briefly described here, the important thing to note is that each organization failed to work harmoniously with the other in mustering the best American Olympic team possible. The USOC was caught in the middle of this persistent problem.

By the early 1960s, interactions between the AAU and NCAA were so poor that the federal government was moved to intervene. On October 26, 1962, Attorney General Robert F. Kennedy invited representatives of the AAU, the NCAA, the USOC, and other organizations involved with amateur athletes (e.g., the YMCA), to a meeting in Washington. The parties reached a preliminary agreement based on sharing power over amateur athletics. However, having initially agreed to the terms, the AAU later reneged on the so-called Washington Alliance. President John F. Kennedy, irked by the AAU's rejection of the agreement and mindful of the approaching 1964 Olympic Games, asked the parties submit to a mediation process headed by Gen. Douglas MacArthur, the iconic World War II general and former president of the USOC (1928). MacArthur's counsel produced an agreement between parties that led to a moratorium on hostilities, at least until the conclusion of the 1964 Olympics.[15]

After the 1964 games, relations between the AAU and the NCAA continued to deteriorate. Although Robert Kennedy's initiative was the first example of federal intrusion into AAU-NCAA Olympic matters, the federal government was reluctant to intervene in amateur athletics, preferring to recommend negotiations rather than demand them. Nevertheless, by 1965 it was clear that some form of external intervention was necessary. The Senate Commerce Committee, chaired by Senator Warren G. Magnuson, began hearings on the "AAU-NCAA sanctioning issue" in 1965. The result was Senate Resolution 147, which authorized Vice President Hubert Humphrey to create a Sports Arbitration Board (SAB) in September 1965 in an effort to resolve the dispute. Theodore Kheel, a renowned labor mediator, was named chair. The AAU and the NCAA responded to the idea of SAB arbitration, which was meant to be binding, with strong reservations and resistance to the concept of matters binding. Nevertheless, the SAB continued its work.[16]

The Kheel Commission, as the SAB came to be known, met frequently over two years. On February 1, 1968, the commission announced its findings during a hearing before the Senate Commerce Committee. The commission had decided to focus solely on track and field, believing that resolution in that sport would establish a blueprint for the resolution of disputes in other sports. It recommended a single organization govern track and field. While the commission was not empowered to legislate the formation of a single organization, its members believed that such an organization had to come from an agreement between the warring factions. Kheel observed that "the element of good faith is absolutely indispensable" if a solution was to be reached. Eric Danoff, who wrote a history of amateur track and field in the United States shortly after the commission concluded its work, observed that in the aftermath of the hearing's declaration, "good faith was not to be found."[17] Because the NCAA and the AAU rejected binding arbitration from the outset, it was impossible to implement any of the commission's major recommendations. In the end, the work of the SAB reverted to yet another session of ineffectual mediation, and the issues at the heart of the AAU-NCAA conflict remained unresolved.

New Federalism

Richard Nixon won the presidential election of 1968 on a platform that included the concept of *New Federalism*. The main idea of New Federalism was to separate government responsibility from problems that were not national.[18] In essence, New Federalism was a form of political devolution that transferred specific powers from the federal government to individual state governments. Nixon's New Federalism was commensurate with the Republican Party principle that the government should not intervene in issues that are not clearly linked to the national interest.[19] New Federalism set the tone for Nixon's presidency.

When Nixon nominated Gerald Ford to replace Spiro Agnew as his vice president on October 12, 1973, Ford was the Republican minority leader in the House of Representatives.[20] In December, Congress confirmed Ford's nomination. Ford supported Nixon's New Federalism. He said, "There is a new spirit at work in this country today and it promises to strengthen and revitalize America. Republicans call it the New Federalism."[21] Thus, when the Watergate scandal led to Nixon's resignation, it was expected that Ford would continue Nixon's New Federalism policies.

Historian Thomas Hunt has noted that "presidents Nixon and Ford were in many ways the most fitting pair of presidents in the nation's history to take on the troubles within American sport." Citing their athletic backgrounds (Nixon played football at Whittier College in California, Ford played center and linebacker for University of Michigan teams that twice won national championships), Hunt speculates that both men were well suited to serve the cause of amateur sport because they understood the importance of athletics.[22] In addition, both Nixon and Ford were political conservatives who were not likely to support federalizing amateur athletics.

Munich Sets the Stage

After Munich, it became obvious that the AAU-NCAA struggle was harming the nation's efforts in the realm of international sport. On October 25, 1972, the NCAA abruptly canceled its membership in the USOC. Reaction was swift. Cecil Coleman, president of the National Association of Collegiate Directors of Athletics, told Gerald Ford in a letter written on November 9 that "only through a White House Congress on Amateur Athletics" that could create a new "super-structure" to coordinate all international athletics could the differences between the sports bodies be settled. Coleman asked Ford to "make this known to President Nixon" if he agreed with this analysis.[23]

A letter from NCAA president Ramer to Ford after the NCAA left the USOC included a 30-page history compiled by the NCAA's International Relations Committee that outlined the often-torturous interrelations among the USOC, the AAU, and the NCAA. Ramer told Ford that he "might be interested in the enclosed history," which would give him information he would need "if Congress decides to take an active interest in this matter." The document concluded that the appropriate solution to the dilemma was the creation of a new Olympic structure that "abandons the present concept of organization control, with its power bloc voting structure and jurisdictional disputes, and returns the United States Olympic movement to the American people on a state basis."[24]

Angered by the NCAA's abrupt departure from the USOC, John B. Kelly Jr., president of the AAU, also wrote to Gerald Ford. Kelly's letter was sharply accusatory; he alleged that a "characteristic fit of pique" on the part of Walter Byers, the NCAA executive director, lay behind the NCAA's action. Kelly also alleged that criminal collusion had occurred within the NCAA. Kelly ended his remarks with a call for Congress to investigate the NCAA. He said that he had "sent letters to every member of the United States Senate, the House of Representatives, and appropriate governmental and private citizens calling for a congressional investigation into the activities and functions of the National Collegiate Athletic Association." Arguing that the NCAA should "not be permitted to ignore Congress as they have in the past," Kelly requested that "a special commission be formed to determine the legitimate scope of the NCAA's activities," and that "such congressional action as is recommended be *binding* upon the NCAA."[25] This letter was the first time in the long and bitter differences between the two organizations that the term "binding" can be interpreted as a call for a higher authority (Congress) to put an end to a long-standing impasse.

A month later, Ford received a second letter from Kelly that again called for Congress to intervene and asked that a commission be formed to investigate the NCAA.[26] The bitter enmity between the two warring parties cast a shadow over any prospect of putting the US Olympic house in order. In addition, each organization steadfastly believed that it was in the right. Neither organization believed it was doing wrong and each organization sought a solution that would give it the power within amateur sport. However, the fact that both groups were calling for congressional intervention improved the chances that binding arbitration might solve the conflict between them.

Righting the Ship

In the aftermath of Munich, three entities set out to solve the country's Olympic dilemma: the Committee for a Better Olympics (CBO), the Senate Commerce Committee, and the White House. The CBO first met on December 10, 1972, at the Palmer House in Chicago.[27] Many high-profile athletes, coaches, administrators, and representatives of amateur sports organizations attended. Their goal was simple: they wanted to revoke the USOC's federally appointed charter and establish a new organization to take its place. At its first meeting, the CBO pledged that it would send proposals to Congress about a restructured USOC. The issues the CBO was interested in were a new body with greater input from athletes, a more efficient use of funds gathered from private donations, and an improvement in America's "sagging international image" in amateur sport.[28] At its second meeting, in February 1973, the CBO put the finishing touches on a proposed constitution for a revised USOC organization and a proposal for a bill to be presented to Congress.[29]

Senator James Pearson, a ranking member of the Senate Commerce Committee, attended the second meeting. Another important guest was present: President Nixon had sent a representative.[30] Attendees at the meeting, however, were startled when Nixon's representative revealed that a presidential commission might be formed to investigate amateur sport.[31] Unbeknown to most, as early as September 1972, in the wake of the Munich Games, the White House had begun seeking a solution to the amateur sports issue.[32]

When the CBO's second meeting adjourned in February 1973, it was evident that four groups were openly voicing positions and agendas related to reforming US amateur sport: the CBO, the NCAA, the AAU, and the USOC. Senator Pearson's presence at the second CBO meeting signaled the entry of a fifth entity, the Senate Commerce Committee. Then the White House quietly entered the discussion about reforming amateur sport when it sent a representative to the second CBO meeting and toyed with the idea of forming a presidential commission.

Choosing Sides

Because the USOC was a federally chartered organization, Congressional action was necessary if reform measures were to be enforced by law. The NCAA demanded Congress investigate the USOC's charter status. In addition, the AAU had demanded that Congress investigate the NCAA. The two entities that had the most power to bring about legislation were the Senate Commerce Committee and the White House.

However, the Senate Commerce Committee and the White House advocated different approaches. The White House preferred to repair the problems with the current system by pursuing a new plan, in keeping with Nixon and Ford's doctrine of limited government involvement in private affairs. The Senate Commerce Committee, in contrast, saw great merit in the Soviet system and leaned toward rejecting the limited-government approach in favor of some form of federal control of amateur athletics. The 93rd Congress of the United States, which met from January 3, 1973 to January 3, 1975, became the primary battleground for this ideological conflict.

The Senate Commerce Committee reexamined the issue from the point when it had stopped trying to settle the dispute through its Sports Arbitration Board in 1968. Building on the recommendations of the Kheel

Commission, the committee formulated a four-point plan: 1) an amateur sports board to award and/or revoke charters for domestic sports federations; 2) a department of facilities and health within that board; 3) a national sports foundation to solicit private contributions with matching federal contributions up to $50 million; and 4) a nine-person commission to review US, participation in the Olympics.[33] The committee proposed two bills, each sponsored by Senator John V. Tunney, a member of the Senate Commerce Committee. The first, the National Olympic Commission Act (S.1018), sought the creation of a new commission to review US participation in the Olympics. It was introduced on February 26, 1973.[34] The other three points in the commission's plan were covered by the Amateur Athletic Act of 1973 (AAA'73, S.2365), which was introduced on August 3, 1973.[35]

Though AAA'73 proposed what some in Congress thought was a plausible solution to the issues plaguing amateur sport, others criticized the bill. One view was that it was "bad legislation which would federalize amateur sports" and thus antithetical to the doctrine of New Federalism.[36] Jerry H. Jones, director of White House personnel, argued that the bill amounted to encroachment by the federal government into "one of our most sacrosanct private efforts."[37] An early draft of the White House plan to establish an Olympic sports commission hinted at the similarities between AAA'73 and the Soviet modus operandi:

> Another widespread concern is the increasing tendency for amateur sports affairs, both here and in international arenas, to honor more in the breach than in the observance [of] the ideal of the Olympic oath—participation "in the true spirit of sportsmanship, for the glory of sport and for the honor of our team."[38]

The phrase "honor more in the breach" insinuated that international entities were subverting the rules of the Olympic Games and bastardizing the Olympic spirit in the quest for victory. Sport policy scholar Laurence Chalip claimed that the nation's prestige hung in the balance. Mimicking the Soviets would be "explicitly unacceptable." Direct federal control of amateur sport was unacceptable, at least to White House officials.[39]

To counter what it felt was bad legislation the Senate Commerce Committee had introduced, the White House pursued two courses of action: it drafted alternative legislation and it sought to block the passage of the Senate Commerce Committee's bills, particularly AAA'73, which Nixon and his staff viewed as anathema to the doctrine of New Federalism. Before it introduced AAA'73, the Senate Commerce Committee had been unsure of its mandate in the amateur sport conflict. Kenneth Cole, an aide to Nixon, wrote a memo before AAA'73 was introduced that recommended that the mandate of the President's Council on Physical Fitness and Sports be expanded to include study of the AAU-NCAA issue. He noted that "the last thing we need is a new Presidential commission" and that the Nixon administration was "committed to limiting—not expanding—the scope of the Federal Government."[40] The White House believed that federal involvement in amateur sport would violate a core principle of the administration. The introduction of AAA'73 in Congress strengthened the White House's resolve to find another way.

Jerry H. Jones sent an important memo to President Nixon on September 17, 1973:

> If the present conduct of amateur athletics activities is allowed to continue, most experts believe that the US will be beaten severely in the 1976 Games, and embarrassed in our bicentennial year. The key to solving the present amateur athletics problems is in the reorganization and reorientation of the US Olympic Committee (USOC), and not in addressing the narrower problem of the AAU-NCAA dispute, nor in the imposition of Federal controls over amateur athletics as is being presently proposed in a Bill in front of the Senate. Thus, this memorandum recommends that you establish a Presidential Commission to study and develop recommendations for Congressional action to amend the Charter and Organization of the USOC.[41]

Numerous early discussions about how to solve the problems with amateur sport were motivated by the necessity for America to show well in its bicentennial year. Three days after Jones wrote his memo, Nixon approved a process that would lead to the creation of a President's Commission on Olympic Sports. However, the commission did not come to fruition for some time.[42]

When Gerald Ford was sworn in as vice president, he was briefed on AAA'73 and the status of the proposed president's commission. He learned that negotiations were ongoing with the senators who were sponsoring the bill to oppose the commission.[43] At an April meeting, Ford "gave his unqualified endorsement to the concept of a Presidential Commission and offered to help in any way he could."[44] Michael Harrigan, one of the architects of the commission, wrote a memo to Ford on May 1, 1974, to tell him of a significant development: the NCAA had decided to throw its support behind AAA'73 and was actively lobbying for its successful passage. Harrigan asked Ford to do three things to move the White House's preferred plan ahead: 1) talk to those who were responsible for securing funding for the White House's commission; 2) discuss the issue with the president; and 3) consider chairing the commission himself.[45]

Nixon approved the creation of a president's commission in late September 1973. This made redundant the bill Senator Tunney had introduced the previous February to create a national Olympic commission rather than a president's commission. In response, the Senate Commerce Committee adjusted AAA'73 (S.2365), removed Tunney's commission, and resubmitted it to the Senate in May 1974 as the "Amateur Athletic Act of 1974" (AAA'74, formally known as S.3500). Sponsored by Senator Pearson, AAA'74 was, for all intents and purposes, identical to AAA'73, save that it no longer called for the creation of a national Olympic commission.[46] Although the NCAA supported the new bill, the AAU, the USOC, and the IOC did not. When Lord Killanin, president of the IOC, was interviewed on the ABC program *Issues and Answers* in February 1974, he frankly stated that the proposed Amateur Athletic Acts would be in "complete contravention" to the Olympic Charter and that if they passed, they ran the risk of rendering the US team ineligible to participate in Olympic Games.[47] Rules 24 and 25 of the charter prohibit domestic governments from interfering with international sports federations. Despite the argument of White House staff that "the Soviet bloc nations appear to violate this rule regularly," the White House opposed AAA'74 for the same reasons it had opposed its almost identical predecessor, AAA'73: it still represented unnecessary federal intervention into an area that the New Federalism construed as decidedly nonfederal.[48]

In May 1974, the White House presented its plan for a president's commission to the House of Representatives instead of implementing it via direct executive action. Representative Jack Kemp, a former star quarterback of the American Football League, acting on behalf of the White House, introduced the bill titled the Olympic Sports Commission Act.[49] The bill was re-introduced the following month with no notable changes.[50] Kemp's bill attempted to "correct the direction and scope" of the commission envisioned in S.1018.[51] For its commission, the White House requested $1.2 million in funding, as opposed to the $50 million S.1018 had requested to fund AAA'73. But because AAA'74 remained active on the Congressional floor, the White House request for funding was denied.[52] Despite opposition from the White House, AAA'74 remained on the docket. A strong lobbying effort by the NCAA kept AAA'74 viable, while the inability of the White House commission to gain funding failed to provide a suitable replacement for it. Action was required to defeat AAA'74, but with the failure of the White House to secure funding for its commission, a different means was required.

Executive Action, the President's Commission on Olympic Sports, and the Amateur Sports Act of 1978

Even though its initial efforts to create a president's commission were not successful, the idea remained alive at 1700 Pennsylvania Avenue. The White House tried a new approach—dismissal of AAA'74 through executive action. A June 1974 memo to Ford from Tod Hullin, associate director of the White House's Domestic Council, requested Ford's support for the idea of recommending that Nixon establish a president's commission by executive order.[53] If this strategy succeeded, it might spell the end of AAA'74.

A month before Nixon resigned, Vice President Ford wrote an article that appeared in *Sports Illustrated.* Titled "In Defense of the Competitive Urge," Ford expressed his public support for the establishment of a president's commission. He argued that there were "few things more important to a country's growth and well-being than competitive athletics" and left no doubt about where he stood on the issue of federal encroachment into amateur sport matters: "Completely regimented, state-supported, state-manipulated athletic programs are not for us. It is a matter of style as well as philosophy." Ford used the opportunity to publicly denounce AAA'74, which he called "anathema" because it implied too much federal control.[54] The *Sports Illustrated* piece was another example of the strong support Ford showed for the establishment of a president's commission.

On August 9, 1974, Nixon resigned and Gerald Ford took the oath of office. As president, Ford focused on finalizing the aims and structure of a president's commission. On 21 August 1974 the White House received word from the Senate indicating that AAA'74 would not be voted upon before the session of Congress ended.[55] This spurred the administration to action. On December 28, 1974, President Ford signed Executive Order 11868, which authorized the creation of the President's Commission on Olympic Sports.[56]

The commission completed its work in early 1977. As Michael Harrigan has pointed out, the commission was successful because it did not frame the problem as another arbitration exercise but rather sought to analyze how amateur sports should be organized to achieve success. It was also successful because it thoroughly analyzed the issue and consulted with numerous athletes, coaches, and administrators. Two of its prominent recommendations were that the USOC become the central coordinating body for amateur sports that compete internationally and that the American Arbitration Association serve as an independent arbiter in all disputes involving amateur sport. The work of the commission was the most powerful factor that

President Ford receiving the final report of the President's Commission on Olympic Sports from commission chair Gerald B. Zornow and executive director Michael Harrigan in the Oval Office, January 4, 1977. *Courtesy of the Gerald R. Ford Presidential Library.*

led to the Amateur Sports Act of 1978, which codified and implemented its recommendations.[57]

The Amateur Sports Act of 1978, enacted through Public Law 95-606, was an amendment to Public Law 805, the USOC's original charter.[58] Because Ford's bid for reelection was unsuccessful, he did not have the honor of signing Amateur Sports Act into law. Instead, President Jimmy Carter signed the act into law on November 8, 1978. The Amateur Sports Act permanently altered the amateur sporting landscape in the United States. One major change was the requirement that all sports become autonomous and incorporate independently. This ended the AAU's control of individual sports and effectively ended its role as a major player in US endeavors in international sport. The fact that the American Arbitration Association became the arbiter in disputes enabled individual national governing bodies to protect their "family rights" under the parental leadership of the USOC. The prerogatives of each national governing body to sanction sports were explicitly detailed, as were the conditions under which the amateur status of an individual or team was determined. The rights of individual athletes were also a large focus of the Amateur Sports Act. After the Act was passed, it became standard practice for athlete to have representation and voting privileges on the boards of directors of national governing bodies, and on the USOC's Board of Directors.[59]

Even though the Amateur Sports Act initiated many positive changes in amateur athletics, it was not without flaws. As Chalip has indicated, the act focused almost entirely on the administration of Olympic sports rather than "sport-for-all."[60] Hunt concluded that the Amateur Sports Act "contributes to the health crisis in the United States by providing limited resources to programs which encourage broader participation in physical exercise." Hunt also notes a lack of adequate opportunities for disabled athletes, an issue Congress addressed when it revised the act in 1998.[61] Finally, the USOC's exclusive "rights ownership" of the Olympic symbols became a point of prolonged contention between the USOC and its parent body, the IOC. Nevertheless, the USOC and the IOC have realized that their fortunes (quite literally) are intertwined.[62]

Conclusion

For almost a century, the administration of amateur sports in the United States was characterized by deeply embedded rivalries for power. A bitter struggle between the NCAA and the AAU compromised US participation in international sporting events, sometimes hindering the performance of Olympic teams, and damaged national pride and prestige. The Munich Olympics in 1972 was a watershed moment in galvanizing attempts to solve the dilemma. Two groups formed to confront the problem: the Senate Committee on Commerce, which advocated partial federal control over amateur sport, and the White House, which advocated limited federal intervention. The two factions engaged in negotiations that ultimately culminated in an executive order by President Gerald Ford that established the President's Commission on Olympic Sports. The commission's recommendations led to the enactment of the Amateur Athletic Act of 1978. This landmark law effectively solved the jurisdictional disputes that plagued US amateur sports. The USOC was given new authority as the coordinating body and sole authority for Olympic sports in America. The passage of the Amateur Sports Act was the culmination of a long and arduous conflict to prevent federal control of amateur athletics in the United States. The framework that emerged as a result of the work of the President's Commission on

Olympic Sports followed the limited federal government doctrine of New Federalism, the hallmark of the Nixon and Ford administrations. Most important, the new framework stymied those who flirted with the idea of emulating the Soviet bloc, enabling the United States to continue to compete in "the American way."

III

Making Men and Defining Women

Femininity, Masculinity, and the Politics of Gender

—5—

"Wolves in Skirts?"

Sex Testing in Cold War Women's Sport

BY LINDSAY PARKS PIEPER

The women worried Avery Brundage. As the American Olympic Committee president, he had first become alarmed about the record-setting performances of muscular female athletes at the Berlin games in 1936. He found the track and field athletes particularly unpleasant and suggested that the International Olympic Committee (IOC) implement a sex test "to make sure they were really 100% female."[1] Although the IOC did not heed his advice, it did appoint him president in 1952. When Brundage took the reins, powerful female athletes continued to irk him; this time, women from the Soviet Union caused his angst. Apprehensive about the appearances of brawny Soviet women, Brundage helped convince the IOC to introduce compulsory sex testing.

Like many Americans, Brundage was not entirely pleased with the advancement of women's sport. As a leading US sport administrator, he repeatedly questioned whether it was appropriate for female athletes to engage in physical endeavors that prioritized power and strength over beauty and grace. For example, while discussing women's athletics after the Berlin games, Brundage commented that "I am fed up to the ears with women as track and field competitors. Their charms sink to less than zero."[2] He maintained similar beliefs when he served as IOC president from 1952 to 1972. Brundage's ideals mirrored the dominant ideology in the United States. Many Americans feared that female physical exertion damaged femininity.

This anxiety increased when the Soviet Union returned to international sport.

Throughout the Cold War, the Soviet Union and the United States disagreed over the appropriateness of female athletes. The Soviet Union encouraged muscularity and bulk as attributes necessary for athletic success. As historian John Turrini argues, "the Soviet Union had egalitarian athletic programs which encouraged mass participation of both men and women and sought to develop fully the most talented, irrespective of gender."[3] In contrast, the United States celebrated petite builds and grace as signifiers of athletic femininity. Or, as *Washington Post* columnist Shirley Povich put it, "our damsels don't have as big of muscles in the same places as the Russian babes, and don't want them."[4] Consequently, throughout the 1950s and 1960s, white US women dominated swimming and diving, while Soviet female athletes controlled athletics, gymnastics, and the medal count.

Manifestations of race, gender, and politics coalesced in Cold War women's sport. When reports of unapologetically muscular Soviet female athletes inundated the United States, many decried the loss of femininity in sport and feared that male imposters had infiltrated women's events. As a result, US residents responded to almost every Soviet achievement with scorn. For example, when shot putter Tamara Press earned multiple medals and set world records under the Soviet flag, the US accounts described her as "big enough to play tackle for the Chicago Bears" and lamented that she "is almost as round as she is tall."[5] Such attitudes led to the introduction of compulsory sex testing in international sport.

This chapter examines the gender and sporting norms in the Soviet Union and the United States that helped officials justify compulsory sex verification. The Soviet women's size and skill convinced the International Association of Athletics Federation (IAAF) that all female competitors needed to prove their womanhood prior to participation. In 1966, the IAAF implemented a "nude parade," which it replaced the following year with a chromosome check. Cold War anxieties persuaded the IOC to follow suit in 1968.

Many in the United States claimed that the Soviet women were the reason for the verification measures. "If the Commies hadn't been guilty of substituting men for women in the first place, the new rule of the IAAF wouldn't have been necessary," complained journalist Frank True in a piece titled "Red 'Wolves' in Skirts."[6] The introduction of sex testing reassured the American public that only "real" women—those who upheld normative notions of white femininity—could compete. This enabled the United States to defend its conventional gender roles in sport, preserve a gendered hierarchy, and regain authority in international competition. US beliefs about gender and sport during the Cold War cast muscular victors as suspicious cheaters and compelled sport policies that hindered athletes and limited the advancement of women.

Women's Sport in the Soviet Union

In addition to the desire of both the Soviet Union and the United States to dominate international sport, both countries regarded the status of its women to be an indication of national supremacy. The Soviet Union depicted capitalism as harmful to American women and used the inability of the United States to promote equal rights and equal pay as evidence. In addition, Soviet propaganda depicted US women as unhappily trapped in domestic life. Historian Helen Laville notes that "the Kremlin argued that if the status of women was indeed a barometer of the progress of a nation, then this status should be understood by her place in politics, economics, and society, not her place in the home."[7] Conversely, the US population described Soviet women as "graceless, shapeless and sexless."[8] Americans further posited that the Soviet Union disrupted the natural gender order by requiring female labor. The difficult physical tasks that Soviet women did increased their muscularity and size, which challenged dominant understandings in the United States of the female physique. These beliefs shaped the reception of women's sport as Cold War athletic forums gained unprecedented international meaning.

Before World War II, the Soviet Union promoted gender equality in all facets of life, including sport. Although the Bolsheviks initially sidelined competitive sport as a pastime of the bourgeois, Soviet leaders eventually recognized the power of elite competitions in international affairs. Sport scholar Rob Beamish explains that "after 1934, the Soviets focused on the bourgeois, competitive, high-performance forms of sports, with the goal of outperforming the capitalist world in this arena."[9] The Soviet system advocated participation for all citizens to improve both individual health and collective military force. "Physical education in our country is an important weapon for educating our youth in the spirit of communism," reported Soviet journalists B. Ivanov and E. Rodikov in 1949. It prepares "the Soviet people for work and for the defense of the socialist Fatherland."[10]

In contrast to the United States and other western countries, the Soviet Union encouraged physical activity for women. Female participation ensured worker productivity, aided in military preparation, and promoted "ideologically correct" forms of physical exertion.[11] "The concept of sports specifically for women was almost redundant because almost all sports, except for boxing and wrestling, were considered to be suitable for women," notes historian

A Soviet propaganda poster encouraging female athleticism.
"Young people—go to the stadiums!" Leonid Fyodorovich Golovanov, 1947.
Courtesy of Alamy Limited.

Kateryna Kobchenko.[12] The Soviet Union celebrated the accomplishments of its female athletes. For example, Vasily V. Parin, one of the Soviet Union's leading physiologists, said of Tamara Press—the athlete the *New York Times* sarcastically described as fit to play tackle in football—that she "throws the discus so far that many men might envy her. Why hide the fact?" He inadvertently hinted at a reason for the disparate accounts between the two nations. "In our everyday life," he noted, "women often bear a bigger physical load in the family than men, where the occupational activity is the same or almost the same."[13] Soviet leaders applauded muscularity in women, and Soviet female athletes consequently excelled in sport.

But inconsistencies also plagued Soviet women. When Leonid Brezhnev assumed power as general secretary in 1964, he endorsed several changes. On the one hand, he instituted substantial financial support to athletic organizations, which helped increase the country's successes in international competitions. On the other, Brezhnev both promoted and discouraged female participation.[14] For example, he prized only certain activities for women, such as gymnastics, and banned other physical competitions. In 1973, the Sports Committee prohibited women from participating in events considered harmful to female reproductive organs, such as judo, soccer, and wrestling.[15] As a result, feminine ideals shifted. During the Brezhnev era, Soviet leaders touted *zhenstvennost*, an inner beauty female athletes possessed that was characterized by compassion, grace, and motherhood. Soviet feminists decried this new norm as contrary to the "equal opportunity utopias of the early Soviet period" and argued that it "represented a superficial and . . . old-fashioned gender stereotype."[16] Nonetheless, under Brezhnev, the Soviet press celebrated feminine female athletes and ignored all sportswomen that were considered "ugly."[17] While this essentially aligned USSR and US gender beliefs, each country continued to laud its women as better than the other's.

Women's Sport in the United States

Although *zhenstvennost* eventually became a celebrated form of sporting femininity in the Soviet Union, the acceptance of female athletes in the United States was historically more restricted. In the early twentieth century, white female physical educators acquired control of women's sport by exaggerating the biological dissimilarities between men and women. Female practitioners argued that the combination of the fragility and inherent inferiority of the female body meant that women should control women's athletic activities. Historian Martha H. Verbrugge notes that these female leaders "staked their programs and authority on female-appropriate exercise."[18] However, by highlighting difference, these physical educators presented a construction of white female athletes as unable to handle male versions of sport. They instead offered moderated versions of athletes who upheld white middle-class femininity.[19]

These prescriptions regarding femininity depicted certain sports as inappropriate for women and therefore off limits. For example, white physical educators deemed track and field to be too strenuous and muscle inducing for proper ladies.[20] Cold War gender and racial norms further shaped the sport as a masculine endeavour. As white women flocked to activities considered feminine, such as diving and swimming, women of color filled the void in track and field. Historian Susan K. Cahn writes that "black women stepped into an arena largely abandoned by middle-class white women . . . and began to blaze a remarkable trail of national and international excellence."[21] For example, in the 1956 Melbourne Olympics, black female US athletes earned three medals in track and field.[22] Black female competitors continued to garner moderate success in athletics for the United States during the Cold War. But even though black women earned medals and scored points, their triumphs reinforced stereotypes that they were less feminine than white women.[23] White Americans interpreted the achievements of black female athletes through the dual lenses of racial and gender ideology.

Although black US women were successful in track and field, their victories did little to offset the dominance of the Soviet women. As Cold War hostilities infiltrated sport, the vitality of the United States came into question. At first, fears that US athletes were physically inept centered on the inabilities of men. When Soviet women helped the USSR edge out the United States in medal counts, however, concerns also slipped into US women's sport. Tensions surfaced between beliefs that it was not appropriate for women to participate in athletic competitions and the need for US female athletes to score points. Historian Jaime Schultz writes that "the 1950s marked a time of intense debate about whether and how to invigorate American women's sport."[24] Female physical educators sought to improve women's performances by organizing more extramural athletic opportunities for college women. However, many of these female leaders simultaneously maintained the belief that female athletes needed to be protected from the exploitation of men's elite sport and thereby upheld modified versions of participation.[25] This seemingly contradictory proposition painted female athletes as simultaneously "admirable and deficient." Female physical educators, Verbrugge argues, "accepted feminine skill but not unfettered athleticism."[26] Consequently, the Soviet women continued to defeat the US women in international contests. Instead of calling upon American practitioners and participants to adjust their athletic framework, many chose to criticize the Soviet women as unnatural cheaters.

American Response to Soviet Female Athletes

When the USSR returned to international competition, the powerful performances of the Soviet women challenged the prevailing athletic and gender norms of the United States. When the Soviet Union joined the European Athletics Championships in 1946, it placed second overall. Strikingly, the Soviet female athletes earned twelve of the nation's seventeen medals. Sweden, which finished first, did so with twenty-two medals earned by men and zero earned by women. Likewise, when the Soviets joined the Olympic Games in 1952, they finished second in the total number of medals, only five fewer than the United States. The Soviets surpassed the United States four years later in Melbourne, 98–74, in Rome, 103–71, and in Tokyo, 96–90. The victories of the Soviet women pushed the nation to the top, setting off alarm bells in the United States. Fearful that masculinized Soviet female competitors unfairly skewed the medal count, the US public condemned the Soviet athletes and advocated for the introduction of sex testing.

Soviet female dominance at the Olympics sparked fears that some competitors were actually men. At the 1952 Helsinki games, the USSR women earned twenty-three of the country's seventy-one medals. In contrast, US women earned eight of the country's seventy-six medals; seven of those eight were for swimming and diving. The United States' lone medal in track and field came from the 4 x 100-meter relay, a race run by a predominantly black squad.[27] Similarly, at the 1960 Rome games, the Soviet women took home twenty-eight medals. The US women earned only twelve: eight in swimming and diving and four in athletics. For the United States, white women collected medals in the pool while women of color did so on the track.[28]

The fact that Soviet women excelled in athletics, an activity considered inappropriate for white women in the United States, prompted many Americans to disparage them. Writing an overview of the Helsinki games for the *Washington Post*, Povich argued that "these 1952 Games wouldn't even have been close between Russia and the United States save for the almost complete dominance of the Russian women in the heftier field events and the gymnastics." But he concluded that "in the non-bicep division . . . in the more graceful swimming and diving events where feminine form counts more than feminine muscle, the American girls were all-conquering."[29] Likewise, in the buildup to the 1956 Olympics, columnist Bill Jauss wrote that although the Soviet women were expected to win several events, "most of the Russian women athletes are far from pretty. They're masculine looking, big-limbed, hard-faced girls, with legs and biceps of an all-American fullback." For those worried that the USSR women might help the Soviet Union exceed the United States in overall medals, Jauss suggested taking comfort in the fact that "our woman athletes, especially swimmers . . . score as well in anatomy statistics as they do in the times and distances of their events."[30] Yet not everyone was so easily dissuaded. US writers responded to the Soviet women's successes by ridiculing how they looked.

Those who were concerned by the appearances of the Soviet female athletes looked to the IOC leadership for a solution. Brundage maintained his negative view of female athletes as IOC president.[31] Three years before his tenure started, Brundage described women's sport as "lukewarm" and argued that "women's events should be confined to those appropriate for women; swimming, tennis, figure skating, and fencing, but certainly not shot-putting."[32] Such beliefs were commensurate with those of many Americans. Some of Brundage's policies as IOC president exhibited his dismissive attitude toward women athletes. For example, in the 1953 session of the IOC, the Executive Board proposed the elimination of women's events.[33] Although the measure did not pass, Brundage suggested again "that women should only be allowed in sports that are appropriate for them."[34] His definition of "appropriate" upheld postwar US attitudes about gender that valued beauty and grace as womanly attributes. The athleticism, power, and strength of the Soviet female Olympians clearly countered this ideal.

Many at home applauded Brundage's efforts. Journalist Arthur Daley called his proposal "magnificent" and a "great idea." He supported the ban on women's participation in international sport because "there's just nothing feminine or enchanting about a girl with beads of perspiration on her alabaster brow, the result of grotesque contortions in events totally unsuited to female architecture."[35] Although the proposal was defeated and women continued to participate in the Olympics, Brundage did not change his mind. He told the *San Francisco Examiner* in 1960 that "if I had my way there'd be no women shot-putters or their like in the competition. . . . I am opposed to seeing them attempt anything to which they are not physically suited." According to Brundage, the better solution was for female Olympians to "stick to such sports as fencing, swimming and gymnastics. These things they do well."[36] Although women continued to compete in track and field, doubts about their femininity and suitability did not dissipate.

The achievements of the Soviet female competitors in track and field, a sport Americans believed to be too grueling and stressful for women, eventually led to whispers of male imposters. Many in the United States believed that women were ill equipped for success in such strenuous events and that individuals who excelled in athletics could not be real women. Such beliefs pushed international sport federations to introduce sex testing. The American public wholeheartedly supported this practice during the Cold War.

Sex Testing in Cold War Sport

The IAAF and the IOC—both of which were western in orientation—also grew worried about the Soviet women's performances in the postwar era. Officials of the IAAF and the IOC erroneously feared that the Soviet Union used male masqueraders to earn medals. Continuing concerns about the appropriateness of track and field for women and the fact that Soviet and black US women dominated the sport persuaded the IAAF to lead the way in sex testing. In 1966, the IAAF began anatomical examinations in all area games and championships.[37] "Sport had no other means of asserting the gender of participants other than having them parade naked in front of a panel of doctors," said Arne Ljungqvist, an IAAF member in the 1970s.[38] Finding the threat credible and incorrectly believing that the IAAF was successfully eliminating imposters, other organizations followed suit and instituted checks.

The IAAF first required testing at the 1966 British Empire and Commonwealth Games in Kingston, Jamaica.[39] British athlete Mary Peters recalled being ordered to lie down, pull up her knees, and remain still while doctors scrutinized her body. It was "the most crude and degrading experience I have ever known in my life," she recalled.[40] Canadian runner Abby Hoffman remembered a manual breast and genital examination.[41] Ignoring the athletes' humiliation and declaring the technique effective for detecting imposters, the IAAF continued to exam participants at the 1966 European Athletics Championships, the 1966 Asian Games, and the 1967 Pan American Games.

The IAAF instituted a chromatin test at the 1967 European Cup track and field event. The technique, also known as the Barr body test or the buccal smear test, was a relatively new method that identified chromosomes to determine sex.[42] Sport officials stipulated that only individuals with XX chromosomes be allowed to participate in women's events. Despite scientific concerns that no single qualifier absolutely denoted sex, including the composition of an individual's chromosomes, the IAAF embraced the test. The international federation checked all female athletes and barred Polish sprinter Ewa Kłobukowska—who had previously passed a visual inspection in 1966—for having a "mosaic" of chromosomes.[43] The IAAF removed her records and barred her from competition.

Olympic leaders interpreted Kłobukowska's "failure" as justification for expanded testing. Brundage repeated his calls for verification and asked, "In view of the sex developments at the recent European Championships in Budapest and the action of the I.A.A.F., should we not have something in our rules on this subject?"[44] French doctor Jacques Thiebault agreed. Regarding the "so-called females who are as strong as oxen"—a not-so-subtle reference to the powerful Soviet athletes—he said that it "is inevitable that sooner or later the real representatives of the weaker sex will feel persecuted and will demand their feminine records be attributed to them."[45] To guarantee that only "real" women competed, the IOC followed the IAAF's lead and introduced sex testing in 1968.

At the Grenoble Winter Olympics, the IOC implemented both sex tests and drug tests, both of which the IOC's Medical Commission oversaw. However, sex verification and anti-doping measures served different ends. Sex testing aimed to unearth male imposters. Anti-doping controls sought to detect prohibited substances. Although sex verification and doping controls existed as separate tests with different intentions, many people conflated the two as achieving a singular purpose: to eliminate unfeminine female competitors. For example, former Medical Commission chair Arthur Porritt said that "there is a very simple test to determine if the athlete is right or wrong" when he described the dual measures.[46] His conflation of the two tests underlines the significance of gender in both sex and anti-doping control. Those who feared masculinized, steroid-ingesting female monstrosities supported compulsory testing.

The Medical Commission checked women's chromosomal patterns to ensure sex segregation and tested urine samples for illegal substances. While only a randomly selected group of women underwent verification in Grenoble as a trial run, all female participants were given the sex text in the 1968 Mexico City Summer Olympics. The IAAF and the IOC continued testing for sex throughout the Cold War.

The US Response to Sex Testing

At first, the US public embraced sex verification. The powerful Soviet victors challenged predominant US understandings of femininity in the early stages of the Cold War, and testing for sex seemed to be a way to return to the previous gendered order. Medical doctor T. R. Van Dellen claimed that "we shall never know the exact number of men who have competed in the Olympics posing as women. But athletes of questionable gender have been common enough to warrant changing the rules."[47] Most US media reports highlighted the appearance of the Soviet athletes instead of discussing the scientific complexities of sex determination. Although the Barr body test detected the composition of an athlete's chromosomes, a majority of the accounts continued to focus on outward expressions of femininity and viewed testing as a way to kick masculine-looking women out of sport. However, some officials and medical practitioners worried about the ethics and legality of the policy. Eventually, as the Cold War cooled, the medical community's opposition led to the termination of compulsory sex verification.

When the IAAF introduced sex testing in 1966 and the IOC followed suit 1968, Americans largely applauded the policies as a way of discouraging suspicious Soviet athletes from participating. For example, when Tamara Press and her sister Irina dropped out of the 1966 European Athletics Championships, citing the illness of their mother, the two world-class athletes faced immediate backlash. Few believed their reason for pulling out of the event. Instead, people suggested that the sisters hoped to avoid the new verification measure. The *Washington Post* claimed that "several top

Russian women athletes . . . refused to compete rather than undergo the sex test."[48] Americans welcomed the idea of watching an Olympics that did not include masculine-looking Soviet women. They believed IAAF president David Burghley's claim that the sex test "has been successful in frightening the doubtful ones away."[49]

The media contrasted the necessity for Soviet athletes to submit to verification with the absurdity of requiring US athletes do the same. The assumption was that while the hefty Olympians of the Soviet Union had compelled the IAAF and IOC to introduce controls, testing the feminine athletes of the United States was a waste of time. Several reports complained about the arbitrary verifications conducted at the 1968 Grenoble Winter Olympics. One Olympic official grumbled that the "random selection did nothing to solve the problem" because the most "obvious" remained untested.[50] Presumably by "most obvious," the official meant those who did not appear suitably feminine by western standards. Conversely, after describing US athlete Karen Budge as "an 18-year-old peachcake" and a "willowy blonde . . . with a figure of a Las Vegas showgirl," several media accounts pointed out the foolishness of requiring that she verify her womanhood. Budge agreed. "It seems a bit ridiculous, and a wasted effort in some ways," she said.[51] Many believed that only women who did not uphold US beauty standards should be required to undergo sex control. Despite the prerequisite that mandated testing for all, including American athletes, the US public appreciated the existence of a test that presumably eliminated gender transgressive women from competition.

In contrast to the positive treatment feminine American athletes received, the US media continued to criticize the Soviet competitors for their masculine appearance. The introduction of sex testing enabled the press to more openly and explicitly criticize the appearances of the Soviet women and other Eastern European participants. "The shoulders on some of [them] are something else," said Jon Romary, US liaison for women athletes in the 1976 Olympics. "Some of the girls can be very masculine looking, and especially in past Games there were some around you wouldn't want to meet in a dark alley."[52] Condemnation of supposedly mannish female athletes abounded. Gone were the subtler references to muscles and bulk; in their place, accounts now more openly accused Soviet athletes of looking like or being men. For example, US athlete Mary Decker repeatedly called her Soviet rival Tatyana Kazankina "Ted" for what she said were "obvious reasons." Decker complained that "when I first ran against her as a young girl in Moscow years ago, I used to beat her in the 800. The girl I ran against now looks like her brother."[53] Sociologist Rebecca Ann Lock notes that being accused of looking like a man is a serious insult to a US woman. "What these kinds of insults reveal is that femininity is aligned with heterosexual attractiveness and one is read as ugly when one's muscularity is close to that of a man's."[54]

US sports officials also focused on the appearances of female competitors to justify the policy. Although Brundage was initially a proponent of sex testing, he later worried about the expense and legality of the procedure of making it compulsory for all female Olympians. As IOC president, he initially suggested delegating oversight to the international federations, the entities recognized by the IOC to administer individual sports worldwide. But with prompting from the IOC Medical Commission, Brundage signed off on verification as the responsibility of the IOC.[55] He then largely distanced himself from the policy, focusing instead on his obsession with amateurism. Still, his opinions about women athletes occasionally resurfaced. After a group of Danish medical authorities protested against sex testing in 1972, arguing that the Barr body test was an unreliable tool for the assessment of sex, Brundage requested clarification from the Medical Commission. He asked if the "eye of a 25 year old would be better" than the current scientific method, insinuating that a young man could verify female Olympians' sex merely by looking at them.[56] His offhand remark underscores his belief that verification measures eliminated unattractive women from competition. In other words, it blocked women who did not conform to western expectations of femininity from mounting the medal podium.

As the media spread details about the implementation of sex testing and sport officials debated whether such testing was necessary, US medical practitioners joined the conversation. University of Iowa urologist Raymond G. Bunge aptly noted in a 1960 *JAMA* article that the demand for verification emanated from Cold War fears. "Probably the whole business arises from an offended American pride," he said.[57] Seven years later, he wrote another piece in *JAMA* that offered advice to the IAAF and the IOC on how to handle the "bewildering dilemma" of sex identification. "Eliminate from competition all those who have a contradiction in their morphological criteria," Bunge suggested. "Allow competition only among those athletes who have no contradiction." Put simply, Bunge agreed that women with biological abnormalities, such as different chromosomal compositions, should be removed from competition. He added that if this seemed too harsh, the IOC could establish two Olympics: "one for the 'normal' men and women and another for the contradictive group."[58] According to Bunge, only "normal" women should be allowed to participate.

Daniel Hanley, a US representative to the IOC's Medical Commission, disagreed. In a 1967 *JAMA* article, he posited that "if you are throwing out everybody with any chromosomal abnormality at all . . . you are wrong." He instead advocated for a visual examination. According to Hanley, the buccal smear test offered the "same conclusion that any near-sighted college boy can come to from a block away."[59] While Hanley opposed the Barr body test as an indicator of sex, his suggested approach still focused on the outward appearances of female competitors. This suggests that chromosomal composition was never the central issue. Rather, requirements about femininity were the reason for testing.

Many Americans continued to support sex verification until the end of the Cold War. As the hostilities between the Soviet Union and the United States decreased, objections from the medical community increased. Although some endocrinologists and geneticists had opposed the singular use of the buccal smear test in sex determination since its introduction in 1967, more vocal practitioners increasingly joined the protest. For example, in 1986, US medical geneticist Joe Leigh Simpson repeated the claim that the singular use of the Barr body test was inadequate and unethical.[60] Likewise, in 1987, sexologist John Money called the practice "arbitrary and totalitarian."[61] By the 1990s, almost all major medical societies within the United States had called for the IOC to end sex testing.[62] The protests convinced the IAAF to abandon the practice in 1992. Only when the IOC's Athletes' Committee recommended to the Executive Board that the policy be abandoned did the IOC drop compulsory testing in 1999.[63]

Conclusion

The Soviet Union and the United States were ideologically polarized superpowers throughout the Cold War. From social dynamics to sporting practices, the two nations conflicted. As sport became a forum for demonstrating superiority, the countries disagreed about the acceptability of women's involvement in athletic endeavors. Whereas the Soviet Union encouraged women to participate in a variety of activities, including those considered masculine, white female athletes in the United States remained hindered by conventional notions of femininity. The imbalance in the performances of US and Soviet women in international competitions stemmed largely from the two countries' different attitudes regarding gender and sexuality. The Soviet state strove to position women as equal to men in all facets of life, including labor and sport. In contrast, the United States viewed female domesticity and femininity as necessary characteristics for US women. These ideologies extended into athletics and limited US women's advancement in any competition considered mannish.

Soviet women thus dominated Cold War sport. Yet rather than celebrate the Soviet competitors' impressive feats, many Americans condemned them as too big, too bulky, and too hefty. After witnessing the impressive Soviet achievements, the IAAF and the IOC decided to verify all female athletes for competition. According to the two organizations, sex testing would eliminate male imposters and ensure fair competition. The driving factor, though, stemmed from a discomfort about the appearances of strong Soviet women competing in women's sport.

The desire to police women's entrance into sport was not entirely sparked by the Soviet Union's victories. Sporadic era examinations occurred in the interwar years before the USSR returned to international sport. But in the context of Cold War tensions, many Americans claimed that the Soviet athletes were the reason sex verification was necessary. The strong, powerful Soviet women became the primary targets because they did not embody US notions of conventional femininity. From the US perspective, sex testing was a necessary tool for defending American gender norms in sport.

Acknowledgement

I thank the Beth Emery Virtual Writing Workshop and Toby Rider and Kevin Witherspoon for the thoughtful editorial feedback on this chapter.

6

America's Team

The US Women's National Basketball Team Confronts the Soviets, 1958–1969

BY KEVIN B. WITHERSPOON

On October 26, 1957, the US women's basketball team defeated the Soviet national team 51–48 to win the World Basketball Championship in Rio de Janeiro, Brazil. The US team, in an effort the press described as "brilliant, magnificent, all-time great, [and] superior defensively as well as offensively," pulled out a thrilling victory after trailing by six points several times in the second half.[1] Aside from being an important landmark in women's basketball history—it was the first game between the US and Soviet teams and only the second Women's World Championship event—the game began a rivalry between the two sides that endured for a more than a decade. The US women's national team went on to play against the Soviets more than forty-five times over the ensuing decade before the contests were abandoned in 1969. These Cold War clashes have largely escaped the notice of basketball historians, who have devoted most of their attention to the later developments of the Title IX era or to the earlier periods of barnstorming and industrial teams.[2] The US-Soviet games, however, provide scholars with a unique opportunity to consider both the place of athletics in the Cold War and the importance of gender within that sphere. In these games, American and Soviet women battled in perhaps the most physical and direct female competition during the Cold War. In an era when conventional gender norms on both sides were thought to be emblematic of social and cultural superiority, the physical nature of these contests became problematic, particularly for American officials, who struggled to achieve a balance between success on the court and upholding traditional American expectations for femininity. Ultimately, as the American team met with defeat against the Soviets more often and as a number of America's top players challenged traditional gender norms, American officials elected to minimize the significance of the women's games and eventually to discontinue them altogether.[3]

Making the Teams: The US and Soviet Teams before 1957

While the US and Soviet women's teams had not met before that championship game in Brazil, they were both on a trajectory toward world dominance. Before the US-Soviet series, the highest level of the American women's game was played by Amateur Athletic Union (AAU) local industrial and small college teams and some independent barnstorming teams. From early in the twentieth century through the 1950s, these teams advanced the evolution of the game, pushing the limits of what was considered acceptable female athleticism, improving in every aspect of the game, and producing progressively greater star players.[4]

By the World War II era, the women's game in the United States was characterized by a series of dynastic teams that one after the other kept raising the bar in terms of national championships won, consecutive games won, and number of players on the national team. During World War II, Nashville's enormous Vultee Aircraft manufacturing plant, the nation's largest airplane builder during the war, sponsored one of the early dynastic teams in women's basketball, the Vultee Bomberettes. The postwar iteration of that squad, Nashville-based Cook's Goldblumes, was the team to beat in the late 1940s. It was followed by Hanes Hosiery out of Winston-Salem, North Carolina, which won three consecutive AAU championships and 102 consecutive games from 1951 to 1954.[5] The Wayland Baptist College Flying Queens ruled in the late 1950s; their record 131-game winning streak was finally broken in 1958. The team that ended that streak, the Nashville Business College "Nabucos," became the dominant team of the 1960's, winning eight straight national championships from 1962 to 1969.[6] Each of these teams produced star players who contributed to the evolution of the women's game, advanced the standard in terms of size and athleticism, and improved skills such as handling the ball, passing, and shooting.[7]

As the Cold War intensified and victory on the court took on heightened significance, AAU and US government officials paid great attention to the roster of the men's team, for whom victory was paramount.[8] In comparison, the roster of the women's team was an afterthought. On international trips, the women's team roster started with the AAU national championship team; it was built around six or seven players from that team and added a handful of top players from the other teams in that year's "final four" at the AAU championships. For games played in the United States, in the interest of saving money on travel, US officials typically matched the best AAU team from the region against the experienced and internationally tested Soviets. Thus, it was players from the Nashville Business College "Nabucos" who faced off against the Soviets most often throughout the 1960s.

During this period, the Soviet team was also improving. Using a strategy similar to that of their other top teams, such as the hockey team and the men's basketball team, the Soviet women's team was built by selecting promising players at a young age, providing them with "jobs" that allowed them as much time to practice as they needed, and eventually assembling an experienced core that stayed with the team year after year. Acclaimed player Skaidrite Smildzinya, for example, was recruited to play for the Tram and Trolley Trust club in Riga at age 16 in 1959 and remained a fixture on the Soviet team throughout the 1960s.[9] Soviet women routinely practiced several hours a day, five days a week, in well-equipped facilities and with outstanding coaches.[10] By 1957, the Soviets had won four consecutive European championships and were ready to challenge the Americans for world supremacy. While they fell short of victory in the 1957 championship, the closely contested final game was indicative of a team on the rise. In fact, the Soviet women would not lose another World Championship title until the American women finally unseated them in 1979.[11]

The US/Soviet Series, 1958–1969

In the Cold War era, the most high-profile sporting clashes between the United States and Soviet Union occurred during the Olympic Games, as evidenced by the controversial 1972 men's basketball gold medal game, the epic 1980 Olympic hockey game, and many others. Women's basketball, however, was not introduced at the Olympics until 1976, and the US-Soviet rivalry was then interrupted by the dueling boycotts in 1980 and 1984. Thus, the women's basketball rivalry played out in secondary competitions, such as the World Championships and—more pointedly for this discussion—a series of tours in which teams from the two nations clashed numerous times over the span of a few weeks. As documented in the growing literature on Cold War sport, these exchanges became hotly contested terrain in the cultural Cold War and victory on the court was regarded as a sign of cultural, economic, political and even military supremacy.[12]

The 1957 World Championship game whetted the appetites of athletes and fans on both sides. Soviet and American officials had been working toward an agreement that would authorize a wide range of social contacts, cultural exchanges, competitions, and expositions designed to "contribute to the normalization and improvement of Soviet-American relations."[13] The Cultural Exchange Agreement was finally signed in January 1958, after several years of sometimes contentious negotiations. Under this agreement, the two sides exchanged visits of doctors, scholars, students, scientists, agricultural experts, artists, musicians, dancers, and all manner of other performers. The agreement also called for mutual visits of athletes and coaches and dual meets in a variety of sports.[14]

The first athletic exchanges, which were scheduled for 1958, included an exchange of weight lifters, a celebrated dual track meet, and a tour of the US men's and women's basketball teams of Eastern Europe and the Soviet Union.[15] The American women's team, anchored by a core of six Nashville Business College players and its coach, John Head, departed on April 20, 1958, for a six-game series in the Soviet Union.[16] The American team struggled early, both with adapting to conditions on the road and with competing with the Soviet team for two games in Moscow, both of which the Americans lost. The players said that the court, the ball, and international rules all required an adjustment. The court was especially problematic: it was built from mill-sawed two-by-fours with gaps between the boards and many chips and uneven edges. Both male and female players commented on the difficulty of adjusting to those uneven floors and the rougher ball, which had raised seams. Even sure-handed dribblers found balls bouncing unexpectedly out of their hands.[17]

After those first two games, the performance of the American women improved. In two games against the Georgian and Estonian national teams in Tiflis and in two more against the Russian Soviet Federation team in Leningrad, the American women prevailed convincingly.[18] The second night in Tiflis presented another unique challenge. The game was played on an outdoor court just after a heavy rainstorm and mounds of sawdust had been dumped on the court to soak up the water.[19]

Cold War overtones were relatively tame in the press after the series, although most reports commented on the contrast in conditions and in how players were treated between the United States and the Soviet Union. In an interview a few days after he returned home, Coach Head suggested that Soviet players visiting the United States the next year might attempt to defect, saying, "The Russians are looking forward to returning our visit and hoping to find a way to stay on when they get here. You just can't imagine the difference in the two countries."[20] In Moscow, the American players were escorted to the May Day military parade, a massive display of Soviet might. While they were duly impressed with the display, some questioned the wisdom of spending such vast amounts of money on weapons when so much of the country was clearly impoverished.[21]

All participants noted that their Soviet hosts treated them well, and in general they emphasized sportsmanship and friendship above wins and losses.[22] Gamesmanship was at a minimum, although *New York Times* writer Max Frankel did report one light-hearted episode. The Soviets may have attempted to get the American players drunk, or at least take the edge off their game, before the third game in the series. "The teams visited the Tiflis champagne factory before the game and tasted of dry, semisweet and semidry products," Frankel recounted. "Vladimir A. Samsonadze, deputy chairman of the Georgia Committee of Physical Culture, remarked at the tasting session that champagne might help to counteract the Americans' superiority at basketball. But it didn't."[23]

The US team was greeted by cheering crowds, which included the Soviet players, and given flowers and gifts at each stop.[24] "In the entire tour I didn't notice a single unhappy incident from either the players or the fans," said Bert Born, a member of the men's team. Shirley Martin, the team's manager and chaperone, noted, "We were enthusiastically treated as V.I.P.'s everywhere we went."[25] Nashville Business College's Margaret (Babe) Holloran said, "When the Soviet girls beat us they did it gracefully and when they lost the crowds still cheered us."[26] As Coach Head explained, though, the trip was heavily scripted and there was no deviation from the plan. All personnel were accompanied by Soviet translators or guides wherever they went and requests to visit sites not on the schedule were politely denied. Head noted, "If we asked to do something they didn't want us to, such as visit their rural districts and ride in the subway, we got this answer—'If it can be arranged.' But it never was."[27] If the Soviets hoped to control what the Americans were able to see, they succeeded only partially, as players and coaches later spoke to the press about the depressed state of the citizens of Moscow and the stunning poverty they observed in the Soviet countryside. Coach Head commented, "I actually do not think [the Russians] believe yet that some of our girls own their own automobiles."[28] In general, players were excited to have had the opportunity to visit but were happy to return home.[29]

In 1959, the Soviets returned to play an eight-game series in various cities across the United States, highlighted by an opening-night overtime thriller the Soviets won in Madison Square Garden, the first time women's basketball had been featured there.[30] As had been the case the previous year, the outcome of the games was secondary to displays of goodwill, although American players such as Nera White and Joan Crawford, who again starred for the US team, must have found the overtime loss difficult to stomach. The sides exchanged gifts: for the Soviets, cigarette lighters, perfume, and makeup; for the Americans, handcrafted Russian dolls called *matryoshkas.*[31] The rest of the series played out in similar fashion, with the American team losing close games to the Soviets.[32]

In 1961, the Americans made their second tour of the Soviet Union, an eight-game series that the two teams split evenly, 4–4. The procedure was similar to the 1958 tour: the US team played two games in Moscow before embarking on a six-game road trip to Kiev, Tiflis, and Leningrad.[33]

While Nera White and Coach Head declined to make the trip, Nashville Business College stars Joan Crawford and Jill Upton anchored the team.[34] As in 1958, players noted that they were treated well, almost too well in one regard. "We had meat, potatoes, carrots, bread, peas and ice cream at every meal, and we were scheduled to eat four times a day. One of the girls gained 14 pounds," said Crawford.[35] Several players felt the Soviets were attempting to fatten them up (and slow them down) by providing so many large, hearty meals. Whether this was an intentional act of sabotage by the Soviets one can only wonder. The players got along well with their Soviet rivals on the court, and despite the sometimes-rugged style of play there were few disagreements. Jill Upton offered a simple explanation for this harmony when she said, "Nobody could understand what anybody else was saying."[36]

What had been up to that point a fairly even contest between the two sides became a one-sided disappointment after that 1961 tour. When the Soviets returned to the United States for an eight-game series in 1962, they won every game—most by embarrassing margins—and the appeal of these exchanges began to wane for the Americans. There was little joy in reporting humiliating defeats. The 1962 series began once again with a game at Madison Square Garden with the Nashville Business College team, which the Soviets won. The Nabucos also lost the next two games, before handing over the task of facing the Soviets to other AAU teams, the Iowa Wesleyans and the Wayland Baptist College Flying Queens. They fared no better, losing every game by 20 points or more. This tour, for the first time, featured a Soviet woman of giant stature, six-foot six-inch Ravela Salimova, and two other players taller than six feet. From then on, the Soviets made a point of stacking their roster with giants, several of whom were over seven feet tall.[37]

The series continued into the late 1960s, with some interruptions, but American interest dwindled. Major newspapers mentioned a 1964 US tour

The 1961 US-Soviet women's basketball game before a packed stadium in Moscow. *Photo courtesy of Jill Upton.*

by the Soviet team on its way to the World Championships in Lima only in passing. The seasoned and talented Soviets swept all five games on US soil, including a 73–27 thrashing of the US national team, which was also on its way to Lima. The press barely mentioned a five-game US tour of the Soviet Union the following year. Even the Americans' sole victory, a 56–51 win over the Leningrad All-Stars, garnered only two sentences in the *New York Times*. In contrast, victories by the Soviet women were front-page news in Moscow.[38] A Soviet sweep of a four-game tour in 1966 marked the last time they visited the United States. Olan Ruble of the AAU was forced to concede after this tour that the Soviet team "is the best women's basketball team that has ever been assembled in the world. They have height, experience, maturity, strength, stamina, agility, speed, precision skill, and team-work."[39] The final American game on Soviet soil was a single game at the end of a nine-game European tour in 1968, which the Soviets won 64–39. One could make no excuses about the inexperience or lack of talent on the American team, which for the first time in many years included the three pillars of the Nashville Business College team, Nera White, Joan Crawford, and Doris Rogers. The Soviets were simply better.

Explaining the Struggles of the US Team

At first glance, it seems surprising that a US team anchored by some of the greatest players of all time struggled so mightily to defeat the Soviets. However, a closer examination of the organization and management of the US team reveals a number of factors that ultimately crippled it. These included the inconsistency of the American team roster compared to that of the Soviets, the challenge of adapting to international rules that differed in critical ways from US rules, and the lack of support and interest from the US government and other bodies.

For a time, the approach to amateurism of the Nashville Business College team and many other AAU teams bore some resemblance to the Soviet model. Unlike college teams, most of the industrial teams placed no limit on eligibility. The company sponsoring the team gave the women jobs, but for the top players their chief responsibility was playing basketball. Players worked, but they also were expected to put in many hours practicing, playing games, and traveling. For a team like the Nabucos, this meant that a core of outstanding players might stick together for years, gradually replacing aging stars with promising young players. In 1969, the six all-stars on the Nashville Business College team included a fifteen-time All-American (Nera White), a thirteen-time All-American (Joan Crawford), and a seven-time All-American (Doris Rogers).[40] Despite the similarities, US politicians and sporting officials accused the Soviets of breaching the rules of amateurism for maintaining a similar system for decades.[41]

However, the AAU system failed to produce a consistently dominant national team. One key difference is that despite a system that seemed to resemble the Soviet system, the American team was still rooted in the concept of freedom of participation. American women were not forced to participate; they did so willingly. At times, they declined invitations to play. Unfortunately for the American team, its best player, Nera White, did exactly that after taking only two international tours. Similarly, her coach, John Head, declined to participate in several international competitions, as did top players from some other teams. Of the top Nashville Business College players, only Joan Crawford played in all the series against the Soviets in the period 1958–1964. The reasons they gave varied. White voiced frustration at the way the teams always seemed to be hastily assembled and given little time to gel. She was also introverted and shy, a condition that intensified as her fame grew. At some point, she had simply had enough of the limelight. Other players noted difficult conditions on some of the trips, poor food, challenges adapting to international rules, sketchy officiating, intestinal troubles, and a variety of other reasons for staying home. Their comments suggest that while for many of these small-town women, an international adventure or two made for a thrilling experience, beyond that, they preferred the comforts of home. Coach Head likely spoke for others when he said after the 1958 tour, "I'm glad to be home. There's no place like it. I'm in no hurry to go back to Russia even if the chance comes."[42] After the 1961 tour, Jill Upton was even more succinct. "Once was enough," she said.[43] Whatever the reasons, the absence of top players from the national squad contributed to a precipitous decline in the US national team's record in international competitions after the early 1960s.

The American women also suffered because they played a fundamentally different game from the Soviets. The rules of the American women's game differed significantly from international rules. For most of the era under discussion, in college and AAU competitions, American women played with sides of six. Each team had to keep two players at each end, and the remaining two players acted as rovers and traversed the entire court. This meant that the play on either end involved four players from each team.[44] The number of dribbles was also limited to three until 1966, which discouraged individual ball-handling and encouraged passing. While such limitations made for some interesting tactical maneuvers, they were rooted in the dated philosophy that women could not physically endure the stresses of a full-court game.[45] The international rules called for a full-court five-on-five game.[46] Players unaccustomed to running the length of the court were now forced to do so, and players who thrived in the open spaces of their customary four-on-four games now had to adjust to the more crowded conditions of a five-on-five game.

The AAU teams struggled for other reasons. Unlike the state-sponsored Soviet teams, American amateur teams were not funded by the government. "The AAU believes in the American Way of life," opined Lyle M. Foster, chair of the AAU Women's National Basketball Committee. "Every youngster with the ability and desire, under proper guidance from AAU officials, will develop according to his [*sic*] own abilities. This is the American way of producing champions. There is no reason for the state regimentation used in some nations."[47] Despite Foster's jab at the Soviet system, over time the limited support the AAU provided for women's sport left the US women at a competitive disadvantage. Throughout the Cold War, financing American teams was a challenge typically left to team owners, whose spending habits varied widely. While Nashville Business College owner and president H. O. Balls invested more liberally than many others, the most generous of them was Claude Hutcherson, who sponsored the women's team at Wayland

Baptist College. Hutcherson also owned a local flying service in Plainview, Texas, and he and his wife Wilda spared no expense in supporting the team, even allowing them the use of four Beechcraft Bonanza airplanes when they traveled, leading to their nickname as the Flying Queens. Claude covered their expenses at top hotels and at fine restaurants, and Wilda made sure the team looked pristine by providing perfectly matched sweaters, traveling suits, and well-styled hair. They became the envy of the women's basketball world. For a time in the early 1950s, the team carried a roster of nearly thirty players.[48]

The US government and national sporting bodies, in contrast, were extremely frugal in their support of women's basketball. In the interest of saving money, the women's "national" team drew largely from the AAU national champion team each year and added one or two players from several other teams around the country. These players, who were thrown together with little opportunity to practice, confronted a seasoned and experienced Soviet national team with a roster that had little turnover. When the Soviet team made its tours of the United States, it usually played games against leading AAU teams from the city or region where the game was played. In short, Soviet dominance after the 1961 series was due in part to the inferior caliber of the US teams they faced.

Women's Basketball and the American Way of Life

Perhaps American officials did not devote more attention to the women's game because female basketball players did not fit the traditional mold of femininity and domesticity that was so central to US gender norms during the Cold War.[49] Historian Linda Ford suggests that "it was obviously not comfortable in the 50's for a lady to be an athlete."[50] Contrary to the idealized vision of the American woman as petite, pretty, and domesticated, many basketball players were tall, muscular, and tough. While the press noted their victories and exploits in AAU play, sportswriters and AAU officials alike struggled to describe the players in ways that conformed to the accepted gender narrative. Historian Helen Lenskyj has observed that US women track stars, who were often lithesome and attractive as well as athletic, "would be forgiven if they did not surpass . . . the [Soviet] performances."[51] US female basketball players were rarely granted such leeway. When the team increasingly failed to win on the court, it became easier to simply ignore the women's games altogether. After the US women were defeated by the Soviet

National Youth (B) team in 1965, one American diplomat in Moscow commented, "It would be far better to simply not send a team at all . . . than to send a second-rate team."[52]

An examination of the lives and backgrounds of the players on the US team indicates that many of them challenged traditional gender norms in a number of ways: they had experienced a rural upbringing, which included both the physical labor of farm life and a tomboy lifestyle that included playing on equal footing with boys, they had fathers and families who supported their athletic pursuits, and they were tall and ungainly in physical appearance.

The US women's national team was led largely by a group of women from small towns, many of them from farming families. Leading players came from towns such as Walnut Grove, Mississippi; Van Buren, Arkansas; and Cross Plains, Ashland City, Seymour, and Lafayette, Tennessee. Rural life provided an ideal setting for the development of female basketball players, and those who have spoken or written about their backgrounds tell remarkably similar stories. Life in the country was robust and active. As young girls, they spent many hours of the day outdoors, running, playing, hunting, or working on the farm, which made them strong, tough, and fearless. Several tell stories of raising cows to show at the state fair, a rite of passage that required not only physical strength but also the courage to stare down a mammoth beast without flinching. Jostling with imposing international players was nothing compared to handling a thousand-pound heifer.[53]

Another common theme in such stories involves being raised with brothers or playing with and against boys. June White Fisher, a high school teammate of Nera White, said, "In grade school, you played with the boys because there never was enough girls big enough to play [by themselves]."[54] Pat Head, better known by her married name of Pat Summitt, recalled a childhood marked by two powerful realities: relentless work in the fields and around the farm and tough, physical basketball games with her three brothers in the hayloft of their barn. "There was no slack in the hayloft. It didn't matter that I was a girl," she wrote in her autobiography.[55]

Finally, most of the women describe a family that permitted or, more often, supported their pursuit of sports. More than one mentioned a father who played ball with them at a very young age. Nera White, the greatest of all, said, "My daddy started playing ball with me when I was three. I can remember playing softball in the sixth grade on a boys' team." When her father lost a leg after an illness, much of the farm work fell on young Nera's shoulders. "When I was at home, I was in charge when we went to the field to work. I had to be the daddy out there."[56] It seems that life on the farm or in small-town America allowed for a softening of some of the gender barriers women encountered elsewhere.[57]

Nera White, the nation's top player, posed the greatest challenge to traditional American gender norms. White, from the small town of Lafayette, Tennessee, is remembered now as the best women's basketball player of that era; some feel she was the best ever.[58] Unlike today's athletes, who typically translate success on the floor to endorsement dollars, fame, and success, White became bitter about the lack of financial opportunities available to her and the painful attacks she suffered on account of her appearance. By the end of her career and through the final decades of her life, she was notoriously bristly and difficult to reach. She gave only a few interviews and nearly boycotted her own induction into the Naismith Memorial Basketball Hall of Fame (which, in 1992, came decades too late by her estimation).[59] Joe Dean, who accompanied the women on the 1958 tour of the Soviet Union, addressed these concerns even while attempting to compliment her decades later, saying of White, "She played like a man; she ran like a man. There was no woman who could match her physically."[60] Not everyone was so complimentary of what were often described as her mannish features. Not only was her play more suited to the men's game of that era—fast, strong, athletic, airborne, aggressive—but her lean and muscular build and often dour, serious face led to criticism from her high school years on. White later said, "By the time I was a junior, I suddenly became aware that I did have a problem and people were making fun of me and it affected me a great deal. I couldn't begin to tell you how much."[61] She eventually became fiercely defensive and withdrew from public activity as much as she could.[62]

The Press and Public Commentary on Women's Games

The media commentary on these games at times reflected the gendered expectations of the era. The national media paid far less attention to the women's games than to the men's; papers such as the *New York Times*, the *Washington Post*, and the *Los Angeles Times* often mentioned the women's games only in the final few sentences of articles otherwise devoted to the men's contests.[63] Writers who did comment on the women's games frequently included references to the players' appearance, emotions, and behavior, especially when the outcome favored the Soviets. Such writers emphasized the feminine qualities of the US players, at times as a way of dismissing their defeats. In an otherwise neutral commentary on the 1958 tour of the Soviet Union, the *Nashville Tennessean* writer Bill Isom awkwardly inserted several sentences about women family members pining for the return of their husbands and children. According to Isom, as the plane taxied to the terminal, Coach Head's wife cried, "Oh, why doesn't it go a little faster!" And one of the players' mothers moaned, "Why don't they hurry up and get off. I just can't wait to see my baby."[64]

Another article attributed the success of the team almost entirely to Coach Head and included a picture of Head as the father/coach encircled by his team.[65] Praise of the coach was not unwarranted, but the coverage of the men's team was generally not treated in the same way. In another article describing the women's game, Bill Scott emphasized that the American players were "young ladies first, fine athletes second."[66] Even those who were sympathetic to female players felt it was important that they maintain their femininity. Des Moines radio commentator Gene Shumate, who was generally enthusiastic about the women's game, explained in 1947, "We've taken to our hearts these lassies who play all-out, race madly hither and yon, but still remember to pause in the midst of a scoring rally to adjust a hair ribbon."[67] When the US team gave sportswriters little to celebrate on the court, they sometimes suggested that the athletic success of the Soviet women came at the expense of suitable feminine traits. One *Washington Post* writer, reflecting on what had become Soviet dominance of the women's game in 1962, jabbed, "The Russian girls, who regularly mop up the court with US women's teams, looked like a collection of shot-putters and javelin throwers transplanted from the Olympic Games." The writer extended his commentary to off-the-court characteristics as well: "None of them wore makeup. All wore silk hose, most of them with crooked seams, low-heel shoes and plain woolen skirts which fell inches below the knee line."[68]

The women's game did not attract as much attention—or as many players nationally—as the men's game, and the entire scope of media coverage and public attention to their games might best be described as small-minded. Even their most high-profile games rarely were played at top venues. Games against the Soviets were sometimes played at places such as Greenbrier High School, and the women's AAU National Championship was held for many years in the remote towns of St. Joseph, Missouri, and Gallup, New Mexico.[69]

Women players suffered some consistent indignities in the way they were treated. Throughout the period, women were required to wear uncomfortable satin uniforms, sometimes tied at the waist in a way that exposed the midriff. While these uniforms were not unseemly or scandalous, they added an element of glamour and "eye appeal" to the women's game. Additionally, both in the press and in organizations like the AAU, the players were frequently called "girls" rather than "women," and articles often emphasized their feminine qualities and tendencies as much as their athletic skill. Throughout this period, the AAU tournament announced both a Most Valuable Player and a beauty queen each year. "Pretty Patsy Epps," wrote *The Amateur Athlete* in 1958, "was crowned queen of the tournament. . . . The queen's lovely attendants were escorted by 'JayCee' men in a colorful ceremony."[70]

Interestingly, it was a final example of sexist treatment that led ultimately to the demise of the Nashville Business College team and, soon after, the decline of AAU play altogether. Throughout the 1960s, many women—and many male supporters—argued that in order to be competitive internationally the United States needed to implement the full-court game for women, a movement that had gained momentum by the late 1960s. H. O. Balls, who had done so much to support women's basketball up to that point, was staunchly opposed to women playing the full-court game. When the AAU adopted the new rules in 1969, Balls disbanded his team and never looked back. With Joan Crawford and Nera White heading into retirement, the Nashville Business College team was probably facing a rebuilding period regardless. But Balls's gendered protest sealed the team's fate. Without several of its biggest stars and its signature franchise, women's AAU basketball quickly receded into the background of American sports.[71]

Conclusion

For a handful of years, an unlikely group of women from the farms and small hamlets of the American countryside stood atop the global basketball scene and provided the United States a string of victories over its Soviet rivals. Confronted with a focused, determined, and well-financed opponent, however, America's amateur teams soon found themselves overmatched. The male-dominated leadership of diplomatic and sporting circles in a nation that did not yet truly respect and treat women as equals gradually diminished support for those games and eventually eliminated them altogether. Thus, these games and the women who played them are symbols not only of the Cold War clash between superpowers but also of the battle for gender equality in the United States.

—7—

To Win One for the Gipper

Football and the Fashioning of a Cold Warrior

BY KATE AGUILAR

> One sees now though, that the stadium is never empty, for the ghosts of past heroes play great games over and over for the Goddess who holds sway for them, as well as she does over the living crowds.[1]
> —Ronald Reagan, "The Stadium" (1931)

In November 1991, dignitaries from around the world gathered to celebrate Ronald Reagan's leadership, life, and legacy at the dedication of the Ronald Reagan Presidential Library and Museum in Simi Valley, California. The 150,000-square-foot library complex overlooks both arid mountains and the Pacific Ocean. The ascent up Presidential Drive to the mission-style building, flanked by banners with portraits of each president, presents a carefully tailored image of American leadership that is quite visibly white and masculine. Upon entering, visitors walk into a lobby where they can purchase tickets to the privately funded museum. A series of quotes then beckons them through cream-colored hallways, past bronze statues of President and Mrs. Nancy Reagan, into a small theater, where a short film orients these quotes to the Reagan storyline. This storyline begins with the "sad tale" of the 1960s and 1970s, followed by a Reagan revolution in which he restored American business and military might, leading to a new "morning in America." Historian Gil Troy describes the Reagan storyline as culminating with "the great party known as the 1980s, when the stock market soared, patriotism surged, the Soviet Union crumbled, and America thrived." The popular narrative highlights Reagan's ability to reinterpret the past in order to create a specific vision for the present, and future.[2]

After the film, visitors are invited to stroll through a series of exhibits. The first few encase childhood memorabilia of the president and introduce his athletic interests. A Republican-red placard emphasizes the importance of Reagan's physical strength for his political career. It reads, "Ronald Reagan loved athletics and the outdoors—his physical energy and vitality were an important part of his success." It is impossible to overlook football as *the* sport that contributed to this vitality, for the exhibit is dominated by an oversized picture of a young Reagan in a football uniform. Next to this picture is a letterman's jacket from Eureka College, where Reagan lettered in football and swimming, and a more appropriately scaled picture of him as a part of the Dixon High School football team.

The exhibit also showcases pieces Reagan wrote in his youth. Two focus on football. The first, "Victory vs. Conscience," "recounts a Dixon High School football game in which a star player chooses honesty over victory and admits to a penalty that costs his team the game." In "The Stadium," which Reagan wrote as a college student in 1931, he describes an empty stadium as "the temple of the great Goddess Youth" where young football players come to terms with "life with its triumphs and defeats, its jeers and praise."[3] Reagan pointed to football as a sport that helped him overcome his insecurities and gave him the confidence to pursue his goals from the time he was a childhood player. His first goal, the story goes, was to wear the purple and white jersey of the Dixon High School football team in Dixon, Illinois. His experiences on high school and college football fields led him to pursue a job as a sports announcer, a job he was qualified for because of the cultural citizenship he had gained through football. His work as a football announcer segued into involvement with other news forms, including entertainment, which opened the door to Hollywood. His work in Hollywood and the tenacity he gained on the gridiron prepared him for political life.[4]

It is surprising, especially considering the rich historical scholarship on Ronald Reagan and the well-documented relationships among football, militarism, and the Cold War, that no scholar has seriously grappled with the role of football in the fashioning of Ronald Reagan. Reagan was not the first American president to draw upon the sport.[5] Appeals to executive authority and demonstrations of manly nationalism go back to the earliest days of the sport and Theodore Roosevelt. Reagan's use of football to shape his political persona drew on this legacy to convey and propagate his own brand of New Right masculinity, a virility clothed in the zero-sum language of the Cold

War.[6] This chapter explores the significance of the sport to the making of the Gipper and how he used football to shape the public memory of his rise from a boy from the Midwest to an American cultural and political icon.

America in Crisis, 1960–1979

Unlike the first decades of the New Deal welfare state, when Americans by and large trusted their government, supported interventionist foreign policy, viewed the government as responsible for economic growth, and gave enormous authority to the president, Roosevelt's Democratic coalition began to break down in the 1960s and 1970s.[7] This coalition was comprised of disparate groups from the South, the middle class, and the labor movement and included whites, African Americans, Latinos, and women. The civil rights and women's movements revealed cracks in the coalition, which was never as cohesive or popular as political opinion conveyed. During the Civil Rights Movement, African Americans and blue-collar whites competed over access to housing, schooling, and employment.[8] The Vietnam War and Watergate eroded faith in leaders, in business and the economy, the military, higher education, and government, and especially in the president of the United States.[9]

The 1970s also ushered in changing views on political affiliation, marriage, religion, crime, family, masculinity, military and civil life, and conspicuous consumption.[10] Although different communities responded to such changes in different ways, the nation as a whole was impacted when President Lyndon Johnson's War on Poverty gave way to President Nixon's War on Drugs. According to historian Dan Baum, the marijuana-toting antiwar protestor became linked to the urban race rioter. He writes, "In the War on Drugs, users would come to provide a bottomless well of villains and scapegoats for administrations looking to unburden the electorate of taxes, shed federal responsibilities, and divert attention from their own failures."[11]

In the Cold War climate of the late 1970s, the attributes Reagan embodied were useful for overcoming the factionalism and supposed national impotence fostered, in part, by the loss of the Vietnam War.[12] The impact of that loss on the American psyche led to the term "the Vietnam syndrome," a phrase that described growing distrust in government and its foreign policy. Another element of this syndrome was the belief that the defeat in Vietnam was largely self-inflicted. Fingers were pointed from all sides as Americans blamed the government for not acting decisively and President Richard Nixon, among others, blamed the media and the antiwar movement for diminishing public support for the war effort. The lack of collective will influenced public opinion about the war and the posturing of national leaders. Two of Reagan's most popular campaign slogans, "Let's make America great again" (1980) and "It's morning again in America" (1984), were a part of a post-Vietnam Reagan reboot that sought to distance itself from collective guilt and impotence.[13]

Reagan's Rise to Prominence

Ronald Reagan believed that the American people had become mentally weak and that both mental and physical might were needed in the face of unrest at home and the Cold War. And he believed that he could be the leader who addressed these problems. His role as the Gipper in the film *Knute Rockne, All American* and his work for the television series *General Electric Theater* had made him a bona fide star. His speech for Arizona senator Barry Goldwater's presidential campaign in 1964 had made him a political force.

In the 1950s, work in film was becoming scarcer for Reagan. As a result, he accepted the position of television host for *General Electric Theater*, a popular anthology series. Reagan estimated that during his eight years as host, he spent twelve to sixteen weeks a year visiting GE plants and speaking to employees. In an October 1987 speech to state government officials and business leaders in Somerset, New Jersey, Reagan described the effect these visits had on his evolving political ideologies. "I have to confess that when I took that job I had a view of business that was fashionable in some circles in those days—an unflattering view," he explained. "But when I visited the plants and met the employees face-to-face, I learned something. I learned that I was seeing then, as I've seen here today, the real source of this nation's economic growth and productivity—not government or bureaucracy."[14] These visits, along with his work with the Screen Actors Guild, led to a change in his ideology and eventually in his political affiliation, away from the New Deal and Democrats to the Republican Party. They also made him a good candidate to speak on behalf of Goldwater, who was crafting a conservative conscience that positioned big government as the problem, not the answer.

Barry Goldwater became the Republican Party's presidential nominee in 1964. He helped shape the agenda of a "new" right that coalesced around distaste for big government.[15] This "new" form of conservatism sought to dismantle New Deal reforms and the post-1930s Democratic voting base it had engendered. Unlike the Roosevelt coalition, which was comprised of disparate groups, this new movement mobilized mostly white, middle-class suburbanites.[16] The central tenets of the New Right were anticommunism, a hands-off approach to economic issues, opposition to the Civil

Rights Movement, and a celebration of "traditional sexual norms."[17] This agenda grew out of the conservative conscience Goldwater articulated in 1960, which called for welfare to become a "private concern," a flat tax, and a seven-point program for winning the Cold War.[18]

Although it was Goldwater who gave voice to this developing New Right, it was Ronald Reagan who came to embody it. Because of his work with GE and his flair for the dramatic, Reagan was invited to speak in support of Goldwater's campaign in California. On October 27, 1964, Reagan delivered a half-hour speech entitled "A Time for Choosing" as a part of the prerecorded television program *Rendezvous with Destiny*. The *Washington Post* recently judged the speech to be one of the four most electric political speeches in American history.[19] At the time, it drew support for Reagan's entrance as a political candidate; he ran successfully for governor of California two years later.[20]

Reagan's commitment to a conservative agenda was evident during his gubernatorial campaign. Reagan centered his 1966 campaign on the decline in morality and respect for authority. His rhetoric routinely focused on sending "the welfare bums back to work" and "[cleaning] up the mess at Berkeley."[21] The governor opposed antiwar protestors and attacked the activism of UC Berkeley students. Historian Rick Perlstein has argued that this focus was a political strategy, as polls showed this activism was initially not an issue for many California voters. Reagan was less interested in the polls and more in the reactions he got from audience members when he made these arguments in his speeches.[22]

In office, his concern with student activism at Berkeley led him to collaborate with FBI director J. Edgar Hoover. Their efforts led to the firing of Clark Kerr, president of the University of California, in 1967. In May 1969, when Berkeley students occupied a piece of university property and created a People's Park to prevent the development of a new sports field, Reagan sent the National Guard to occupy the campus for two weeks. And under Reagan's watch, one student died, another was blinded by tear gas, and many more, including residents and schoolchildren, were affected in the largest deployment of tear gas during the Vietnam War protests.[23]

Football and Reagan's Political Methodology

While Governor Reagan's methods were controversial, many conservatives applauded him for using force to put radical students in their place. *San Francisco Chronicle* cartoonist Bob Bastian depicted the governor as a football player who took on the student movement through his tackling of

President Kerr. The cartoon implied that Reagan had demonstrated his mental and physical fortitude through his handling of UC Berkeley, attributes that were also necessary for the sport. Regardless of the intent of Bastian's cartoon—which most likely was to mock the president's overt show of force—the image of Reagan in uniform shows how significant the narrative of football was to popular perceptions of his masculinity and Cold War leadership.

This political cartoon perhaps drew from popular misperceptions of the brawny college football player (and his coach) as the "true Americans," in contrast to their "wild-hair hippy" counterparts. Football historian Michael Oriard writes, "Looking back, someone today might conclude that to play football in the 1960s was to choose authoritarian discipline over personal freedom, violence over peace and love, and the war in Vietnam over revolution at home."[24] *Life* magazine supported this view, referring to counter-protestors of the 1968 Columbia student movement as members of "the jock faction."[25]

Coaches and, somewhat ironically for this political cartoon, university presidents, also promoted this perspective. Washington State University coach Jim Sweeney called football a "fortress that has held the wall against radical elements." University of Connecticut president Homer Babbidge described the school's football players as "aware of the importance of law and order and discipline" and referred to short hair as a "visible sign of deeply held traditional values."[26] Oriard's research debunks the binaries of brawn versus brain and football player versus student protestor by showing that black athletes were central to the radicalism of the 1960s and 1970s. Nevertheless, such misperceptions strengthened the hypermasculine rhetoric of the Cold War, positioning all those who opposed or were indifferent to the war as effeminate and un-American.[27] Scholars of football Jeffrey Montez de Oca and Kurt Edward Kemper argue that football became a more powerful image of Cold War masculinity than other sports because of its warlike quality, including the forceful capturing of territory and a willingness to go head to head with adversaries.[28]

As a politician, Reagan used football to craft a public image of conservative masculinity that celebrated brawn and bravado.[29] Cultural historian Daniel Marcus explores how Reagan used nostalgia to produce his own version of the past in order to articulate a vision for the 1980s. He describes public memory as a "key act of social power when one group determines narrative over others."[30] Reagan associated himself with the popular roles of football player, the cowboys of the Old West, and the Vietnam veteran action hero John Rambo, implying that he was an action hero in his own right. In a remark that was not aired but was picked up during a national address from the Oval Office, Reagan famously proclaimed, "Boy, after seeing 'Rambo' last night, I know what to do next time [a hostage situation] happens."[31] He appealed to this militaristic, muscular masculinity to differentiate himself from President Jimmy Carter and position himself as "decisive, tough, aggressive, strong, and domineering."[32] His history as a football player helped cultivate this hypermasculinity, creating an image that he believed made him suitable for war and leadership.

Reagan as "The Gipper"

On May 17, 1981, President Ronald Reagan demonstrated grit when he addressed the University of Notre Dame in his first public appearance outside Washington, D.C., following an assassination attempt.[33] The *Chicago Tribune* described the 70-year-old as "jaunty and upbeat on his return to the scene of his favorite motion picture role."[34] The iconic role was that of football legend George Gipp in the 1940 film *Knute Rockne, All American*. The film immortalized both the coach, Knute Rockne, and the college standout, portrayed by Reagan. The Chicago paper's headline, "A ND Diploma for the 'Gipper,'" conflated the president and the role.[35]

Reagan's love of football and the courage and idealism that George Gipp embodied are what drew him to the part. He was a relatively unknown actor in the late 1930s and securing the role of Gipp was a "young actor's dream." In his speech, Reagan told how he answered a *Variety* magazine ad for actors, only to be told that the film required a big name and a more physical presence. Reagan submitted a photo of him in his college football uniform to prove that he had the physicality for the role. Producer Hal Wallis granted him a screen test as a result of the photograph.[36] This story, which Reagan recycled throughout his political career, became important to his self-fashioning as an action figure with the presence and grit to lead.

Reagan frequently referred to the Gipper. After his 1980 election to the presidency, for example, he sent a letter to Notre Dame's president, Rev. Theodore Hesburgh, that said that "playing the Gipper was a turning point in my career. He and Notre Dame have a very secure place in my heart."[37] Reagan also spoke of the role in his 1981 commencement address at Notre Dame, a school that has won eleven national championships and boasts seven Heisman winners and 117 All-Americans.[38] "Now, I'm going to mention again that movie that Pat and I and Notre Dame were in, because it says something about America," Reagan said.[39] He continued, "First, Knute Rockne as a boy came to America with his parents from Norway. And in the few years it took him to grow up to college age, he became so American that

President Reagan holding the Gipper jersey at a campaign rally in Endicott, New York, September 12, 1984. *Courtesy Ronald Reagan Library.*

here at Notre Dame, he became an All-American in a game that is still, to this day, uniquely American." He went on to connect the image of the football squad to another "band of men"—the Founding Fathers—"who rose to such selfless heights" to birth American democracy and invited Notre Dame graduates to see him as their coach who could help them obtain total victory in a Cold War.[40]

Reagan's commencement speech used football as a cultural lens for demonstrating the dominance of the United States.[41] Sociologist Jeffrey Montez de Oca contextualizes football as both a "ritual and symbol of the nation." Through the sport, the individual assimilates into the nation-state. In order to achieve what Montez de Oca defines as cultural citizenship, the individual has to learn the "technical knowledge" of the game and its customs, or "cultural knowledge."[42] He defines football as a "technology of citizenship" where people display their competence as citizens through popular culture. The citizen fulfills his or her cultural obligations by learning the game and is given the right to power when they excel at it.

The centrality of men to the game made the sport important to conceptions of American leadership in the 1980s. For some, including leaders of the Soviet Union who took notice of the speech, Reagan's Notre Dame address was a clear message about his resilience and that of the American people. Historian Bradley Birzer contends that perhaps the ten most important words of his presidency were spoken in that moment, "ten words that changed the entire course of American foreign policy since Truman implemented it in the middle 1940s: 'The West will not contain communism; it will transcend it.'" Birzer defines the speech as a major foreign policy address.[43]

Reagan reflected on the lives of Knute Rockne and, later, George Gipp in this address to illustrate the nationalism embedded in the game. The men and the sport embodied attributes integral to American citizenship: self-discipline, sacrifice, mental and physical toughness, and honor. He also used the sport to fashion himself as the quintessential masculine leader of the period. Football mattered to Reagan personally and to his and others' fashioning of him as a political player.

Football and Reagan's Presidency

By the time he gave the Notre Dame commencement speech, Reagan had already taken on the notion of a "Vietnam syndrome" in a campaign speech at the Veterans of Foreign Wars Convention in August 1980. There he declared, "There is a lesson for all of us in Vietnam. If we are forced to fight, we must have the means and the determination to prevail or we will not have what it takes to secure the peace. And while we are at it, let us tell those who fought in that war that we will never again ask young men to fight and possibly die in a war our government is afraid to let them win."[44] The point was clear: Reagan had not fallen prey to the syndrome and he was willing to create and facilitate a game plan that would let the nation win. Reshaping the narrative around a more overt form of masculinity was a part of this game plan. He also "presided over the biggest peacetime defense buildup in history, from high-tech weapons systems to larger training ranges and military pay increases."[45]

The emphasis among scholars on Reagan's role in the demise of communism remains divided. Some argue that "Reagan essentially won the cold war, that he intended to win it, and that as president he conceived and carried out a coordinated campaign to achieve this objective," while others contend that "internal Soviet conditions and decision making" led to its fall. Regardless, Reagan's image as a cold warrior derived from his willingness to go head to head with the Soviets, made all the more compelling by the fall of the Soviet empire a mere ten months after he left office.[46]

Scholars from the first camp show that Reagan began to flex his Cold War muscles long before he took political office, when he spoke out against the "red threat" while he was in Hollywood.[47] Paul Kengor shows this hard-bodied masculinity at work through the invasion of Grenada and other "economic warfare" that supported anti-communist leaders in Central America and the Caribbean.[48] The Gipper's refusal to back down from an arms race led historian George H. Nash to conclude that "even the academic disparagers of Reaganite 'triumphalism' seem inclined to grant the Gipper at the very least the 'best supporting actor' in Gorbachev's drama and that Reagan's policies helped to push the Soviet Union toward irreversible reform."[49] Nash's reference to the Gipper allowed him to draw upon the image of Reagan on the gridiron, willing to go to battle.

Football was critical in suggesting Reagan's physical presence, despite the fact that he was the oldest president. Throughout his presidency, he took the attention away from his age by emphasizing his physical pursuits. In December 1983, for example, the president wrote an article for *Parade* magazine entitled "How to Stay Fit: The President's Personal Exercise Program," in which he jokingly asked fitness guru Jane Fonda to move aside. He referred to his high school and college football play as a part of the reason physical fitness continued to come naturally to him.[50]

This reference was not unique. A cursory search of all the presidential speeches housed in the Reagan Library reveals that Reagan referred to football at least 189 times.[51] In the speeches archived on the *American Presidency Project* website, presidents mentioned football 1,022 times. In the presidential speeches on this website, only President Barack Obama referred to the sport more often than Reagan.[52]

Both Reagan and journalists used the sport to shape him as a political player long before he was elected president. In a February 1969 article about how other governors rejected Reagan's tough stance on dealing with student activists, the *Boston Globe* said that "Ronald Reagan lost one for the Gipper yesterday."[53] In a 1968 article in the *Chicago Tribune* about whether or not Governor Reagan would run for president, journalist Chesly Manly described Reagan first as a former college football star.[54]

In his 1988 autobiography, Reagan's adopted son Michael also discussed the impact the sport had on his father, including his view of masculinity. Michael was from Reagan's first marriage to actress Jane Wyman. While the father and son admittedly had a tenuous relationship, Michael referred to the role sport played in bringing the two together. He wrote of how important it was to Reagan that Michael was not a "sissy" and Reagan's belief that football could help make him a "real boy."[55]

In Ronald Reagan's second autobiography, he elaborated on what the sport had taught him. Reagan wrote, "I loved playing on the line: For me, it was probably a marriage made in heaven. It's as fundamental as anything in life—a collision between two bodies, one determined to advance, the other determined to resist; one man against another man, blocking, tackling, breaking through the line."[56] Football as both a personal memory and a part of a public script positioned him as someone who was willing to and capable of going toe to toe against a political adversary.

His knowledge of and love for football also quite literally changed his fate. When he graduated from college, Reagan had no idea what he wanted to pursue professionally. Inspired by a love for sport and an interest in the newly created role of radio sports announcer, Reagan found himself at WOC radio in Davenport, Iowa. He asked to speak to the program director but was turned away because no announcer positions were available. While he was waiting for an elevator, Reagan was overheard mumbling about what one had to do to get a *sports* announcer job. The program director, Pete MacArthur, supposedly shuffled after him, yelling, "Hold on, you big bastard. . . . What was that you said about *sports* announcing?" When Reagan explained that he was interested in working as a *sports* announcer, Pete asked, "De ye know anything about football?" Reagan's ability to announce a fictitious game on the spot led to his hiring. He announced the Iowa-Minnesota football game that weekend.[57]

This type of improvisation got Reagan his next big break. He moved over to WHO radio station in Des Moines after WOC closed. There he followed a number of sports, which included Chicago Cubs baseball. Reagan began following the Cubs out to Pasadena, California, for their spring practice in 1935. In California, he met a friend he knew from conducting interviews for WHO and confessed his love of acting. In 1937, this friend offered Reagan an opportunity with her agent to see if he had what it took to succeed in show business. After finishing his "pitch," as Reagan called it, the agent reportedly picked up the phone and called a casting director for Warner Brothers.[58]

I am not the first to suggest that a script mattered to Reagan. Scholars of his political career and his presidency speak often of how he used popular culture, including his work as an actor, to connect with the public. Presidential historian Gil Troy notes that "Ronald Reagan was a man of standard formats, reassuring Americans by following the scripts they loved."[59] Reagan used football as a powerful and beloved script to standardize the masculinity of the period.

Reagan also used football to shape public perceptions of his manhood and his leadership. In his recollection of his impromptu interview with WOC radio, Reagan described how he chose to relive one of his own games from his Eureka College football days. While doing so, Reagan notably changed a personal blunder into a prominent block that converted him into the star. Susan Jeffords, who has analyzed how Reagan spun popular scripts to emphasize a particular version of himself as "hard bodied," argues that "Reagan learned a vital political lesson: that the success of the story, especially a story in which he could figure as a hero, was more important than any facts involving the events themselves."[60] As with his 1964 speech for Barry Goldwater, "A Time for Choosing," his public memory of football, both fact and fiction, was more important for how it made Americans feel about his physicality than the truth about what that physicality could actually achieve.

Football helped order Americans' relationships to the nation-state, preparing men, often white men, for military service and political leadership. It is not surprising that those paid to analyze Reagan's presidency drew from the same scripts Reagan used. In a CBS News publication that was put together shortly after his death, correspondent Dan Rather wrote, "In the public role of the presidency, Ronald Reagan knew how to personify the American spirit of the times, and reflect it back to an American public that generally liked what it saw."[61]

Not surprisingly, the CBS News collection emphasized Reagan's identity as a football player. The second image of Reagan in the book, following a traditional portrait, is that of him throwing a football in the role of George Gipp. *Los Angeles Times* staff writer Johanna Neuman describes how the president got the nickname the Gipper, along with his other nickname "The Great Communicator." He used football to communicate his and America's dominance. The picture following the one of him as the Gipper is one of him and Nancy walking in Honolulu, Hawaii, during a layover en route to an economic summit. The 1986 photo, in which Reagan throws a football to someone off camera, "shows good throwing form," the caption says.[62]

In another essay, "American Dreamer," Jon Meacham and others describe the importance of football for Reagan's political evolution: "The myth of the triumphant Gipper is a powerful one, but Reagan was more complex than his legend suggests. The man who rode to the rescue of a dispirited country started out as a shy child. The Manichean cold warrior was driven by a sentimental yearning for peace. The captivating charmer in public had little interest in the lives of other people, and no close friends." And yet, "Always competitive, he chose football over baseball and remembered the pleasure he found in exerting force."[63] Scholars have long recognized the significance of overt masculinity to the president's political narrative, including his positioning of himself alongside the action figures of the period such as Rambo and as a rogue cowboy willing to take on the establishment. Because he chose football, however, the shy child became an effective cold warrior.

Conclusion

Reagan used football to fashion himself as mentally and physically fit to lead. He may have loved the game. There is no reason to doubt that he did. To show himself as a real or model American man most fit to overcome "the Vietnam syndrome," Reagan may have also looked to a historical and cultural space that celebrated violence, masculinity, whiteness, performance, and the nation-state, a space that sought to mold men into action heroes ready to defend the American way of life. His and others' repetitive use of this script indicates its cultural weight. This chapter argues that analysis of football can help us understand the range of Reagan's strategies and how he used sport to craft a public memory of him as most fit to lead Americans in a Cold War. It has strived to show how and why Reagan and those closest to him focused on the game—a sport tied to a particular narrative of racial, masculine leadership and American militarism during the Cold War—to make clear how he like the sport embodied certain forms of vigor and nationalism for the 1980s.

Historian Richard Neustadt argues that the real power of any president is the power to persuade.[64] The cultural significance of Ronald Reagan as "the Gipper" is how artfully he employed popular culture as a political script, in particular through the sport of American football. Reagan's nuanced understanding of football as a cultural site that uniquely prepared American men for war and his positioning of himself as a football star shows how astutely he deployed this cultural icon to craft himself the rightful leader of the United States and its military. In this sense, the Gipper identity proved far more than useful; it was powerful. If persuasion is the ability of a president to show how his interests align with those of others, Reagan's use of "the Gipper" created a playbook for American presidents centered on the power of football to gain Americans' trust.

Historian Douglas Brinkley, who edited Reagan's diaries, reflected on a White House dinner in May 2010 that President Barack Obama invited presidential historians to for a working supper. Brinkley, who published his experience in *Time* magazine, was surprised that the president was less interested in talking about the legacies of historical heavyweights like Abraham Lincoln or John F. Kennedy. Instead, Obama spoke affectionately of the work of Ronald Reagan. "There are policies and there is persona, and a lot can be told by persona," Brinkley wrote. "Obama is approaching the job in a Reaganesque fashion."[65]

The goal of this chapter is to show how much the Reagan mantle—the Reagan script—was inspired by sport, how carefully he forged a political persona through American football and the identity of "the Gipper," and how important this image was and remains to his political success and legacy. It is not surprising, then, that the tagline in Brinkley's *Time* article says, "Now Obama is fashioning his own presidency to follow the Gipper's playbook." Nor is it surprising that the article juxtaposes a picture of Reagan about to throw a football in the Oval Office alongside an image of Obama also in the Oval Office with a football in hand. This work carefully shows why such images are no accident. They are the product of a president who recognized the weight of certain cultural images and influenced mass media and the viewing public to define leadership through this lens. As the Gipper, Reagan created a playbook that presidents still follow. He has left the stadium, but the game continues.

—IV—

Addressing the "Achilles Heel"

Race and the Cold War at the Periphery

— 8 —

"An outstanding representative of America"

Mal Whitfield and America's Black Sports Ambassadors in Africa

BY KEVIN B. WITHERSPOON

On January 22, 1955, Mal Whitfield blitzed the field in an exhibition 400-meter race. Whitfield crossed the line some ten meters ahead of his competition, who had a perfect view of his back and the bottom of his track spikes as they kicked up high at the end of his somewhat unorthodox but famous long, graceful stride. His victory was not unexpected. Whitfield was at the height of his prowess at that time. He was already a two-time Olympic champion in the 800 meters, had taken the bronze in the 400 meters in 1948, and was in training for what he hoped to be his third Olympics. His competition that day, however, was somewhat unusual. He had not beaten a group of fellow Olympic hopefuls or top NCAA talent. Instead, he was chased by an enthusiastic group of several dozen young Zambian runners. Whitfield was in Northern Rhodesia—as it was called at that time—as part of a State Department–sponsored tour that took him to more than a dozen countries in Africa, Europe, and the Middle East.[1]

While Whitfield's name is less familiar than other great African American athletes of his generation—Jackie Robinson, Althea Gibson, Rafer Johnson, Wilma Rudolph, Muhammad Ali, and others—in the late 1940s and early 1950s he was a fixture in the sports headlines. It was not only his celebrity and athletic ability, however, that attracted State Department officials to his services. Whitfield proved to be an ideal athlete-diplomat: curious, patient, articulate, cheerful, flexible, and supportive of America's mission abroad. So successful were his foreign tours that the State Department called upon Whitfield four times from 1947 to 1963 for visits abroad that typically lasted several months. He also made dozens of shorter excursions for international exhibitions and track meets. His services were in highest demand in Africa, where Whitfield eventually became a full-time sports ambassador after his athletic career drew to a close, spearheading the development of what became elite track programs in nations such as Kenya and Ethiopia. Whitfield retired as the Cold War ended in 1989, having served abroad for more than forty years.[2]

Whitfield is unique among the black athletes who participated in the American sports diplomacy program for at least two reasons: his career as a diplomat spanned the pre- and post–Civil Rights era, beginning before Jackie Robinson broke baseball's color barrier in 1947 and ending long after the Black Power movement had subsided; and he made the transition from athlete to diplomat more thoroughly than anyone. While many of the sports diplomats were diplomats in name only, Whitfield truly embraced the role, immersing himself in the culture, politics, and lifestyle of the nations he visited. Whitfield's career provides a compelling case study that encapsulates the varied experiences of the African American sports diplomats, a one-man example of the evolution from what historian Damion Thomas has called "the good Negro"—the largely cheerful and compliant black athlete of the 1950s—to the more militant black athlete of the late 1960s.[3]

Black Athletes and the American Sports Diplomacy Program

Scholars who explore the significance of Cold War sport have largely—and appropriately—focused their energies on studying the Olympics, by far the largest and most prominent international sporting event.[4] It should be noted, however, that sporting events at every level took on heightened significance in this era. As the Cold War deepened, both sides developed extensive sports diplomacy programs, not only meeting each other in a series of high-profile track meets, swim meets, and matches in a variety of other sports but also sending out their own athletes as emissaries around the world.[5] These athletes became soldiers on the front lines of the Cold War, struggling to win the hearts and minds of citizens in nations whose loyalties were yet to be determined. For the United States, these efforts coalesced into an extensive program of sports specialists whom the State Department sent abroad on hundreds of sports tours over the duration of the Cold War, primarily to regions of the world on the periphery of the Cold War, such as Latin America, Southeast Asia, and Africa.[6]

The State Department employed African American athletes from the earliest days of the Cold War. Black athletes such as the Harlem Globetrotters, Althea Gibson, Rafer Johnson, Arthur Ashe, and many others helped promote the US government's message that the United States was a nation that offered equality to all citizens, regardless of race. In his essential book on this subject, *Globetrotting: African American Athletes and Cold War Politics*, Damion Thomas argues insightfully that black athletes in the 1950s and early 1960s generally accepted the proposition that while the United States was far from perfect in its racial policies, it was making progress. In fact, as athletes, they were involved in the aspect of American life that seemed to be moving toward racial equality most rapidly: sports. Even Cassius Clay, only a few years before becoming known as one of the most radical black athletes, declared his belief at the 1960 Rome Olympics that "the USA is still the best country in the world."[7]

From the perspective of the almost exclusively white male leadership of the US State Department, successful and famous African American athletes were a potentially powerful tool for the State Department's mission of neutralizing negative press abroad about race in the United States. As the Civil Rights Movement gained momentum and scenes of violence and repression of protestors circulated widely around the globe, US officials abroad faced constant scrutiny about America's racial policies at home. The message of America as a bastion of freedom, equality, and democracy did not seem to gibe with reports of lynchings, hasty trials, and the denial of basic human rights. The Soviet propaganda machine was quick to capitalize on such reports and frequently referred to the hypocrisy of the American stance on race. Black athletic diplomats, whom audiences understood as having prospered under the American system, reinforced the US government's message of fairness and equality for all, even if life on the American home front for such athletes did not live up to the image they projected abroad.

Using African American athletes as foreign specialists was just one component of the US government's carefully crafted propaganda campaign to influence international perceptions of America's race problem. From the State Department's perspective, African American were especially desirable for a variety of reasons. First, not only did black athletes help defuse criticism of racism in America but also athletes were not overtly political. They could be brought into a region without a specific political agenda, and often as not local officials welcomed them as a positive influence. Just by being there, the athletes opened the door for more serious discussions to come. As Whitfield himself noted, sport "teaches us . . . that in many areas of the world where our accustomed diplomacy doesn't work, or where we are simply not welcome (except as sports figures or entertainers), the United States may have to use new techniques to achieve its international goals."[8] Second, athletes communicated as much with their physical abilities and exploits as with words. In many cases, demonstrations were done before a large audience involving little speech; movements were acted out, usually to the delight of the crowd. An East African official observed one such example during Whitfield's 1957 African tour: "Mal, in his practical workout on the track, demonstrated common faults that had the crowd in fits of laughter, and then Mal took over the 'mike' to explain in his own wonderful technique how these common faults can be remedied and eventually used to help the other athletes along the road of track and field skills. The crowd showed their appreciation of this demonstration by a wonderful ovation."[9] Thus, athletes bridged language barriers and communicated more easily than others could. Finally, in some cases athletes arrived as international celebrities. Local dignitaries and even average citizens were aware of their exploits and were eager to see and hear them.

Among the first African American athletes to travel the world were the appropriately named Harlem Globetrotters, whom the State Department sent abroad beginning in 1951. Secretary of State Dean Acheson noted the public relations potential of the Globetrotters' tours: "The Department feels that there are unlimited possibilities for racial understanding and good will in the visits of these teams . . . which may provide an effective answer to Communist charges of racial prejudice in the USA."[10] The Globetrotters' legacy as racial pioneers is mixed, however, as their international prestige was accompanied by their troubling reliance on clowning, trickery, and performances that were reminiscent of minstrelsy. While winning games (usually against white opponents) and dazzling audiences with their tremendous ball-handling and shooting skills, the Globetrotters did it all while smiling, laughing, and clowning, conveying the appearance of happiness. Whatever discontent they might have felt over poor working and traveling conditions, low pay, and personal shame and unhappiness at the nature of their performances, it was hidden from the public behind what appeared to be smiles of joy.[11]

State Department officials were especially eager to deploy African American athletes to Africa, where they hoped a shared history and shared cultural heritage offered a point of commonality with people whom white American diplomats struggled to reach. A September 1965 State Department report based on a survey of all diplomatic posts noted the African nations' "eagerness to be guided by some more competent power." The report predicted that "teams or individuals who demonstrate, conduct clinics, pass on the advantages resulting from the experience and resources available in the United States, would meet with enormous success . . . The situation in Africa is fraught with possibility."[12] The belief that black Americans would readily connect and identify with average African citizens did not always bear fruit. On a 1970 tour of Africa, Arthur Ashe expressed some frustration about the State Department's expectation that he would naturally connect with Africans, saying, "I'm a stranger here."[13] Others did describe some natural connection with Africa, such as Kareem Abdul-Jabbar, who commented during a tour of Africa in 1971 that "this is going to be like getting a chance to go to the fountainhead, so to speak. It's going to be, really, a pleasure."[14]

Mal Whitfield: "An outstanding representative of America"

No American athlete was so thoroughly invested in the diplomatic program as Malvin "Mal" Whitfield, a five-time Olympic medalist in the 400-and 800-meter run at the 1948 and 1952 Olympics. In 1955, the time of the race described in the introduction, Whitfield the athlete was already an accomplished diplomat. He had completed his first diplomatic tour eight years earlier, a brief tour of Europe with nine other AAU track athletes in 1947 and had traveled the world extensively as part of his athletic career and his service in the military, which spanned World War II and the Korean War.[15] Deeply committed to his diplomatic service and especially the development of sport in Africa, Whitfield made it his full-time career after failing to qualify for the 1956 Olympics.

State Department officials interested in calming international criticism of racism in the United States immediately recognized the potential appeal of an athlete such as Whitfield. The biography and background of the Olympic champion fit neatly into the narrative of racial progress and equality that the Department promoted. Born of mixed race in Texas in 1924, Whitfield was raised in Los Angeles by his sister after both of his parents died while he was a child. He attended Thomas Jefferson High School with a student body he described as extremely diverse. "We had harmony," Whitfield says, "and everybody was supportive of one another."[16] He generally did not experience or witness the abject racism he might have experienced in the South or elsewhere.

Whitfield was a gifted athlete and excelled in every sport he tried, including baseball, football, and track. His devotion to track was sparked in 1932, when he and some friends sneaked into the Los Angeles Memorial Coliseum to watch the Olympics being held there and saw Eddie Tolan beat Ralph Metcalfe in the 100-meter sprint. From then on, he said, "I knew I wanted to run in the Olympics."[17] After he graduated from high school in 1943, in the midst of World War II, Whitfield was drafted into the armed forces. That was the beginning of a decorated military career of nearly ten years. He served with the Tuskegee Airmen, a group of African American fighter pilots. He was recalled to service during the Korean War and served as a tail gunner on twenty-seven missions from 1950 to 1952. From 1944 to 1950, interspersed with his military service, Whitfield attended Ohio State University. While, as he described, there were "very few blacks on campus," his experience at Ohio State was relatively benign.[18] At the same time, he found his life moving in directions that were unfamiliar to his friends and peers in Los Angeles and at Ohio State. "Beginning in 1946," he writes, "my life had taken a new turn. I had traveled extensively as new doors were opened to me through sports."[19]

Those new doors included starring turns at two Olympics—London in 1948 and Helsinki in 1952—where Whitfield's international reputation as a true track star was secured by winning five medals in the 400 and 800 meters and the 4 x 400-meter relay. As impressive as his Olympic achievements were, Whitfield's greatest years may well have been 1953 and 1954, between the Helsinki and Melbourne Olympics. During that period, Whitfield became a mainstay in sports pages around the country and the world as he broke and re-broke world records in his signature race, the 800 meters and in races of 500, 600, and 880 yards.[20] For a time, Whitfield's name was mentioned alongside elite milers such as Wes Santee and Roger Bannister as a possible candidate to break the four-minute mile (a feat first accomplished, of course, by Bannister in 1954).[21] This string of record-breaking performances and the fact that he was "held in high regard by contestants in this country and abroad, popular with fellow athletes and officials and most cooperative in assisting youngsters who request information on training," led to his recognition as the winner of the James E. Sullivan Award in 1954. He was the first African American to win this prestigious award, which the Amateur Athletic Union gives to America's top amateur athlete each year.[22]

It was in the midst of his track career that Whitfield began his long tenure in the foreign service. Even while training for three Olympics and completing his studies at Ohio State University, Whitfield logged many months of service abroad. After failing to qualify for a third Olympics in 1956, Whitfield retired from his own athletic career and turned to the work of coaching and motivating others. He had already begun the transition from athlete to diplomat; in 1955, he fulfilled a three-month appointment in Africa. He later joked that "three months turned out to be more than a quarter century of involvement in African sports programs." In 1956, he won a million-dollar grant from the Mobil Oil Company to hold a training camp for seventeen African states in West Africa. For the next thirty-three years, save for a few visits home, he lived abroad.[23]

For State Department officials, Whitfield nearly perfectly represented the idealized racial vision they sought to portray abroad. He was not only an athletic champion but also a decorated veteran of two wars. Further, Whitfield's background in the military and his time at Ohio State not only demonstrated that he had the restraint and discipline to follow orders but also that he was accustomed to working in an integrated environment and under white leadership. Just as Branch Rickey had selected Jackie Robinson as the man to break Major League Baseball's color barrier in part because of his experience at UCLA and in the military, State Department officials saw promise in Whitfield.[24]

Reports from the Department's foreign agents reflect both the expectations they had for Whitfield and the overwhelming belief that he had fulfilled those expectations. Dave Albritton, the office manager in Cologne, Germany, wrote of Whitfield's 1953 visit, "Mal Whitfield conducted himself as a gentleman at all times while he was with us." He had even helped straighten out two of his teammates who had gotten drunk and raised hell on the visit.[25] Following Whitfield's 1955 visit to Kenya, an official raved, "One noticed surprise and pleasure that any one man could combine such outstanding athletic prowess with such ability and charm in public-speaking, lecturing, and broadcasting."[26] Such opinions are aptly summarized by an Iranian official, who wrote, "Whitfield was in every way an outstanding representative of America."[27]

From "Good Negro" to Black Power: The Evolution of Mal Whitfield

On many occasions during these tours, Whitfield deftly fielded questions about race issues in the United States. Joseph C. Kolarek, public affairs officer in Belgrade, Yugoslavia, noted one such instance: "Whitfield's answers were of considerable propaganda value. . . . In emphasizing the difference in interests and attitudes of various sections of the United States, Whitfield, especially since he is a Negro, indirectly but effectively made the point that the Negro problem in the United States is regional rather than national."[28] And Richard L. Jones, who was stationed in Monrovia, Liberia, noted after Whitfield's lengthy stay in 1957 that "Whitfield [showed] to the best advantage a representative American Negro whose contribution to the American way of life is recognized throughout the US."[29] Noting examples like this, Damion Thomas argues that "Mal Whitfield's personal success as an African American was crucial to achieving his mission: altering international perceptions of the United States." From the perspective of the State Department, Whitfield was fulfilling this mission in stellar fashion. From its vantage point, Whitfield was indeed a "good Negro."[30]

But how did Whitfield perceive his own mission on such tours? "My job," he said, "was to conduct a series of athletic training programs talking about its importance in everyday life. . . . We emphasized what it means to represent your country in international competition. I talked about the Olympic Games and loyalty to your country and community."[31] Whitfield did not perceive that his mission was to change international views on racism, even if those sending him abroad did. Race had not been a source of crippling setbacks or attacks for Whitfield. He had not been scarred by racism in the way some of the other black athletes of his generation had. When he did speak publicly on the matter, his tone was hardly combative. For example, 1956, when he accepted his appointment as the vice-chair of the Los Angeles County United Republican Precinct Organization, he said, "I am delighted with the very real gains in the field of civil rights made during the Eisenhower-Nixon administration."[32]

The American public was thus accustomed to a largely subdued and cooperative Whitfield during the era when he was most prominently in the spotlight. Yet living abroad—primarily in Africa—through the most dynamic years of the civil rights struggle in the United States gradually changed Whitfield's is views. In addition to a variety of tours throughout Africa, Whitfield held long-term positions as the sports advisor to the president of the Assembly in Liberia, the head of the Department of Physical Education at the University of Nigeria, and athletic advisor in Somalia and Kenya.[33] Whitfield also hosted many other African American athletes as they toured Africa. He escorted Bill Russell through Liberia, Lee Evans through Kenya, and toured five nations with Muhammad Ali leading up to the 1980 Olympics. All told, he spent time in more than fifty African nations and coached many of the greatest Olympians from the continent, including Olympic gold medalists Kipchoge "Kip" Keino, Degage "Mamo" Wolde, Abebe Bikila, and Miruts Yifter.[34]

He did another tour for the State Department in 1963 that took him to many underdeveloped nations, such as Laos, which he noted as perhaps the most dangerous country he had ever visited.[35] Despite a host of organizational challenges, Whitfield drew from many of these experiences an

Mal Whitfield demonstrating his sprinter's stance to interested viewers in Luang Prabang, Laos, May 1963. *Courtesy of the University of Arkansas.*

incredible sense of optimism and hope, especially in the nations of post-colonial Africa. In the space of just a handful of years, Whitfield witnessed in such nations the creation of sports programs that started with nothing and grew into programs that produced topflight international athletes.[36]

At the same time, he found himself increasingly frustrated with his treatment by white managers, whether in the diplomatic realm or in the infrastructure of American athletics. He harbored deep-seated resentment about a matter that probably cost him the Sullivan Award in 1953. That year, Whitfield and several other American athletes were investigated for breaking the rules of amateurism while on an international tour. Whitfield was eventually exonerated, and he won the Sullivan Award the following year. Wes Santee and several other high-profile athletes were not so lucky, and the AAU barred them from international competition for one year.[37] Years later, the incident still bothered Whitfield.[38]

He returned to the United States only for one brief interlude: the March on Washington in 1963. He left the difficult but rewarding atmosphere of Africa to face an atmosphere of highly charged racial tension in the United

States. The violence of the early months of 1963—which were punctuated by images of fire hoses and attack dogs turned upon peaceful protestors in Birmingham—had fueled the momentum for the massive march that summer. So motivated was Whitfield to attend the protest that he flew back to the states, left his young family in Los Angeles, and drove on his own across the country to Washington, D.C. Whitfield recalled, "I felt that I had to do this, because I had seen all these positive changes in the governments of Africa when they became independent. I expected similar progress here at home."[39]

Whitfield was part of a broader evolution in the mindset of many black athletes, who gradually came to reject the view that sport was a positive force in the movement toward black equality. Over time, as the Civil Rights Movement made progress on the home front and as black activists became more outspoken, black athletic ambassadors began to co-opt elements of the tours and derive personal enrichment and pleasure from the experience, sometimes at the expense of the State Department's broader mission. Even African American athletes who largely accepted the premise that athletics played a positive role in advancing the black race often developed their own views of the tours. Athletes such as Bill Russell, Wilma Rudolph, and Kareem Abdul-Jabbar expressed such sentiments during or after their foreign tours. Rudolph described her 1963 trip to Africa this way: "I just felt at home. . . . I just went out like I belonged there. They accepted me and that's what I wanted them to do. And whatever they wore, I wore."[40] Beyond simply doing the bidding of the State Department, African American athletes used such journeys for their own ends, such as communing with the African people and visiting the homeland of their ancestors.

By the mid-1960s, after the violence of the early Civil Rights Movement, the attacks with fire hoses and police dogs in Birmingham, the assassination of John F. Kennedy, and a host of other discouraging events, many black athletes turned away from the State Department's party line. Instead of accepting sport as a symbol of racial progress in the United States, black athletes expressed frustration at the slow pace of change and limited progress within the realm of sports. Eventually, the Black Power movement of the late 1960s broke altogether with the idea that the United States was improving.[41] As exemplified by NBA stars Kareem Abdul-Jabbar and Oscar Robertson, who participated in a trouble-filled tour of Africa in 1971, black athletes by the early 1970s were no longer likely to serve as willing agents of American propaganda.[42]

Thus, when Whitfield returned to the public eye in the mid-1960s, he assumed a much more aggressive stance than he had previously, to the surprise of many who were familiar with his earlier work. Most famously, Whitfield authored a stunning article published in *Ebony* magazine in March 1964 that advocated that black athletes boycott the upcoming Tokyo Olympics. "For the most part," Whitfield wrote, "Negro athletes have been conspicuous by their absence from the numerous Civil Rights battles around the country."[43] It was time, in his estimation, to get involved.

He gave several reasons for his support of this drastic measure, but perhaps most eloquent—bringing to mind Martin Luther King Jr.'s speech from the March on Washington—was his statement that "it is time for America to live up to its promises of Liberty, Equality and Justice for all, or be shown up to the world as a nation where the color of one's skin takes precedence over the quality of one's mind and character."[44] As a black American living abroad, Whitfield had witnessed and experienced dramatic social progress. He had seen peoples who had been thrown from the repression of colonialism into the chaos of independence striving in fits and starts to find greatness from within. He was now seeing the United States almost as a foreigner himself, and what he saw disappointed him. Ironically, a visit to South Africa—still under the system of apartheid—fortified these feelings. Because of his diplomatic status, Whitfield enjoyed the finest accommodations, food, and transportation of his many journeys abroad. This gave him access to privileges black South Africans could never have. "I remember thinking," he wrote, "about my not having these liberties . . . in the United States. I was free to go wherever I chose, without anticipating any serious problems."[45] His position that African American athletes should boycott the 1964 Olympics derived from the contrast between the freedoms and privileges he enjoyed in Africa and the struggles of African Americans at home to secure basic civil and human rights.

Whitfield, perhaps less aggressively, also supported the Black Power movement that was evolving in the late 1960s. His previous frustrations were merely confirmed by another incident that occurred before the 1968 Mexico City Olympics. Whitfield was scheduled to join the Ethiopian team that he had been coaching. At the last minute, however, he was told he would not be allowed to travel with the team, as he was designated as America's "Sports Affairs Officer for the whole of Africa," rather than the sports officer for a single country. After that, Whitfield said, "I began to side with the Black Power athletes." [46] Whitfield maintained this more militant stance. He backed two black athletes, Marshall Dill and Herb Washington, who left the American track team while touring Africa in 1973, claiming that white officials were favoring the white athletes on the team.[47] Despite his frustration, he still hoped for change and progress from the country he had long supported. "I was still loyal and dedicated to my country," he says, "but I was upset, because there had not been equality, even before and during my time of being a popular personality while waving the red, white and blue flag around the world. I waved that flag, because I believed in the principles of democracy."[48]

Conclusion

Mal Whitfield personifies the complexities of the State Department program that sent black athletes abroad to enhance international acceptance of American policies. Whitfield transformed from "good Negro" to black radical, mystifying many American officials who had come to rely upon him as one of America's finest representatives. As one who participated in and closely observed the workings of the State Department programs, Whitfield ultimately came to doubt their motivations and effectiveness and to support other black athletes who challenged the system. By the late 1960s, Whitfield—and many others—seemed to support Harry Edwards's words in his autobiographical account, *The Revolt of the Black Athlete* that white supervisors treated African American athletes like "black super-animals," to be used like "pieces of equipment," and discarded when their usefulness expired.[49]

Ultimately, the State Department's practice of employing prominent black athletes began to unravel. After more than a decade of faithful service with little to show for it, black athletes could no longer support the American government's propagandistic view of racial harmony and progress. Too often, athletes who celebrated such concepts during their international trips returned to segregation, racism, and violence in the United States. The Harlem Globetrotters—the clown princes of basketball—privately complained of working under oppressive conditions for little pay with no chance of capitalizing on their talents in the professional league.[50] And Mal Whitfield, whom many saw as an ideal representative of the United States abroad, was pursued on trumped-up charges that he had broken the rules of amateurism, waited years too long for recognition such as the Sullivan Award, and struggled for years to advance in white-dominated US diplomatic circles. Far too many others recalled racist incidents from their upbringing, racist epithets used by white coaches, and even violence and intimidation.[51] Black athletes ultimately chose to reject a system that failed to live up to the image of equality, freedom, and harmony it projected to the rest of the world.

9

"One of the greatest ambassadors that the United States has ever sent abroad"

Wilma Rudolph, American Athletic Icon for the Cold War and the Civil Rights Movement

BY CAT ARIAIL

"Wilma has been one of the greatest ambassadors that the United States has ever sent abroad," announced Louis J. Fisher, president of the Amateur Athletic Union (AAU), when he presented Wilma Rudolph with the 1961 James E. Sullivan Award. Rudolph was the first African American female athlete to receive the prestigious award, which honored "the amateur athlete who, by performance, example and good influence, did the most to advance good sportsmanship throughout the year."[1] Rudolph emerged as an icon of American athleticism at the 1960 Rome Olympics, where she won gold in the 100-meter, in the 200-meter, and as the anchor leg for the US women's 4 x 100-meter relay team. Her triple gold track triumph was a first for an American female athlete and a first for a black female athlete. In the summer of 1961, she returned to the tracks of Europe, threatening to break world records as she represented the United States in a series of dual track meets against the Soviet Union and other European nations.

These international athletic achievements and her national successes made Rudolph a more than worthy recipient of the Sullivan Award. But was she, as Fisher proclaimed, "one of the greatest ambassadors" ever to represent the United States? In 1963, the State Department seemed to validate Fisher's estimation when they named Rudolph an American sports specialist and sent her on a goodwill trip to French West Africa. Why did the state officials and the officials of American sport consider a young black female athlete such a suitable ambassador?

Throughout the Cold War, the United States proclaimed the superiority of democracy, insisting that a democratic society, unlike a communistic one, provided rights, privileges, and opportunities to all. However, the direct-action civil rights movement effectively exposed the gap between the rhetoric and reality of American democracy. Officials in the US government and other institutions thus sought to reconcile the demands of the Cold War with those of the movement for civil rights. Sport presented an effective space for this propaganda project. The United States and the Soviet Union shared the belief that sport was a proxy for the nation's character and capacity.[2] By way of their victories, American athletes, especially African American athletes, advertised the "cultural diversity, political freedom, and social mobility" characteristic of the "American way of life" to allied and unaligned populations.[3] For the primarily white officials of state and sport in the United States, the successes of African American athletes seemed to demonstrate that despite enduring evidence of racial discrimination, American democracy encouraged black Americans to reach their potential in sport and in other realms.

As an athletically successful yet feminine African American, Wilma Rudolph was perfectly suited for the demands of the historical moment. Due to long-held stereotypes, many whites felt that African American women represented the antithesis of femininity. Yet, somewhat curiously, the American press, along with numerous government and sports officials, celebrated Rudolph for her femininity. Her achievement, attractiveness, and racial identity made her a powerful representative of the possibilities for progress in a democratic American society. That she also had overcome childhood poverty and polio further underscored the opportunities offered by American democracy. Whether she was competing as an unofficial athletic ambassador on the track or serving as the State Department's cultural ambassador in Africa, she presented an idealized portrait of the American way of life. Rudolph's story illustrates how ideas about race, gender, and sport were central to the United States' navigation of the contradictions of the Cold War and civil rights movement, allowing the nation to claim that it practiced the values of democracy and equality that it preached. However, Rudolph intimately experienced the limitations of her symbolism. The attributes that made her an appealing representative of the best of America, namely her race and gender, were barriers that prevented her from living the life she advertised.[4]

"We Really Showed Out": The Tennessee State Tigerbelles Join the Cold War

Remarkably, Wilma Rudolph did not run until age twelve. Born in 1940 in Clarksville, Tennessee as the twentieth of twenty-two children, she suffered from polio and a variety of other illnesses as a child. From the age of five, she wore metal leg braces, so only could she watch neighborhood children participate in sprint races and pick-up basketball games. When she finally was able to participate in these activities, Rudolph quickly displayed precocious athletic ability. When she was playing basketball for Burt High School, she caught the eye of referee Ed Temple, who was also the coach of the Tennessee State University (TSU) Tigerbelle track team.[5] In 1953, Temple assumed head coaching duties at TSU. He soon established the Tigerbelles as the dominant force in American women's track and field. Temple perfected the model Cleve Abbott had established at Tuskegee Institute in the mid-1930s that used a combination of athletics and academics to uplift young black women.[6] In 1955, the Tigerbelles won their first National AAU Championship, then set their sights on the 1956 Olympic Games. Temple invited the promising young Rudolph to join his team as they trained for the 1956 National AAU Championship and Olympic Trials. Rudolph contributed to TSU's junior AAU title and earned a spot on the 1956 US women's Olympic track and field squad, one of a record six Tigerbelles who represented the United States in Melbourne.[7]

At the Olympics, Rudolph competed in the 200 meters and the 4 x 100-meter relay. While she failed to advance to the 200-meter final, she joined Mae Faggs, Isabelle Daniels, and Margaret Matthews, all products of TSU, to win the bronze in the relay. That year the women's track and field team gave their most successful performance since the 1936 Olympic Games in Berlin. In addition to the bronze the relay team won, Tuskegee's Mildred McDaniel won gold in the high jump and Willye White, also of TSU, won silver in the long jump.[8] Yet enduring sexism and racism prevented Rudolph and her teammates from earning acclaim outside the African American sport community. Nevertheless, Temple considered 1956 to be the foundation for the future successes his athletes would achieve.[9]

At the inaugural US-USSR dual track meet in Moscow in the summer of 1958, the Tigerbelles built upon this foundation. That meet provided an opportunity for athletes from the United States and the Soviet Union to foster friendship and understanding through sport, albeit while trying to assert the athletic superiority of their respective nations. Many presumed that the

American women would not contribute to the nation's sporting supremacy, but as Temple later proclaimed, "We shocked the US men and we shocked us. We didn't know we was good. But we really showed out."[10] Coached by Temple, African American track women scored four victories.[11] Even though the Soviet female athletes defeated their American counterparts by a score of 63 to 44, the surprisingly strong showing earned this cohort of young black women acclaim. The AAU praised their performance in *Amateur Athlete*, its official magazine: "Our girls, while outscored by their vaunted opposition 63 points to 44, nevertheless did considerably better than many had expected and won four of their 10 events."[12] The *Chicago Defender* likewise boasted that "Uncle Sam's girls humiliated the husky competitors by winning two of the first five events in the women's competition."[13]

The language used in these plaudits indicates that the excitement the performances of African American female track athletes inspired extended beyond their athletic talent. In contrast to the Soviet "women," they were "girls." Temple at one point quipped that he wanted his female athletes to be 'foxes, not oxes,' underscoring his espousal of the politics of respectability.[14] Similar to the leaders of civil rights demonstrations, who required activists to dress in their Sunday best, Temple demanded that his athletes present and comport themselves in a feminine manner in order to gain broader social acceptance.[15] Although Temple's policy was paternalistic, he believed that a feminine presentation would guard against overtly racist attacks. Furthermore, ensuring his athletes were "foxes" also discouraged accusations of mannishness, which had long worked to discredit women athletes, especially black women athletes who competed in the traditionally masculine sport of track and field.[16]

US officials intent on demonstrating that the nation was fulfilling its democratic values viewed Temple's Tigerbelles as a powerful counter to accusations of American racism. In the Cold War battle for hearts and minds, the Soviet Union distributed images around the world of the violent resistance of white Americans to the movement for civil rights, aiming to undermine US claims about the promises of democracy. The success of black athletes seemed to present an alternative narrative about race in America, enabling US government officials to claim that violent reactions to the Civil Rights Movement were isolated incidents.[17] Thus, the clash of the priorities of the cultural Cold War and the demands of the movement for civil rights made the moment right for Wilma Rudolph. At the 1960 Summer Olympics in Rome, she established herself as an exceptionally athletic and attractive young African American woman, which, in turn, made her "one of the greatest athletic ambassadors" to suit up for the United States.

"The Quintessence of Olympian Effort": Icon of Feminine Athleticism

Rudolph was in peak form when the competitions in Rome began. Even though she turned her ankle before her first heat in the 100 meters, she coasted through the qualifying rounds and entered the final as the presumptive favorite. These expectations did not faze her as she toed the starting line for the 100-meter final and the 80,000 fans in the stadium chanted "Vilma!" When the gun sounded, Rudolph started clean and, as she described in her 1977 autobiography, "When I reached fifty meters, I saw that I had them all, and I was just beginning to turn it on. By seventy meters, I knew the race was mine, nobody was going to catch me."[18] And no one did. Rudolph finished five yards ahead of Great Britain's Dorothy Hyman and Germany's Jutta Heine.

She also demonstrated her superior ability in the 200-meter sprint, again besting Heine and Hyman to capture her second gold. In the 4 x 100 meters, Martha Hudson, Barbara Jones, and Lucinda Williams ran the first three legs before passing the baton to Rudolph. The trio had established a comfortable lead, but a bobbled baton exchange between Williams and Rudolph appeared to put their gold in jeopardy. Alex Haley, the noted African American author, described the resulting drama for *The Rotarian*: "Wilma had to stop to grasp it and a gasp went from the crowd. Germany's Jute [*sic*] Heine was flying two strides away. But now Wilma's great, scissoring, incredible strides began to burn up the track. She came abreast of Jute Heine . . . pulled slightly ahead . . . and burst the tape in first place."[19] Rudolph remembered the celebratory chaos that erupted after the victory:

> After the playing of "The Star-Spangled Banner," I came away from the victory stand and I was mobbed. People were jumping all over me, pushing microphones into my face, pounding my back. I couldn't believe it. Finally, the American officials grabbed me and escorted me to safety. One of them said, "Wilma, life will never be the same for you again." He was so right.[20]

But more than changing the circumstances of her own life, she changed the perception of female athletes and of African American women generally.

As Temple later recognized, "She has the ability, the naive charm, and charisma that endeared people to her. She, I suppose more than any other runner, opened up the modern door of track for women."[21] American publications offered effusive estimations of Rudolph. "The quintessence of Olympian effort was expressed in the lissome, straining figure of this 20-year-old American girl as she sprinted explosively across the finish line," declared *Life*.[22] The *New*

Wilma Rudolph competing in the 200 meters at the 1960 Rome Summer Olympic Games. *Courtesy of the International Olympic Committee.*

York Times described Rudolph as the "queen of the 1960 Olympics," deeming her "a slender beauty whose eyes carry a perpetual twinkle."[23] *Sports Illustrated* wrote, "A slender 5 feet 11 inches, Wilma Rudolph can command a look of mingled graciousness and hauteur that suggests a duchess."[24] These quotations convey the combination of athleticism and attractiveness Rudolph possessed that captivated sports fanatics in the United States and abroad. She appeared to be embodied evidence of American equality.

Although popularly understood as uniquely exceptional, Rudolph represented the culmination of the "Temple Way." Her athletic excellence and feminine image was the product of careful cultivation, as Temple, who served as the sprint coach for the 1960 US women's track and field team, ensured that Rudolph and her teammates were not only prepared to succeed athletically but also to look attractive while doing so. However, it was US Cold War priorities and the historical circumstances of the civil rights movement that made Rudolph an affective and effective American icon.

The fact that Rudolph exceeded expectations of race, gender, and athleticism gave her great symbolic power. Despite the fact that civic leaders within the African American community embraced the politics of respectability, white people continued to promote negative stereotypes that portrayed

African American women as lascivious and dishonest, denying them the qualities of conventional femininity.[25] As a young black woman who participated in the traditionally masculine sport of track and field, Rudolph seemed an unlikely candidate to contest this stereotype. Yet it was the implicit belief in the unfemininity of African American women that made the feminine Rudolph an appealing representative of American opportunity. By presenting a positive image of African American women, she likewise advertised a favorable image of American society, demonstrating that a democratic society appeared to allow all persons to achieve their potential. Society columnists for African American newspapers embraced Rudolph as a model of femininity. "The ultra femininity of Wilma Rudolph, Olympic track star, was a delightful surprise," proclaimed Thomasina Norford in the *New York Amsterdam News*. The *Afro-American*'s Lula Garrett included Rudolph in her "'60's Top Ten," choosing her and the other nine women on the list "because of the strictly feminine subtlety with which they initiated moves that have or will have national and international influence."[26]

More significantly, white women's publications and mainstream organizations also celebrated Rudolph for her femininity. "I've seen Wilma Rudolph run like a gazelle, walk like a queen and smile like an angel," wrote the *Ladies' Home Journal*.[27] *Mademoiselle* named Rudolph one of their "10 Young Women of the Year."[28] The General Mills company presented her with a plaque for her "contribution to American womanhood."[29] The General Mills honor best captures her significance. She was not just an admirable representative of black American womanhood; she was a representative of all American women. Placing Rudolph in this symbolic role not only expanded the boundaries of American womanhood, but also contested accusations of American racial inequality. And because of the international acclaim Rudolph received, the alternative image of American femininity she presented had the potential to gain more purchase.

Sport publications from across Europe celebrated Rudolph, referring to her affectionately as "La Gazelle Nera" ("The Black Gazelle") and "La Perle Noire" ("The Black Pearl").[30] London's *Daily Express* exclaimed that "the name of Wilma Rudolph, the flamingo-legged American heroine, is indelibly imprinted on these Games by the medals she won with feet that seemed to caress the track as she moved past the old barriers of pace."[31] A commentator for the British Broadcasting Corporation described her as "the girl with an easy kind hearted smile" who "moves with unthinking grace of a gazelle" and "broke the tape with a dream-like smile on her face."[32] The response to Rudolph throughout the US track and field team's post-Olympic tour in Western Europe brought the young athlete more attention. According to

Sports Illustrated, "Autograph hunters jostled her wherever she went, and she was deluged with letters, gifts, telegrams, and pleas that she stay where she was or come to a dozen cities where she wasn't."[33] The Victorian Women's Amateur Athletic Association in Melbourne sought to inject Australian women's track with such excitement by inviting Rudolph to compete in the country in early 1961.[34] Israel and Trinidad offered similar opportunities.[35] Although none of these trips came about, the invitations indicate the level of Rudolph's appeal around the world. By the time she returned to Tennessee, she reportedly had received more than seventy-five marriage proposals from domestic and international suitors.[36] Among other honors, a German sport magazine, *ISK*, selected Rudolph as "top athlete of the year" over Armin Hary, Germany's gold medal winner in the men's 100 meters.[37] In the summer of 1961, when Madame Tussaud's museum in London installed a wax sculpture of Rudolph, she was the first American athlete to receive this tribute.[38]

As these celebrations evince, Rudolph had emerged as an unofficial ambassador of American democracy. The combination of her feminine identity, athletic achievements, and personal story appealed to an array of audiences, allowing her to advertise an inclusive image of American society. After witnessing the national and international responses to Rudolph, the US government sought to tap into her potential as a vehicle for propaganda. In 1961, the United States Information Agency (USIA), a government organization that spread pro-American propaganda, produced a film about Rudolph titled *Wilma Rudolph: Olympic Champion*. The film emphasized her ability to overcome childhood illness to achieve athletic and academic success and presented her as a figure of American individualism who symbolized the possibilities available to all, regardless of race or gender, in a democratic society.[39]

The State Department, which also wanted to take advantage of Rudolph's appeal, organized a goodwill tour to India and other Asian nations for her.[40] Since the mid-1950s, the State Department's Cultural Exchange Program had sent African American artists and athletes abroad, employing the likes of Louis Armstrong and Jesse Owens to demonstrate American racial equality.[41] But few African American female athletes had participated in these efforts. In the fall of 1955, tennis champion Althea Gibson toured Southeast Asia with Karol Fagores, a white female tennis player noted for her beauty, and two male tennis players.[42] The following spring, Mae Faggs, Rudolph's mentor at TSU, and Karen Anderson, a young white female javelin thrower, traveled with six male track stars to Central Africa to compete in local meets and conduct exhibitions.[43] Because of her popularity, Rudolph seemed the perfect candidate to become the third black female athlete to serve as a cultural diplomat. Although her trip to the Far East fell through, she remained on the State Department's radar. She instead spent the summer of 1961 as an informal athletic ambassador, tearing up the tracks of Europe as a member of the AAU's summer track and field tour.

Wilma Rudolph as Athletic Ambassador

The third annual US-USSR track meet was the centerpiece of the 1961 AAU summer tour, with head-to-head track meets against Poland, West Germany, and Great Britain to follow. Rudolph confidently told sportswriters, "I've never been to Russia and I'm looking forward to it. I am sure I'll be in top shape in about a week."[44] She proved that she was in more than "top shape." In front of the more than 70,000 fans in Lenin Stadium, Rudolph equaled the 100-meter world record, seemingly unhindered by the muscle strain that had limited her preparation. The *New York Times* reported that "Miss Rudolph was clearly in command of the women's 100 meters after the first thirty meters. She sped home a comfortable winner."[45] She followed her dominating win by anchoring a world-record 4 x 100-meter relay effort. After Willye White, Ernestine Pollards, and Vivian Brown completed the relay's first three legs, the US team trailed the Soviets. Rudolph then bumbled the baton pass from Brown, falling five yards behind Tatiana Shchelkanova. Yet, as *Sports Illustrated* wrote, Rudolph "closed very slowly for the first 30, 40, 50 yards. But then something happened. Wilma went zoom. She passed Shchelkanova as if the Russian were nailed to the track and won by three yards."[46] Despite Rudolph's pair of stunning performances, the Soviet team defeated the US women. "But with Wilma equaling her 100-meter world record and helping set another in the 400-meter relay—and capturing the hearts of Muscovites as she had captured the hearts of Romans—no one was too concerned over the final score," *Sports Illustrated* judged.[47] This statement conveys the important, albeit unofficial, role Rudolph played: her ability to offer a captivating image of American democracy to international audiences took priority over the inability of US women to claim athletic victory.

In the US teams' next dual meet in Stuttgart, West Germany, she confirmed her athletic and symbolic value. Rudolph thrilled more than 50,000 West German track fans, turning in a scintillating 100-meter effort to set a new world record of 11.2 seconds. The *New York Times* reported that the crowd "cheered her lustily for many minutes," a noteworthy degree of acclaim, for, as the *Times* noted, "in Europe, female track stars normally command no more interest than in America."[48] Rudolph elicited similar interest among over 70,000 fans in Warsaw, where she again won the 100 meters and anchored the US team to a win over Poland in the 4 x 100-meter relay.[49] At the United States' final meet in London, Rudolph did not race in the 100-meter, receiving a well-deserved break to rest the hamstring she pulled during her world record run in Stuttgart. In order not to disappoint the more than 21,000 fans in White City Stadium, she ran the anchor leg in the 4x100-meter relay. However, because her teammates had established such a dominating lead, Rudolph did not have to race at top speed, and she claimed the victory with ease.[50]

The impressive record Rudolph compiled earned her the 1961 James E. Sullivan Award and AAU President Fisher's statement that she "has been one of the greatest ambassadors the United States has ever sent abroad."[51] Named after one of the founders of the AAU, the Sullivan Award defined ideal American athletic identity, celebrating the amateur athlete "whose ability and character combined have had the greatest influence during the year in advancing the standards of sportsmanship."[52] Until 1954, an African American athlete had never won the award. That year, Mal Whitfield, a middle-distance runner who had won gold in the 800 meters at the 1948 and 1952 Olympic Games while also serving in the Air Force during World War II and the Korean War, broke the Sullivan Award's racial barrier. The following year, Harrison Dillard, a gold medalist in the 100-meter sprint in London and 110-meter high hurdles in Helsinki who also had served in World War II, received the honor.[53] The fact that both these men had military backgrounds indicates the degree to which national service, whether athletically or militarily, made an athlete, especially an African American athlete, worthy of the nation's most vaunted athletic award.[54]

In 1959, Lucinda Williams, Rudolph's Tigerbelle teammate who had won a trio of gold medals at the Pan-American Games in Chicago and captained the US track women for that year's dual meet with the Soviet Union, became the first African American female athlete to earn a Sullivan nomination.[55] In 1960, Rafer Johnson, who had established a new world record in the decathlon at the Rome Olympics, became the third African American to capture the Sullivan Award.[56] Like Johnson, Whitfield, and Dillard, Rudolph served larger symbolic needs. As the first black female athlete and first female track athlete to win the award, she presented a positive image of American athleticism that implicitly refuted accusations of racism.

In the summer of 1962, Rudolph further established herself as America's leading athletic icon. That year Palo Alto, California, hosted the fourth US-USSR dual meet, attracting the second largest crowd in US track and field history. Rudolph again asserted herself as one of the nation's most valuable competitors. In the 100 meters, she unleashed another exciting come-from-behind win. Although she was trailing Mariya Itkina at the 80-meter mark,

Rudolph "put on an explosive burst of speed to capture the 100-meter dash by eight feet."[57] She provided a similar thrill in the 4 x 100-meter relay. While Willye White, Edith McGuire, and Vivian Brown had kept the United States within striking distance of the Soviets, Rudolph clinched the win, "taking off a shade behind Galina Popova, [then outspeeding] her by three yards."[58] Vivian Brown gave the US women a third victory by securing a surprising win in the 200 meters.[59] But Rudolph was the star of the event. *Sports Illustrated* proclaimed: "In action or repose, red or red-white-and-blue, black or white, male or female, no one in Palo Alto could match the incomparable Wilma Rudolph for effortless grace and poise."[60]

During a subsequent AAU-sponsored track and field tour of Sweden, Rudolph displayed her combination of athleticism and attractiveness, delighting Swedish track enthusiasts in Gothenburg, Hässleholm, Malmö, and Oslo in what popularly was referred to as the "Wilma Rudolph Tour."[61] According to Jo Ann Terry, a fellow Tigerbelle who joined Rudolph in her tour of Sweden, "They just loved her. They had posters up with a big picture of Wilma." Rudolph told the *Afro-American*, "We played to full houses everywhere and I never got so many flowers in all my life."[62] After Rudolph again captivated track fans with her brand of feminine athletic excellence, the US government decided formally to take advantage of her potential as an ambassador.

Wilma Rudolph, American Sports Specialist

In the spring of 1963, the State Department nominated Rudolph to serve as an American Sports Specialist in Senegal, Mali, Ghana, Upper Volta, and Guinea.[63] The previous African American female athlete ambassadors, Althea Gibson and Mae Faggs, had participated as members of goodwill tours with other athletes. Rudolph, as an American Sports Specialist, traveled to French West Africa as a lone representative of the United States, an assignment that suggests that the State Department recognized that Rudolph seemed to singularly embody an idealized image of American democracy. She was the first and only African American female athlete to receive this designation. Statements from documents on the specialist program capture how government officials hoped the program would function. "We have taken the phrase 'life, liberty, and the pursuit of happiness,' a phrase that seems to epitomize American aspirations, and we have grouped around this phrase those aspects of American life which guide us in the selection and orientation of the individuals who will participate in the program," declared "The Officer's Guide on Division for Americans Abroad," which described the American Sports Specialist program.[64] A 1963 report on the program asserted that "the American Specialist represents in his own field of competence some aspect of American excellence, but he also attempts to answer a broad range of questions about America, correct misconceptions of America and generally to bolster American leadership of the free world."[65]

In the mid-1960s, the State Department completed a study on how sports could advance US foreign policy goals that revealed more about the motives for sending Rudolph and other athletes to Africa. Following the African independence movements of the late 1950s and early 1960s, both the United States and the Soviet Union sought to sway newly autonomous African nations to their side in the Cold War, and sport was a potentially effective vehicle in this battle for hearts and minds.[66] The study determined that although the majority of African nations harbored a "considerable to great" interest in sports, Africans viewed the United States as "a competent but distant power—acknowledged but irrelevant." The "almost inevitable conclusion" was "that it would be to the advantage of the United States to increase diplomat efforts in this direction," the report writer concluded.[67] For the State Department, Rudolph was the perfect candidate for the task. Government officials hoped that her identity as a successful black female athlete would counter Soviet critiques of US racism.[68]

Reports of Rudolph's 27-day tour indicate that she fulfilled these expectations. The trip began in Dakar, Senegal, where Rudolph received an enthusiastic welcome from US ambassador Philip Kaiser and his wife and a crowd of Senegalese citizens.[69] Over the following week, she acted as a "goodwill sports representative" at the African Friendship Games.[70] Rudolph told reporters, "I am very happy to be here although this is the first time that I am attending an important track meet without participating in it."[71] Rudolph also served as an honored guest of President Leopold Senghor at the inaugural soccer match in the nation's new Liberty Stadium. Senghor reportedly practiced his English with Rudolph, while she shared her scant knowledge of French with him.[72] Rudolph later gave advice about sprinting techniques to African female athletes participating in the Friendship Games, telling the press that "I thought they needed more help."[73] She also offered advice about nutrition and diet with the Senegalese female athletes. While Rudolph emphasized how important it was for an athlete to find the diet that individually suited her, the admiring African athletes desired to emulate their American instructor exactly. "Unfortunately, the women wanted to adopt my diet," Rudolph reported.[74]

When she traveled to Ghana, where she found a group of well-equipped and experienced female athletes, Rudolph suggested that two Ghanaian female athletes were as talented as American women.[75] After a State Department official asked her about a potential competition between American and Ghanaian female athletes, she replied, "They wouldn't be too far behind. But I'm sure in the sprints that American women could win."[76] In addition to athletic instruction, Rudolph also offered academic advice, encouraging her listeners to cultivate a "sound mind in a sound body."[77] After she left Ghana, a local sportswriter excitedly wrote, "Wilma Rudolph, American women's sprint champion and 1960 triple gold medal winner, concluded a four-day visit here last week declaring that she had seen many potential world class athletes in Ghana. She said she would be willing to return to help train competitors."[78]

She next visited Mali, again sharing advice about athletics, education, and nutrition with female athletes at secondary schools and training camps.[79] According to the US ambassador stationed there, Rudolph was "the undisputed main attraction at every public appearance," noting that she was "recognized immediately, warmly applauded, and constantly besieged with requests for autographs."[80] President Keita of Mali expressed appreciation for Rudolph's visit, telling her, "We believe your presence will stimulate development of sports among our young people."[81] Rudolph then traveled to Guinea, where she visited the Ministry of Sports and the Ministry of Education. She completed her tour in Upper Volta, where American ambassador Thomas Estes and the Upper Volta youth and sports minister hosted receptions for her.[82] Before leaving the continent, she told reporters and citizens, "My trip is proof in effect that the United States is interested in the development of sports in Africa."[83]

State Department officials praised Rudolph's diplomatic performance. Tony Merrill, a State Department official who conducted a series of debriefing interviews with Rudolph, enthused, "I must tell you that the reports coming in from all our posts and our embassies and our ambassador said you were a remarkable representative of our country."[84] Nicholas Rodis, special assistant for athletic programs at the State Department, echoed Merrill's opinion. In an article in *Amateur Athlete*, he referred to Rudolph as a "working diplomat in the finest sense," complimenting her for communicating "to the young and very proud developing nations of Africa that the United States was interested enough in the Pan-African Games [*sic*] to send one of its best athletes."[85]

Rudolph performed the symbolic labor the nation asked of her expertly. The combination of athleticism and attractiveness that had captivated so many in the United States and Europe also proved effective in West Africa. Rudolph later said that she received more than fifty marriage proposals while she was in Africa.[86] The Young Pioneers, Ghana's leading track club, named her an honorary member.[87] Although the effusive embrace of Rudolph does not mean that Africans adopted an improved opinion of the United States, the State Department deemed Rudolph's specialist service an unqualified success. [88] Developments in the Civil Rights Movement likely influenced the positive responses to Rudolph's diplomacy. Her time in Africa coincided with the arrest of Martin Luther King Jr. in Birmingham, Alabama and the subsequent release of his "Letter from Birmingham Jail." State Department officials did not refer to this event or other civil rights developments when they evaluated Rudolph's effectiveness as a State Department sports specialist. However, this context gave her service greater meaning. Across West Africa, her presence presumably presented a picture of American democracy that countered reports of American resistance to racial progress. She ostensibly demonstrated that, in the words of Merrill, a young African American woman could be "a walking flag of the United States of America."[89]

Conclusion

Though she served as a representative of an idealized version of the American way of life, Rudolph was excluded from its bounties. As Temple later noted, Rudolph "didn't get nothing except a pat on her back and a couple of banquets" for her service for the United States, both on and off the track.[90] Rudolph was a powerful symbol of an idealized narrative about the benefits of democracy because she seemed to have transcended the burdens and barriers of race and gender. Yet the popular image of Rudolph rendered invisible how these burdens and barriers had and would influence her life prospects. In her 1977 autobiography, she wrote "you get scars deep inside of you that sometimes never heal."[91] Scars inflicted by racism and sexism were also part of the American way of life. And sport, for all its symbolic power, could not heal them.

—10—

Defying the Cultural Boycott

Arthur Ashe, the Anti-Apartheid Activist

BY DAMION L. THOMAS

After a historic visit to South Africa in 1973, Arthur Ashe, the top-ranked Black tennis player in the world, prepared to leave the country. As he waited at the airport, an unfamiliar man browsing in the terminal's newspaper shop quietly approached Carole Dell, a member of Ashe's entourage. The man had a message that he wanted to relay to Ashe. Given the South African government's restrictions on activism, the unnamed messenger had to be cautious. If caught, he could be jailed or put in exile. Despite the risks, the man informed Dell that another man would leave a newspaper in the waiting room with an important message meant for Ashe. He asked Dell to collect the newspaper and give it to Ashe once the airplane was in flight.

In his 1981 autobiography *Off the Court*, Arthur Ashe recounted this incident. Tucked inside the newspaper was a photograph with a note on the back from one of South Africa's most notable leaders: Winnie Mandela, the wife of freedom fighter Nelson Mandela. At the time, Mr. Mandela was serving a life sentence in prison. The note thanked Ashe for what he was doing and reminded him that "the best you can do is ask the South Africans what you can do to help in their struggle."[1] Mandela's note struck at the core of the two issues that surrounded his controversial trip: which methods were best suited to end racial oppression and why Ashe was interested in the South African anti-apartheid movement.

Ashe's involvement in the anti-apartheid movement is complicated. Scholarly accounts and Arthur Ashe's own reflections on the issue tend to focus on his exclusion from the prestigious South African Open.[2] Heretofore, scholars have not given primacy to Arthur Ashe's divergent ideas about racial struggle and advancement as the principal reasons for his involvement in the anti-apartheid movement. Arthur Ashe was a Black conservative. However, black conservatism was in decline in the United States in the late 1960s as the more aggressive Black Power Movement began to set an agenda for the black freedom movement in the United States. Ashe was uncomfortable with the brashness and confrontational posturing of the Black Power Movement, but he felt an increasing desire to be socially active.

African Americans who criticized US foreign policy in Africa faced harsh rebuke during the early days of the Cold War. For example, both Paul Robeson and W. E. B. Du Bois lost their ability to travel internationally because of their refusal to temper their opposition to US support of colonialism. By 1968, however, many of the harshest Cold War-era restrictions that had limited African Americans activists' ability to draw connections between the oppression of African Americans and those suffering under colonial rule throughout the African Diaspora had waned. Still, many African American athletes chose not to participate in the anti-apartheid movement after South Africa was banned from the 1964 Olympics. Yet Ashe intensified his commitment to fighting apartheid in South Africa despite staunch, largely uncritical support of the apartheid regime by one of South Africa's most important Cold War allies: the US government. Although criticism of US policy in Africa was less likely to garner condemnation from US officials, many African Americans were reluctant to join the international movement against apartheid. Given those fears, Ashe's stand was bold.[3] Ashe's conservatism put him at odds with most Black South Africans who were demanding the immediate removal of the apartheid regime. In contrast, Ashe advocated incremental change in South Africa. The anti-apartheid movement's cultural and economic boycott of South Africa was inconsistent with Ashe's conservative beliefs about how to bring about social change. But his beliefs would be challenged by Black South Africans, the very people he wanted to empower.

A Different World

World War II caused a fundamental shift in world affairs: racial discrimination would no longer be ignored by international political bodies. The war to defeat Nazi Germany raised awareness about how far racist ideologies could lead countries if international agencies, multinational political bodies, and internationally minded individuals did not intervene. Between 1945 and 1960, forty countries representing a quarter of the world's population gained independence from colonial powers. These new nations were determined to push the newly formed United Nations into becoming a political body that would address colonialism and racial discrimination.[4]

In 1960 alone, seventeen African states were admitted to the United Nations. The Year of Africa inspired hope that independence would sweep the entire continent. Both these liberation movements and the international Black Power and Black Consciousness Movements fostered a "fever for independence" that extended into even South Africa and Rhodesia, the most resistant regions on the continent. Many began to mistakenly believe that the governments in both countries would recognize that independence was going to be the new way of life throughout Africa and allow majority rule.[5]

UN member nations from Africa, Asia, and the Middle East were inspired by the Charter of the United Nations, which supported sovereignty and the human rights of all peoples. Because of the efforts of UN representatives from these nations, as historian Thomas Borstelmann has noted, South Africa was the first nation to have its racial practices "rebuked by an international council," a demonstration "that the world was changing."[6] Despite these global ideological shifts, South Africa increased its support for racial discrimination in the post–World War II era.

Apartheid, the system of legal racial separation in South Africa, began in earnest after the National Party won a surprise victory in the 1948 national election. White South Africans worried about losing their jobs to lower-paid Blacks and Afrikaner farmers feared a severe labor shortage as massive numbers of Blacks began to migrate from the countryside and into the industrial centers of Johannesburg, Cape Town, and Port Elizabeth. Exploiting these fears, the National Party campaigned on a platform of *swart gevaar*, or "black peril," promising to send Blacks out of the cities and back to the countryside in the hopes of creating a true Afrikaner homeland. Afrikaner nationalism swelled in the aftermath of World War II, and whites appeared ready to permanently separate themselves from the Black majority, which accounted for over 88 percent of the population. After the National Party's victory, the new prime minister, D. F. Malan, said, "For the first time, South Africa is our own. May God grant that it always remains our own."[7] Despite efforts to eradicate apartheid, white minority rule remained in place for the next forty-five years.

The United States and South Africa

Both the United States and South Africa struggled with the issue of race. Both nations endured turbulent domestic unrest and racial strife during the 1950s and 1960s, and both nations continue to be burdened by the legacies of racial segregation and racism. As apartheid in South Africa increasingly restricted Blacks throughout the 1950s and 1960s, African Americans in the United States made important advances in the movement for civil rights: the integration of baseball in 1947, the integration of the military in 1948, the 1954 Supreme Court decision in *Brown v. Board* of Education, and the 1957 desegregation of Central High School in Little Rock, Arkansas were important milestones toward providing African Americans with equal treatment.[8] Later, the US Congress passed the Civil Rights Act of 1964, which mandated equality in public accommodations, and the Voting Rights Act of 1965 guaranteed the right to register to vote to African Americans.

Despite these achievements, the United States became increasingly racially polarized throughout the late 1960s. This, in turn, hindered US efforts to assume a leading role in world affairs after the onset of the Cold War. By the late 1940s, reports from diplomatic posts made it clear to US government officials that segregation was having a negative impact on its foreign policy. American officials around the world noted that developing nations were aware of and strongly disapproved of US racial segregation. Numerous influential American figures including Walter White, Richard Nixon, A. Philip Randolph, Paul Robeson, Eleanor Roosevelt, and Secretary of State Dean Rusk publicly stated that the biggest single burden that the United States carried in its foreign policy negotiations was its domestic policy of racial discrimination. Pointedly, Henry Cabot Lodge, the US ambassador to the United Nations, acknowledged that racism was the nation's "international Achilles heel" because nations of color saw the denial of rights to African Americans as a reflection of the nation's attitude toward all people of color.[9]

Soviet Union representatives drew connections between capitalism and racial discrimination in the United States and imperialism and the exploitation of people of color worldwide, making effective use of US segregation to undermine US foreign policy efforts throughout the African Diaspora. In the late 1940s, State Department officials estimated that almost half of Soviet propaganda focused on racial discrimination in the United States.[10] Rusk noted with exasperation, "Frequently we find it next to impossible to formulate a satisfactory answer to our critics in other countries."[11] The passage of civil rights legislation in the United States was designed to show that US policies were supportive of the liberation of all people of color worldwide.[12] These extraordinary steps were taken after worldwide condemnation had threated US influence.

Similarly, instances of race-based oppression in South Africa had reverberations across the globe. On May 21, 1960, when a crowd of 5,000 gathered for a peaceful demonstration at a police station in Sharpeville, a Black township just thirty miles from Johannesburg, police opened fire on the protesters, killing 69 and wounding nearly 200. This incident became known as the Sharpeville massacre. The Dwight D. Eisenhower administration stated that it considered the massacre to be "an internal South African matter." The state-sponsored brutality amplified international attention.[13] Because the US government and other western states were unwilling to forcefully stand against the violence, many nongovernmental agencies and prominent individuals attempted to raise international awareness about the horrors of apartheid. The anti-apartheid movement, one of the largest global activist movements of the twentieth century, was a massive, sprawling international effort. Participants included government officials, business leaders, churches, the United Nations, colleges and universities, labor unions, athletes, artists, and the media.[14]

Within the United States, the American Committee on Africa (ACOA) was the largest lobbying organization that focused on African affairs during the mid-1960s. In 1965, this group led efforts to draft the "Declaration Against Apartheid," which became a central document for the US anti-apartheid movement. The declaration signaled support for the liberation movement's call for isolating South Africa as a tool in the fight against apartheid. More than sixty US artists and entertainers, including Harry Belafonte, Sammy Davis Jr., Nina Simone, Ed Sullivan, Henry Fonda, and Leonard Bernstein, immediately agreed to abide by the cultural boycott of South Africa by refusing to perform there.[15] Martin Luther King Jr. indicated his support for the international boycott later that year at a Human Rights Day event in New York.

Although anti-apartheid activism assumed many different forms, as the "Declaration Against Apartheid" suggested, one of the most significant developments was the cultural boycott. The call for such a boycott, which was first articulated in the mid-1950s, gained increasing international support in the early 1960s among athletes because the sports world was impacted by the entrenchment of apartheid. White-controlled sports bodies in South Africa enacted color bans in their constitutions. T. E. Donges, the South African minister of the interior, articulated the government's apartheid sports policy in 1956, announcing that racial mixing was prohibited among Black and white athletes, coaches, and sports administrators. In addition, the policy barred nonwhites from the playing fields, stands, and stadiums where whites competed.[16]

Perhaps there was no bigger sign of the importance of the growing momentum of the anti-apartheid movement in sports than the number of important sporting organizations that banned South Africa from international competitions in the 1960s and 1970s. In 1963, the International Olympic Committee (IOC) informed the South African National Olympic Committee that if it did not renounce racial discrimination and select an integrated team, it would be barred from the 1964 Olympics. When South Africa refused to alter its policies, the IOC rescinded South Africa's invitation to compete at the 1964 Summer Olympic Games in Tokyo. When the IOC flirted with allowing South Africa back into the Olympics for the 1968 Mexico City Games, the Soviet Union, the Olympic Project for Human Rights, the Organization of African Unity, and a number of Asian countries said they would boycott. Because of their mobilization, South Africa was banned from the banned until the 1992 Olympics in Barcelona.[17] Following the lead of the IOC, momentum for the cultural boycott continued to grow in the sports world. By the end of 1970, South Africa had been suspended or expelled from international competition in a number of sports, including cricket, tennis, basketball, soccer, cycling, fencing, weightlifting, track and field, boxing, gymnastics, and wrestling. When South Africa was expelled from the Davis Cup, the premiere national competition in tennis, Arthur Ashe said that the suspension was "a pretty sad, but just decision."[18]

Ashe sought to participate in sporting contests on South African soil after South Africa had been banned from a number of international competitions. In the late 1960s, the South African Open was among the most prestigious tournaments in tennis. Because the International Lawn Tennis Federation sanctioned it, Arthur Ashe believed that he had a right to compete in the tournament despite South Africa's domestic laws. However, Ashe frequently criticized South Africa in press conferences and before congressional committees and the United Nations. He also expressed solidarity with Black liberation movements during his tour of Africa for the State Department in 1970. Because of this, South Africa rejected his repeated requests for a visa, stating that Ashe's intentions were not just to play tennis but to also be a "dangerous black militant; a rabble rouser intent on destroying apartheid and fomenting unrest among nonwhites." Government officials believed that Ashe wanted to visit South Africa so he could "engage in political activity," as evidenced by his "outright unfriendly and threatening attitude to South Africa."[19] Even though he was repeatedly denied a visa, Ashe continued to push South Africa to reform.

To the surprise of Arthur Ashe and many others, South African prime minister B. J. Vorster announced a change in the country's sports policy in early 1971 in response to international pressure. The new rules permitted nonwhite South Africans to compete in international athletic events abroad and within South Africa. Most notably, these changes would allow Black athletes to compete in tennis, golf, and track and field events. In the ensuing months, the apartheid regime promised to allow some form of integrated track and field competitions and invited an integrated baseball team from the United States to the country.[20] The two most high-profile athletes to benefit from this change were Evonne Goolagong, an Australian Aborigine tennis star, and Lee Elder, an African American golfer who competed in events in South Africa in 1971.[21]

Evonne Goolagong's trip demonstrates how sports became a tool South Africa used to try to influence international perceptions of the country. Alf Chalmers, president of the South African Tennis Union, invited Goolagong to participate in the South African championships in the spring of 1971. The decision to invite Goolagong and not Arthur Ashe was designed to buttress the South African government's claims that they banned Ashe because of his political activism rather than because of his race. The ways the new policy rules were applied continued to suggest that Ashe should be barred for expressing solidarity with liberation movements and criticizing South Africa. In contrast, Goolagong was not outwardly politically hostile toward the South African government and did not offer harsh condemnation of the government and its policies. Many viewed her visit as a shift to the center and a harbinger of more rights and freedoms for Blacks in South Africa as the government became more liberal.[22]

Some international sports organizations looked upon these changes approvingly. In a surprise move, the Davis Cup committee voted to invite South Africa to compete in the 1972 tennis tournament in response to Goolagong's visit. The committee suggested that her visit demonstrated that South Africa was taking sufficient steps to integrate its sports competitions. The formal vote was 5–2 in favor of readmission. The United States was one of the five nations who backed South Africa. This move showed those who supported a cultural boycott that some in the West were eager to find reasons to offer South Africa the benefit of the doubt.[23] Thus, South Africa could make small changes in policy that international sports bodies interpreted as important symbols of advancement.

Significantly, US government officials emphasized these minimal steps in an attempt to limit international condemnation of South Africa because South Africa was one of the United States' most important allies in the fight to contain communism.[24] Instead of championing the independence movement in South Africa, the United States viewed the apartheid regime as a force of stability and a protector of western institutions and values on the African continent. As the National Party took power in 1948, it relied upon its close identification with the West to extend its apartheid policies.

The Cold War Alliance

As Donald Culverson has argued, South Africa used its Cold War alignment with the United States and other western powers to pursue "a comprehensive system of laws and regulations to secure white supremacy, solidify racial segregation, control movement of black labor, and suppress emergent black political activity." The white minority that governed South Africa believed that anticommunism and white supremacy complemented each other. South Africa's fervent anticommunism emerged from the practice of labeling those who advocated for majority rule as communist. Because South Africa was the most prominent anti-communist nation in Africa, it was evident in the early days of the Cold War that national security concerns, instead of alleviating racial oppression, would dominate US foreign policy toward South Africa. This was the case from the Truman administration through to the Reagan administration.[25]

Demand for natural resources also drew the United States and South Africa together as Cold War allies. The West needed access to South African raw materials to help rebuild Europe after World War II. In addition, western countries wanted to increase their access to raw materials that were essential for making bombs. Equally important, by working with South Africa, the United States hoped to hinder the Soviet Union's ability to acquire the minerals it needed to compete with the US arsenal. Uranium was a crucial resource in the arms race and limiting Soviet access to it became a goal of the United States. South Africa's promise to sell uranium only to the United States and Great Britain in 1950 helped US policymakers realize that as the Cold War intensified, it needed "South Africa more than South Africa needed them." Thus, for American officials, the apartheid regime in South Africa was of "unique significance."[26]

Even as he pushed South Africa to reform, Arthur Ashe was aware of US foreign policy toward South Africa and understood why Cold War concerns would keep US officials from leading efforts to transform South Africa. The realities of the alliance between the United States and South Africa, Ashe argued, caused many people to write off the anti-apartheid movement as "hopeless." In *Off the Court*, Ashe acknowledged that South African natural resources such as uranium, diamonds, cobalt, magnesium, and gold were "critically needed" and were essential to determining "the balance of power in the world." Ashe wrote, "The West does not want South Africa to change too much" because of the fear that a Black-run government in South Africa might embargo these natural resources and thus shift global power toward the Soviet Union.[27]

South Africa's strategic significance as a Cold War ally caused the United States to pursue a "middle road" strategy: the United States acknowledged colonized people's right to self-determination but also suggested that "premature independence" could be detrimental to US, European, and South African interests. The United States was fearful that access to essential materials would be curtailed by the South African government if they supported majority rule in the race-torn nation. Yet as nations in Africa gained their independence, the United States wanted to make sure that it did not alienate this new, important voting bloc at the United Nations. It was clear that the "middle road" position would be tilted toward the United States deepening its collaboration with the apartheid regime by defending South Africa at United Nations hearings and signing a nuclear cooperation agreement to extend the use of atomic energy. The two nations also agreed to a mutual defense pact that called for joint naval exercises and the deployment of a joint satellite tracking system.[28]

Ashe Visits South Africa

Why did Ashe decide to become actively involved in the anti-apartheid movement in South Africa? For one thing, he believed he had a right to play in the International Lawn Tennis Federation–sanctioned South African Open tournament. He also believed that Black South Africans deserved greater rights and freedoms. In addition to these pull factors, important push factors caused Ashe to make the anti-apartheid movement the focus of his public activism in the late 1960s and early 1970s instead of addressing racial issues in the United States. As the militant Black Power movement shifted the African American struggle for greater rights and freedoms away from integrationism and conciliatory approaches to racial reform, Ashe was vexed. As his fame increased, he wanted to use his platform to advance civil rights. Uncomfortable with the Black Power movement's confrontational tactics, he turned to the anti-apartheid movement because he believed it would be a better fit with his conservative beliefs.[29]

Those beliefs were evident long before Ashe became involved in the anti-apartheid movement. In 1967, as a 24-year-old tennis phenomenon, Arthur Ashe published his first memoir, *Advantage Ashe*. In it, Ashe took a very conservative position on the direct action campaigns civil rights leaders called for. Ashe maintained that he had "learned to blend into the background" rather than participate in social protests. Even though he revered Dr. Martin Luther King, he was critical of the tactics of the Civil Rights Movement. Ashe believed that the "best chance [for an African American] to advance is to get himself an education somehow and prove his worth as an individual." Ashe concluded that African Americans were trying to "ram ourselves down people's throats." Ashe said, "I'm not a marcher. I'm not a sign carrier." Instead, he argued that "quiet negotiation and slow infiltration" were the most promising measures for African Americans, because they would "never advance far by force, because we're outnumbered ten to one."[30] Even though Black South Africans constituted an overwhelming majority in South Africa, Ashe adopted a similar perspective on the South African fight against apartheid.

Given his conservatism, Ashe believed that maintaining contact with South Africa was preferable to the UN-sanctioned goal of cultural isolation. However, before Ashe received permission to enter South Africa, he sought advice about whether he should go from a number of activists and politicians, including Andrew Young, Sargent Shriver, and Barbara Jordan. Most encouraged him to go, but perhaps Andrew Young had the most impact on him. Later, Ashe described Young as a "conciliator committed to the cause, someone who could haggle, bargain, and compromise with whites."[31]

In many respects, Ashe's description of Young is how he wanted to be perceived. Fundamental to his beliefs about social change was the notion that "progress and improvement do not come in big chunks, they come in little pieces, and the sooner people accept this the better off they'll be." This idea was at the heart of his philosophy of social change, and a few emerging white leaders in South Africa, such as Minister of Sports Dr. Piet Koornhof, cemented Ashe's belief in that approach. In his memoir, *Portrait in Motion*, Arthur Ashe recalled his opinions on the minister: "Koornhof is widely considered to be the most intelligent member of the Cabinet and the comer in the National Party, heir apparent to Prime Minister Johannes Vorster." Despite limited reforms in South Africa, Ashe found common ground with Koornhof. In fact, his misplaced belief that Koornhof was reflective of the rise of moderation in racial oppression in South Africa kept Ashe actively engaged in defying the cultural boycott. Ashe continued his praise of Koornhof, "What other government . . . anywhere in the world has felt obliged to place the most promising member of the government in charge of its athletic program? Usually that area is a political backwater." Ashe saw an opportunity for an alliance with Koornhof, but that meant he would have to conform to Koornhof's request to be less critical of the African nation. Ashe was advised "not to drop any more H-bombs on Johannesburg," a reference to a statement he made during a London news conference that he wanted to bomb the city where the South African Open was held.[32]

Even as activists warned him that he would be merely window dressing if he competed in the 1973 South African Open, Ashe remained committed to the gradualist philosophy he had developed during the Civil Rights Movement. "Tokenism is always the way it starts out," Ashe argued. "Because when anything starts, you're not going to start with waves of people coming in. You start with one or two and then it will be opened up."[33] Ashe's philosophy about how best to combat apartheid was drawn from his experiences with the Civil Rights Movement. However, Ashe's message that "small concessions incline towards larger ones" faced strong, intense, and unrelenting critique from Black South Africans during his visit to the pariah state.[34]

The tension between Ashe's approach and the one of most Black South Africans favored was evident on the first day of his visit. That evening, the United States Information Service (USIS) hosted a reception in his honor that sixty Black journalists attended. These journalists "suffered the indignities of apartheid every day and watched as the government banned or jailed their friends and colleagues and would not sit quietly as Ashe lectured them on the value of taking small steps," historian and Ashe biographer Eric Hall explained. Ashe was rebuked as an Uncle Tom and was told to stay away. "Your presence delays our struggle" some of the scribes in the crowd shouted. "Go back to New York!"[35]

During the reception Ashe had talked about the Civil Rights Movement and how the actions of Rosa Parks and Martin Luther King Jr. and the Montgomery bus boycott had led to change. The journalists informed him that Parks and King would have been jailed or banned in South Africa if they organized acts of civil disobedience. The reporters' message was clear: the Civil Rights Movement did not provide a strategy that would work in South Africa. "We don't want equality," one woman argued. "We were dispossessed. We want our land back." The reporters seemed to suggest that Ashe's belief that his visit to South Africa could lead to change was naïve. "If we isolate them, they're forced to change," another reporter shouted out, "cut off South Africa, boycott it!" Because it was so difficult to challenge apartheid from within during the early 1970s, the role of the international community was paramount. The negative responses Ashe encountered revealed the tension between the tactics he believed in and the strategy most Black South Africans favored.[36]

Strong opposition to his visit was evident again when Ashe engaged with another predominantly Black crowd of journalists after giving a tennis clinic in Soweto Township. Ashe and his entourage drove thirty miles outside Johannesburg to visit one of the designated areas were Black South Africans could live. There, he was accused of being complicit in the repression of Black South Africans by visiting. Aware that the South African government would use his trip to try to sway international opinions on apartheid a small crowd gathered around him chanted, "Go home! Leave us alone!" The tennis star was denounced as a sellout and a stooge. After his initial encounter with the reporters at the USIS reception, Ashe had prepared himself for the fact that Black South Africans would likely speak in opposition to his visit, but the level of hostility that Ashe faced made him "sense real rage." He felt like an "outsider, a meddling outsider." The situation became more intense when a group of students began to confront another group of students who were challenging Ashe for visiting South Africa. As one group asked Ashe to leave, another one called out, "God bless you Arthur Ashe."[37]

The rift in Black South African opinions over Arthur Ashe's trip was evident in the responses of Don Mattera and Dennis Brutus, two outspoken critics of apartheid. Mattera, a poet and writer who had recently been banned from the country for nine years for engaging in anti-government activity, attended the USIS reception as a reporter for the *Johannesburg Star*. Years later, Mattera described how the South African government intimidated him to punish him for his opposition to the apartheid regime. "My house was raided more than 600 times," he said. He was "detained more than 200 times" and "was tortured on more occasions than I can remember." Even though he had suffered under the apartheid regime, Mattera did not attack Ashe. After the other reporters left, Ashe pointedly asked Mattera: "Do you think I should have come?" Mattera responded, "We need to be periodically assured that people in the rest of the world still understand and care." Mattera felt that Ashe's presence was a show of solidarity and compassion.[38]

Dennis Brutus, in contrast, was staunchly opposed to Ashe's decision to defy the boycott and made his opposition to Ashe's trip clear when Ashe sent him a letter in early 1972, asking if he should come to visit South Africa. In 1963, Brutus had been arrested for fomenting rebellion and was shot in the back during an attempted prison escape. He was returned to prison and was eventually allowed to emigrate to England under the condition that he never return to South Africa. In exile, Brutus continued to fight for the end of apartheid. He believed in the boycott, in direct action, and in isolating South Africa. In his opinion, Ashe was naïve for thinking that his visit could influence the apartheid government. He also thought that Ashe had made a mistake by agreeing to not criticize the South African government during his trip. Ashe's silence allowed the press and the government to control the narrative of the meaning of his trip.[39]

Most important, Brutus thought that Ashe had developed a relationship with Piet Koornhof that was too cozy. He argued that Ashe's trust in the South African leader was misplaced and that Koornhof was using him to present the facade of "progress." Similarly, William Cotter, writing for *Africa Report,* stated that Ashe has "displayed wishful thinking" because of his belief that South Africa's limited concessions with regard to multiracial sports could lead to political reform. In spite of the small changes Koornhof and the government made to blur racial lines in the nation's sports infrastructure, apartheid remained entrenched in South Africa. Ashe had misinterpreted Koornhof's support of minor reforms in sports as evidence that he would work to end apartheid throughout South African society.[40]

Conclusion: Joining the Cultural Boycott

In 1976, a tragedy occurred in Soweto Township, which Ashe had visited during his first trip in 1973. Police murdered 170 teens during the Soweto uprising that year, during which 20,000 Black high school students staged a series of protests. After that, the already disillusioned tennis star was compelled to change his then wavering position. Ashe was forced to admit that his defiance of the cultural boycott had not produced the impact he had sought.[41]

Until the Soweto uprising, Ashe believed the US Civil Rights Movement offered important insights into how to wage the struggle in South Africa. In 1975, Ashe was moving toward the conclusion that the differences between the two countries were more profound than he originally thought: "When the [United States] Supreme Court came out with [the 1954 *Brown v. Board of Education* decision] it was the same as saying that inherent in our Constitution was the theory that we are all equal. That is not inherent in the Constitution of South Africa," Ashe told *The Black Scholar.*[42] Instead of continuing to take trips to South Africa, Ashe decided to join the cultural boycott.

In the late 1970s, he became involved in TransAfrica, a research organization that Black members of the US Congress had established to study issues relating to Africa and to lobby for legislation that would restrict US economic, political, and cultural partnerships between the United States and South Africa. It was the only think tank in the United States controlled exclusively by African Americans. In 1983, Ashe, Harry Belafonte, Ruby Dee, Ossie Davis, Tony Randall, Gregory Hines, and others announced the formation of Artists and Athletes against Apartheid. "If you go to Johannesburg or Sun City and play to audiences, extracting inordinate amounts of money for your services and leaving little behind, by your presence, you are encouraging apartheid," Belafonte declared. One of the main goals of the group, Ashe said, "was to persuade athletes and entertainers not to perform" in South

A PUPIL learns from a master. Arthur Ashe, one of the top Ame ican tennis stars, currently on an African tour, is seen here coaching 10-yea -old Joash Kongo, a standard III pupil at Kileleshwa Primary School in Nairobi. This picture was taken at the University tennis courts when Ashe held a coaching session for the students.

Kongo's father works at the University. After the coaching Mr. Ashe presented a tennis racket to Joash.

Ashe is due to arrive in Kampala on October 29 for a three-day visit.

Arthur Ashe giving a schoolboy a tennis lesson in Nairobi in 1976. *Courtesy of the University of Arkansas Archives.*

Africa. As a result of his activism, the number of foreign sports people visiting South Africa during the mid-1980s continued to drop.[43]

When Arthur Ashe stepped onto the tennis court at the South African Open in 1973 in defiance of a worldwide boycott against South Africa, his main goal was to win. He wanted to beat his white opponents and destroy stereotypes about Black people because he believed that such actions would eventually destroy apartheid and racism in South Africa. He counted every small win as part of important larger gains. However, through his experiences in South Africa, he learned that merely winning your own cause could lead to losing a bigger battle. As Winnie Mandela reminded him in that anonymously delivered note, activists are obligated to ask people what they want before they engage in activism on their behalf. After a tumultuous relationship with Black South Africans, Arthur Ashe finally learned that true activism does not always mean leading, that it can also mean standing behind and in solidarity with people as they seek freedom on their own terms. By the end of the 1970s, Ashe had become a strong proponent of the cultural boycott of South Africa.

—V—

Manipulating the Five Rings

Public Diplomacy, Statecraft, and the Olympic Games

—11—

Sport Is Not So Separate from Politics

Diplomatic Manipulation of Germany's Postwar Return to the Olympic Movement

BY HEATHER L. DICHTER

The International Olympic Committee (IOC) and international sport leaders have long espoused the idea that sport and politics are separate. However, they have, in fact, always been closely entangled. IOC members have often engaged with their governments—and not just those members from communist states. Even in the democratic West, IOC members routinely corresponded with their governments and, in some cases, had served their governments in earlier roles, establishing close relationships that predated their Olympic service. Avery Brundage, perhaps the most vocal person in international sport on the topic of the separation of sport and politics, quietly and frequently corresponded in the early years of the Cold War with the US State Department regarding international sport and politics, often seeking advice from officials and informing them about attitudes within the IOC. Foreign service officers sent reports of these conversations back to the United States, sometimes all the way to the secretary of state, and the department sought to influence Brundage and the IOC to act in ways that supported its policies in an increasingly divided world.

One of the sporting issues that greatly concerned the State Department was the return of Germany to the international community as the Cold War began. During World War II, factions had developed within the US government about how to treat a defeated Germany. Instead of harsher treatment, the four occupation powers agreed to divide Germany after the war.[1] Denazification was the driving factor behind many of the policies of the Allies, including Allied Control Directive 23 on the Limitation and Demilitarization of Sport in Germany.[2] Denazification ultimately ran into several logistical problems, and the western Allies soon realized they needed competent and skilled Germans to help with the reconstruction of the country and its economy.[3]

Cold War divisions—which ran right through Germany—accelerated the efforts of the United States, Britain, and France to incorporate a new democratic and peaceful Germany in international relations. The three western Allies sought to return a peaceful and democratic Germany to the international system and, as the split with the Soviet Union hardened, in the western camp. The US government supported international alliances such as the European Coal and Steel Community, the (failed) European Defence Community, and the North Atlantic Treaty Organization to anchor the new Federal Republic of Germany (FRG, officially established in 1949, commonly known as West Germany) with western democracies and prevent future wars. Helping Germany return to international sport organizations such as the International Olympic Committee thus coincided with the western Allies' overall aims for the postwar German state.

In countries that have an official sports minister, a close relationship exists between international sport delegates and the government, but the United States has never had such a position. Instead, its government has left the oversight of sport almost entirely to private organizations. To this day, the United States is one of a handful of countries whose government does not fund its Olympic and elite athletes. The 1978 Amateur Sport Act is one of the rare instances of government involvement, but this piece of legislation primarily established the national sport structure and did not fund national governing bodies or the United States Olympic Committee. These organizations still maintain a nonprofit status in the United States.[4] The federal government's hands-off approach was especially visible in the decade before World War II. The 1932 Los Angeles Olympics received no funding from the government because of the Great Depression. That year, President Herbert Hoover was the first head of state who did not open an Olympic Games. For the 1936 Olympics, it was sport organizations and the press—not the federal government—that debated whether the United States should send athletes to the controversial Olympic Games in Nazi Germany.[5]

The State Department's actions at the beginning of the 1950s mark a significant shift in the attitude of US diplomats regarding international sport. Through meetings and correspondence with Avery Brundage and J. Brooks B. Parker, US members of the IOC, US members of High Commission for

Occupied Germany (HICOG) and officials in the State Department worked to ensure that international sport supported US foreign policy. Although US diplomats acknowledged the independence of private sport organizations, they still tried to influence IOC members to take actions that supported America's position that the Federal Republic of Germany was the legitimate postwar German state. This specific example of American postwar policy regarding Germany, although covering a very short period of time, demonstrated the State Department's new postwar willingness to use international sport to achieve its aims.

The International Olympic Committee did not accept Germany back into the world of international sport until May 1951.[6] The Nazi past of many German sport leaders created problems for both the western powers and the IOC. The two-year delay in the IOC's formal recognition of the German National Olympic Committee (NOC) was the result of the intense activity by diplomats in the US State Department, the British Foreign Office, and the High Commission for Occupied Germany related to the composition of the NOC. (While members of the French delegation were present at tripartite meetings and expressed their opinions about Germany's participation in the Olympics, they did not work as strenuously behind the scenes as their British and US counterparts because wartime activities had compromised two of their IOC members.[7])

American and British concerns about the Nazi pasts of some German sports officials as the latter pushed the IOC to recognize Germany again demonstrate the problems the Allies faced in implementing denazification.[8] The State Department ultimately subverted postwar occupation goals to the politics of the Cold War as it became heavily involved in Germany's reentry into the Olympic Movement. The desire of the US and British governments for international acceptance of a democratic Germany prompted their foreign ministry officials and diplomats to work closely with IOC members to facilitate Germany's return, even if it meant the continued presence of German sport leaders with questionable Nazi pasts. The German NOC celebrated its return to the Olympic Movement as its own achievement,[9] but the efforts of US and British officials facilitated this reacceptance because of the hardening of the Cold War.

New Germany, New National Olympic Committee

Because the Allies occupied Germany after the war, the German state and all national organizations ceased to exist, including all national bodies that governed sport. This lack of sovereignty prompted the IOC and all international federations to stop recognizing Germany's membership. The four occupying powers controlled their respective zones through military governments that approved clubs and organizations at the local level and later at the provincial (*Land*) level. Interzonal or national organizations were forbidden until 1949, when the three western zones combined into the Federal Republic of Germany. With the formation of a national government and resumption of sovereignty, the western Allies formally ended their occupations and shifted their powers from military governments to diplomatic representatives via the High Commission, which continued to influence the new German state. This transfer of power to Germans took place on September 21, 1949, when Chancellor Konrad Adenauer presented his cabinet to the three high commissioners.

During the months between the decision to merge the three zones and the formal establishment of the Federal Republic of Germany, groups across the zones began working together to form national organizations. Sport leaders held several meetings to determine the structure of German sport, and representatives from all three military governments oversaw this process.[10] These actions resulted in the refounding of the German National Olympic Committee in September 1949, just two days after the new German government was established in the new capital of Bonn. The country's new president, Theodor Heuss, spoke on the second day, expressing his satisfaction that Germany again had an Olympic Committee.[11] The chancellor's office sent a message welcoming the preparations undertaken for Germany's participation in the next Olympics. All of the members of the National Olympic Committee whom the new government welcomed had become adults before the Nazis came to power.[12] The Allies had granted amnesty from denazification procedures to individuals born after January 1, 1919, as young people could not be held responsible for the rise of Nazism.[13] However, Nazis had so thoroughly co-opted sport in Germany that the men who now comprised the NOC were likely tainted by some level of cooperation with the Nazis from their role as sports leaders during the Third Reich.

Less than a month after the National Olympic Committee formed, a HICOG report expressed concern that although the occupation powers and German sport leaders had agreed that the members of the NOC would be democratically elected, "German officials at Bonn have recently appointed a committee of the former 1936 Olympic Committee members for this purpose." The report continued: "This move has incenced [*sic*] not only the Occupation officials concerned, but the democratic element among German sports leaders who have worked on this agreement."[14] From the US perspective, the Germans had established a National Olympic Committee without respecting the democratizing aims of the occupation. Even more troubling was the failure of the policy of denazification among the core leaders of sport administration in Germany.

The primary objections concerned the two German members of the International Olympic Committee: Duke Adolf Friedrich von Mecklenburg and Karl Ritter von Halt, who had been IOC members since 1926 and 1929, respectively. Ritter von Halt, from Bavaria, had assisted with Germany's bid to host the 1936 Olympics and had been president of the Garmisch-Partenkirchen Winter Games. In the 1930s, he had risen rapidly to higher positions in both international sport and the SA (Stormabteilung). As a director of the Deutsche Bank, he had provided funds to SS (Schutzstaffel) leader Heinrich Himmler and was part of his inner circle. By 1938, Ritter von Halt resigned from a four-year term as president of the International Amateur Handball Federation, but he still held positions as a member of the IOC, a member of the International Amateur Athletic Federation Executive Council, the president of the German Bobsleigh Association, and a vice-president of the International Federation of Bobsled and Tobogganing. Ritter von Halt was also head of track and field under the centralized Nazi sport system, and he was the final Reichssportführer as the Third Reich fell in 1945. This last position was one reason the Soviets imprisoned him. They did not release Ritter von Halt until February 1950, and then only as a precondition of joining the IOC themselves.[15]

The Duke of Mecklenburg's actions during the Third Reich are not as well documented. He served as governor of Togoland from 1912 to 1914. During World War I, he earned an Iron Cross from Austria-Hungary. In April 1918, some leading Baltic Germans, Estonians, and Latvians requested that he become the head of state of a United Baltic Duchy, but the proposal did not come to fruition. The Duke of Mecklenburg had also played a leading role in the Colonial Society (Kolonial-Gesellschaft), which sought to reclaim the colonies Germany lost in the Treaty of Versailles. During the Weimar Republic and the Third Reich, the Duke of Mecklenburg traveled around the world, particularly to Africa and South America, to help improve trade relations with Germany and to speak with communities of emigrant Germans, albeit not in an official capacity.[16] The Duke of Mecklenburg's participation in sport was typical of an aristocrat with many sporting interests. He participated in equestrian sport, automobile races, and the famous Blau-Weiß tennis club in Berlin. Because he was the brother-in-law of Queen Wilhelmina of the Netherlands, however, his connections to exiled European royalty had led to his dismissal from any posts under the Nazis.[17]

Diplomatic Pressure

The Americans were not the only people concerned about Germany's new NOC and its long-standing IOC members. The British diplomatic corps also had reservations, and other IOC members—especially from countries Nazi Germany had occupied—did not want to work with men who had served the Third Reich. The US and British high commissioners raised concerns about these German sport leaders with members of Adenauer's government in an attempt to convince them to change the NOC leadership to make it acceptable to the Allies and to the international community. The high commissioners knew they could not force changes on the new sovereign German state, but they wanted the international community to quickly accept the country as a bulwark against communism.

Germans hoped to convince the IOC to readmit them at its 1950 annual congress in Copenhagen. In preparation for that meeting, Chancellor Konrad Adenauer asked US high commissioner John J. McCloy to garner US IOC member Avery Brundage's support for Germany's readmission. The chancellor, who understood the US government's aims for Germany, was "convinced that Mr. Brundage will agree to do this when he finds out that you [McCloy] are in favor of readmittance of Germany to International sport relations and particularly to [the] International Olympic Committee." The Allies had used local sport to further their political aims since 1945, and Adenauer was shrewd enough to subtly remind the high commissioner that his request would enable the Americans to broaden their influence in Olympic affairs.[18] McCloy informed the State Department that he "agree[d] in principle to German membership," suggesting that the US embassy in Copenhagen should assist with the matter. Although McCloy felt that the composition of Germany's Olympic committee was unsatisfactory, he stated that "the matter of its membership will be taken up separately" from the decision to readmit Germany to the IOC.[19] McCloy's support for Germany's IOC recognition was in line with the tripartite commission's recommendation to press for Germany's membership in international organizations,[20] but he emphasized that the members of the NOC had to be acceptable as this body would represent the new Germany on the international stage. The State Department supported McCloy's suggestion regarding the involvement of foreign service officers at the US embassy in Copenhagen, which is exactly what happened. Embassy officials told Brundage that the high commission wanted Germany to be readmitted to international sport governing bodies so German athletes could participate in the 1952 Helsinki Olympics.[21]

The British government also used a similar strategy of consulting with diplomats in their own embassies about the Cold War implications of the Federal Republic of Germany's role in international sport. At the IOC's meeting in Copenhagen, British member Lord David Burghley read a letter he had received from General Brian Robertson, the British high commissioner, who expressed hope that the IOC would welcome Germany back into international sport, as "it is the best means that we can provide to show the German youth that their cooperation is required for the re-attainment of peace and the contact with the youth of other nations." The IOC provisionally recognized the German Olympic Committee at the Copenhagen meeting with the understanding that a separate meeting of members of the IOC and the NOC would address any remaining concerns.[22]

Just days before the Copenhagen meeting, the issue of the NOC had arisen in one of the high commission's subcommittees. The Political Affairs Committee (PAC) agreed to inform Brundage "that German participation in the 1952 games was favored, but that it was understood that the Germans who were members of the Committee were politically undesirable and that it was hoped they could be prevailed upon to resign."[23] PAC members recognized that as the face of German sport, the new National Olympic Committee could not resemble Germany's authoritarian and Nazi past. This appearance was critical to alleviate the fears of the smaller European countries and to prevent more criticism from the communist states that former Nazis were running West Germany. Although most PAC members believed that the Duke of Mecklenburg and Ritter von Halt should resign their positions on the IOC, they knew that meddling in a completely domestic organization would be viewed negatively both within Germany and abroad. The British member of the committee drafted a paper that was highly influenced by his discussions with one of the British members of the IOC. It stated that "the choice of members of the German Committee is entirely a German matter and that it would, therefore, be undesirable for the Allied High Commission to intervene officially." To facilitate Germany's reentry into international sport, the British member recommended that they should advise the German chancellor's office "personally and informally" to suggest that the Duke of Mecklenburg resign his position on the IOC.[24]

While the first draft of the paper primarily addressed the Duke of Mecklenburg, a revised version delved into the backgrounds of many NOC members, revealing that the entire executive committee was neither democratic nor denazified. This version of the document seemed to redeem the Duke of Mecklenburg; it stated that his "political record appears to be untarnished by Nazism." In contrast, the document said, several other NOC members "had played a considerable role in Nazi organizations." PAC members objected to individuals who had held posts in the 1936 Olympic organizing committee or had been a member of the Nazi Party or its affiliated organizations. PAC now stated the compromised individuals who should resign were Ritter von Halt (president), Peter "Peco" Bauwens and Max Danz (vice presidents), Carl Diem (secretary), Willi Daume (treasurer), and Guido "Guy" Schmidt (ski representative). In addition, PAC members believed allegations that the NOC was self-appointed and "does not enjoy the confidence of the majority of democratic German sportsmen."[25] In essence, the PAC believed that sport leaders in Germany had accepted Nazism and therefore had led the general population astray through their participation in sport activities. While these men may have been sufficiently denazified for everyday life, they were not acceptable as representatives of German sport to the international community. PAC members recommended that all members of the National Olympic Committee who had held positions in the 1936 Olympic organizing committee resign, that the two German representatives to the IOC resign, and that all vacated positions be filled through elections of "uncompromised representatives of German sport."[26]

The Allied high commissioners—John J. McCloy, France's André François-Poncet, and Sir Ivone Kirkpatrick, Robertson's successor—considered the recommendations of the PAC and worked unofficially behind the scenes to obtain favorable outcomes within the IOC that were in line with Allied goals in Germany. The high commissioners addressed the issue of Germany's sport leaders less than two weeks before National Olympic Committee officials planned to travel to Lausanne to meet with IOC members. Because US intelligence discovered that Diem, Ritter von Halt, Bauwens, and Daume had all falsified their travel documents and that charges against them were pending, the matter presented a sense of urgency. At the high commissioners' meeting on August 17, 1950, McCloy asked if all agreed that they suggest to Adenauer that Germany's chances at recognition would greatly improve if the organizers of the 1936 Olympics were not members of the new German Olympic Committee.[27] A brief that had been prepared for Kirkpatrick raised the point that National Olympic Committee membership was "presumably revocable," whereas International Olympic Committee membership was for life, presenting "difficulties in securing the withdrawal of the Duke of Mecklenburg and of von Halt if they cannot be persuaded to retire voluntarily."[28] Kirkpatrick preferred that the suggestion to the chancellor take the form of a statement of fact from which Adenauer could draw his own conclusions, reminding the high commissioners that their concern was foreign affairs and not the role of the sporting ministry. François-Poncet agreed, and McCloy presented the suggestion in their meeting with Adenauer later that day.[29]

That afternoon Adenauer and the high commissioners discussed several issues regarding Germany's position within the international system, including the European Defence Community, German rearmament, the possibility of an East German-Soviet invasion of West Germany, and the German Olympic Committee. During the occupation all four Allies had emphasized demilitarization, but after the Cold War began and particularly after the Korean War broke out, the western Allies wanted some form of West German rearmament so the Federal Republic could defend itself. However, the idea of rearming did not have widespread support within Germany, including from Adenauer. Because the Federal Republic of Germany was only eleven months old and had been "created out of nothing," Adenauer argued, controversial plans such as rearmament could not be rushed.[30] Yet this same uncertainty about Germany's place in the international community could be removed if the country participated in a positive setting on the world stage, such as in international sport. When the high commissioners informed Adenauer of the efforts to secure German participation in the Olympics and their suggestions about the membership of the National Olympic Committee, the chancellor expressed concern and promised to cooperate.[31]

Adenauer fully grasped the importance of the Olympic Games as a powerful international setting for a country to present itself to the world and understood that the Federal Republic of Germany could not afford to be excluded from another Olympiad. Four days before the German delegation (of unsatisfactory individuals) was scheduled to meet with the IOC in Lausanne, Adenauer reported to the high commission that he had contacted the NOC and "taken steps that the composition of the delegation be changed to conform to your wishes." Carl Diem, Karl Ritter von Halt, Willi Daume, and Max Danz had been removed from the trip to Switzerland.[32] Adenauer requested that the new delegation—Walter Kolb, Peco Bauwens, and Robert Lingnau—be granted travel documents immediately, as none of these men had been members of the Nazi Party.[33] The National Olympic Committee bowed to the pressure from both the federal government and US authorities so that Germany could gain unconditional recognition from the IOC.[34]

In late August 1950, the German delegation pleaded its case in Lausanne for full recognition.[35] After apologizing for the inhumanities (*Grausamkeiten*) perpetrated by the criminal Nazis, tarnishing of the name of Germany, the delegates provided information on the status of German sport and expressed the desire of German youth to participate in the Olympic movement again. They also detailed the measures the high commission (although not the chancellor) had taken to prevent the original German delegation—including its two IOC representatives—from appearing in Switzerland. The IOC members at the meeting in Lausanne recommended that the entire IOC grant full recognition to Germany at its congress the following year in Vienna. They also recommended that Germany be allowed to participate in the 1952 Olympic Games in Helsinki. Only once did an IOC member raise the issue of compromised individuals continuing in their roles on Germany's NOC.[36] Col. P. W. Scharroo, from the Netherlands, had led the defense of Rotterdam and, with a heavy heart, had surrendered the city to the Germans in 1940.[37] The Dutch and Belgian members in particular repeatedly voiced their opinions, in their home countries and at IOC meetings, that the return to the Olympic movement of Germany with its compromised individuals was unacceptable and that their own countries would boycott the games.[38] Yet when Scharroo raised his objection, his colleagues basically ignored him. The next speaker (Swiss representative Albert Mayer) replied that if the German sport representatives had the trust of the German youth, then the IOC should not interfere with the German NOC's affairs.[39]

Although Germany's return to the Olympic movement only needed formal approval by the entire International Olympic Committee in Vienna in 1951, Germany's IOC members again faced anti-German sentiment. Some IOC members still wanted to exclude the German members from the meeting. Knowing that the IOC members in Lausanne had recommended that Germany be readmitted, the Duke of Mecklenburg and Karl Ritter von Halt intended to travel to Vienna for the meeting. IOC president J. Sigfrid Edström asked IOC chancellor Otto Mayer whether any objections to their participation might arise, although he personally felt it would be "quite natural" because of the impending recognition.[40] Mayer replied that while earlier he would have said that they should attend, now he thought "that Western Germany will be recognized if our German members do not come, but there will be more difficulties if they are present. This press campaign is coming especially from Norway and Sweden and is reproduced by certain German Press also." With Oslo the site of the 1952 Winter Games and East Germany pushing for its own recognition, the IOC could not afford the negative publicity, particularly in the communist East German press, that would follow if they allowed former Nazis to resume their membership. In addition, Mayer raised the point that some members still harbored animosity toward Germany and its IOC members. Taking all of these factors into consideration, Mayer concluded that "their absence is more suitable for the sake of everything."[41] However, when the Belgian member, Rodolphe W. Seeldrayers, insisted on excluding the German IOC members from the Vienna meeting,

Edström responded that "our rules say that no discrimination is allowed against anyone on grounds of politics. We must stick to that. We cannot any longer preclude German sport from the Olympic games."[42] The IOC had excluded Germany before the founding of the Federal Republic because no German state existed, but now that one did, the IOC had to act according to its rules.

Although the IOC permitted the Duke of Mecklenburg and Ritter von Halt to attend the meeting, political problems appeared to prevent them from participating in Vienna. Austria and its capital were, like Germany, under quadripartite control, and both men feared for their safety should they travel to Vienna, particularly as Ritter von Halt had already been held in Soviet prisons for a few years.[43] Although they had been denied travel visas, they crossed the border into Salzburg and called Edström, claiming that they had to be at the meeting to discuss the East German issue. Edström, with the help of Brundage and the US embassy, obtained entry visas for them, and they were at the IOC meeting where Germany resumed its participation in the Olympic movement.[44]

IOC Members behind the Scenes

Germany's return to the IOC was a direct result of the behind-the-scenes intervention of the US government, which had clearly shifted its opinions regarding Ritter von Halt and the Duke of Mecklenburg. In October 1950, IOC member Brundage wrote to McCloy to attest to the non-Nazi character of Ritter von Halt and Diem with the hope of permitting these two men to continue leading German sport.[45] When McCloy had not replied after eight months, Brundage contacted the State Department directly. The State Department and HICOG communicated with each other—but not with Brundage—about the progress of the NOC and the Nazi associations of its leaders. In July 1951, HICOG informed the State Department that "the situation had taken on a confidential and political phase, the factors of which could not be divulged to Mr. Brundage."[46] That "confidential and political phase," however, was a need to brush aside the problematic nature of denazification in order to address a more pressing concern: the developing Cold War, which in this context meant preventing the IOC from recognizing East Germany. The Korean War had globalized the Cold War by moving beyond Europe's borders, and the IOC's recognition of the USSR in 1951 had brought the Cold War into the realm of international sport. The western Allies knew that it was only a matter of time before the Soviet Union and its satellite states began to push for East Germany in sport. Shortly before the IOC's

Vienna meeting, East Germany had established its own National Olympic Committee. Support for East German recognition among Communist Bloc nations forced the IOC, and the international federations, to make a decision about readmitting the Federal Republic of Germany.[47]

In addition, the US IOC members in Vienna, particularly J. Brooks B. Parker, were speaking regularly with staff at the US embassy there. Parker is perhaps one of the least known—or even the most unknown—American who has served as an IOC member. The IOC elected him at its Copenhagen meeting in May 1950, and he died from a heart attack in November 1951, the day after hosting a luncheon in his hometown of Philadelphia for IOC president J. Sigfrid Edström.[48] Parker, a fencer on the 1920 and 1924 US Olympic teams, had worked for the US government in several capacities. From 1914 to 1916, he was assistant director in the Bureau of War Risk Insurance in the Treasury Department; in 1916, he was the assistant secretary for the American-Mexican Joint Commission on Arbitration (in the State Department); and in 1938, he served as the technical advisor to the US delegation at the Fourth Diplomatic Conference on Air Law in Brussels.[49] Thus, Parker's election to the IOC was a tremendous asset to the State Department—they now had an inside man on the committee. In May 1951, Parker informed the US embassy in Vienna about the possibility that the IOC would recognize East Germany at its congress so he could obtain advice from Washington. However, he reported a few days later that the IOC had dismissed this question.[50]

Despite Avery Brundage's continued promotion of the separation of sport and politics in his extensive correspondence, particularly after he became IOC president 1952, he routinely consulted with the US State Department and its embassies and consulates. Following the negotiations with the East and West Germans regarding their participation in the 1952 Olympic Games, Brundage met with the US consulate general in Geneva to report on these discussions. These developments "were gratifying to the Department, which was greatly pleased by the reports it had of the role played by Mr. Brundage in taking care of a potentially difficult situation."[51] In August 1951, Brundage wrote to the secretary of state to thank him for the State Department's assistance in Vienna, Geneva, Bern, and Copenhagen, where diplomats in US embassies had provided advice regarding West German recognition and the Soviet Bloc's efforts to recognize East Germany.[52]

This letter from Brundage to the secretary of state illustrates a change in the position of the United States Olympic Association (USOA), that Parker articulated in a meeting at the State Department the summer after the IOC's meeting in Vienna. Parker requested that an embassy official in Oslo be prepared to offer guidance when the IOC next met. The State Department noted

At a luncheon in Philadelphia hosted by US IOC member J. Brooks B. Parker (second from left) to honor IOC president J. Sigfrid Edström (second from right) in November 1951, Mayor Bernhard Samuel (far left) presents the key to the city to Edström with local businessman Arthur C. Kaufmann (far right). *Courtesy of J. Sigfrid Edströms arkiv, fotoalbum 102, Riksarkivet, Stockholm, Sweden.*

that Parker had "made a rather important statement regarding a change in [the] policy" of the USOA, which "had decided to abandon its long standing policy of operating without reference to or consultation with the United States government and had decided to maintain in the future closer association with the Department of State, and to request guidance from it in connection with international olympic meetings, negotiations, etc."[53] This change in the USOA's policy marked a clear departure from its public position that sport and politics should be separate. Behind the scenes, Parker and Brundage maintained a clear line of communication with State Department officials to help direct IOC actions to align with US political aims.

Parker continued to consult with the State Department about new individuals nominated for IOC membership. In 1951, he requested information from the State Department about Konstantin Andrianov, the recently elected IOC member from the Soviet Union, and Vladimir Stoychev, the proposed member from Bulgaria. The State Department provided him with biographies about both men, noting Stoychev's many athletic and political accomplishments, including his two-year position as the Bulgarian political representative in Washington from 1945 to 1947, noting that he was not known to be a member of the Communist Party.[54] Similarly, when the IOC hoped to increase the number of members from Latin America, Parker wrote to the State Department asking for recommendations and information about each person. He noted that "the American group is anxious to bring more of the Latin American countries into this work, but only of course if the proper individuals can be found."[55] Parker and the other members of "the American group" did not want to select Latin American members who would vote with the Soviet Bloc, which by 1951 was already introducing their own political agenda at IOC meetings.

Conclusion

The IOC's recognition of the Federal Republic of Germany in 1951 ended the demands of the High Commission of Occupied Germany for further denazification of German sport in conjunction with the change in western policies as a result of the deepening Cold War. Nevertheless, Germany's new National Olympic Committee had to contend with the US State Department's agendas with regard to the committee's membership and its fight for IOC recognition, even though these aspects were seemingly internal affairs for Germans and the international sporting community. Although the western Allies viewed sport as a way to teach German youth how to be democratic, sport leaders who had held positions of power in Nazi Germany resumed their positions after the war because of their expertise and their contacts with the international community. Western officials regarded these leaders as reliable enough if they could demonstrate that their work had begun before the Nazis took power and that they had tried to protect sporting ideals from Nazi corruption. US State Department officials and their British and French colleagues ultimately reversed their earlier assessments about German sport leaders in order to ensure that Germany could support the western stance in the Cold War.

By preventing a separate recognition of East Germany, Brundage was clearly maintaining the US political position, which supported its West German ally, within the IOC.[56] The State Department continued its efforts to prevent the issue of East German recognition from arising at the 1953 IOC meeting in Mexico City. State Department representatives met with Karl Ritter von Halt and US Olympic official J. Lyman Bingham, and Brundage assured a Mexico City embassy officer that "he had been successful in deferring the East Germany and Communist China participation in the games for another year and he added that while he had been successful in sidetracking this issue for the past six years, he felt that at the next Conference the Committee would find it extremely difficult, if not impossible, to evade this issue further."[57] While many sportsmen in the twentieth century continually espoused the clear separation between sport and politics, their actions presented a different reality from their public statements. Even in 1956 as Brundage met with a representative from the German embassy in New York regarding the preparation for the all-German Olympic team, Brundage began the conversation by reiterating that "he had always attempted to avoid being drawn into political controversy in connection with the Olympic Games."[58] Yet the eagerness with which the US members of the IOC—including Brundage—corresponded with their governments gives their rhetoric about the apolitical nature of sport a hollow ring.

Parker's accession to the IOC pleased State Department officials because they finally had someone who provided them with inside information and consulted with them regarding political matters. He could help influence the actions of international sports officials so their actions would coincide with US political aims. However, this relationship was cut short with Parker's sudden death. Throughout the Cold War, the German government worked closely with its IOC members and leading sport officials, especially to counter the growing strength of East Germany. Indeed, the State Department continued to work, both directly and through its embassies, to reinforce its position with US delegates to international sports federations.[59] With Germany's return to the Olympic movement, western powers achieved their political aims within the realm of international sport, particularly as Cold War lines hardened. As staunch supporters of the Anglo-American way of life, western members of the IOC acted as the supporters of and surrogates for American and British foreign policies.

—12—

Sport and American Foreign Policy during the 1960s

BY THOMAS M. HUNT

From its inception, the Cold War was fought on a variety of fronts, which, fortunately, never extended into direct military confrontation between the United States and the Soviet Union. Instead, the two superpowers avoided armed interchanges in favor of more subtle applications of power. During these years, the American containment doctrine expanded its original focus on political and military applications of power to also encompass cultural dimensions. The resulting propaganda campaign included the development of an athletic rivalry between the United States and its communist rivals.

This chapter argues that the years of Lyndon B. Johnson's presidency served as an important transition period between competing visions of American sport policy. Johnson's immediate predecessors in the White House, Dwight D. Eisenhower and John F. Kennedy, believed in the necessity of a broad-based national fitness campaign to reverse the country's declining levels of physical fitness. Later, Presidents Richard Nixon and Gerald Ford focused on the need for reform among the country's amateur sport bodies in order to increase American competitiveness in international competitions. In the interim, members of the Johnson administration struggled with how best to use sport as a means of influence in the Cold War. Their endeavors, however, were relatively uncoordinated. This can be partly explained by a federalist political ideology in the United States whereby "minor" affairs such as sport are traditionally seen as outside the jurisdiction of the national government. Even when the Cold War stimulated involvement with the issue, the importance of athletics to federal policymakers was limited. Hampered by an expensive war in Vietnam, the Johnson administration was focused on its Great Society program. Nevertheless, American sport played a part in the administration's struggle to win the hearts and minds of the world.

Manipulating the 1964 Olympic Festivals

From the onset of the Johnson presidency, the successes of Soviet bloc teams in international events drew members of the Johnson administration away from issues of national physical fitness. Worried that it "looks like we're going to do badly" in the upcoming Tokyo Olympic games, Attorney General Robert Kennedy told Johnson in May 1964 that "we could do much better than we have done in the past." He suggested that the administration undertake a study with the aim of creating a "program or suggestion in the field of athletics."[1]

In July 1964, Kennedy published his thoughts in what amounted to a sports manifesto for the American people. "Part of a nation's prestige in the cold war is won in the Olympic Games," he began. "Nations use the scoreboard of sports as a visible measuring stick to prove their superiority over the 'soft and decadent' democratic way of life." According to the attorney general, it was "thus in our national interest that we regain our Olympic superiority."[2] Members of Congress also expressed concern about the country's position in sport. Senator Hubert Humphrey issued a sharp warning about the devastating effects of continued Soviet dominance: "The Russians are feverishly building toward what they expect to be a major Cold War victory in 1964: a massive triumph in the Tokyo Olympics." Humphrey added that "the Red propaganda drums will thunder out in a worldwide tattoo, heralding the 'new Soviet men and women' as 'virile, unbeatable conquerors' in sports—or anything else."[3]

After President Johnson took office, Humphrey expounded on the destructive effects of a long-standing feud between America's Amateur Athletic Union and National Collegiate Athletic Association. He wrote to Johnson that "you may wish to consider appointment of a White House commission on Sports. It could help prevent an all-out 'war' which threatens to break out between amateur sports groups."[4] The United States Olympic Committee (USOC) was also troubled by the antagonism. "If we could just go back to an alliance between the AAU and the NCAA," USOC president Kenneth Wilson lamented, "everything necessary for a complete Olympic development could be accomplished."[5] Representative Louis Wyman, a Republican from New Hampshire, likewise told President Johnson that "our continuing defeats at the Olympic Games are a matter of concern to all Americans, regardless of political party." Wyman recommended that Johnson "appoint a study group, composed of knowledgeable men and women in this field, to report to you concerning this subject as soon as reasonably possible."[6]

Wyman was not aware that the Interagency Committee on International Athletics had already been created to "collect, exchange, and review information concerning amateur athletic matters."[7] Chaired by Nicholas Rodis, special assistant for athletic programs in the State Department's Bureau of Educational and Cultural Affairs, the committee sought to coordinate the efforts of the different federal agencies that were interested in sport. Dissatisfaction with the existing conditions also led to a collaborative effort between the USOC and the Johnson administration in enlisting the support of a private consulting firm, the Arthur D. Little Corporation, which was headed by former lieutenant general James Gavin. Several of the firm's associates met with US sports officials and federal representatives to consider the idea of an amateur sports foundation.[8] USOC official Franklin Orth was enthusiastic about the plan. He argued that efforts to harmonize amateur athletics in the United States needed public support, pointing out that the Soviet government had spent an estimated $1.2 billion on athletics in 1963 alone as part of "the policy of the Kremlin in the unrelenting battle to win men's minds."[9]

On June 12, 1964, President Johnson met with Kennedy and Gavin.[10] In a follow-up letter to Gavin, Johnson asked the company to begin its investigation and said that their deliberations "on the problem of achieving excellence in sports in this country were most helpful."[11] Although not much could be done before the 1964 Tokyo Games, in April 1964, William P. Bundy, assistant secretary of state for East Asian and Pacific Affairs, sent a suggestion "in regard to *exploitation* of the 1964 Olympics in Tokyo." Given the "intense interest in sports among youth in the underdeveloped countries and particularly in Asia," he proposed that the United States Information Agency (USIA) and the Voice of America "might with advantage develop an all-out program of coverage of the Games." Bundy continued, "If film treatment could in the course of things show a degree of friendly fraternization between American Olympic teams and their counterparts from Asia and Africa this would add to interest."[12] The message was lost on USIA director Carl Rowan, however. He released a cable asserting that "the Games have relatively little relevance to USIA psychological objectives so that only limited selective coverage is regarded as justified."[13]

In contrast, the State Department recognized the potential propaganda value of the competitions. Martin McLaughlin, an official in the Bureau of Educational and Cultural Affairs, sent a memorandum to Rodis stating, "I don't feel [Rowan's message] is altogether responsive to the suggestions

[Bundy] made."[14] Rodis replied that "there will be world-wide saturation coverage of the Olympic Games. Would this not . . . indicate the interest and importance the nations of the world place on the Olympics?" Rodis also supported linking USIA coverage to the bureau's cultural presentations and specialist programs that sent American athletes and coaches abroad to assist the sports programs of other countries. "I believe it would be of benefit," Rodis wrote, "if developing nations . . . were aware that the United States has enough interest in one of their members to help them improve their sports image."[15]

On May 18, 1964, President Johnson received a memorandum that proposed the use of the National Aeronautics and Space Administration's Syncom II satellite for a global broadcast of the Olympics. The memo informed him that "the Japanese are extremely anxious to pursue the project and have continued to pressure senior officials in the Department of State." The State Department considered "it important for reasons of international relations that these broadcasts be made possible."[16] Johnson was apparently unimpressed and initially failed to approve the initiative. According to presidential assistant Larry O'Brien, Representative Joseph Karth, the ranking member of the House Science and Astronautics Committee, was "very disturbed at what he understands to be a White House rejection of a proposal to transmit the Olympic games." Connecting the proposed broadcast with the space race against the Soviet Union, Karth "emphasized the importance of this proposal to US-Japanese relations—the psychological impact this would have on maintaining the US image of space supremacy."[17] White House aide Horace Busby then hit upon an issue that the president could not overlook. "The Olympic Games will be conducted in October at the peak of the 1964 presidential campaigns," he reminded Johnson. "The telecasts—if technically well-done—would be a matter of pride for all Democratic candidates, and would also give the Administration an opportunity to identify with *youth, athletics, international cooperation*, et al."[18] The president relented, and on October 7, 1964, informed the world of the operation. "It is heartening," he declared, "that the Olympic Games—a symbol of peaceful competition among nations—can be seen simultaneously by those actually present and by peoples throughout the entire world."[19]

Alongside such constructive ideas were more sinister schemes to "manipulate" international sport. Such an opportunity presented itself when the Indonesian government denied Israeli and Taiwanese athletes entry into the country when it hosted the 1962 Asian Games. The International Olympic Committee (IOC) responded by suspending Indonesia's membership. Indonesian president Sukarno announced his country's withdrawal from the Olympic movement and made plans for a rival set of competitions called the Games of the New Emerging Forces (GANEFO).[20] In short order, the Democratic People's Republic of Korea's vociferous support of GANEFO sparked the imagination of American officials.

A North Korean threat to boycott the 1964 games astonished the American embassy in Seoul, given that the "regime [in Pyongyang] has put a tremendous amount of effort into securing an invitation to the Tokyo games and into building a strong team." This development was welcome, however, as "it is clear that the boycott threat will have the effect of further souring North Korea's relations with the IOC."[21] A proposal to exploit the situation was immediately put forward. In May 1964, the US ambassador to the Republic of Korea, Samuel Berger, sent a telegram to Secretary of State Dean Rusk recommending that American diplomats draw the IOC's attention to the North Korean government's public denigrations of. "There is a possibility," Berger declared, "that [the] strident and defiant tone of broadcasts may stiffen [the] IOC's . . . determination [to] keep North Korean GANEFO participants out o[f] [the] 1964 Olympics."[22] Several days later, Rusk cabled the American embassy in Switzerland and requested that it make the IOC aware of the North Korean rhetoric.[23] In the end, six North Korean athletes were denied entry to the Olympic village.[24] While it is difficult to attribute these results to US diplomacy, the outcome was particularly satisfying, especially since the IOC had just accepted North Korea's national Olympic committee.[25]

Federal Fitness Campaigns

US athletes performed surprisingly well at the 1964 Olympics, and US officials believed that their country had received a propaganda boost. Two days before the conclusion of the games, Special Assistant Rodis told Representative Wyman that "our team has done a job way beyond our fondest expectations."[26] Despite such perceptions, some US officials recognized that reform of the country's athletic organizations had to begin if the success of the Tokyo games was to continue. Representative Robert Michel declared in a message to Johnson that "the raging controversy between the A.A.U. and the N.C.A.A. . . . will not be settled without some outside pressure. . . . We surely want the very best team to go against the Russians and it would be tragic . . . [if our best athletes] should be denied a place on the US team."[27]

The Kennedy administration had tried neutral arbitration as a strategy for resolving the conflict between the NCAA and the AAU.[28] Johnson was not satisfied with the results of that process and wanted to consider other strategies. Presidential aide Bill Moyers informed a colleague that General

Gavin's analysis of "a program of fund raising through a private foundation to develop better performances by US athletes in international meets . . . seems to be going fairly well."[29] The approach was apparently influenced by a 1960 report Gavin had received from Great Britain titled "Sport and the Community" that advocated a combination of government funds and private contributions as the best way to strengthen the capabilities of athletes.[30] The general's study proposed a variety of recommendations that centered on a publicly funded national amateur sports system.[31]

By May of 1965, Gavin had submitted his findings and recommendations to the White House. Johnson responded that "my staff is reviewing your recommendations, and will continue to do so in order that we may do everything in our power to create the greatest possible athletic opportunity for all Americans."[32] Gavin distributed the report to the USOC Board of Directors and planned to approach the editors of *Sports Illustrated* about an article on the topic. However, the president preferred that the study remain confidential.[33]

Johnson ultimately decided against implementing the recommendations of the study. The president, according to White House aide Jack Valenti, was "faced with [so] many pressing problems, both in the international and domestic fields . . . that there has not been the opportunity to give thought to the matter."[34] While this communication did not clearly convey the president's political reasons for rejecting Gavin's recommendations, his staff was more open in their communications with each other. For example, a June 21, 1965, memorandum from presidential assistant Harry McPherson to Valenti said that the "NCAA and AAU are intransigent, power-mad, and wholly self-seeking." He concluded that "the President's name should not be used to urge anything we aren't certain to get."[35]

Several members of Congress disagreed. In August of 1965, the Senate Committee on Commerce, chaired by Warren Magnuson, held a hearing on the status of track and field in the nation. Problems in the sport were particularly salient at the time; the NCAA had prohibited a number of collegiate athletes from competing at that year's dual US-Soviet track meet in Kiev, Ukraine.[36] Magnuson declared that "at stake, ultimately, is our continued ability to demonstrate in the Olympic Games that fitness and zest for voluntary competition are the hallmarks of a free and democratic society."[37] While Magnuson hoped "that [the NCAA and AAU] will voluntarily agree to some form of continuing arbitration," the committee was "prepared to go even farther."[38] To prevent intrusion in their affairs by a congressional committee, the two organizations quickly agreed to a suspension of hostilities and an arbitration proceeding.[39] However, the quarrel would not be resolved until Congress passed the Amateur Sports Act in 1978.

In 1965, the Johnson administration turned its attention to the sports programs the President's Council on Physical Fitness managed. In November, Johnson remarked that "the struggles to preserve freedom and to advance human hopes and aspirations will not be won by nations whose citizens let themselves grow soft and weak."[40] That June, the results of a national youth fitness test had demonstrated a marked increase in the fitness of American children.[41] Galvanized by this progress, the president announced the creation of the Presidential Physical Fitness Award Program. "It is essential that our young people develop their physical capabilities," Johnson stated. "Sports and other forms of active play promote good health and help provide our country with sturdy young citizens equal to the challenges of the future."[42]

The connection between such mass-based initiatives and elite athletics was never far from the surface. Attorney General Nicholas Katzenbach wrote to retired baseball star Stan Musial, consultant to the president on physical fitness, that "while I realize that physical fitness programs and competitive amateur athletics are not necessarily the same, there may be considerable overlap."[43] Paul Miller, an official in the Department of Health, Education, and Welfare, proposed a formal coupling of the two issues. He first called for the creation of a national physical fitness and sports center that "would tie the sports development program to the Great Society" in order to "provide a stimulus for development of significant Governmental programs." He also suggested, as others had previously, that a new national sports foundation "would key in on our poor Olympic performance."[44]

In March 1968, President Johnson signed Executive Order 11398, which added the words "and Sports" to the title of the President's Council on Physical Fitness. The order also raised the status of the council within the federal government. Until that time, the council had been led by the secretary of health, education, and welfare, but the executive order made the vice-president the chair.[45] Johnson challenged the body to "develop national goals and programs to promote sports and fitness in America."[46] USOC executive director Arthur Lentz immediately recognized the benefits that might accrue to his organization. "With the Vice President at the head," he stated, "we'll move faster to improve our overall stature in Olympic competition."[47] As Lentz predicted, Vice President Humphrey attempted to use the council as a vehicle for revitalizing the nation's Olympic stature. "I want to see a great national competition, from the smallest hamlet to the biggest city," he stated. Although Humphrey believed that the federal government

A 1968 poster for the President's Council on Physical Fitness.
Courtesy of the University of Arkansas.

should not take too active a role, he felt that "we can get local government and private groups working together." Recognizing the potential impact on his organization, Lentz noted that this was "the kind of federal support we've been looking for."[48]

Sports Tours and Cultural Diplomacy

By 1965, the State Department had become increasingly aware of the potential of athletics to stimulate cultural contacts with other peoples. In September of that year, the department released a study on the subject with an announcement that "United States foreign policy objectives can be achieved to some extent through the medium of sports." After analyzing the past successes and problems of US athletic initiatives while they were abroad, it concluded that "a. most of the world is 'sports-conscious'; b. that athletic activities are the least suspicious approach to youth; c. that in some countries sports bear a close relationship to politics."[49] The State Department had already been sending athletes overseas as cultural ambassadors for years. With an annual budget of approximately $250,000, it had sent around ten athletic groups abroad each year from 1963 to 1967.[50] These teams put on public exhibitions that highlighted the skill of American athletes. While such demonstrations were important, the department was also interested in workshops for local teams. "These groups," according to Rodis, "visit schools in out-of-the-way places, affording a maximum of contact between American athletes and their host country counterparts."[51] US officials stationed abroad repeatedly cited the visits as among the most successful methods through which contacts with local populations could be established.[52]

US officials also believed that US teams could be used to undermine the Soviet grip on its satellite countries. The 1965 study declared, for instance, that "many Poles want the United States to defeat the Soviet[s] and are emotionally upset over any US loss to the Soviet[s]."[53] The American Legation in Budapest, Hungary, likewise reported that spectator sentiment at the 1965 World University Games was decidedly pro-American: "Every American victory is greeted by an ovation out of proportion to those accorded other teams." More significantly, "there has been not only a noticeable coolness towards Soviet victories . . . but an undercurrent of hostility on occasion." Such sentiments were loudly pronounced by the approximately 10,000 Hungarian spectators who watched the US college basketball team defeat its Soviet opponent.[54]

Athletic coaches also visited foreign nations under the Department of State's American Specialists program.[55] In 1966, fifty-seven sports specialists traveled overseas.[56] One of them, Joey Bouchard, a physical education instructor from Maine, spent seventy-nine days in Mali during which he conducted clinics in four different cities. As a result, a diplomat at the US embassy in Bamako, Mali's capital, expressed his belief "that [a] year-long association between Americans and Malians could produce not only good basketball, but good personal relationships."[57] Athletic coaches also visited foreign nations under the Department of State's American Specialists program.[58] US officials in Tehran described basketball coach Donald Linehan's stay in Iran as a coup for America's relationship with the country. "Coach Linehan's tour was extremely worthwhile," they declared. "He . . . faced a number of problems far removed from the basketball court with concern, skill and, we feel, a degree of long-term success."[59]

Despite such successes, the number of athletic tours abroad began to decline in the late 1960s along with a general deemphasis of cultural programs. The resources afforded to these undertakings had been under threat since at least 1964, when Congress began to contemplate a reduction in the appropriations for the State Department's cultural exchange initiatives.[60] J. William Fulbright, chair of the Senate Committee on Foreign Relations, wrote to President Johnson in May that year to express "deep concern over the current financial prospects and future status of our official educational and cultural exchange program."[61] Johnson agreed, writing to Senator John McClellan that "it would be a mistake for a program of this quality to be drastically curtailed at this time."[62]

As time went on, though, the federal government became distracted by issues that required more immediate results than cultural programs could provide. The House Appropriations Committee stated in its report on the 1969 appropriation bill that "[the cultural exchange program] was an area in which substantial reductions could be made in view of the present financial situation."[63] In 1968, the Republican Party, in an ironic twist to its traditional fiscal conservatism, chastised the Johnson administration for its short-sightedness. The White House received a draft declaration from the Republican Coordinating Committee's Task Force on the Conduct of Foreign Relations that claimed that "it is our Party that originated this nation's first concerted overseas information policy and program, and it is Republicans who have consistently called for major improvements in this critical field. We now call for still greater efforts." Lamenting the "tarnished American image" abroad, the declaration argued for a reorganization of the country's foreign activities so that "long-range educational and cultural programs, which need far greater emphasis, should be transferred from the Department of State to USIA." The statement concluded "that the current administration is unwilling or incapable of performing responsibly and imaginatively."[64]

In fiscal year 1968, the State Department's budget for sports was reduced by 42 percent from the previous year, and in 1969 it was reduced again.[65] Indeed, by fiscal year 1969, the budget for the entire cultural presentations program was less than half of what it had been just five years earlier.[66] Highlighting the effects of these reductions in February 1968, Deputy Assistant Secretary of State Jacob Canter was forced to deny a request by Glenn Ferguson, the US ambassador in Nairobi, for a sports tour for Kenya. Despite the "ample evidence that our athletic personalities have enjoyed a large measure of success abroad . . . " Canter replied, "we are not able to program more people in this field."[67] By the time President Johnson left office, the cultural program that had funded sport tours had become so limited that a State Department analysis concluded, "The effect of the FY 1969 budget reductions has been to retain a skeleton program with little flesh on the bone."[68]

Civil Rights, National Image, and the 1968 Mexico Olympics

Whatever the diminishing resources for its cultural programs, the Johnson-era State Department recognized the prospective value of the 1968 Mexico City Olympics for American prestige. In February 1967, the Mexico City Olympic Organizing Committee publicly announced that a cultural exhibition would accompany the athletic competitions.[69] Fearful that the Soviet Union would use the exhibition to undermine American influence, US ambassador to Mexico Fulton Freeman argued that the United States needed to mount an outstanding cultural presentation.[70] A later decision by Cuba to send a large entourage increased Freeman's perception about the Cold War implications of the exhibition.[71] Freeman envisioned that the State Department and USIA could coordinate displays on art, history, folklore, film, nuclear weapons, and space that could compete with the attractions the Communist Bloc nations would present.[72] President Johnson even expressed interest, declaring that "the revival of the cultural phase of the Olympiad is a significant occurrence.... I want to express America's delight in being able to take part."[73]

Because the Bureau of Educational and Cultural Affairs had such limited funds, a series of interagency meetings were held that included officials from the USIA, NASA, the Atomic Energy Commission, and the Smithsonian Institution.[74] In September 1968, State Department official Asbury Coward traveled to a USOC Board of Directors meeting in Chicago to relay the government's plans. Stating that "I don't think anybody envisioned either the dimensions of it [the cultural event] or the importance the Mexicans were going to attach to it," he went on to describe "a pretty major operation."[75] The variety of attractions eventually pleased Freeman.[76] "What was accomplished," he wrote to Washington, "was, considering the limitation of funds, good, and permitted the US to participate to a far greater extent than original pessimist estimates indicated." Indeed, he went on, "the four cultural presentations completely funded by the Department were of high, if not top quality, and performed well."[77]

The United States also sent several coaches to Mexico to help train Mexican athletes and fellow coaches.[78] In May 1966, Ambassador Freeman sent an urgent telegram to Washington requesting an initiative to "counteract increased Communist Bloc country penetration in the Mexican Olympic Committee sports program." Nine coaches from the communist world were already working in Mexico, he warned; seven more were expected in the near future. An effort by the State Department to provide American coaches would be "interpreted as an expression of goodwill; it would show the value of close cultural ties with the United States; and would significantly enhance the US image."[79] The fruits of the coaches' labors impressed Freeman. "The work of the US coaches," he wrote, "would appear to have been extraordinarily productive, and results exceeded best expectations."[80]

Not everything went as well for the United States at the Mexico City Olympic Games, however. During the Cold War, successful African American athletes were seen as examples that challenged the Soviet Union's criticism of a racial divide in the United States. An American victory in the 1964 US-Soviet dual track and field meet by an all-black team prompted Department of Labor official John W. Leslie to write to the White House to suggest that "in view of the headlines on racial strife, it would seem to me an appropriate action for the president to call in this biracial group of American athletes who, working together, beat the Soviet Union."[81] Throughout the 1960s, however, African Americans had been mobilizing to protest the racial situation in their country.

Protests by African Americans were a particularly sensitive issue for the Johnson presidency, which fashioned itself as the most progressive administration in American history. By 1968, heavyweight champion boxer Cassius Clay had become anathema to many white Americans and a hero to those in the Civil Rights Movement. Renaming himself Muhammad Ali in accordance with Islamic tradition, Clay refused to be inducted into the armed forces and was subsequently convicted of knowingly and willfully avoiding military service.[82] When he registered as a conscientious objector, he described the mixture of racial injustices and religious convictions that informed his decision. "I'm expected to go overseas to help free people in South Vietnam," Ali asserted, "and at the same time my people here are being brutalized and mistreated, and this is really the same thing that's happening over in Vietnam."[83]

During this period, some black athletes grew interested in boycotting the 1968 Olympic Games. Harry Edwards, a professor at San Jose State College, became the leader of this movement, which became known as the Olympic Project for Human Rights.[84] Edwards listed four major objectives: first, to stage a major international demonstration against discrimination in the United States; second, to expose the use of African American athletes as instruments of political propaganda; third, to establish a connection between black athletes and the wider African American community; and fourth, to educate the African American community about the costs of unthinking involvement in the white-dominated athletic system.[85] Edwards called for the removal of IOC president Avery Brundage, the banishment of South Africa and Northern Rhodesia from the Olympic movement, and the reinstatement of Ali as the world heavyweight boxing champion.[86] Announcing that on November 23, 1967, a group of black athletes would vote on whether to boycott the games, Edwards proclaimed that the oppression of blacks in the United States was equal to that found in South Africa. He said, "America has to be exposed for what it is."[87]

After learning of the boycott proposal, USOC president Douglas Roby condemned Edwards as a self-serving obstacle to the Olympic ideal. "The fellow that's heading this . . . is making a strenuous effort to attract attention to himself, and he is sort of a rabble rouser and he is trying to create a scene and he is looking for a vehicle and direct attention to himself."[88] The Johnson administration was also concerned. Bureau of Educational and Cultural Affairs official Asbury Coward personally discussed the situation with former black Olympians and supported the idea of putting an African American on the USOC Board of Directors.[89] Vice President Humphrey also took action: he used the Council on Physical Fitness and Sports as an instrument for obtaining appointments for African Americans in the nation's sport organizations.[90] The USOC, in contrast, decided to take a wait-and-see approach. Referring to the possibility that an African American might come onto USOC managerial team, Roby said, "I'd hate to see a man put on the Board just because his skin was dark."[91]

The boycott movement in the United States joined a larger protest when South Africa was readmitted into the Olympic movement in the spring of 1968.[92] Edwards's reaction was sharp: the IOC had "virtually said the hell with us. Now we'll have to reply let Whitey run his own Olympics."[93] In a statement to the American Committee on Africa, he announced, "I am deeply opposed to the presence of South Africans or Southern Rhodesians as team members . . . at international sporting events. . . . Black athletes will refuse to participate in the Olympic Games if [the two countries] . . . are permitted into the Games while racism still exists at any level."[94] Tommie Smith, a world-record sprinter at San Jose State, added that the situation was "lousy" and that "you cannot rule out the possibility that we Negro athletes might boycott the games."[95] Eager to win points in the developing world, Soviet officials condemned IOC president Brundage, who was American, for "juggling facts" in "the unsavory role of defender of the racists."[96] After the Mexican government, which was worried about the effects of a boycott, called for an emergency meeting, the IOC gave in by voting to expel South Africa from the Olympics in April 1968.[97]

The somewhat mollified American athletes altered their initial plans in favor of a symbolic protest. During the Olympic victory ceremony for the 200-meter sprint, Tommie Smith and John Carlos, the American gold and bronze medalists, raised their fists in protest as the American national flag was hoisted. The IOC immediately informed the USOC that the sprinters should receive prompt punishment for their "political" action. While the USOC initially preferred to issue a minor warning, the IOC insisted that immediate expulsion of the two sprinters from the competitions was the minimum requirement if the entire US team to avoid suspension.[98] The USOC Executive Committee conceded and asked Smith and Carlos to leave Mexico.[99] Tensions between the USOC and the nation's athletes grew when several Olympians announced that they would refuse to compete when they heard of the penalties. Leon Coleman, an African American hurdler from Boston, said that "we're pretty much agreed if one of us goes home, everybody'll go home."[100] In the end, though, Smith and Carlos convinced their colleagues to continue and the events concluded with only one additional—and rather small—American demonstration.[101]

Initial press reports indicated that the US government was involved in seeking harsh measures for the runners.[102] In contrast to such rumors, the US embassy in Mexico actually warned USOC officials against overreacting and expressed a desire that Smith and Carlos be allowed to remain.[103] At the White House, National Security Advisor Walt Rostow was informed of the situation and received notice that the embassy was prepared to intervene if tensions between black Olympians and the USOC threatened the prestige of the United States.[104] Although no such action was taken, several Latin American Olympic delegations condemned the protest as an example of disrespect to Mexico. Puerto Rican official Felicio Torregrosa stated that "it is hard for Latin Americans to understand the attitude of the Negro athletes because in our countries we do not have . . . [such] racial conditions. But, regardless . . . politics should not be brought into the Olympic Games." Soviet track coach Gabriel Korobkov—not surprisingly—drew attention to the situation with an assertion that "it's too bad. They are supposed to be free people."[105]

In the end, the Johnson administration could do little in the realm of athletics to counteract Smith and Carlos's symbolic demonstration. It did attempt to publicize the president's meeting with George Foreman, an African American gold medalist in boxing at the 1968 games. Foreman was an attractive figure for the White House both because he was a product of the administration's Job Corps program and because he had loudly broadcast his patriotism in Mexico. In his proposal that Johnson should meet Foreman, Office of Economic Opportunity Director Bill Kelly asserted that "instead of clenching his fist in protest at Mexico City, George waved an American flag."[106]

Conclusion

The 1968 Olympics thus exemplified the ambivalent nature of federal sport policy during the Johnson presidency. On the one hand, the US government attempted to reinforce its image abroad by providing coaches to Mexico and by participating in a cultural exhibition at the games. The effects of these initiatives were somewhat dampened, however, when several African American athletes at the competitions protested the shortcomings of the Johnson administration. These results illustrate the uncertain nature of sport in US culture in the 1960s. While governmental officials believed that competitiveness in international athletics demonstrated national vitality, sports could also be used to reveal problems in American society.

The president himself vacillated between advocating efforts designed to enhance the efforts of US athletes in elite competitions and supporting programs geared toward broad participation and national fitness. In the end, torn between such seemingly contradictory goals, the Johnson administration failed to address either approach adequately. As a result, proposals such as the national amateur sports foundation were never implemented. While it is easy to exaggerate the significance of sport to American policymakers, waging the Cold War at cultural levels endowed international athletics with a unique degree of importance for government officials. Rightly or wrongly, they perceived sport as an instrument for both promoting US interests and negating critiques of US racial realities from the country's enemies.

13

In Defense of a Neoliberal America

Ronald Reagan, Domestic Policy, and the Soviet Boycott of the 1984 Los Angeles Olympic Games

BY BRADLEY J. CONGELIO

On September 5, 1983, just before 8:00 pm, President Ronald Reagan entered the Oval Office after spending the entirety of the Labor Day holiday in his swimming trunks poolside, feverishly writing a speech. Now trim and proper in his favored blue suit, the president took his place behind the desk made of wood from the HMS *Resolute* and stared intently at the teleprompter between two large television cameras. The Oval Office lights dimmed. At the conclusion of the countdown, Reagan—affectionately and endearingly referred to as the Great Communicator—stared into the heart of a nation that was both shocked and full of a new rage toward the Soviet Union. Just five days before, the Kremlin had ordered a Soviet fighter jet to shoot down Korean Airlines flight 007, killing all 269 people aboard the plane, including one member of the US Congress and sixty other Americans. The United States was now on a dangerous precipice. For many Americans, the KAL 007 disaster realized their worst fears about Soviet atrocities. Reagan's words and actions regarding KAL 007 were vitally important in assuaging American anger. In his speech, Reagan called the Soviet action an "act of inhuman brutality." Reagan continued:

> But, despite the savagery of their crime, the universal reaction against it, and the evidence of their complicity, the Soviets still refuse to tell the truth. They have persistently refused to admit that their pilot fired on the Korean aircraft. Indeed, they have not even told the Russian people

> that a plane was shot down. The Soviet Government calls the whole thing an accident. I call it murder.[1]

Reagan's speech provided startling details about the callousness of the Soviet Union in the minutes leading up to the authorization to fire:

> Let me repeat the stark words of the Soviet pilot himself after signaling that his missile warheads were locked on the airliner: "I have executed the launch. The target is destroyed. I am breaking off attack."

Reagan urged his fellow Americans to "steadfastly gird ourselves for what John F. Kennedy called the 'long twilight struggle.' We must see the Soviets as they are, rather than as some would like them to be."

Approximately 2,600 miles away, the Los Angeles Olympic Organizing Committee (LAOOC)—headed by businessman Peter Ueberroth—were acutely aware that Reagan's response to the downing of KAL 007 had major implications for the planning process for the Los Angeles Games. Prior to the KAL 007 incident, the LAOOC and the Soviet Union had been embroiled in contentious negotiations. The Kremlin had made several demands that had to be met before it would allow Soviet athletes to set foot on US soil: 1) that Soviet Aeroflot flights transporting the national Olympic team be permitted to land at Los Angeles International Airport after a stop in Cuba; 2) that the Soviet Union be allowed to dock a luxury cruise ship in Long Beach Harbor to serve as the official Olympic Village for Soviet athletes and administrators; and 3) that the LAOOC or the US government pay for more than $500,000 worth of security equipment and personnel to protect Soviet athletes and interests for the duration of the 1984 Olympics. The LAOOC had waited for Reagan's response to KAL 007 to see if convincing the Soviet Union to attend the 1984 Olympics was going to become an even more herculean task.

American Anger and Reagan's Response to KAL 007

Only hours after the attack on KAL 007 took place, President Reagan received a memo on official White House letterhead. Calling the president by his first name, the author, identified only as "Jus," wrote:

> This is no time for sanction; no way you can get even on this dastardly act. Let the act itself stand as punishment. Make use of this tragic incident, it substantiates everything you have been saying all these years about the Russians—that they are bastards and sons of bitches not to be trusted, and that we must increase our military strength or they will continue such reckless abuses.[2]

President Reagan addresses the nation after the Soviet attack on Korean Airlines Flight 007. *Courtesy of the Ronald Reagan Library.*

By noon on September 2nd, less than 24 hours after KAL 007 was shot down, the White House had received 1,900 telephone calls and 1,800 telegrams and mailgrams related to the incident. Anne Higgins, the director of Reagan's Office of Correspondence, was responsible for organizing incoming calls and letters and passing along the most pressing to the president. The first telegram she presented to Reagan grasped the solemnity of the matter immediately. The telegram, written by the parents of Irene Steckler—a passenger aboard KAL 007—argued that the deaths of their daughter and her husband Stuart "were the results of the Soviet Union violating every concept of human rights" and that it was "an act of murder that cannot remain unpunished." The distraught parents did not want a swift and firm response to the Soviets as an act of personal revenge. Rather, they asked that Reagan choose a reaction that would "deter the Soviet Union from further committing such wanton murder."[3]

Another telegram Higgins's staff chose to show the president was from John Noble of Muncy, Pennsylvania. Noble wrote, "Having been a prisoner of the Soviet Union for 10 years, I want to encourage you to take the firmest possible stand against the Soviets for their latest act of inhumanity in shooting down a civilian airliner."[4] Soviet occupation forces had arrested Noble and his father in Dresden, Germany, ostensibly for spying. Noble spent ten years in the Soviet Gulag system.[5] Remembering his time as a Soviet prisoner, Noble told Reagan that "only the strongest retaliation will be understood by the Godless communists."[6]

Some Americans asked the president how he could "justify selling grain to murdering Russians" and said that the United States could not "sit back silently for the sake of foreign exchange."[7] Others said that they would be willing to "pay $4 for a loaf of bread" if the grain deal came to an immediate halt.[8] Douglas and Cathy Albrecht said that Reagan should close all "Aeroflot offices in the US," expel all "Soviet personnel," and cancel all "Aeroflot landing rights under the US jurisdiction" except for emergency landings. They also wanted Reagan to immediately revoke the "hundreds of licenses issued to Soviet fishing vessels" and cancel all cultural exchanges between the two countries.[9]

Reagan took swift and decisive action against the Soviet Union and Aeroflot. In his speech, Reagan noted that his administration was "suspending negotiations on several bilateral agreements" that were under consideration prior to the incident.[10] Reagan's actions were much more severe than he outlined in the speech. In a letter to the Civil Aeronautics Board, Reagan wrote:

> The Soviet attack on Korean Air Line Flight 7 on Sept. 1 1983, which resulted in the loss of 269 innocent lives, called for a united, firm, and measured response from the international community. Toward this end, I have initiated a number of measures in coordination with other nations . . . I have determined that it is in the essential foreign policy interest of the United States to take resolute action against the Soviet air carrier Aeroflot.[11]

The president forbade US carriers from booking connecting flights with Aeroflot and required them to sever any and all ties with the Soviet company. He also ordered that Aeroflot close its offices in New York and Washington, D.C., and stipulated that the Soviet employees of both offices be expelled from the United States.[12]

These actions created clear obstacles for the LAOOC. In a memorandum dated December 9, 1983, Richard Levine, a member of Reagan's National Security Council, wrote that because of the "President's KAL decision," the State Department and "other concerned agencies" were to reject all "Soviet proposals" regarding Aeroflot flights and vessels in Long Beach Harbor.[13] However, Reagan made no immediate decision regarding the Soviet Union's requests related to the Olympics.

The Ban the Soviets Coalition

US citizens also took action to express their anger. Seven days after KAL 007 was shot from the sky, the Soviet cruise ship *Novokuibyshevsk* was forced to anchor in a channel just short of the Los Angeles Harbor "after a telephone threat was made against the ship."[14] Kenneth Cho, one of many protestors of Korean descent, argued that "like a grown adult who plays with a 3-year-old, the Soviets . . . attacked a defenseless jet plane, and they should be punished." Valdis Pavlovskis, the president of the Baltic American Freedom League, announced that his organization would "not rest until President Reagan" banned "all Soviet goods from our shores, and close[d] the Soviet Consulate in San Francisco."[15] The Baltic American Freedom League later called the Soviet Union an "outlaw nation" and organized a semi-successful boycott of vodka throughout the United States.[16]

Four California businessmen led by David Balsiger formed a group called the Ban the Soviets Coalition on September 26, 1983, a group the Soviet Union argued was "threatening violence against Soviet athletes."[17] Ban the Soviets Coalition was a right-wing faction composed largely of evangelical Christians and East European émigrés. It was a small but vociferous group. Balsiger, an advertising executive who had campaigned unsuccessfully for a seat in the US House of Representatives, felt that the Olympics were a significant component of Soviet foreign policy, culture, and society. Ban the Soviets Coalition was focused on "depriving the Soviets of the use of the Olympics for propaganda purposes."[18]

Balsiger and his group obtained the assistance of a member of the California state senate, John T. Doolittle, whom Balsiger announced was a "national co-organizer."[19] Doolittle sponsored a resolution in the California legislature that asked President Reagan and Congress to "take appropriate actions to ban the Soviets from the 1984 Olympic Games." Balsiger remarked that "considering that California is the host state of the 1984 Olympics, it took tremendous courage by Senator Doolittle and his colleagues to pass this resolution which we hope will become the model for other states."[20] However, the assistance from the California state government rapidly eroded. Shortly after approving the resolution, California lawmakers revoked it, arguing that they had been "unaware of the proposed sanction against the Soviet Union" written into the document. Balsiger argued that the backtracking legislature had been "sucked into becoming Soviet apologists at the beckoning of the Los Angeles Olympic Organizing Committee."[21]

Balsiger also contended that "various terrorist activities" would likely be carried out by "5,000 KGB agents and operatives" who would be descending on "Southern California disguised as Olympic spectators, with assignments to include spying, subversion, and recruitment of agents to buy, steal, or search out US high technology secrets." It is a matter of debate whether or not Balsiger believed the far-fetched scenarios he was spouting. His goal was to further agitate the simmering fury over the idea that the Soviet Union might participate in the 1984 Olympics. Balsiger also criticized the federal government for "being ready to grant unrestricted travel privileges to Soviet Olympic journalists, most of which," he claimed, were "actually KGB agents wanting open access to high tech manufacturing areas of Southern California."[22]

In a letter to Michael K. Deaver, Reagan's deputy chief of staff and the official White House liaison to the 1984 Los Angeles Olympics, Balsiger claimed that the "ethnic, religious, political, social, education, and veterans organizations" that made up the Ban the Soviets Coalition maintained "a sphere of influence" that extended to "30 to 40 million people—the good people of America who still believe that principle and the value of human lives take precedence over sporting events." He argued that the Ban the Soviets Coalition was constructed of the "same group" that had backed Reagan's successful 1980 presidential campaign, and informed Deaver that ignoring the coalition's requests would result in a substantial lack of support in the president's bid for reelection in 1984.[23]

Members of the Ban the Soviets Coalition, whom Ueberroth deemed to be "a group of nobodies," started mailing leaflets and letters directly to Marat Gramov, the leader of the Soviet state sports committee in Moscow. As Ueberroth recalled, "the literature used inflammatory language and promised to greet the Soviet athletes with anti-Soviet demonstrations." One leaflet graphically depicted an American eagle clawing the back of a Russian bear.[24] The Ban the Soviets Coalition claimed that the letter-writing campaign was only the "first of several aggressive actions" and said that the group planned to continue its attempts to "directly and indirectly influence the Soviets to scuttle their Olympic participation plans." Balsiger claimed that he was attempting "to tell the Soviets that they're not really welcome here but if you do come, don't blame us if you reap the whirlwind."[25]

Reagan Signs Off on All Soviet Requests

On January 31, 1984, in an official action memorandum for the president, Robert McFarlane, Reagan's national security advisor, outlined the Soviets' requests vis-à-vis the Olympics. He began by noting that all involved government agencies agreed that "granting the requests for Aeroflot would require suspending the application of sanction applied to the Soviets following the

KAL shootdown." Suspending the sanction would further anger an American citizenry that was still clamoring for even more severe punishment for the KAL 007 incident. McFarlane also noted that all involved agencies agreed that the Soviet requests raised serious "national security concerns."

McFarlane told the president that "all agencies" recommended that the Aeroflot flights "be granted for the specific purpose of bringing the Soviet Olympic family to Los Angeles, but without the right to land elsewhere in the US or to carry third-country passengers." The national security advisor also reported that government agencies had no objections to "brief calls" from a Soviet vessel to "deliver and, subsequently, pick up equipment and passengers." However, agencies were "strongly opposed to allowing the ship to stay at the Pier in Long Beach Harbor during the Games, primarily because of the potential for electronic eavesdropping." McFarlane reminded Reagan that "no other country" had been granted "permission to keep a ship in port during the Olympics, and so long as we allow no one else in port during the Olympics . . . we should be able to defend refusal of this request as non-discriminatory." McFarlane concluded his summary of his survey of government officials by informing Reagan that "although the Soviets are likely to press the point, we believe that permission should not be granted."

The memo included four recommendations for President Reagan to either approve with a checkmark and his initials or disapprove. The initial recommendation had little to do with the Soviet request:

> That the Olympic Games in Los Angeles be treated as a special event, for which every effort should be made to treat the Soviets on a non-discriminatory basis, unless overriding interests of national security require special arrangements.

Reagan checked this recommendation and initialed "OK." He also approved of McFarlane's second recommendation:

> That Aeroflot be allowed to operate special flights to support their Olympic team, but without the right to transport third-country nationals or to land at intermediate stops in the US

The third recommendation read:

> That the Soviet ship be allowed to enter Long Beach Harbor before and after the Olympics, but not to remain at the pier during the Games, unless such a privilege is granted to other countries.

Reagan did not approve this recommendation as written. He edited it to read:

> That the Soviet ship be allowed to enter Long Beach Harbor before and after the Game, ~~but not~~ *and* to remain at the pier during the Games *subject to the establishment of all possible measures designed to minimize intelligence loss,* ~~unless~~ *and that* privilege is granted to other countries.[26]

Reagan's decision went against the advice of many in his administration as McFarlane had outlined in the introduction to the action memorandum. He ignored the request of the Central Intelligence Agency, the United States Coast Guard, and local Los Angeles law enforcement that he refuse to allow the Soviet ship to stay in the Long Beach Harbor.

Reagan's response to the fourth recommendation in McFarlane's memo is perhaps the most telling illustration of his position on the Soviet requests. The final recommendation of the memorandum read:

> That the LAOOC be instructed to ask the Soviets to submit their requests through normal diplomatic channels.[27]

Reagan wrote "no" next to this recommendation, thus decreasing the likelihood that politics would intertwined with the Olympic Games in Los Angeles. Reagan further cemented his decisions when he signed National Security Decision Directive Number 135 (NSDD 135) approximately two months later.

> The United States desires the complete success of the 1984 Summer Olympic Games and seeks to ensure the full and equitable participation of all accredited members of the Olympic Family in accordance with Olympic rules and applicable laws of the United States. We will also ensure the safe passage of Soviet Aeroflot flights to and from our country and visit of the Soviet vessel Gruzia to the Long Beach Harbor area.

Reagan's friendly signals to the Soviet athletes, however, included some stipulations. He required that the aircraft "be subject to boarding for Customs and other inspections as a condition for entry to the United States." He also required "US Escort crews for each Aeroflot flight" to "ensure Soviet compliance with all US routing procedures." The *Gruzia* was to be treated as a "commercial . . . not a public vessel" and was to be "subject to boarding and searches at such times as necessary by the Coast Guard or other authorities." In addition, "radio transmission from the *Gruzia* was to be highly prohibited while it was berthed in Long Beach harbor."[28]

On March 14, 1984, Deaver wrote to Ueberroth to deliver the news of NSDD 135. Noting that he was writing on behalf of President Reagan, Deaver reiterated "the United States Government's firm commitment to the complete success of the 1984 Summer Olympic Games to be held in Los Angeles." Deaver was "pleased" to inform Ueberroth "that the United States Government" was "agreeable to a reasonable number of Olympic-related charter flights by the Soviet airline 'Aeroflot' and to the berthing of the Soviet passenger vessel '*Gruzia*' in Long Beach Harbor during the Games."[29]

Even with the stipulations attached to Reagan's decision, it was a significant change in his position regarding matters with the Soviet Union. Many were perplexed by the fact that Reagan, who had built a political career on anti-Soviet rhetoric, had suddenly changed course and become amenable to the requests of the Soviets.

Explaining Reagan's Cold War Reversal

There are several theories as to why Reagan set aside decades of aggressive speech about the Soviet Union in order to make sure the USSR could participate in the 1984 Los Angeles Olympic Games. Historian Robert Edelman argues that the 1984 Olympics were an event that "portrayed the world's most powerful leader as a man of peace." Diplomat John W. Kimball argues that as a "former Governor of California," Reagan would have been remiss if he did anything that "would hurt the Los Angeles effort" to "facilitate the entry of all Olympic participants."[30]

It is also reasonable to conclude that Reagan accepted the Kremlin's requests in order to stay in compliance with the Olympic Charter. His decisions ensured that the Olympic Games remained free of both international affairs and politics. World leaders and governments have historically bent to the will of the International Olympic Committee. During the 1960 Winter Olympics in Squaw Valley, California, for example, the United States allowed athletes from Communist Bloc nations with which it did not have diplomatic ties to enter the country after the International Olympic Committee threatened to withdraw the event from the California ski resort. Even Adolf Hitler, the German dictator, was not impervious to the power of the IOC; he was forced to give his personal assurances that Jewish athletes would be permitted to compete on the German Olympic team at the 1936 Games in Berlin.[31]

These popular explanations for Reagan's decision making will not be disputed here. However, another possible explanation is rooted in Reagan's economic philosophy. As Rick Gruneau and Robert Neubauer argue, Reagan's chief domestic policy goal was to "strengthen economic freedom, on the basis of a conception that feared the political as well as economic consequences of growing governmental controls." To achieve this goal, Reagan slashed the income tax rate in the Economic Recovery Tax Act of 1981, even though it produced a "crippling loss of federal government revenue." By the end of 1981, Reagan's economic measures had "pushed the US economy into the worst recession since the 1930s. . . . Yet, while damning in the eyes of many, the Reagan administration's self-imposed recession and fiscal crisis were essential to consolidating a longer-range neoliberal project" and moving ownership of the national economy out of the government's hands and into the private sector. The Reagan administration desperately needed a "private sector win," and the financial success of the Los Angeles Olympics, a "private enterprise Olympics," would be just that. During the 1984 presidential race between Reagan and Democratic opponent Walter Mondale, it became evident that the success of the Los Angeles Olympic Games as a "form of private enterprise dramatized the available political choices in a populist and highly accessible manner." Thus, for Reagan, a financially successful Los Angeles Olympics would provide "common-sense evidence of the superiority of the private sector over the ability of the government to solve problems and provide important services."[32]

Reagan understood that the Olympic Games could be even more profitable than the LAOOC was predicting if the Soviet Union participated. Fighting the Cold War on athletic fields and in arenas around Los Angeles would undoubtedly increase ticket sales, television viewership, local tourism, and sales of Olympic-related merchandise. Reagan's agreement to all of the Soviets' demands in exchange for their attendance at the Olympics was perhaps a pragmatic decision calculated to bring greater financial success for the 1984 Los Angeles Olympics and thus provide concrete proof that his neoliberal economic agenda could succeed.

The 1984 Los Angeles Olympics, by any measure, were a financial success. Ueberroth, a shrewd and calculating businessman, sold the television rights for the Los Angeles Olympics to ABC for $225 million and netted another $500,000 for the radio rights. Moreover, the existing sporting infrastructure in southern California allowed the LAOOC to operate on a much smaller budget than any other modern Olympic Organizing Committee. Ueberroth used the dormitories at UCLA and USC as the Olympic Village. The biggest cost for facilities involved the construction of a swimming pool and velodrome, both of which were covered by private investors in return for sponsorship and naming rights. Even ancillary events brought in revenue. The Olympic torch relay, for example, netted a $10.9 million sponsorship agreement from AT&T. Interest in supporting the games was so intense that Ueberroth later claimed that he turned away a number of potential sponsors. Shortly after the festival concluded, Ueberroth explained that the event netted a $215 million profit for the LAOOC and noted that "the surplus shocked the world."[33]

In the aftermath of the Los Angeles Olympics, President Reagan began

President Reagan and Nancy Reagan with Nadia Comaneci and Juan Antonio Samaranch during the opening ceremonies of the 1984 Olympic Games. *Courtesy of the Ronald Reagan Library.*

to include references to his neoliberal economic philosophy in his speeches about the Olympics by "drawing analogies between champion athletes and the spirit of American entrepreneurship."[34] Mark Dyreson and Matthew Llewellyn argue that the success of the Los Angeles Olympics restored "American faith in the nation."[35] The financial success of the 1984 Olympics was an indicator that Reagan's aggressive economic policies were beginning to take root and proof to skeptics about his neoliberal agenda that the policy could be successful in America.

In a radio address to the nation on August 18, 194, Reagan spoke of American gymnast Mary Lou Retton who had the "courage and opportunity to work hard." He said that because of her dedication she was able to "not only perform great feats" but also help "pull all of us forward as well." Reagan articulated his belief that the fact that American progress was the result of both "spirit and willingness of the heart" had been largely disregarded in the 1970s. Instead, he said, the "establishment" had been too busy "demanding more power for the government, more bureaucracy" and more spending and taxes. Reagan said that what the country had witnessed at the Olympic Games revealed something "very important about America—we believe in ourselves, we're hungry for real opportunity, and we're up to any challenge." He told his listeners that "America's destiny" was back in their hands and said that if they worked "harder and earn more than before" their reward would be "greater" than it ever was.[36] The analogy between Reagan's neoliberal agenda and the 1984 Olympics was clear: if American citizens worked hard as American athletes and the LAOOC had, they too could find untold amounts of success. Lindsay Parks Pieper argues that the financial success of the LAOOC and the success of US athletes at the Los Angeles Olympics "legitimized" the "neoliberal project in the United States."[37]

In his campaign for reelection in 1984, Reagan continued to draw comparisons between the success of US athletes and the LAOOC to his desire to shift ownership of the American economy to the private sector. At a rally in Hackensack, New Jersey, on October 26, 1984, Reagan said that the "United States was never meant to be a second-best nation" and that "like our Olympic athletes, this nation should set its sights on the stars and go for the gold." Noting that lowering tax rates "led to the best expansion in 30 years," Reagan argued that giving American citizens more control over the direction of the economy would provide American workers the "tools they need" to "outproduce, outcompete, and outsell anyone, anyplace in the world."[38] President Reagan echoed the same message when he spoke to the employees of Westinghouse Furniture Systems in Grand Rapids, Michigan. Reagan argued this his administration's policy of neoliberalism had reversed the "trends that had been building for the few years" prior and "proven the gloom and doomers wrong."[39] Indeed, the "free enterprise" sporting festival that the Los Angeles Olympics represented were "celebrated by conservatives as confirming the values of the Reagan years." America needed to "shoot for the stars, strive for the best" and like the Los Angeles Olympics and American athletes, "go for it."[40]

Conclusion

Reagan's decision to agree to all the Soviet Union's demands in exchange for their potential attendance at the 1984 Los Angeles Olympic Games was surprising, especially in the context of the nation's angry mood after the downing of Korean Airlines Flight 007. In the end, there does not seem to be one singular explanation for Reagan's action. The most salient explanation is likely his pragmatic approach to the presidency in order to achieve his foreign and domestic policy goals. Having the Soviet Union attend would have been powerful propaganda and would have been politically expedient. If he had succeeded in convincing the Soviets to attend the Los Angeles Olympics, the 1984 games would have been even more successful financially than they were. His comments about the success of the Olympics during his campaign for reelection suggest that economic considerations informed his decision to agree to the Soviets' requests vis-à-vis the Olympics. Reagan was interested in portraying the 1984 Olympics as a massively successful private enterprise and using them as evidence of the effectiveness of his neoliberal economic policies.

—CONCLUSION—

Olympic Spectacles in the Next "American Century"

Sport and Nationalism in a Post–Cold War World

BY MARK DYRESON

In the visitor center at Fort McHenry, one of the leading shrines of nationalism in the United States, sport dominates the Cold War sections of the museum displays. Tourists flock to Fort McHenry in urban Baltimore to connect with two of the most powerful symbols of American patriotism—the flag and the national anthem.[1] In 1814, during the Battle of Baltimore, a local lawyer named Francis Scott Key who witnessed the British navy's tenacious shelling of the citadel marveled that after an all-day and all-night assault, dawn revealed the Stars and Stripes still fluttering above the American redoubts.[2]

Scott quickly penned a poem about the US flag flying over Fort McHenry. Its stanzas were liberally sprinkled with language about American democratic values such as "land of the free" and "home of the brave" and martial theatrics such as "rockets' red glare" and "bombs bursting in air." Key gave the verses to his brother-in-law, a Baltimore judge, who set Key's words to the popular tune of a well-known drinking ditty. A few months after the shelling of Fort McHenry, the song, originally titled "The Defence of Fort McHenry" had become the "Star-Spangled Banner." It quickly developed into a staple of Fourth of July festivities and other patriotic events. The US Congress made it the national anthem in 1931, in the midst of the bleakest days of the Great Depression.[3]

Although the original flag that flew over Fort McHenry is now one of the central attractions of the Smithsonian's National Museum of American History in Washington, D.C.,[4] Fort McHenry remains hallowed ground for Americans seeking to explore the roots of their patriotic mythology—the only National Park Service monument that has the designation "Historic Shrine."[5] The small gallery in the visitor center explores the historical development of both the flag and the song as national icons, offering a timeline of the "Stars and Stripes." Sporting images dominate the brief section on Cold War manifestations of the flag and the anthem. In the 1968 entry, the instantly recognizable photograph of Tommy Smith and John Carlos standing in black-gloved protest atop the medal stand at the Mexico City Olympics while the American flag soared and the national anthem swelled depicts a defiant narrative of the tumultuous 1960s.[6]

In the 1980 entry, a large photograph of American flags waving joyously amid the strains of star-spangled triumph as the US Olympic hockey team upsets the heavily favored Soviet squad at the Lake Placid winter games in what has come to be known as "the miracle on ice" sets a different tone.[7] The caption contains one error, however. It reads: "Intense Cold War rivalry between the world's two superpowers is symbolized by their clash in the hockey final of the Winter Olympics. The U.S.A. beats the U.S.S.R. to take the gold." The "miracle" that propelled the underdog Americans over the mighty Soviet hockey machine took place not in the gold medal final but in the second-to-last game of the round-robin tournament that determined the final standings. The United States had to beat Finland a few days later to secure the gold medal. Nevertheless, the larger point, that the "intense Cold War rivalry between the world's two superpowers" was somehow symbolized by what transpired in a hockey game cannot be overshadowed by a misremembered detail at Fort McHenry.[8]

These paired displays of Cold War sport highlight contrasting interpretations of the national flag and the national anthem in American culture during the long struggle with the Soviet empire. During the Cold War, the flag and the anthem were deployed for protest and patriotism, for criticism and celebration. Significantly, it is sport rather than politics or economics or even war that provides the Cold War frames for these public interpretations of American history. As the essays in this volume reveal, sport, particularly international spectacles and especially the Olympic games, served as front lines in the long struggle between the United States and the Union of Soviet Socialist Republics. As the Fort McHenry displays reveal, sport symbolized the fundamental parameters of the Cold War.

This collection adds to a growing list of studies that highlight the power of sport in shaping Cold War culture. During the past decade, many historical works have located sport at the heart of what Americanists have dubbed the cultural Cold War.[9] In chronicling this cultural clash, historians have finally admitted that sport served as one of the main battlefields in the long struggle between the US-led Western Bloc and the Soviet-led Eastern Bloc. A growing catalog of insightful books have made it impossible to teach Cold War history without paying attention to sport. They include Damion Thomas's *Globetrotting: African American Athletes and Cold War Politics*, Thomas Hunt's *Drug Games: The International Olympic Committee and the Politics of Doping, 1960–2008*, Kevin Witherspoon's *Before the Eyes of the World: Mexico and the 1968 Olympic Games*, and Toby Rider's *Cold War Games: Propaganda, the Olympics, and US Foreign Policy*, to name just a few.[10] Sports scholars Robert Edelman and Christopher Young have recently hosted not just one but three sterling international conferences devoted entirely to Cold War sport, in Moscow, New York City, and Cambridge. Three volumes of original essays will soon be published as a result of these conferences, which were sponsored with a grant from the Woodrow Wilson Center.[11]

These projects and others have revealed the central role sport and other cultural developments played in Cold War rivalries. Basketball, blue jeans, and the Bolshoi Ballet were in some ways as significant as spycraft, hydrogen bombs, and proxy wars in understanding the nature and the depth of the struggle between the rival superpowers and their allies. That understanding has taken some time for scholars to recognize, as was the case for those who lived through the Cold War. Indeed, in 1941, Henry Luce, the founder of the Time, Inc. empire who would later become an ardent American Cold Warrior, proclaimed in an essay on the eve of America's entry into World War II that the twentieth century was destined to be the "American Century," presaging the general sentiments of US Cold War ideology. Luce contended that "American jazz, Hollywood movies, American slang, American machines and patented products, are in fact the only things that every community in the world, from Zanzibar to Hamburg, recognizes in common."[12] A decade and a half later, with the Cold War raging, Luce added two other ingredients to that litany of forces that were creating an American-style global village. "We have the H-Bomb, and we have *Sports Illustrated*," Luce boasted in 1954, the year he debuted the magazine that would become a leading American chronicler of American sporting culture. In fact, Luce contended, when people around the world engaged in the "pursuit of happiness," it invariably had "something to do with sport."[13]

Luce's 1954 sermonette on the power of both weapons of mass destruction and sporting habits to Americanize the globe links Cold War ideologies of sport to older traditions in American history. It echoes the bellicose martial and athletic rhetoric of Theodore Roosevelt, who at the beginning of the twentieth century touted US naval power and American dominion in international sporting contests such as the Olympic games as signals that the new century would be dominated by the emergence of the United States as a world power.[14] As the eminent historian of nationalism E. J. Hobsbawm has contended, during the first half of the twentieth century, sport became one of the world's most potent forces for shaping national identities. Hobsbawm ranked sport just behind war in the nationalist toolkit.[15] Historians of Cold War sport have increasingly recognized this longer lineage connecting international sporting contests to the intense nationalism of the decades that preceded the great rivalry that split the globe into Western and Eastern blocs. They find precursors to Cold War trends in Nazi Olympics, heavyweight prizefights, and World Cup soccer matches.

From 1945 to the early 1990s, star-spangled banners and hammer and sickle flags provided symbolic backdrops at Cold War sporting clashes. The Cold War provided rich narratives for framing athletic struggles and shaping interpretations of how what happened in sporting encounters revealed the fundamental dichotomies that divided East and West. The last of the Cold War Olympic games was held in one of the fractious epicenters of the conflict, Seoul, on the divided Korean peninsula, where East and West had long faced off in a seemingly permanent stalemate. In this final episode, the communist regimes seemed to cement their claims to athletic superiority. The Soviet Union won 132 total medals, including 55 golds, while its powerful satellite state, the German Democratic Republic (better known as East Germany), took second place with 102 total medals, 37 of them gold. The US managed only third place, with 94 total medals, 36 of which were gold. Host South Korea finished a distant fourth, with 33 overall medals, including 12 gold. In Olympic venues, the Soviets and their allies appeared poised to create an enduring dominion.[16]

Just a few years later, in 1991, the Cold War abruptly fizzled out as the USSR suddenly evaporated. Without the specter of an antagonistic Soviet empire and its satellites to challenge Americans for global supremacy, the United States entered a post–Cold War universe in which neither miracles on ice nor black-gloved Olympic protests seemed to remain as possibilities around which to weave national narratives. It proved impossible to generate a rivalry against a generic Unified Team, as the strange agglomeration of former Soviet states that competed at the 1992 winter games in Albertville and the 1992 summer games in Barcelona were dubbed. The hammer and sickle disappeared from official ceremonies, replaced by the utilitarian Olympic flag. The "State Anthem of the Soviet Union" was no longer heard at medal ceremonies, replaced by a multitude of anthems of the independent former Soviet republics, heralding victories by Armenian, Azerbaijani, Belarussian, Georgian, Kazak, Kyrgyzstani, Moldovan, Tajik, Turkmen, Ukrainian, and Uzbek Olympic champions.

Even the fact that the Unified Team beat the United States in the number of both gold medals (45 to 37) and overall medals (112 to 108) at Barcelona and finished a close second to a reunified German squad in Albertville (Germany won 10 gold medals and 26 overall medals; the Unified Team won 9 gold and 23 total medals) could not reignite the East-versus-West rivalry that had made Olympic stadiums Cold War battlefields since the end of World War II.[17] Beginning at the 1996 Atlanta Olympics, the United States built a commanding lead (44 gold, 101 total) over their most powerful former Soviet rival, Russia (26 gold, 63 total),[18] while the other former Soviet states scrambled for gold medals far down in the national rankings, behind even Ethiopia.[19] At the Sydney Olympics in 2000, the Russians gave the United States a tussle (the Americans edged the Russians 37 to 32 in gold medals and 93 to 89 in overall medals).[20] Since Sydney, however, the Russians have faded substantially in the standings.[21]

As the former Soviets declined in the Olympic standings, the United States looked for new rivals. Initially, a reunited Germany seemed the mostly likely challenger to the Americans. After East and West Germany reunited in 1990, many athletic experts expected that the Germans would field powerful national teams. East Germany, with a population of less than one-tenth of that of the United States, finished third in the overall medal count at Munich in 1972 and then second and ahead of the United States in Montreal in 1976. It also finished second in Moscow in 1980 (with the United States boycotting) and again at Seoul in 1988. Indeed, the German Democratic Republic earned a well-deserved reputation as both an athletic powerhouse and a bastion of state-sponsored performance enhancement. Combining East Germany's athletic machine with a robust West German program, some observers contended, would make the new Germany a potent threat to US supremacy. After reunification, the regions that had comprised East Germany, which accounted for only 20 percent of the population of reunited Germany, continued to provide far more Olympic medalists than the western regions. In Barcelona in 1992 and Atlanta in 1996, a reenergized German team finished third in the national standings. Since then, however, Germany has managed no better than fifth place in the summer games, although it has done much better at the winter games, finishing first or second in every winter games except Lillehammer in 1994 (where they were third) and Sochi in 2014 (where they were a distant sixth).[22]

Still, a reunified Germany, which is firmly ensconced in the post–Cold War orbit of the West, did not emerge as a consistent rival for the United States. Western powers also have not delivered rivals. Occasionally, a major US ally such as France, Australia, Great Britain, Italy, South Korea, or Japan has cracked the top five in overall medal counts, especially when it has hosted the Olympics. Australia garnered a fourth-place finish when it hosted at Sydney in 2000 and followed up with another fourth place at Athens in 2004. Great Britain finished third when it hosted in London in 2012 and then followed up with a surprising second-place finish at Rio de Janeiro in 2016.[23] Unsurprisingly, the top of the medal standings have come to resemble the Group of Seven (the United States, Canada, Germany, France, Great Britain, Japan, and Italy) or other lists of the leaders that dominate the global economy in the twenty-first century (the G7 plus China, Russia, Brazil, and Australia, for example).[24]

While staunch western allies dominate the pack that distantly trails the United States in post–Cold War Olympics, regimes that are openly hostile to American dominion such as the "Axis of Evil" triumvirate—North Korea, Iran, and Iraq—that President George W. Bush identified in his 2002 State of the Union speech, as well as other thorns in the side of US supremacy such as Libya and Syria have not made a significant mark at the Olympics. One exception to that trend has been Cuba, an Olympic powerhouse during the Cold War and after. Punching far above its weight class, the tiny Caribbean nation ranked as high as fourth and not lower than ninth in the world in a span that begins with the 1976 Montreal games and ends with the 2000 Sydney games (Cuba boycotted the 1984 Los Angeles games and the 1988 Seoul games). Cuban athletes also bested American rivals in head-to-head matchups in sports the United States regards as significant, especially in boxing, baseball, and track and field. Since 2004, however, the Cuban Olympic machine's medal production has fallen dramatically as the collapse of the Soviet empire curtailed the massive aid the USSR once provided for its Cuban ally.[25]

The collapse of the USSR left China in the position of the globe's leading communist power, and the Chinese have emerged in the new world order as the most substantial threat to American hegemony across a wide variety of fronts, including at the Olympics. China came relatively late to the Olympics, sending tiny and unrepresentative teams first to Los Angeles in 1932 and then to Berlin in 1936.[26] After the communists came to power in the civil war that followed World War II, the People's Republic of China sent a one-person squad to Helsinki in 1952 and then dropped out of Olympic competition for several decades, finally reappearing in the 1980 winter games in Lake Placid and then at the summer games in Los Angeles four years later. The world's most populous nation turned in a surprising fourth-place finish in the 1984 medal count and followed that up with a string of solid performances in the 1990s. A decade after the Soviet empire disappeared, China redoubled its Olympic commitments and ignited a rivalry with the United States, moving from a third-place finish in Sydney in 2000 to a second-place finish in Athens in 2004. In 2008, China hosted the Olympics in Beijing and took home the most gold medals, besting the United States by a margin of 51 to 36. In the overall medal count, the United States remained on top with 112 medals to China's 100.[27] In London in 2012, the Chinese team again finished a close second to the United States. In 2016 at Rio, the Chinese fell to third place, behind the United States and Great Britain.[28]

In the post–Cold War Olympics, China has clearly emerged as a replacement for the Soviets as the most significant foil for US teams in international arenas. If the Olympics played a central role in the cultural Cold War that raged between the United States and the USSR, they have served a similar function since the 1990s in framing the emerging economic, political, and social rivalries between the People's Republic and the American republic. The Chinese clearly recognize that they have inherited the old Soviet mantle in Olympic challenges to US hegemony. "'Sports is the only way China can win the culture war,'" argued Chinese Olympic official Wei Jizhong in the midst of the race for the top spot on the medal tables at the 2012 London games.[29]

Four years earlier, when Beijing hosted the Olympics, the Chinese launched a major salvo in the developing Sino-American sporting culture war. In their home games, the Chinese became the first nation other than the United States and the old USSR to top the national gold medal chart since 1936, when Nazi Germany performed the same trick. In Beijing, the Chinese triumphed in the gold medal tabulation while the United States won the total medal count. Both nations claimed Olympic victory based on the medal counts that favored them. The United States stressed the overall count as more significant, while China crowed about its gold medals. American apologists also stressed that US athletes won vastly more medals in events that the world really cared about, such as track and field, swimming, soccer, and basketball. China, the American observers scoffed, won a bounteous share of medals in "judged sports" such as diving and gymnastics, where Beijing's home crowds could intimidate the officials. Another group of American boosters complained that China's "Plan 119," which focused Chinese efforts on medal-rich individual sports that US athletes typically ignored such as archery, rhythmic gymnastics, badminton, canoeing and kayaking, diving, shooting, trampoline gymnastics, table tennis, and weightlifting, amounted to a nefarious scheme to twist the results in China's favor.[30]

American critics contended that not only did China fare poorly in many of the events that the world allegedly considered legitimate tests of national fiber, such as track and field, soccer, basketball, and swimming, but that China's athletes also struggled in the newer action sports that were supposedly the creation of a transnational community of like-minded young people from every region of the world.[31] With the exception of a silver and a bronze at Beijing and a bronze at London in women's beach volleyball, Chinese athletes generally lagged behind in these new and trendy Olympic disciplines—mountain and BMX cycling, triathlon, windsurfing, beach volleyball, and a host of other fashionable winter pastimes that signal the increasing Californization of the Olympics.[32]

The Californization of the Olympics, a pattern in which one particularly attractive version of the American good life has been sold to the world by connecting Olympic sport to lifestyle choices and consumer products, has roots that date back to at least the 1920s, when Americans linked their prowess in Olympic swimming pools to the nation's thriving cultural production industry and marketed the fashions and sentiments of California beach culture to the globe's eager consumers. The Californization of the Olympics surged as the Soviet Empire unraveled. Soviet ideology, far more comfortable with the Spartan austerity of biathlon, the wintertime display of prowess in cross-country skiing and rifle marksmanship, than with the glitz and mercantilism of snowboarding, was no longer an impediment to American interest groups who beginning in the 1990s vastly expanded the footprint of Californization with the blessing of the profit-seeking International Olympic Committee.[33]

In all probability, the incorporation of a host of new and telegenic adventure sports with roots in California and deep connections to American consumer culture would have met considerably stiffer resistance from the Soviets and their allies if the USSR had not collapsed and the Cold War had continued. Indeed, instead of decrying these new Olympian entertainments as scourges of bourgeois commerce, China, a communist polity deeply enmeshed in the new global capitalism that has thrived since the 1990s, has manufactured BMX cycles and mountain bikes and has sold them not only to western customers but also to its own burgeoning market of consumers.

Chinese Olympic BMX riders and mountain bikers signal the eagerness of the regime to embrace global markets and the radical shifts in ideology regarding consumerism that have taken place since the end of the Cold War.[34]

In comparison with the Soviet Union, China has not proven to be a stalwart resistor to Californization or other forms of Americanization at the Olympics. Nor, despite their golden moment in 2008 at Beijing, have the Chinese yet proven to be an adversary that can consistently defeat American teams in overall medal counts. They have not matched the Cold War–era Soviet squads that from 1952, when the USSR made its Olympic debut, to 1988, the last time the Soviets fielded an Olympic team, won 1,007 overall medals and 393 gold medals in summer and winter games to clearly surpass the US total of 774 overall medals and 315 golds.[35] Since the end of the Cold War, China has won 221 gold medals and 562 overall medals at summer and winter Olympic games.[36] In that same span, the United States has won 374 gold medals and 999 overall medals.[37] In the post–Cold War Olympic universe, as in so many other arenas, the United States stands as the lone global super power.

Fort McHenry's "Stars and Stripes" timeline of nationalism uses another illustration from the Olympics to signal this new American dominion. It features a Baltimorean who was born in 1985, just six years before the Cold War abruptly faded. An image of Michael Phelps on the medal stand at the 2008 Beijing games against a backdrop of the national flag, bejeweled by one of the multitude of gold medals he won, dominates the post–Cold War display. The use of Phelps's victorious visage to illustrate nationalism in US culture in the post–Cold War world clearly highlights the distance between the time of "Miracles on Ice" and the era after the Soviet empire crumbled. No longer did plucky American underdogs occasionally upset Soviet athletic machines. In a new world with just one remaining superpower, the United States seemed entirely unbeatable, as close to omnipotent in Olympic arenas and on world stages as a human organization could become.[38]

On one level, the achievements of Michael Phelps signify the power of the United States in a world without true rivals. Phelps made his Olympic debut at the Sydney games in the summer of 2000, nearly a decade after the Soviet Union had disappeared from the Olympic stage. At the age of fifteen, Phelps did not manage to reach the medal stand. Over the next four Olympics, at Athens in 2004, Beijing in 2008, London in 2012, and Rio de Janeiro in 2016, he became the medal-winningest Olympian of all time, hauling in an incredible 28 medals—including an astonishing 23 golds and 3 silvers and 2 bronzes. Phelps's victories made him a global icon and a local and national patriotic hero, as his inclusion on Fort McHenry's timeline of nationalism signifies.[39]

Phelps symbolized the United States in a post–Cold War era in which the super power of which he was a citizen towered over all other nations. In fact, so monumental were Phelps's accomplishments that when he announced his retirement after the Rio Olympics, an astonished media corps could not muster individual comparisons to put his career in perspective. Instead, it launched a series of comparisons as if the "Baltimore Bullet" were a nation in and of himself. The press gushed that the nation of Phelps, rendered variously as the "Republic of Phelps" and "Phelpsphanistan," ranked somewhere from 32nd to 38th (some counted total medals, some just the golds) in the all-time Olympic rank since the world began counting at the inaugural 1896 games. Most of the stories in this vein put Phelps alongside South Africa and Brazil, regular Olympic powers, and ahead of such nations as Argentina, Mexico, India, and even sprinting sensation Jamaica (and Usain Bolt, a triple gold medalist in three consecutive Olympics, 2008, 2012, and 2016).[40]

In the history of Olympic swimming, Phelps had all by himself won more medals than such Olympic aquatic luminaries as the Netherlands, Japan, Germany, and Great Britain. All by himself, Phelps had won more medals in swimming than the old Soviet Union, the former great rival to the United States, whom Phelps had never actually faced in the pool, although he had taken on a few Russians. Counting Phelps's total of golds in his four medal-winning games from 2004 to 2016, the American prodigy ranked 13th in the world, ahead of such solid Olympic performers as Spain, Brazil, Norway, Canada, Sweden, Cuba, Greece, Romania and the Netherlands. Put another way, the "Republic of Phelps" finished 16th in the national totals at Athens in 2004, 10th in Beijing in 2008, 20th in London in 2008, and 19th in Rio de Janeiro in 2016.[41]

When he returned to racing in 2017, Phelps apparently could not find a suitable human challenger. Having conquered a Sovietless world, Phelps had moved on to better competition. He ended up pitted against a great white shark as the lead feature in the Discovery Channel's wildly popular program *Shark Week*. In fact, Phelps raced a CGI version of the fearsome beast, much to the chagrin of some viewers who apparently thought Phelps was actually going to get in the water with the relentless predator.[42] Although the "Republic of Phelps" failed to earn a gold in the cross-species Olympics Hollywood staged, he will be cashing in for decades as a global icon of consumerism, much as his fellow American swimmer and wrestler of alligators Johnny Weissmuller did nearly a century ago as Hollywood's original Tarzan. Phelps is the latest example of the Californization of the Olympics; he has translated his global swimming fame into new material for the American entertainment industry. Though he has yet to relocate to California (he lives in Phoenix and helps Bob Bowman, his former club coach, in the swim program at Arizona State University), he has married a former Miss California and seems destined to spend more time in the dream factories of Hollywood starring with Great Whites and other creatures.[43]

The post–Cold War Olympics have continued to provide stages for American teams to craft narratives about American exceptionalism and project images to dazzle the rest of the world. Older scripts that celebrate melting pots and immigrants as sources of American dynamism have been reanimated to suit twenty-first-century sensibilities, as in the celebrations of Mexican Americans and African Americans winning winter gold in Salt Lake City in 2002 and the honoring of Sudanese immigrant Lopez Lomong with flag-bearer duties at the opening ceremonies of the 2008 Beijing games. The Olympic games also continue to serve as forums for attempts to promote American racial reconciliation and equality, from the legendary Muhammad Ali's starring role in lighting the flame at the 1996 Atlanta games to multiple-gold-medal-winning gymnast Simone Biles carrying the Stars and Stripes at the closing ceremonies of the 2016 Rio de Janeiro games. In addition, the Olympics continue to provide opportunities to celebrate the achievements of American women, as in 2012 when the media highlighted the fortieth anniversary of Title IX by stressing that female athletes earned significantly more medals than male athletes as the United States once again ranked at the top of the national performance lists.[44]

The post–Cold War Olympics no longer have national rivals for the United States that truly threaten the historic claims Americans have made that victory in medal tabulations at Olympic venues translates into proof of American superiority in the world. Without the Soviets and their East German confederates to challenge American claims, Michael Phelps is left to challenge great white sharks in CGI spectacles. The United States seems destined to continue abundant medal hauls, but a repeat of the miracle on ice seems an unlikely prospect as the Olympics continue into their second century.

Notes

Introduction: Sport and American Cold War Culture

1. George Orwell, "You and the Atomic Bomb," *Tribune*, October 19, 1945, Orwell's italics.

2. Daniel Yergin, *Shattered Peace: The Origins of the Cold War and the National Security State* (Boston: Houghton Mifflin Company, 1977).

3. Joseph M. Jones, *The Fifteen Weeks* (New York: Viking Press, 1955), 141.

4. Kenneth Osgood, *Total Cold War: Eisenhower's Secret Propaganda Battle at Home and Abroad* (Lawrence: University Press of Kansas, 2006), 2. See also Walter L. Hixson, *Parting the Curtain: Propaganda, Culture, and the Cold* War (New York: St. Martin's Press, 1997); Hans Krabbendam and Giles Scott-Smith, eds., *The Cultural Cold War in Western Europe, 1945–1960* (London: Frank Cass Publishers, 2003); Frances Stoner Saunders, *Who Paid the Piper? The CIA and the Cultural Cold* War (London: Granta Books, 1999); David Caute, *The Dancer Defects: The Struggle for Cultural Supremacy during the Cold War* (Oxford: Oxford University Press, 2003); and Reinhold Wagnleitner, *Coca-Colonization and the Cold War: The Cultural Mission of the United States in Austria after the Second World* War (Chapel Hill: University of North Carolina Press, 1994).

5. John F. Kennedy, "A Bold Proposal for American Sport," *Sports Illustrated*, July 27, 1964, 13.

6. David B. Kanin, "Superpower Sport in Cold War and 'Détente,'" in *Sport and International Relations*, edited by B. Lowe, D. B. Kanin, and A. Strenk (Champaign, Ill.: Stipes Publishing Company, 1978), 249–262; Stephen Wagg and David L. Andrews, "Introduction: War Minus the Shooting," in *East Plays West: Sport and the Cold War*, edited by Stephen Wagg and David L. Andrews (New York: Routledge, 2007), 19.

7. Barbara Keys, *Globalizing Sport: National Rivalry and International Community in the 1930s* (Cambridge, Mass.: Harvard University Press, 2006).

8. For more on sport in the Soviet Union after 1945, see Jenifer Parks, *Red Sport, Red Tape: The Olympic Games, the Soviet Sports Bureaucracy, and the Cold War* (Lanham, Md.: Lexington Books, 2017). For studies of sport in Eastern European communist countries, see the special issue of *International Journal of the History of Sport* 26, no. 4 (2009).

9. For more on these anxieties, see Joseph Turrini, *The End of Amateurism in American Track and Field* (Urbana: University of Illinois Press, 2010); and Erin Redihan, *The Olympics and the Cold War, 1948–1968: Sport as Battleground in the US–Soviet Rivalry* (Jefferson, N.C.: McFarland & Company, 2017).

10. Odd Arne Westad, *The Global Cold War: Third World Interventions and the Making of Our Times* (Cambridge: Cambridge University Press, 2005).

11. Melvyn P. Leffler, "The Emergence of an American Grand Strategy, 1945–1952," in *The Cambridge History of the Cold War*, vol. 1, *Origins*, edited by Melvin P. Leffler and Odd Arne Westad (Cambridge: Cambridge University Press, 2010), 68–72.

12. Joseph S. Nye, "Public Diplomacy and Soft Power," *Annals of the American Academy of Political and Social Science* 616 (March 2008): 94–109.

13. The best study on this is Nicholas Evan Sarantakes, *Dropping the Torch: Jimmy Carter, the Olympic Boycott, and the Cold War* (New York: Cambridge University Press, 2011).

14. See Roy Clumpner, "Federal Involvement in Sport to Promote American Interest or Foreign Policy Objectives, 1950–1973," in *Sport and International Relations*, edited by B. Lowe, D. B. Kanin, and A. Strenk (Champaign, Ill.: Stipes Publishing Company, 1978), 400–452; Thomas M. Domer, "Sport in Cold War America, 1953–1963: The Diplomatic and Political Use of Sport in the Eisenhower and Kennedy Administrations" (PhD diss., Marquette University, 1976); Thomas M. Hunt, "American Sport Policy and the Cultural Cold War: The Lyndon B. Johnson Presidential Years," *Journal of Sport History* 33, no. 3 (2006): 273–297; Nicholas Evan Sarantakes, "Moscow versus Los Angeles: The Nixon White House Wages Cold War in the Olympic Selection Process," *Cold War History* 9, no. 1 (2009): 135–157; Harold E. Wilson Jr., "The Golden Opportunity: Romania's Political Manipulation of the 1984 Los Angles Olympic Games," *Olympika* 3 (1994): 83–97; Brad J. Congelio, "Reagan's Rapprochement: A Brief Analysis of the Reagan Administration and the 1984 Olympics," *Journal of Olympic History* 21, no. 3 (2013): 46–50; Toby C. Rider, *Cold War Games: Propaganda, the Olympics, and US Foreign Policy* (Urbana: University of Illinois Press, 2016); Toby C. Rider, "Filling the Information Gap: Radio Free Europe-Radio Liberty and the Politics of Accreditation at the 1984 Los Angeles Olympic Games," *International Journal of the History of Sport* 32, no. 1 (2015): 37–52; Damion Thomas, *Globetrotting: African American Athletes and Cold War Politics* (Urbana: University of Illinois Press, 2012); Kevin B. Witherspoon, "Going 'to the Fountainhead': Black American Athletes as Cultural Ambassadors in Africa, 1970–1971," *International Journal of the History of Sport* 30, no. 13 (2013): 1508–1522; and Kevin B. Witherspoon, "'Fuzz Kids' and 'Musclemen': The US-Soviet Basketball Rivalry, 1958–1975," in *Diplomatic Games: Sport, Statecraft, and International Relations Since 1945*, edited by Heather L. Dichter and Andrew L. Johns (Lexington: University Press of Kentucky, 2014), 297–326.

15. Rider, *Cold War Games*. For more on this cooperative "state-private network," see Scott Lucas, "Beyond Freedom, Beyond Control: Approaches to Culture and the State-Private Network in the Cold War," *Intelligence and National Security* 18, no. 2 (2003): 53–72.

16. See Stephen J. Whitfield, *The Culture of the Cold War* (Baltimore, Maryland: The John's Hopkins Press, 1991).

17. Tony Shaw and Denise Youngblood, "The Cinematic Cold War," *Sport in the Cold War*, podcast episode 1, accessed March 16, 2017, http://digitalarchive.wilson-center.org/resource/sport-in-the-cold-war/episode-01-the-cinematic-cold-war; Russ Crawford, *The Use of Sports to Promote the American Way of Life during the Cold War: Cultural Propaganda, 1945–1963* (Lewiston, N.Y.: Edwin Mellen Press,

2009); John Massaro, "Press Box Propaganda? The Cold War and *Sports Illustrated*, 1956," *Journal of American Culture* 26, no. 3 (2003): 361–370.

1. Projecting America

1. John N. Washburn, "Sport as a Soviet Tool," *Foreign Affairs* 34, no. 3 (1956): 490–499.

2. Sport-related propaganda produced by the US government is mentioned briefly in Kenneth A. Osgood, *Total Cold War: Eisenhower's Secret Propaganda Battle at Home and Abroad* (Lawrence: University Press of Kansas, 2006), 263–264; and Walter L. Hixson, *Parting the Curtain: Propaganda, Culture, and the Cold War* (New York: St. Martin's Press, 1997), 136.

3. These themes include race relations, gender, religious freedom, the family, and capitalism. For more on the themes of US propaganda, see Laura A. Belmonte, *Selling the American Way: US Propaganda and the Cold War* (Philadelphia: University of Pennsylvania Press, 2008.)

4. Laura A. Belmonte, "Exporting America: The US Propaganda Offensive, 1945–1959," in *The Arts of Democracy: Art, Public Culture, and the State*, edited by Casey Nelson Blake (Philadelphia: University of Pennsylvania Press, 2007), 123. The US government defined propaganda, or information, as "any organized effort or movement to disseminate information or a particular doctrine by means of news, special arguments or appeals designed to influence the thoughts and actions of any given group." Quoted in Frances Stoner Saunders, *Who Paid the Piper? The CIA and the Cultural Cold War* (London: Granta Books, 1999), 4.

5. See Heather L. Dichter and Andrew L. Johns, eds., *Diplomatic Games: Sport, Statecraft, and International Relations since 1945* (Lexington: University Press of Kentucky, 2014).

6. Hixson, *Parting the Curtain*, 10–11; Nicholas J. Cull, *The Cold War and the United States Information Agency: American Propaganda and Public Diplomacy, 1945–1989* (Cambridge: Cambridge University Press, 2008).

7. "The Kremlin's Intensified Campaign in the Field of Cultural Affairs," *Department of State Bulletin*, December 3, 1951, 903.

8. Alfred Dick Sander, *Eisenhower's Executive Office* (Westport, Conn.: Greenwood Press, 1999).

9. "The Soviet Athlete in International Competition," *Department of State Bulletin*, December 24, 1951, 1007–1010.

10. Quote in "Soviet Paper Links Sports in US To War," *New York Times*, September 21, 1949, 4. For examples of government officials commenting on Soviet accusations about American sport, see George Kennan to Secretary of State, July 18, 1952, Box 5167, 861.4531/7-1852, Central Decimal Files, 1950–54, Department of State Central Files (hereafter RG 59), National Archives and Records Administration (hereafter NARA), College Park, Maryland; and McSweeney to Department of State, February 15, 1952, Box 4371, 800.4531/2-1552, Central Decimal Files, 1950–54, RG 59, NARA.

11. "Evidence of Professionalism in Soviet Sports," June 16, 1955, Box 2, "Intelligence Bulletins, Memorandums and Summaries, 1954–56," Office of Research and Intelligence, Record Group 306, Records of the United States Information Service (hereafter RG 306), NARA.

12. Toby C. Rider, *Cold War Games: Propaganda, the Olympics, and US Foreign Policy* (Urbana: University of Illinois Press, 2016), 3–4.

13. Damion L. Thomas, *Globetrotting: African American Athletes and Cold War Politics* (Urbana: University of Illinois Press, 2012), 90–93.

14. Rider, *Cold War Games*, 157, 166.

15. "Use of Sports Subjects in USIE Output," n.d., Box 4371, 800.4531/10–351, RG 59, Central Decimal File, 1950–54, NARA.

16. Belmonte, "Exporting America," 126.

17. For more on early attitudes toward sport in the United States, see Mark Dyreson, *Making the American Team: Sport, Culture, and the Olympic Experience* (Urbana: University of Illinois Press, 1998).

18. See "US President Dwight D. Eisenhower Ardent Golfer," Box 26, "#28: USIS Sports Packet, October 1956," Feature Packets with Recurring Subjects, 1953–59, RG 306, NARA.

19. "World Series," *Air Bulletin*, September 2, 1947, Box 1, "Department of State Air Bulletin," USIS Feature Via Airmail Thru World Affairs Bulletin, RG 306, NARA.

20. "National Pastime," *Air Bulletin*, April 5, 1948, Box 1, "Department of State Air Bulletin," USIS Feature Via Airmail Thru World Affairs Bulletin, RG 306, NARA.

21. "Foreign Sports in the United States," 1951, Box 5, Movie Scripts, 1942–1965, RG 306, NARA.

22. "Soccer Gains Popularity in the United States," *USIS Feature*, March 20, 1952, Box 3, (1) "USIS Features Via Airmail," USIS Feature Via Airmail Thru World Affairs Bulletin, RG 306, NARA.

23. T. L. Barnard to Dunning, Morris, Edwards, Kohler, LaBlonde, and Johnson, n.d., Box 4371, 800.4531/10–351, Central Decimal Files, 1950–54, RG 59, NARA.

24. "Punches for Charity," Box 25, "#2: USIS Sports Packet, July 1954," Feature Packets with Recurring Subjects, 1953–59, RG 306, NARA.

25. See "Interim Report: Consideration of US Position in Connection with 1956 Olympic Games," April 17, 1956, Box 112, (3) "OCB 353.8 (Amusements and Athletics) June 1954–April 1956," White House Office, National Security Council Staff: Papers, 1948–61 (hereafter WHO NSC Papers), OCB Central File Series, Dwight D. Eisenhower Presidential Library (hereafter DDEL), Abilene, Kansas.

26. "Olympic Code Requires Athletes to Have Amateur Standing," *USIS Feature*, April 3, 1952, Box 3, (1) "USIS Features Via Airmail," USIS Feature Via Airmail Thru World Affairs Bulletin, RG 306, NARA.

27. For a discussion of policy, see "Interim Report: Consideration of US Position in Connection with 1956 Olympic Games"; and Osgood, *Total Cold War*, 255–257.

28. "Comments with Regard to Soviet and Satellite Participation in the Olympic Games," appended to Walter Stoessel to Department of State, July 10, 1952, Box 4372, 800.4531/7-1052, Central Decimal Files, 1950–54, RG 59, NARA; and Laura A. Belmonte, "A Family Affair? Gender, the US Information Agency, and Cold War Ideology, 1945–1960," in *Culture and International History*, edited by Jessica C. E. Gienow-Hecht and Frank Schumacher (New York: Berghahn Books, 2003), 83, 85.

29. See the cartoon drawing of Karl Schwenzfeier in Box 25, "#24: USIS Sports Packet, June 1956," Feature Packets with Recurring Subjects, 1953–59, RG 306, NARA.

30. "The Reverend Robert E. Richards US Pole-Vaulter," *USIS Feature*, February 28, 1952, Box 3, (2) "USIS Features Via Airmail," USIS Feature Via Airmail Thru World

Affairs Bulletin, RG 306, NARA; "Mermaid with Stamina," Box 25, "#2: USIS Sports Packet, July 1954," Feature Packets with Recurring Subjects, 1953–59, RG 306, NARA; Belmonte, "Exporting America," 131.

31. Andrew L. Yarrow, "Selling a New Vision of America to the World: Changing Messages in Early US Cold War Print Propaganda," *Journal of Cold War Studies* 11, no. 4 (2009): 31–40.

32. "Sport of Sailing Enjoyed by Thousands in the United States," *USA Life Bulletin*, October 31, 1951, Box 2, (2) "USA Life Bulletin," USIS Feature Via Airmail Thru World Affairs Bulletin, RG 306, NARA.

33. "US Now Has 5,358 Golf Courses," Box 27, "#31: USIS Sports Packet, June 1957," Feature Packets with Recurring Subjects, 1953–59, RG 306, NARA.

34. Quoted in Saunders, *Who Paid the Piper?* 289.

35. "'Jersey Joe' Walcott, Heavyweight Boxing Champion," *USA. Life Bulletin*, August 22, 1951, Box 2, (2) "USA Life Bulletin," USIS Feature Via Airmail Thru World Affairs Bulletin, RG 306, NARA.

36. For more on race and US propaganda, see Osgood, *Total Cold War*, 275–285.

37. "Major Sammy Lee Voted Outstanding US Amateur Athlete of 1953" (note to public affairs officer), Box 2, "#13: USIS Special Youth Packet, April 1954," Feature Packets with Recurring Subjects, 1953–59, RG 306, NARA. For more on racial discrimination and sport in America, see David K. Wiggins, "'Black Athletes in White Men's Games': Race, Sport, and American National Pastimes," *International Journal of the History of Sport* 31, no. 12 (2014): 181–202.

38. "The American Negro in Baseball," Box 1, "#4: USIS Special Youth Packet, July 1956," Feature Packets with Recurring Subjects, 1953–59, RG 306, NARA.

39. For more on gender and US propaganda, see Belmonte, "A Family Affair?" 83; and David J. Snyder, "Domesticity, Rearmament, and the Limits of US Public Diplomacy in the Netherlands during the Early Cold War," *Journal of Cold War Studies* 15, no. 3 (2013): 47–75.

40. "Carol Heiss Aims for World Figure Skating Title," Box 25, "#19: USIS Sports Packet, January 1956," Feature Packets with Recurring Subjects, 1953–59, RG 306, NARA. See also Ashley Brown, "Swinging for the State Department: American Women Tennis Players in Diplomatic Goodwill Tours, 194159," *Journal of Sport History* 42, no. 3 (2015): 289–309.

41. "Sam Fox Sparks Basketball Interest in Turkey," Box 25, "#19: USIS Sports Packet, February 1956," Feature Packets with Recurring Subjects, 1953–59, RG 306, NARA.

42. Harold L. Howland to Frank Dennis, March 28, 1956, Box 112, (3) "OCB 353.8," OCB Central File Series, WHO NSC Papers, DDEL.

43. See for instance, Armin Meyer to Department of State, January 18, 1955, Box 93, File 8, Bureau of Educational and Cultural Affairs Historical Collection, University of Arkansas, Fayetteville, Arkansas (hereafter BECAHC); Gene Karst to Department of State, June 25, 1956, Box 92, File 14, BECAHC.

44. "A.A.U. Tours Gain Praise from State Dept. Official," *Amateur Athlete* 29, no. 1 (1958): 9.

45. See Ralph Block to Richard Walsh, November 19, 1951, "Private Enterprise Cooperation, 1952–53," Box 4, Office of Administration, 1952–55, RG 306, NARA.

46. "Swimming Prospects for the 1952 Olympics," *USIS Feature*, June 12, 1952,

Box 3, (2) "USIS Features Via Airmail," USIS Feature Via Airmail Thru World Affairs Bulletin, RG 306, NARA.

47. "The United State Prepares for the 1952 Olympic Games," *USA Life Bulletin*, December 5, 1951, Box 2, (2) "USA Life Bulletin," USIS Feature Via Airmail Thru World Affairs Bulletin, RG 306, NARA.

48. Rider, *Cold War Games*, 6–7.

49. George V. Allen to All Principle USIS Posts, January 4, 1960, Box 2239, 800.4531/1-460, Central Decimal Files, 1960–63, RG 59, NARA. For the book, see John V. Grombach, *Olympic Cavalcade of Sports* (New York: Ballantine Books, 1956). Interestingly, Grombach was head of POND, a secret US Army intelligence unit, during World War II. See Peter Grose, *Operation Rollback: America's Secret War behind the Iron Curtain* (New York: Houghton Mifflin Company, 2000), 42.

50. "Interim Report: Consideration of US Position in Connection with 1956 Olympic Games."

51. "The Soviet Athlete in International Competition," *Department of State Bulletin*, December 24, 1951, 1007.

52. "Terms of Reference for OCB Working Group on 1956 Olympics," February 20, 1956, Box 112, (2) "OCB 353.8," OCB Central File Series, WHO NSC Papers, DDEL.

53. "Principles to Assure Coordination of Gray Activities," May 14, 1954, in *United States Declassified Documents Reference System* (Woodbridge, CT, 1992), document number 486.

54. W. J. Convery Egan to Department of State, May 21, 1951, Box 5252, 862A.453/5-2151, Central Decimal Files, 1950–54, RG 59, NARA.

55. "Sport behind the Iron Curtain," 4–5, September 1955, FO 975/82, Foreign Office: Information Research Department: Information Reports, Public Record Office: The National Archives, Kew, England; "Olympics 1956," November 4, 1955, Box 112, (1) "OCB 353.8," OCB Central File Series, WHO NSC Papers, DDEL.

56. "Hungarian Athlete Tells of Treatment behind Iron Curtain," Box 25, "#17: USIS Sports Packet, November 1955," Feature Packets with Recurring Subjects, 1953–59, RG 306, NARA. Interestingly, doping was not a prevalent theme in US propaganda. Although performance-enhancing drugs were being widely used in the 1950s, the issue had not yet erupted in the global sport community. In the final decades of the Cold War, however, western critics accused the communists of doping when, in fact, it was practiced by athletes in many western countries, including the United States. See Paul Dimeo, *A History of Drug Use in Sport: Beyond Good and Evil* (London: Routledge, 2007), 87–104.

57. "Polish Refugee Track Performer Draws Attention of US Sports Fans," Box 27, "#36: USIS Sports Packet, June 1957," Feature Packets with Recurring Subjects, 1953–59, RG 306, NARA.

58. For more on the challenges of assessing the effectiveness of US propaganda, see Osgood, *Total Cold War*, 9–10.

59. Driver to USIA, April 10, 1956, Box 12, "Olympics–1956," Office of Research and Intelligence, Headquarter Subject Files, 1955–70, RG 306, NARA.

60. William Bourne to Mr. Berding, September 30, 1954, Box 112, (1) "OCB 353.8," OCB Central File Series, WHO NSC Papers, DDEL.

61. Weathersby to USIA, April 11, 1956, Box 12, "Olympics–1956," Office of Research and Intelligence, Headquarter Subject Files, 1955–70, RG 306, NARA.

62. "Conclusions and Recommendations of the President's Committee on Information Activities Abroad–Chapter VI," December 1960, in *United States Declassified Documents Reference System* (Woodbridge, CT, 1990), document number 2216.

2. From Football to the Blacklist

1. Val Adams, "Bill Cosby of 'I Spy' Wins TV Emmy," *New York Times*, May 23, 1966, 68.
2. Adams, "Bill Cosby of 'I Spy' Wins TV Emmy." In a piece Lampell wrote for the *New York Times* almost two months later, he claimed that his line was, "I think I ought to mention I was blacklisted for ten years." See Millard Lampell, "I Think I Ought to Mention I Was Blacklisted," *New York Times*, August 21, 1966, 109.
3. Adams, "Bill Cosby of 'I Spy' Wins TV Emmy," 68.
4. Lampell, "I Think I Ought to Mention I Was Blacklisted."
5. Lampell, "I Think I Ought to Mention I Was Blacklisted." A good source for Lampell's connection with the Communist Party USA is Ronald D. Cohen, "Millard Lampell: Blacklisted," *American Communist History* 9, no. 3 (2010): 293–313.
6. Lampell, "I Think I Ought to Mention I Was Blacklisted."
7. Jon Pareles, "Millard Lampell, 78, Writer and Supporter of Causes, Dies," *New York Times*, October 11, 1997, B7.
8. For a study of the influence of the 1934 Production Code on the motion picture industry, see Thomas Doherty, *Pre-Code Hollywood: Sex, Immorality, and Insurrection in American Cinema, 1930*–1934 (New York: Columbia University Press, 1999); and Thomas Doherty, *Hollywood Censor: Joseph I. Breen and the Production Code Administration* (New York: Columbia University Press, 2007).
9. Cohen, "Millard Lampell," 302.
10. For a study of John R. Tunis's works, see Michael Oriard, *King Football: Sport and Spectacle in the Golden Age of Radio and Newsreels, Movies and Magazines, the Weekly and the Daily Press* (Chapel Hill: University of North Carolina Press, 2001), 109–110.
11. For a study of Francis Wallace's attacks on college football, see Oriard, *King Football*, 111–119, 129.
12. In *King Football*, 155, Oriard briefly mentions Reeve's "The Pigskin Heart."
13. Robert Penn Warren's 1946 novel *All the King's Men* is based on the life of Louisiana governor Huey P. Long, a politician who closely associated himself with Louisiana State University football and a man who bears some similarity to T.C. McCabe. The best nonfiction account of Long's political career is Richard D. White Jr., *Kingfish: The Reign of Huey P. Long* (New York: Random House, 2006).
14. Earl H. Blaik with Tim Cohane, *You Have to Pay the Price* (New York: Holt, Rinehart and Winston, 1960), 312.
15. See Michael Oriard, *Reading Football: How the Popular Press Created an American Spectacle* (Chapel Hill: University of North Carolina Press, 1993), 191–192.
16. Kurt Edward Kemper, *College Football and American Culture in the Cold War Era* (Urbana: University of Illinois Press, 2009), 27.
17. See Oriard, *King Football*, 155–156.
18. Kemper, *College Football*, 40–41. Also see Oriard, *King Football*, 146–153;

Murray Sperber, *Shake Down the Thunder: The Creation of Notre Dame Football* (New York: Henry Holt, 1993), 464–483; and Murray Sperber, *Onward to Victory: The Crises that Shaped College Sports* (New York: Henry Holt, 1998), especially Part 3, "Knute Rockne—All-American: American Myths and College Sports" and Part 2, "The Best Defense Is a Good Offense."

19. Oriard, *King Football*, 153.

20. Bosley Crowther, "College Football Is 'Exposed' in *Saturday's Hero*," *New York Times*, September 12, 1951, 37.

21. Sperber, *Onward to Victory*, 137–146.

22. Crowther, "College Football Is 'Exposed' in *Saturday's Hero*."

23. Quoted from Susan Doll, "Saturday's Hero," film article, TCM, n.d., accessed November 10, 2016, http://www.tcm.com/this-month/article.html?isPreview=&id=296744%7C296753&name=Saturday-s-Hero.

24. For an account of Larry Doby's life in Paterson, New Jersey, see Thomas Moore, *Pride Against Prejudice: The Biography of Larry Doby* (Westport, Conn.: Greenwood, 1998).

25. Cohen, "Millard Lampell," 295.

26. Pareles. "Millard Lampell, 78, Writer and Supporter of Causes, Dies."

27. Cohen, "Millard Lampell," 295.

28. Mike Landon [Millard Lampell], "Is There a Fuhrer in the House?" *The New Republic*, August 12, 1940, 212–213.

29. Millard Lampell, "Not So Free Election," *The New Republic*, October 21, 1940, 549.

30. Cohen, "Millard Lampell," 295.

31. Lampell quoted in Cohen, "Millard Lampell," 295–296.

32. Cohen, "Millard Lampell," 296.

33. Michael Denning, *The Cultural Front: The Laboring of American Culture in the Twentieth Century* (London: Verso, 1996), xvii–xviii. Also see Rachel Clare Donaldson, *I Hear America Singing* (Philadelphia: Temple University Press, 2014), 38–39.

34. Doherty, *Hollywood's Censor*, 167.

35. Lee Hays quoted in Donaldson, *I Hear America Singing*, 79.

36. Lampell, "I Think I Ought to Mention I Was Blacklisted."

37. Lampell, "I Think I Ought to Mention I Was Blacklisted." For a thorough study of the Almanac Singers, see Cohen, "Millard Lampell"; and Donaldson, *I Hear America Singing*.

38. Bess Lomax quoted in Cohen, "Millard Lampell," 296.

39. Many of the lyrics Lampell wrote for the Almanac Singers can be found online. See "The Songs of the Almanac Singers," www.woodyguthrie.de/Almanac.html; "Ballad of October 16th (Millard Lampell)," www.folkarchive.de/oct16.html; and "Millard Lampell Lyrics," awww.lyricsondemand.com/m/millard lampelllyrics/.

40. See Edward Ericson, "Karl Schnurre and the Evolution of Nazi-Soviet Relations, 1936–1941," *German Studies Review* 21, no. 2 (1998): 263–283.

41. Cohen, "Millard Lampell," 296. In *Where Have All the Flowers Gone: A Musical Autobiography* (Bethlehem, Pa.: Sing Out, 1997), Pete Seeger remembers the show airing in January 1942.

42. Quoted in Cohen, "Millard Lampell," 297.
43. See Seeger, *Where Have All the Flowers Gone*, 28.
44. Lampell quoted in Cohen, "Millard Lampell," 298.
45. Quoted in Nancy Lynn Schwartz, *The Hollywood Writers' War* (New York: Knopf, 1982), 136.
46. Schwartz, *The Hollywood Writers' War*, 137.
47. Thomas F. Brady, "*Long Way Home* Bought for Film," *New York Times*, November 1, 1947, 11.
48. Ted Morgan, *McCarthyism in Twentieth-Century America* (New York: Random House, 2003), 328–330.
49. Schwartz, *The Hollywood Writers' War*, 280–281.
50. Cohen, "Millard Lampell," 300.
51. Clarence Woodbury, "Can You Spot a Communist?" *American Magazine* 152 (September 1951): 34–35, 112–116, 118. For a discussion of the radio and television shows, see Thomas Patrick Doherty, *Cold War, Cool Medium: Television, McCarthyism, and American Culture* (New York: Columbia University Press, 2003), 142–148.
52. C. P. Trussell, "McCarran Inquiry Unit Says Reds Control Radio Guild," *New York Times*, August 28, 1952, 1.
53. Lampell, "I Think I Ought to Mention I Was Blacklisted."
54. Millard Lampell, *The Hero* (New York: Julian Messner, 1949), 4.
55. Lampell, *The Hero*, 8.
56. Lampell, *The Hero*, 189.
57. Lampell, *The Hero*, 8.
58. Walter Byers, *Unsportsmanlike Conduct: Exploiting College Athletes* (Ann Arbor: University of Michigan Press, 1995), 53–55. Also see Howard P. Chudacoff, *Changing the Playbook: How Power, Profit, and Politics Transformed College Sports* (Urbana: University of Illinois Press, 2015), 8–9.
59. Lampell, *The Hero*, 9.
60. Oriard, *King Football*, 276.
61. Lampell, *The Hero*, 4.
62. Lampell, *The Hero*, 35.
63. Lampell, *The Hero*, 34.
64. Lampell, *The Hero*, 7.
65. Lampell, *The Hero*, 7.
66. Lampell, *The Hero*, 5.
67. Lampell, *The Hero*, 18–19.
68. Lampell, *The Hero*, 31.
69. Lampell, *The Hero*, 151–152.
70. Lampell, *The Hero*, 123.
71. Lampell, *The Hero*, 112–113.
72. Lampell, *The Hero*, 66.
73. Lampell, *The Hero*, 88.
74. Lampell, *The Hero*, 89.
75. Lampell, *The Hero*, 179.
76. Lampell, *The Hero*, 176.
77. Lampell, *The Hero*, 186.

78. Lampell, *The Hero*, 189–190.
79. Lampell, *The Hero*, 190.
80. Crowther, "College Football Is 'Exposed' in *Saturday's Hero*."
81. Lampell, *The Hero*, 221.
82. Lampell, *The Hero*, 220.
83. Lampell, *The Hero*, 222.
84. Lampell, "I Think I Ought to Mention I Was Blacklisted."
85. Lampell, "I Think I Ought to Mention I Was Blacklisted."
86. Lampell, "I Think I Ought to Mention I Was Blacklisted."
87. Howard Taubman, "White House Salutes Culture in America," *New York Times*, June 15, 1965, 1.
88. Carl Sandburg quoted in Lampell, "I Think I Ought to Mention I Was Blacklisted."

3. The "Big Arms" Race

1. "Michael Phelps Says He Never Faced a Completely Clean International Field," *BBC News*, March 1, 2017.
2. Notable examples of historical works that focus on doping during the Cold War include John Hoberman, *Mortal Engines: The Science of Performance and the Dehumanization of Sport* (New York: The Free Press, 1992); Thomas Hunt, "Sport, Drugs, and the Cold War: The Conundrum of Olympic Doping Policy, 1970–1979," *Olympika* 16 (2007): 19–41; Thomas Hunt, *Drug Games: The International Olympic Committee and the Politics of Doping, 1960–2008* (Austin: University of Texas Press, 2011); and Thomas Hunt, Paul Dimeo, Florian Hemme, and Anne Mueller, "The Health Risks of Doping during the Cold War: A Comparative Analysis of the Two Sides of the Iron Curtain," *International Journal of the History of Sport* 31, no. 17 (2014): 2230–2244.
3. Steven Ungerleider, *Faust's Gold: Inside the East German Doping Machine* (New York: Thomas Dunne Books/St. Martin's Press, 2001).
4. For a useful discussion of the term doping, see the introduction in Verner Møller, *The Doping Devil* (Copenhagen: Gyldendal, 2008).
5. John Gleaves, "Manufactured Dope: How the 1984 US Olympic Cycling Team Rewrote the Rules on Drugs in Sports," *International Journal of the History of Sport* 32, no. 1 (2015): 89–107.
6. See John Hoberman, "History and Prevalence of Doping in the Marathon," *Sports Medicine* 37, nos. 4–5 (2007): 386–88; John Gleaves, "Doped Professionals and Clean Amateurs: Amateurism's Influence on the Modern Philosophy of Anti-Doping," *Journal of Sport History* 38, no. 2 (2011): 237–254; and Paul Dimeo, "Why Lance Armstrong? Historical Context and Key Turning Points in the 'Cleaning Up' of Professional Cycling," *International Journal of the History of Sport* 31, no. 8 (2014): 951–968.
7. Jenifer Parks, "Red Sport, Red Tape: The Olympic Games, the Soviet Sports Bureaucracy, and the Cold War, 1952–1980" (PhD diss., University of North Carolina at Chapel Hill, 2009), 14.
8. Michael Krüger, Christian Becker, and Stefan Nielsen, *German Sports, Doping, and Politics: A History of Performance Enhancement* (Lanham, Md.: Rowman &

Littlefield, 2015); Paul Dimeo, Thomas M. Hunt, and Richard Horbury, "The Individual and the State: A Social Historical Analysis of the East German 'Doping System,'" *Sport in History* 31, no. 2 (2011): 218–237.

9. Barbara Keys, *Globalizing Sport: National Rivalry and International Community in the 1930s* (Cambridge, Mass.: Harvard University Press, 2007), 245.

10. Susan Grant, *Physical Culture and Sport in Soviet Society: Propaganda, Acculturation, and Transformation in the 1920s and 1930s* (London: Routledge, 2012); Vassil Girginov, "Capitalist Philosophy and Communist Practice: The Transformation of Eastern European Sport and the International Olympic Committee," *Sport in Society* 1, no. 1 (1998): 122.

11. Parks, *"Red Sport, Red Tape."*

12. James Riordan, "The USSR and Olympic Boycotts," *International Journal of the History of Sport* 5, no. 3 (1988): 352.

13. James Riordan, "Russia and Eastern Europe in the Future of the Modern Olympic Movement," in *Critical Reflections on Olympic Ideology: Second International Symposium for Olympic Research, edited by* Robert Knight Barney and Klaus V. Meier (London, Ont.: International Center for Olympic Studies, University of Western Ontario, 1994), 3.

14. Evelyn Mertin, "Presenting Heroes: Athletes as Role Models for the New Soviet Person," *International Journal of the History of Sport* 26, no. 4 (2009): 469.

15. Mertin, "Presenting Heroes," 475.

16. Parks, *"Red Sport, Red Tape,"* 66.

17. Girginov, "Capitalist Philosophy and Communist Practice," 118–148.

18. David F. Gerrard, "Playing Foreign Policy Games: States, Drugs and Other Olympian Vices," *Sport in Society* 11, no. 4 (2008): 459–466; Dimeo et al., "The Individual and the State."

19. Ungerleider, *Faust's Gold.*

20. John Gleaves and Matthew Llewellyn, "Sport, Drugs and Amateurism: Tracing the Real Cultural Origins of Anti-Doping Rules in International Sport," *International Journal of the History of Sport* 31, no. 8 (2014): 839–853.

21. "Russians Sniffed Some Suspicious Stuff," *New York Times*, July 29, 1952, 24.

22. Hunt, *Drug Games*, 5.

23. Seymour Topping, "Soviet Chief Sets 2 Olympic Goals," *New York Times*, August 10, 1960, 40.

24. Verner Møller, "Knud Enemark Jensen's Death during the 1960 Rome Olympics: A Search for Truth?" *Sport in History* 25, no. 3 (2005): 452–471.

25. Mark Dyreson, *Crafting Patriotism for Global Domination: America at the Olympic Games* (London: Routledge, 2009).

26. Keys, *Globalizing Sport*, 75.

27. Alison Wrynn, "The Athlete in the Making: The Scientific Study of American Athletic Performance, 1920–1932," *Sport in History* 30, no. 1 (2010): 121–137.

28. Steve W. Pope, *Patriotic Games: Sporting Traditions in the American Imagination, 1876–1926* (Oxford: Oxford University Press, 1997), 46.

29. Hunt, "Sport, Drugs, and the Cold War," 19–41.

30. "Effect of Drugs to Aid Athletes Studied by US," *New York Times*, August 22, 1976, https://www.nytimes.com/1976/08/22/archives/effect-of-drugs-to-aid-athletes-studied-by-us-panel-of-us-olympic.html.

31. J. B. Strasser and Laurie Becklund, *Swoosh: The Unauthorized Story of Nike and the Men Who Played There* (New York: Harper Business, 1993).

32. For the creation of Athletics West, see Strasser and Becklund, *Swoosh*, 273.

33. Toby C. Rider, *Cold War Games: Propaganda, the Olympics, and US Foreign Policy* (Urbana: University of Illinois Press, 2016).

34. Gerald R. Ford, "In Defense of the Competitive Urge," *Sports Illustrated*, July 8, 1974, 17.

35. Thomas Hunt, "Countering the Soviet Threat in the Olympic Medals Race: The Amateur Sports Act of 1978 and American Athletics Policy Reform," *International Journal of the History of Sport* 24, no. 6 (2007): 796–818.

36. Bil Gilbert, "Something Extra on the Ball," *Sports Illustrated*, June 30, 1969.

37. Jack Scott, "It's Not How You Play the Game, but What Pill You Take," *New York Times*, October 17, 1971, SM40.

38. "Morning Briefing: Team Physiologist Claims Nearly All US Weightlifters on Steroids," *Los Angeles Times*, July 16, 1972, D2.

39. Gleaves, "Manufactured Dope."

40. Neil Amdur, "Race Relations Crisis Poses Serious Threat to Olympic Games," *New York Times*, August 20, 1972, S1; Stuart Auerbach, "Steroids: Superdrugs That Create Supermen, or Havoc?" *Washington Post*, August 20, 1972, D1.

41. Auerbach, "Steroids: Superdrugs That Create Supermen, or Havoc?" D1.

42. An exhaustive account of the reproduction of Ziegler's claim is nearly impossible. However, the following examples illustrate additional instances where journalists and scholars cite Ziegler's story as provenance that linked the Soviet Union to anabolic steroid use: Terry Todd, "The Steroid Predicament," *Sports Illustrated*, August 1, 1983; John D. Fair, "Olympic Weightlifting and the Introduction of Steroids: A Statistical Analysis of World Championship Results, 1948–72," *International Journal of the History of Sport* 5, no. 1 (1988): 96–114; Charles E. Yesalis, *Anabolic Steroids in Sports and Exercise* (Champaign, ILl.: Human Kinetics, 2000); and Joseph M. Berning, Kent J. Adams, and Bryant A. Stamford, "Anabolic Steroid Usage in Athletics: Facts, Fiction, and Public Relations," *Journal of Strength & Conditioning Research* 18, no. 4 (2004): 908–917.

43. Todd, "The Steroid Predicament"; John D. Fair, "Isometrics or Steroids? Exploring New Frontiers of Strength in the Early 1960s," *Journal of Sport History* 20, no. 1 (1993): 124.

44. John Hoberman, *Testosterone Dreams: Rejuvenation, Aphrodisia, Doping* (Los Angeles: University of California Press, 2005), 2.

45. Paul Dimeo, *A History of Drug Use in Sport 1876–1976: Beyond Good and Evil* (New York: Routledge, 2007). 72.

46. Hoberman, *Testosterone Dreams*, 2.

47. Dimeo, *A History of Drug Use in Sport*, 72.

48. Marcel Reinhold and John Hoberman, "The Myth of the Nazi Steroid," *International Journal of the History of Sport* 31, no. 8 (2014): 871–183, 878.

49. Auerbach, "Steroids: Superdrugs That Create Supermen, or Havoc?" D1. For the inclusion of a "few drinks," see Todd, "The Steroid Predicament."

50. Reinhold and Hoberman, "The Myth of the Nazi Steroid," 877.

51. Fair, "Isometrics or Steroids?" 4.

52. Grimke quoted in Fair, "Olympic Weightlifting and the Introduction of Steroids," 4.

53. Ziegler quoted in Fair, "Isometrics or Steroids?" 4.

54. Auerbach, "Steroids: Superdrugs That Create Supermen, or Havoc?" D1.

55. Jim Murray, "Russians Pull a Fast One," *Los Angeles Times*, September 3, 1972, B1.

56. Neil Amdur, "Use of Drugs at Olympics Found to Be Widespread," *New York Times*, November 10, 1972, 27.

57. Hunt, "Sport, Drugs, and the Cold War," 19–41.

58. *Commission of Inquiry into the Use of Drugs and Banned Practices Intended to Increase Athletic Performance* (Ottawa: Canadian Government Publishing Centre, 1990), accessed March 13, 2018, http://publications.gc.ca/collections/collection_2014/bcp-pco/CP32-56-1990-1-eng.pdf.

59. Paul Attner, "Three Training Centers to Bring the 20th Century to US Athletes," *Washington Post*, June 9, 1977, D1.

60. Attner, "Three Training Centers to Bring the 20th Century to US Athletes."

61. Amdur, "Use of Drugs at Olympics Found to Be Widespread," 27.

62. Nancy Scannell, "Today's Addiction for Athletes Is Vitamins," *Washington Post*, December 27, 1977, D3.

63. Attner, "Three Training Centers to Bring the 20th Century to US Athletes," D1.

64. For example, see Michael Strauss, "Czechoslovakia Forfeits for Drug Use," *New York Times*, February 13, 1976, 53; "Trace of Drug Costs Soviet Skier Medal," *Washington Post*, February 10, 1976, D1; Neil Amdur, "Mounting Drug Use Afflicts World Sports," *New York Times*, November 20, 1978, C1.

65. Hunt, *Drug Games*.

66. Amdur, "Mounting Drug Use Afflicts World Sports," C1.

67. "The Newswire: Soviet Swimmer Fails Drug Tests, Stripped of Medal," *Los Angeles Times*, August 29, 1978, F4.

68. Neil Amdur, "The Drug Game Threatens International Amateur Sport," *New York Times*, November 4, 1979, S1.

69. Amdur, "Mounting Drug Use Afflicts World Sports," C1.

70. Barry Lorge, "A Thoroughly Modern Athlete," *Washington Post*, May 27, 1979, A1.

71. Lorge, "A Thoroughly Modern Athlete."

72. Barry Lorge and Thomas Boswell, "Steroid Effects Debated While Use Proliferates," *Washington Post*, May 27, 1979, D5.

73. Jan Todd and Daniel L. Rosenke, "'The Event That Shook the Whole World Up': Historicizing the 1983 Pan-American Games Doping Scandal," *International Journal of the History of Sport* 33, nos. 1-2 (2016): 164–185.

74. Craig Neff, "Caracas: A Scandal and a Warning," *Sports Illustrated*, September 5, 1983, accessed March 13, 2018, http://www.si.com/vault/1983/09/05/619517/caracas-a-scandal-and-a-warning.

75. Neff, "Caracas: A Scandal and a Warning."

76. "Pan Am Cleanup Sends Out Olympic Signal," *Washington Post*, August 24, 1983, D1.

77. "Pan Am Cleanup Sends Out Olympic Signal."

78. Todd and Rosenke, "'The Event That Shook the Whole World Up.'"

79. Elliott Almond, Julie Cart, and Randy Harvey, "Cheating on Anabolic Steroids Is Also a Question of Ethics and Morality," *Los Angeles Times*, February 1, 1984, B8.

80. Gleaves, "Manufactured Dope," 89–107.

81. John Feinstein, "Doctor Says Steroid Patients Have Won Medals," *Washington Post*, August 10, 1984, F4.

82. John J. MacAloon, "Steroids and the State: Dubin, Melodrama and the Accomplishment of Innocence," *Public Culture* 2, no. 2 (1990): 41–64.

83. Michael Janofsky, "Soviet Sports Official Explains Stance on Drugs," *New York Times*, November 27, 1988, S2.

84. Michael Janofsky, "US And Soviet Union Approve Plan on Drug Testing of Athletes," *New York Times*, November 22, 1988, A1.

85. Christine Brennan, "Kerr Says He Prescribed Steroids for Some '84 Olympic Medalists," *Washington Post*, June 20, 1989, E1.

86. Associated Press, "Soviet Doping Widespread," *Los Angeles Times*, March 24, 1989, AF6.

87. For a story about the secret Russian doping laboratory, see Elliot Almond, "How Russian Doping Scandal Reverberates in Bay Area," *Mercury News*, May 13, 2016.

88. Neil MacFarquhar, "Putin's Swift Reaction to Doping Report Blames Anti-Russian Politics," *New York Times*, July 19, 2016, B11.

4. Preserving "the American Way"

1. See Laurence Chalip, "Sport and the State: The Case of the United States of America," in *Sport . . . The Third Millennium: Proceedings of the International Symposium, Quebec City, Canada, May 21–25, 1990*, edited by Fernand Landry, Marc Landry, and Magdeleine Yerlès (Sainte-Foy: Les Presses de L'Université Laval, 1991), 243–250; and Laurence Chalip, "Policy Analysis in Sport Management," *Journal of Sport Management* 9, no. 1 (1995): 113.

2. For a general historical overview, see Joseph M. Turrini, *The End of Amateurism in American Track and Field* (Urbana: University of Illinois Press, 2010), 136–148; and Eric Danoff, "The Struggle for Control of Amateur Track and Field in the United States–Part I," *Sport History Review* 6, no. 1 (1975): 43–85. For an analysis of the Amateur Sports Act against the backdrop of the "Soviet threat," see Thomas M. Hunt, "Countering the Soviet Threat in the Olympic Medals Race: The Amateur Sports Act of 1978 and American Athletics Policy Reform," *International Journal of the History of Sport* 24, no. 6 (2007): 796–818.

3. See Stephen R. Wenn, "A Long and Winding Road: IOC/USOC Relations, Money, and the Amateur Sports Act," *Olympika: The International Journal of Olympic Studies* 24 (2015): 146.

4. Barbara J. Keys, *Globalizing Sport: National Rivalry and International Community in the 1930s* (Cambridge, Mass.: Harvard University Press, 2006), 158–180.

5. "The Great Gold Robbery," *Los Angeles Times*, September 11, 1972.

6. "Olympic Ideal Big Loser at Munich," *Washington Post*, September 11, 1972.

7. "The Great Gold Robbery," *Los Angeles Times*, September 11, 1972. For more on Soviet-America basketball rivalry, see Chris Elzey, "Munich 1972: Sport, Politics and Tragedy" (PhD diss., Purdue University, 2004); and Kevin B. Witherspoon,

"'Fuzz Kids' and 'Musclemen': The US-Soviet Basketball Rivalry, 1958–1975," in *Diplomatic Games: Sport, Statecraft, and International Relations since 1945*, edited by Heather L. Dichter and Andrew L. Johns (Lexington: University Press of Kentucky, 2014), 297–326.

8. Chalip, "Sport and the State," 245–246.

9. Turrini, *The End of Amateurism in American Track and Field*, 138.

10. Jerry H. Jones to the President, September 17, 1973, Box 83, Folder "Physical Fitness and Sports, President's Council on," Gerald R. Ford Vice Presidential Papers, Gerald R. Ford Library, Ann Arbor, Michigan (hereafter GFL).

11. Earl Ramer to Gerald Ford, December 4, 1972, Box 154, Folder "Olympics," Gerald R. Ford Vice Presidential Papers, GFL. Attached to this letter was a report composed by the NCAA's International Relations Committee titled "United States Olympic Crisis: The Problem That Won't Go Away."

12. Danoff, "The Struggle for Control of Amateur Track and Field in the United States–Part I," 49.

13. The overview of the AAU-NCAA dilemma and its history in the following paragraphs was written using the Sports Arbitration Board's Congressional Hearing reports (US Congress, Senate, Committee on Commerce, *Sports Arbitration Board Report: Hearing Before the Committee on Commerce, 90th Cong., 2nd sess., 1 February 1968*, Box 154, Folder "Olympics," Gerald R. Ford Vice Presidential Papers), GFL; Danoff's work; and the NCAA's "United States Olympic Crisis," all of which draw from Arnold Flath, *A History of Relations between the National Collegiate Athletic Association and the Amateur Athletic Union of the United States, 1905–1963* (Champaign, Ill.: Stipes Publishing, 1964).

14. Robert K. Barney, Stephen R. Wenn, and Scott G. Martyn, *Selling the Five Rings: The International Olympic Committee and the Rise of Olympic Commercialism* (Salt Lake City: University of Utah Press, 2002), Chapter 2.

15. Flath, *A History of Relations between the National Collegiate Athletic Association and the Amateur Athletic Union of the United States, 1905–1963, 287–310; Sports Arbitration Board Report, 21–22.*

16. "United States Olympic Crisis."

17. Danoff, "The Struggle for Control of Amateur Track and Field in the United States–Part I," 78–85.

18. Sidney M. Milkis and Michael Nelson, *The American Presidency: Origins and Development, 1776–2007*, 5th ed. (Washington: CQ Press, 2008), 342–344.

19. Chalip, "Policy Analysis and Sport Management," 5.

20. The Twenty-Fifth Amendment, which was adopted on February 10, 1967, empowered the president to nominate a replacement for vice president.

21. News Release, Republican Dinner, September 22, 1973, Box D35, Folder "Republican Dinner, Petoskey, MI, September 22, 1973," Ford Congressional Papers: Press Secretary and Speech File, GFL.

22. Hunt, "Countering the Soviet Threat in the Olympic Medals Race," 803–804.

23. Cecil N. Coleman to Gerald Ford, November 9, 1972, Box 154, Folder "Olympics," Gerald R. Ford Vice Presidential Papers, GFL.

24. Ramer to Ford, December 4, 1972.

25. Remarks of AAU president John B. Kelly Jr., November 1, 1972, Box 154, Folder "Olympics," Gerald R. Ford Vice Presidential Papers, GFL, our italics.

26. John B. Kelly Jr. to Gerald Ford, December 1, 1972, Box 154, Folder "Olympics," Gerald R. Ford Vice Presidential Papers, GFL.

27. "Hal Connolly: American Dream Is a Nightmare," *Chicago Tribune*, December 11, 1972.

28. "Break Up of USOC Looms as Only Alternative," *Hartford Courant*, February 1, 1973.

29. "New Group Seeking Control of US Olympic Movement," *Chicago Tribune*, February 20, 1973.

30. "Consider New USO.C. Plan in Meeting Here," *Chicago Tribune*, February 18, 1973.

31. "New Group Seeking Control of US Olympic Movement."

32. Mike Harrigan to Bill Casselman, April 22, 1974, Box 74, Folder "Amateur Sports Legislation," Gerald R. Ford Vice Presidential Papers, GFL.

33. Jerry H. Jones to the President, September 17, 1973, Box 83, Folder "Physical Fitness and Sports, President's Council on," Gerald R. Ford Vice Presidential Papers, GFL.

34. "S.1018–National Olympic Commission Act," *Congress.gov*, accessed March 13, 2018, https://www.congress.gov/bill/93rd-congress/senate-bill/1018.

35. "S.2365–Amateur Athletic Act," *Congress.gov*, accessed March 13, 2018, https://www.congress.gov/bill/93rd-congress/senate-bill/2365.

36. Ken Cole, memorandum to Staff Secretary, July 20, 1973, Box 37, Folder "Olympic Sports, President's Commission on (1)," F. Lynn May Files, Gerald R. Ford Library, GFL.

37. Jones to the President, September 17, 1973.

38. Statement by the President: Olympic Sports Commission, fifth draft, November 19, 1973, Box 83, Folder "Physical Fitness and Sports, President's Council on," Gerald R. Ford Vice Presidential Papers, GFL.

39. Chalip, "Policy Analysis in Sport Management," 6–7.

40. Cole to Staff Secretary, July 20, 1973.

41. Jones to the President, September 17, 1973.

42. Michael T. Harrigan and Steven R. Mead to Tod Hullin, May 29, 1974, Box 37, Folder "Olympic Sports, President's Commission on (1)," F. Lynn May Files, Gerald R. Ford Library, GFL.

43. Mike Harrigan to the Vice President, January 17, 1974, Box 83, Folder "Physical Fitness and Sports, President's Council on," Gerald R. Ford Vice Presidential Papers, GFL.

44. Michael T. Harrigan to Russ Rourke, February 27, 1975, Box 27, Folder "Olympic Sports, President's Commission on," John O. Marsh Files, Gerald R. Ford Library, GFL.

45. Mike Harrigan to the Vice President, May 1, 1974, Box 83, Folder "Physical Fitness and Sports, President's Council on," Gerald R. Ford Vice Presidential Papers, GFL.

46. "S.3500–Amateur Athletic Act," *Congress.gov*, accessed March 13, 2018, https://www.congress.gov/bill/93rd-congress/senate-bill/3500.

47. "Issues and Answers," *Olympic Review*, nos. 78–79 (1974): 191–194.

48. Mike Harrigan, "Summary and Current Status," 8, n.d., Box 74, Folder "Amateur Sports Legislation," Gerald R. Ford Vice Presidential Papers, GFL.

49. "H.R.14938–Olympic Sports Commission Act," *Congress.gov*, accessed March 13, 2018, https://www.congress.gov/bill/93rd-congress/house-bill/14938.

50. "H.R.15241–Olympic Sports Commission Act," accessed March 13, 2018, *Congress.gov*, https://www.congress.gov/bill/93rd-congress/house-bill/15241.

51. Bob Mathias and Robert Mendes, *An American Odyssey: The Bob Mathias Story* (New York: Sports Publishing, 2001), 168–169.

52. Harrigan to Mead and Hullin, May 29, 1974.

53. Tod R. Hullin to the Vice President, June 19, 1974, Box 224, Folder "Amateur Athletics," Gerald R. Ford Vice Presidential Papers, GFL.

54. Gerald Ford, "In Defense of the Competitive Urge," *Sports Illustrated*, July 8, 1974, 16–23.

55. Barry Roth to Bill Casselman, August 21, 1974, Box 12, Folder "FG 205: President's Council on Physical Fitness and Sports," Kenneth A. Lazarus Files, GFL.

56. Tod Hullin to Ken Cole and Jim Cavanaugh, January 4, 1975, Boxes 5–6, Folder "RE 14: Olympics," White House Central Files Subject File, GFL.

57. Michael T. Harrigan, "A Class Act," *The Olympian*, January 1989, 9–13.

58. Public Law 95–606, 92 Stat. 3045 (1978).

59. For a more detailed overview of the implementation of the Amateur Sports Act and the transition from the President's Commission on Olympic Sports to the Amateur Sports Act, see Harrigan, "A Class Act," 9–15.

60. Chalip, "Sport and the State," 244–245.

61. Hunt, "Countering the Soviet Threat in the Olympic Medals Race," 808–809.

62. Wenn, "A Long and Winding Road," 3–4.

5. "Wolves in Skirts?"

This chapter is based on research completed for *Sex Testing: Gender Policing in Women's Sports* (Urbana: University of Illinois Press, 2016). Whereas *Sex Testing* provides an international overview of gender verification by chronicling the practices of the IAAF and IOC from the 1920s to the present, this chapter focuses specifically on US sport officials—notably Avery Brundage—and media responses during the Cold War.

1. "Change of Sex," *Time*, August 24, 1936, 39–40.

2. Quoted in Kevin B. Wamsley, "Womanizing the Olympic Athletes: Policy and Practice during the Avery Brundage Era," in *Onward to the Olympics: Historical Perspectives on the Olympic Games*, edited by Gerald P. Schaus and Stephen R. Wenn (Waterloo: Wilfrid Laurier University Press, 2007), 277.

3. Joseph M. Turrini, "'It Was Communism versus the Free World': The USA-USSR Dual Track Meet Series and the Development of Track and Field in the United States, 1958–1985," *Journal of Sport History* 28, no. 3 (2001): 433.

4. Shirley Povich, "This Morning," *Washington Post*, July 29, 1958, A18.

5. Arthur Daley, "Sports of the Times: The Red-Faced Reds," *New York Times*, October 23, 1964, 47; Paul Zimmerman, "Men's Hopes Dim, Gals' Bright," *Los Angeles Times*, August 24, 1960, C1.

6. Frank True, "Red 'Wolves' in Skirts?" *Sarasota Herald Tribune*, September 13, 1966, 17.

7. Helen Laville, "Gender and Women's Rights in the Cold War," in *The Oxford Handbook of the Cold War*, edited by Richard H. Immerman and Petra Goedde (Oxford: Oxford University Press, 2013), 529.

8. Robert L. Griswold, "'Russian Blonde in Space': Soviet Women in the American Imagination, 1950–1965," *Journal of Social History* 45, no. 4 (2012): 881.

9. Rob Beamish, *Steroids: A New Look at Performance-Enhancing Drugs* (Santa Barbara, Calif.: Praeger, 2011), 43.

10. B. Ivanov and E. Rodikov, "Bourgeois Cosmopolitans in Sports Literature," *Current Digest of the Russian Press*, April 5, 1949, 55–56.

11. Alison Rowley, "Sport in the Service of the State: Images of Physical Culture and Soviet Women, 1917–1941," *International Journal of the History of Sport* 23, no. 8 (2006): 1314–1340.

12. Kateryna Kobchenko, "Emancipation within the Ruling Ideology: Soviet Women in Fizkul'tura and Sport in the 1920s and 1930s," in *Euphoria and Exhaustion: Modern Sport in Soviet Culture and Society*, edited by Nikolaus Katzer, Sandra Budy, Alexandra Köhring, and Manfred Zeller (Frankfurt: Campus Verlag, 2010), 255–265.

13. V. Parin, "We are Domesticating the Universe," *Current Digest of the Russian Press*, July 10, 1963, 19–21.

14. Anke Hilbrenner, "Soviet Women in Sports in the Brezhnev Years: The Female Body and Soviet Modernism," in *Euphoria and Exhaustion: Modern Sport in Soviet Culture and Society*, edited by Nikolaus Katzer, Sandra Budy, Alexandra Köhring and Manfred Zeller (Frankfurt: Campus Verlag, 2010), 298–299.

15. Jim Riordan, "The Rise, Fall and Rebirth of Sporting Women in Russia and the USSR," *Journal of Sport History* 18, no. 1 (1991): 195.

16. Hilbrenner, "Soviet Women in Sports in the Brezhnev Years," 300.

17. Stefan Wiederkehr, "'. . . If Jarmila Kratochvilova Is the Future of Women's Sports, I'm Not Sure I'm Ready for It,'" in *Euphoria and Exhaustion: Modern Sport in Soviet Culture and Society*, edited by Nikolaus Katzer, Sandra Budy, Alexandra Köhring and Manfred Zeller (Frankfurt: Campus Verlag, 2010), 320.

18. Martha H. Verbrugge, *Active Bodies: A History of Women's Physical Education in Twentieth-Century America* (Oxford: Oxford University Press, 2012), 53.

19. Jaime Schultz, *Qualifying Times: Points of Change in US Women's Sport* (Urbana: University of Illinois Press, 2014), 73.

20. Sarah Jane Eikleberry, "More than Milk and Cookies: Revisiting the College Play Day," *Journal of Sport History* 41, no. 3 (2014): 467–486.

21. Susan K. Cahn, *Coming on Strong: Gender and Sexuality in Twentieth-Century Women's Sport* (Cambridge: Harvard University Press, 1994), 111–112.

22. Millie McDaniel finished first in the high jump, Willye White placed second in the long jump, and Isabelle Daniels, Wilma Rudolph, Mae Faggs Starr, and Margaret Matthews Wilburn earned bronze in the 4 x 100-meter relay.

23. Jennifer H. Lansbury, *A Spectacular Leap: Black Women Athletes in Twentieth-Century America* (Fayetteville: University of Arkansas Press, 2014).

24. Schultz, *Qualifying Times*, 86.

25. Schultz, *Qualifying Times*, 84–89.

26. Verbrugge, *Active Bodies*, 206.

27. Mae Faggs, Catherine Hardy, Barbara Jones, and Janet Moreau earned gold in the 4 x 100-meter relay.

28. In swimming and diving, the medals earned included: Lynn Burke, gold in the 100-meter backstroke; Carolyn Schuler, gold in the 100-meter butterfly; Chris von Saltza, silver in the 100-meter freestyle and gold in the 400-meter freestyle; Joan Spillane, Shirley Stobs, Carolyn Wood, and von Saltza, gold in the 4 x 100-meter freestyle relay; Burke, Patty Kempner, Schuler, and von Saltza, gold in the 4 x 100-meter medley relay; and Paula Jean Myers, two silvers in the three-meter springboard and the ten-meter platform. In athletics, the medals earned included: Earlene Brown, bronze in the shot put; Wilma Rudolph, two golds in the 100-meter and 200-meter; and Martha Hudson, Barbara Jones, Rudolph, and Lucinda Williams, gold in the 4 x 100-meter relay.

29. Shirley Povich, "This Morning," *Washington Post*, August 4, 1952, 8.

30. Bill Jauss, "US Girls Add Beauty to Olympic Games," *Washington Post*, November 11, 1956, C3.

31. Scholarly accounts of Brundage's views on female athletes differ somewhat. Mary Henson Leigh argues that Brundage initially held a pragmatic opinion about women's entrance into sport. As the head of the AAU in the 1920s, he believed female athletes would inevitably compete and that sport organizations should accept their inclusion and implement safeguards. Leigh suggests that his ideas changed in the 1930s, possibly because of increased sponsorship in track and field and that by 1953, he mostly opposed women's events. See Leigh, "The Enigma of Avery Brundage and Women Athletes," *Arena Review* 4 (1980): 1121. Allen Guttmann argues that Brundage's antipathy toward women has been exaggerated and claims that concerns about amateurism and the reduction of the Olympics superseded his thoughts about female competitors; Guttmann, *The Olympics: A History of the Modern Games* (Chicago: University of Illinois Press, 1992). Carly Adams disagrees with the view that Brundage's aversion was overstated and argues that his actions as a leading sport official "clearly indicate his unfavorable position concerning female sport" (145); Carly Adams, "Fighting for Acceptance: Sigfrid Edström and Avery Brundage: Their Efforts to Shape and Control Women's Participation in the Olympic Games," in *The Global Nexus Engaged: Past, Present, Future Interdisciplinary Olympic Studies: Sixth International Symposium for Olympic Research*, edited by Kevin B. Wamsley, Robert K. Barney, and Scott G. Martyn (London, Ontario: International Centre for Olympic Studies, 2002): 143–148.

32. Quoted in Leigh, "The Enigma of Avery Brundage," 16.

33. Scholars offer differing perspectives on the motivations for this proposal. According to Allen Guttmann, the IOC Executive Board, including Brundage, worried about the rapid growth of the Olympic Games. Concerns about commercialization, breaches of amateurism, and the ability of cities to organize an increasing number of events encouraged the IOC to consider reducing the Olympic program. According to Guttmann, Brundage viewed the exclusion of women as a potential way to solve the problem. See Guttmann, *The Games Must Go On: Avery Brundage and the Olympic Movement* (New York: Columbia University Press, 1984), 194. Carly Adams disagrees. She argues that Brundage's private correspondences show an inherent disdain for women's sport. See Adams, "Fighting for Acceptance," 145–146.

34. "Meeting Minutes of the International Olympic Committee Session in Mexico City, 1953," Archives of the International Olympic Committee, Olympic Studies Centre (hereafter OSC), Lausanne, Switzerland.

35. Arthur Daley, "More Deadly than the Male," *New York Times*, February 8, 1953, S2.

36. Prescott Sullivan, "The Low Down—Brundage Says Olympics Should Be for Men Only," *San Francisco Examiner*, May 9, 1960, Scrapbook Number 12B: Avery Brundage—General, 72, Avery Brundage Collection, University of Illinois Archives, University Library, University of Illinois at Urbana-Champaign (hereafter Brundage Collection).

37. Donald T. P. Pain to Johann Westerhoff, December 14, 1967, IAAF Correspondence, 1967–1975, Archives of the International Olympic Committee, OSC Archives.

38. Arne Ljungqvist, *Doping's Nemesis* (Cheltenham: SportsBooks Limited, 2011), 183.

39. Arthur Porritt to Avery Brundage, November 10, 1966, Commission Medicale Correspondence, 1960–1967, OSC Archives.

40. Mary Peters, *Mary P: Autobiography* (London: Stanley Paul & Company, 1974), 56–57.

41. Mary Jollimore, "Gender Bender Hunt Not Necessary in the Olympics," *The Globe and Mail*, June 15, 1992.

42. Murray L. Barr and Ewart G. Bertram, "A Morphological Distinction between Neurones of the Male and Female, and the Behaviour of the Nucleolar Satellite during Accelerated Nucleoprotein Synthesis," *Nature*, April 30, 1949, 676–677.

43. "Mosaic in X & Y," *Time*, September 29, 1967.

44. Avery Brundage to Arthur Porritt, November 1, 1966, Box 104, IOC Commissions and Committees—Medical Commission, Part III, 1966–1969 Folder, Brundage Collection.

45. "Minutes of the Meeting of the Medical Commission, July 14–17, 1968," Box 89, IOC Meetings, 1968, IOC Meetings—67th Session Folder, Brundage Collection. Thiebault was later a member of the IOC's Medical Commission.

46. "Male Hormones Outlawed: Sex, Doping Tests Set for Olympians," *Washington Post*, May 9, 1967, D2.

47. T. R. Van Dellen, "How to Keep Well," *Chicago Tribune*, October 15, 1968, 16.

48. "Male Hormones Outlawed."

49. David Burghley to Johann Westerhoff, January 10, 1967, Biography and Correspondence of David Burghley, OSC Archives.

50. "1-in-5 Test of Sex Said 'Ludicrous,'" *Washington Post*, February 3, 1968, D1.

51. Shirley Povich, "This Morning," *Washington Post*, February 5, 1968, D1; "Sex Test: Olympic Girl Skiers 'Amused, Chagrined,'" *Los Angeles Times*, February 3, 1968, A6.

52. Sally Quinn, "The Sex Test," *Atlanta Constitution*, July 25, 1976, 8D.

53. Jim Murray, "You'd Never Think She Is One of Them," *Los Angeles Times*, December 29, 1981, D1.

54. Rebecca Ann Lock, "The Doping Ban: Compulsory Heterosexuality and Lesbophobia," *International Review for the Sociology of Sport* 38, no. 4 (2003): 405.

55. Lindsay Parks Pieper, *Sex Testing: Gender Policing in Women's Sports* (Urbana: University of Illinois Press, 2016), 77.

56. Avery Brundage to Alexandre de Mérode, April 24, 1972, Box 105, Commissions, IOC Commissions and Committees—Medical Commission, 1970–1973, Brundage Collection.

57. Raymond G. Bunge, "Sex and the Olympic Games," *JAMA: The Journal of the American Medical Association* 173, no. 12 (July 23, 1960): 196.

58. Raymond G. Bunge, "Narration: Sex and the Olympic Games No. 2," *JAMA: The Journal of the American Medical Association* 200, no. 2 (June 5, 1967): 267.

59. Daniel F. Hanley, "Medical News, Chromosomes Do Not an Athlete Make," *JAMA: The Journal of the American Medical Association* 202, no. 11 (December 11, 1967): 55.

60. Joe Leigh Simpson, "Gender Testing in the Olympics," *JAMA: The Journal of the American Medical Association* 256, no. 14 (October 10, 1986), 1938.

61. John Money to Myron Genel, September 29, 1987, Correspondence Regarding the Petition by the "Heinonen Sixteen" on Gender Verification, March–April 1994, Papers of Andrew Ferguson-Smith, University of Glasgow Archives.

62. The American Academy of Pediatrics, American College of Obstetricians and Gynecologists, American College of Physicians, American Medical Association, American Society of Human Genetics, and the Endocrine Society publicly opposed sex testing. Pieper, *Sex Testing*, 171–172.

63. Pieper, *Sex Testing*, 174–175.

6. America's Team

1. Tennie McGhee, "US Girls Capture World Basketball Championship with Comeback Spirit," *Amateur Athlete*, December 1957, 8–9.

2. For the most thorough study of AAU basketball, see Robert W. Ikard, *Just for Fun: The Story of AAU Women's Basketball* (Fayetteville: University of Arkansas Press, 2005). See also Christine A. Baker, *Why She Plays: The World of Women's Basketball* (Lincoln: University of Nebraska Press, 2008); Pamela Grundy and Susan Shackelford, *Shattering the Glass: The Remarkable History of Women's Basketball* (Chapel Hill: University of North Carolina Press, 2007); Linda Ford, *Lady Hoopsters: A History of Women's Basketball in America* (Northampton, Mass.: Half Moon Books, 2000); Joan S. Hult and Marianna Treckell, eds., *A Century of Women's Basketball: From Frailty to Final Four* (Reston, Va.: American Alliance for Physical Health, 1991); and Janice A. Beran, *From Six-on-Six to Full Court Press: A Century of Iowa Girls' Basketball* (Iowa City: University of Iowa Press, 1993), 149–162.

3. The differing views of gender in the USSR and the United States extended to their views of women in sport. See Lindsay Parks Pieper, *Sex Testing: Gender Policing in Women's Sports* (Urbana: Illinois University Press, 2016), 35–59.

4. For more on the evolution of women's basketball in the early twentieth century, see Baker, *Why She Plays*; Ikard, *Just for Fun*; Hult and Treckell, *A Century of Women's Basketball*; and Ford, *Lady Hoopsters*, 52–88. While they were never participants in the US-Soviet series, African American women did play college and AAU ball, at times with great success. See Rita Liberti, "'We Were Ladies, We Just Played

Basketball Like Boys': African American Womanhood and Competitive Basketball at Bennett College, 1928–1942," *Journal of Sport History* 26, no. 3 (1999): 567–584; and Grundy and Shackelford, *Shattering the Glass*, 92–95.

5. Bob Hampton, "Hanes Girls Style Revolutionizes Basketball," *Amateur Athlete*, April, 1953, 17; Ikard, *Just for Fun*, 72.

6. For further evidence of the NBC's dominance, see Bill Isom, "Nashville Wins Fourth Straight A.A.U. Title," in *AAU Basketball Guide 1965* (Indianapolis: Amateur Athletic Union, 1965), 5–7; Bill Isom, "Nashville Does It Again," in *AAU Basketball Guide 1966* (Indianapolis: Amateur Athletic Union, 1966), 5–6.

7. Ikard, *Just for Fun*. See also Grundy and Shackelford, *Shattering the Glass*, 85–103; Ford, *Lady Hoopsters*, 63–88. For a first-person perspective on the Wayland Baptist College team, see Patsy Neal, "Basketballs, Goldfish, and World Championships," in *A Century of Women's Basketball: From Frailty to Final Four*, edited by Joan S. Hult and Marianna Treckell (Reston, Va.: American Alliance for Physical Health, 1991), 345–353.

8. Kevin Witherspoon, "'Fuzz Kids' and 'Musclemen': The US/Soviet Basketball Rivalry, 1965–75," in *Diplomatic Games: An International History of Sport and Foreign Relations since 1945*, edited by Heather Dichter and Andy Johns (Lexington: University Press of Kentucky, 2014), 297–326.

9. "Skaidrite Smildzinya: New Skipper of the Latvian Team," *Basketball*, December 1965, 14–15; "Scanning Sports," *Soviet Life*, October 1966, 64; Gerald Yelensky, "A Tall Men's Game," *Soviet Life*, April 1962, 64.

10. Lyle M. Foster, "Soviet Basketball Teams Tour the USA.," in *Women's National AAU Basketball Championship 1963, Official Souvenir Program* (1963), 24, author's personal collection.

11. For a broader view of women's sport under totalitarian regimes, see Allen Guttmann, *Women's Sports: A History* (New York: Columbia University Press, 1991), 172–188.

12. See Damion Thomas, *Globetrotting: African American Athletes and Cold War Politics* (Urbana: University of Illinois Press, 2012); Toby C. Rider, *Cold War Games: Propaganda, the Olympic, and US Foreign Policy* (Urbana: University of Illinois Press, 2016); Ashley Brown, "Swinging for the State Department: American Women Tennis Players in Diplomatic Goodwill Tours, 1941–59," *Journal of Sport History* 42, no. 3 (2015): 289–309; and Kevin B. Witherspoon, "Going 'to the Fountainhead': Black American Athletes as Cultural Ambassadors in Africa, 1970–1971," *International Journal of the History of Sport* 30, no. 13 (2013): 1508–1522.

13. Soviet official Georgi Zarubin quoted in Walter Hixson, *Parting the Curtain: Propaganda, Culture, and the Cold War, 1945–61* (New York: St. Martin's Press: 1997), 152.

14. Ibid; Joseph M. Turrini, "'It Was Communism Versus the Free World': The USA-USSR Dual Track Meet Series and the Development of Track and Field in the United States, 1958–1985," *Journal of Sport History* 28, no. 3 (2001): 427–471. Organization of the basketball exchanges is described in Lyle M. Foster, "Women's Basketball Committee Report," in "Amateur Athletic Union of the United States, 71st Annual Convention, Minutes 1958," 7, 32–33, LA84 Foundation Archives, Los Angeles, CA.

15. "A.A.U. Plans Set for Soviet Swap," *Amateur Athlete*, April 1958, 5; "US Basketball Squads Leave for Six-Game Series in Russia," *New York Times*, April 21, 1958, 30; "Russ Pledge Warm Greeting for Yanks," *Los Angeles Times*, April 14, 1958, C3.

16. *Nashville Tennessean*, May 9, 1958, 28, 45; "US Court Stars Play in Russia," *Amateur Athlete*, May 1958, 5.

17. Larry Taft, "At Home, Alone: Nera White joins Basketball Hall of Fame, But Finds Solace Only in Her Corner of World," *Nashville Tennessean*, May 10, 1992, 6C; "US Cagers Praise Soviet Sportsmanship," *Nashville Tennessean*, May 11, 1958, 2E; William J. Jorden, "US Men Rally to Win in Moscow Basketball," *New York Times*, April 26, 1958, 12.

18. *Nashville Tennessean*, May 9, 1958, 28, 45.

19. Shirley Martin, "US Women's Court Team in USSR," *Amateur Athlete*, June 1958, 14–15; "Russian Basketball Players to Tour US in '59," *New York Times*, May 7, 1958, 45; "Two US Court Teams Triumph," *Los Angeles Times*, April 29, 1958, C2; "US Routs Russians in Basketball," *Washington Post*, April 29, 1958, A20.

20. Bill Isom, "Reds Not Well Off, But Gracious Hosts," *Nashville Tennessean*, May 11, 1958, 5E.

21. Taft, "At Home, Alone."

22. "How Russian Press Reported on the American Basketballers," *New York Times*, April 27, 1958, 238.

23. Max Frankel, "American Basketball Teams Triumph to Cheers of 25,000 in Tiflis," *New York Times*, April 29, 1958, 35.

24. "A.A.U. Basketball Teams Cheered in Moscow on Arrival by Soviet Jet," *New York Times*, April 22, 1958, 44; "Tiflis Warms Up to US Athletes," *New York Times*, April 28, 1958, 29.

25. "Returning Women's Team Hails Soviet 'Red-Carpet' Treatment," *New York Times*, May 9, 1958, 31; "Russians Will Play in US," *Washington Post*, May 7, 1958, D3.

26. Harold K. Milks, "Cage Tour Success, Reds to Return Visit," *Nashville Tennessean*, May 9, 1958, 29.

27. Bill Isom, "Reds Not Well Off, But Gracious Hosts," *Nashville Tennessean*, May 11, 1958, E5.

28. *Nashville Banner*, May 14, 1958, *Nashville Banner* clipping file, NBC, Nashville Public Library; "Local Girls' Team Returns from Russia," *Nashville Banner* clipping file, NBC, Nashville Public Library.

29. *Nashville Tennessean*, May 11, 1958; *Nashville Banner*, May 15, 1958, 54; Bill Isom, "NBCers Enjoyed Russian Tour, Glad to be Back," *Nashville Tennessean*, May 9, 1958, 45; Victor Kuprianov, "Basketball USA-USSR," *Soviet Life* 23 (1958): 62–63.

30. Pam Clark, "Nera Hoping to Be 1st Woman in Naismith Hall," *Nashville Banner*, August 9, 1982, *Nashville Banner* clipping file, NBC, Nashville Public Library. Nera White was always frustrated that others credited a 1975 game between Immaculata College and Queens College as the "first women's basketball game ever played at Madison Square Garden." Historians perpetuated this false claim; see Karra Porter, *Mad Seasons: The Story of the First Women's Professional Basketball League, 1978–81* (Lincoln: University of Nebraska Press, 2006), 6.

31. Howard M. Tuckner, "American Men Set Back Soviet Five but US Women Bow at Garden," *New York Times*, November 27, 1959, 45.

32. Louis Effrat, "Soviet Athletes Arrive for Tour," *New York Times*, November 24, 1959, 48; Howard M. Tuckner, "Russians' Coach Says Goodwill, Not Score, Counts Here Tonight," *New York Times*, November 26, 1959, 60; "Soviet Men's Five Loses, Women Win," *New York Times*, November 30, 1959, 35.

33. "Touring A.A.U. Fives Will Assemble Here," *New York Times*, April 12, 1961, 51; "US Cagers Tip Russians in Pair," *Nashville Tennessean*, May 3, 1961, 26; "Lucas Vaults US Cagers over Soviets," *Nashville Tennessean*, May 4, 1961, 52; "US Cagers, Soviets Split Pair of Games," *Nashville Tennessean*, May 7, 1961, 3E; "N.B.C.'s Crawford Paces US Girls," *Nashville Tennessean*, May 8, 1961, 23.

34. "Back from Russia," *Nashville Banner*, May 12, 1961, *Nashville Banner* clipping file, NBC, Nashville Public Library; "NBC Tour behind the Iron Curtain," *Nashville Tennessean*, May 13, 1961, 10.

35. Tom Powell, "Cagers Say Home's Best," *Nashville Tennessean*, May 13, 1961, 10.

36. Ibid; Lyle M. Foster, "USA Basketball Teams Tour the USSR and Sweden," *Women's National A.A.U. Basketball Championships, Official Souvenir Program* (1962), 24; Beran, *From Six-on-Six to Full Court Press*, 149–162; "Reds Vow to Beat US in '64," *Washington Post*, May 13, 1961, A13.

37. "N.C.A.A. Boycotts Soviet Tour Here," *New York Times*, October 17, 1962, 66; "Soviet Quintets Arrive for Tour," *New York Times*, November 6, 1962, 41; Joseph M. Sheehan, "Soviet Quintets Face US Tonight," *New York Times*, November 8, 1962, 66; "Russian Men Beat US 68–59; Soviet Women Triumph, 51–40," *New York Times*, November 13, 1962, 48; "US Men Trounce Soviet Five, 85–60, but Visiting Women's Team Defeats Americans, 70–43," *New York Times*, November 25, 1962, 232; "Soviet Five Bows to US Men, 86–71, Russian Women Win Eighth Straight as Tour Ends," *New York Times*, November 27, 1962, 47; Foster, "Soviet Basketball Teams Tour"; "Russian Cagers Win, Yankee Tosses Punch," *Los Angeles Times*, November 23, 1962, C9; Byron Roberts, "Soviet Basketballers Tall, Too, but Have Problems with Defense," *Washington Post*, November 10, 1962, C9.

38. "USA National Women's Basketball Team in Moscow," Airgram from AmEmbassy Moscow to Department of State, April 27, 1965, Box 407, Folder EDX US/USSR, 4/1/65, Department of State Central Files, RG 59, National Archives and Records Administration, College Park, Maryland (hereafter NARA).

39. Olan G. Ruble, "Russians Blank US Girls," *Amateur Athletic Union of the US, Official Basketball Guide, 1966–67*, 8–11.

40. Ikard, *Just for Fun*, 214.

41. The literature recounting the fierce debate over amateurism in this era is vast. Perhaps the most comprehensive study is Matthew P. Llewellyn and John Gleaves, *The Rise and Fall of Olympic Amateurism* (Urbana: University of Illinois Press, 2016).

42. Bill Isom, "Reds Not Well Off, but Gracious Hosts," *Nashville Tennessean*, May 11, 1958, 5E.

43. Powell, "Cagers Say Home's Best."

44. George Sherman, "How Girls' AAU Rules Differ from Men's Basketball," *Women's National A.A.U. Basketball Championship, Official Souvenir Program* (1963), 35. For more on the evolution of the rules, see Mildred Barnes, "Coaching and Game Reflections, 1940s to 1980s," in *A Century of Women's Basketball: From Frailty*

to Final Four, edited by Joan S. Hult and Marianna Treckell (Reston, Va.: American Alliance for Physical Health, 1991), 335–344; Jaime Schultz, *Qualifying Times: Points of Change in US Women's Sport* (Urbana: University of Illinois, 2014), 74–76; Paula Welch, "Interscholastic Basketball: Bane of Collegiate Physical Educators," in *Her Story in Sport: A Historical Anthology of Women in Sports*, edited by Reet Howell (New York: Leisure Press, 1982), 424–431; and Jan Beran, "The Story: Six-Player Girls' Basketball in Iowa," in *Her Story in Sport*, 552–563.

45. Vince Prygoski, *Worst to First: Or, a Shocking Tale of Women's Basketball in Motown* (Denver: Outskirts Press, 2006); Beran, *From Six-on-Six to Full Court Press.*

46. Shelley Lucas, "Courting Controversy: Gender and Power in Iowa Girls' Basketball," *Journal of Sport History* 30, no. 3 (2003): 281–308; Ford, *Lady Hoopsters*, 73–88.

47. Lyle M. Foster, "The A.A.U. Celebrates its Diamond Jubilee," *Women's National A.A.U. Basketball Championship, Official Souvenir Program* (1963), 29.

48. Jeré Longman, "Before UConn, There Was Wayland," *New York Times*, December 18, 2010, SP1; Neal, *Basketballs, Goldfish, and World Championships*, 50–63; Ikard, *Just for Fun*, 105–106.

49. See Schultz, *Qualifying Times*, 84–101; Joan S. Hult, "Introduction to Part II," in *A Century of Women's Basketball: From Frailty to Final Four*, edited by Joan S. Hult and Marianna Treckell (Reston, Va.: American Alliance for Physical Health, 1991), 207–222; Jennifer Hargreaves, *Sporting Females: Critical Issues in the History and Sociology of Women's Sports* (New York: Routledge, 1994), 164; Guttmann, *Women's Sports*, 189–206.

50. Ford, *Lady Hoopsters*, 82.

51. Helen Lenskyj, *Out of Bounds: Women, Sport & Sexuality* (Toronto: The Women's Press, 1986), 86.

52. "USA National Women's Basketball Team in Moscow."

53. Neal, *Basketballs, Goldfish, and World Championships*, 39–43.

54. Gary Quinn, "Country Girls Had a Tough Row to Hoe," *Nashville Banner* clipping file, Nashville Public Library; "It's Official: White in Hall," *Nashville Tennessean*, March 12, 1992, 8.

55. Head had a successful career as a player before going on to even greater success as a coach; she retired from the University of Tennessee as the all-time winningest college basketball coach. See Pat Summitt with Sally Jenkins, *Sum It Up: A Thousand and Ninety-Eight Victories, a Couple of Irrelevant Losses, and a Life in Perspective* (New York: Three Rivers Press, 2013), 37.

56. Taft, "At Home, Alone."

57. Taft, "At Home, Alone." Historian Janice A. Beran describes similar stories of rural Iowan girls and their experiences in *From Six-on-Six to Full Court Press*, 44–49.

58. Gary Quinn, "Nera White's Legacy: 'In a Class by Herself,'" *Nashville Banner*, March 10, 1992, E1; Tom Wood, "White Earns 17th All-American Title," *TN Sports*, September 25, 1980, 59.

59. Larry Taft, "Coping with the Cruelty," *Nashville Tennessean*, May 10, 1992, 7C.

60. Quinn, "Nera White's Legacy."

61. Taft, "Coping with the Cruelty."

62. Clark, "Nera Hoping to Be 1st Woman in Naismith Hall"; Taft, "At Home,

Alone"; Logan Horn, "Remembering Nera White," *Macon County Times*, April 20, 2016; Emily Langer, "Nera White, Early Superstar of Women's Basketball, Dies at 80," *Washington Post*, April 15, 2016, 2C; Sam Roberts, "Nera White, Hall of Fame Basketball Star of 1950's and '60s, Is Dead at 80," *New York Times*, April 16, 2016, A22; Mike Organ, "In Hot Pursuit of Women's Basketball Great Nera White," *Nashville Tennessean*, April 5, 2014, A1; Ford, *Lady Hoopsters*, 84–85.

63. A review of these newspapers over the period under consideration reveals only a handful of articles discussing the women's games beyond a few sentences. Papers reflecting a stronger local interest in women's basketball, such as the *Nashville Tennessean* and the *Nashville Banner*, typically devoted greater attention to the women's games.

64. Bill Isom, "NBCers Enjoyed Russian Tour, Glad to be Back," *Nashville Tennessean*, May 9, 1958, 45.

65. "The Girls Won by a Head," *Nashville Tennessean*, May 9, 1958, 45.

66. Bill Scott, *Women's National A.A.U. Basketball Championship, Official Souvenir Program* (1963), 35.

67. Baker, *Why She Plays*, 83.

68. "Soviets Strive to Catch Americans in Basketball," *Washington Post*, November 7, 1962, D2.

69. Ikard, *Just for Fun*.

70. Lyle M. Foster, "Nashville Wins Women's Basketball Champ Title by Upsetting Queens," *Amateur Athlete*, May 1958, 32. In 1959, the queen was the "beautiful and charming Elaine Carter," and so on. See also Lyle M. Foster, "National A.A.U. Women's Basketball Championship, 1958–59," *Official A.A.U Basketball Guide 1959*, 30.

71. Wendy Smith, "Business of Winning," *Nashville Tennessean*, December 27, 1999, 10C; Larry Taft, "Before the Lady Vols, There Was NBC," *Nashville Tennessean*, March 4, 2012, 7X.

7. To Win One for the Gipper

1. Edmund Morris, *Dutch: A Memoir of Ronald Reagan* (New York City: Modern Library, 2000), 99.

2. Gil Troy, *Morning in America: How Ronald Reagan Invented the 1980's* (Princeton, N.J.: Princeton University Press, 2007), 12–13.

3. Morris, *Dutch*, 99.

4. Ronald Reagan, *An American Life: The Autobiography* (New York: Simon and Schuster, 2011), 34.

5. Dwight Eisenhower, John F. Kennedy, Richard Nixon, and Gerald Ford all played football, and Ford was nominated the University of Michigan's most valuable player in 1934; see John S. Watterson, "Political Football: Theodore Roosevelt, Woodrow Wilson and the Gridiron Reform Movement," *Presidential Studies Quarterly* 25, no. 3 (1995): 555.

6. The work of Steven Belletto shows how the zero-sum language of the Cold War was a product of "the game theory narrative," in which the Cold War was reduced to a two-person game—the United States versus the Soviet Union—and total victory was required by one side to ensure the defeat of the other. For more on this

concept, see Steven Belletto, "The Game Theory Narrative and the Myth of the National State," *American Quarterly* 61, no. 2 (2009): 333–357. For more on the language of the Cold War, see Jeffrey Montez de Oca, *Discipline and Indulgence: College Football, Media, and the American Way of Life during the Cold War* (New Brunswick, N.J.: Rutgers University Press, 2013).

7. Steve Fraser and Gary Gerstle, *The Rise and Fall of the New Deal Order, 1930–1980* (Princeton, N.J.: Princeton University Press, 1990).

8. Thomas Byrne Edsall with Mary Edsall, *Chain Reaction: The Impact of Race, Rights, and Taxes on American Politics* (New York: W. W. Norton & Company, 1992), 6.

9. Edward D. Berkowitz, *Something Happened: A Political and Cultural Overview of the Seventies* (New York: Columbia University Press, 2007).

10. For more on these changing viewpoints, see David Frum, *How We Got Here: The 70s, the Decade that Brought You Modern Life— For Better or* Worse (New York: Basic Books, 2000); and Bruce Schulman, *The Seventies: The Great Shift in American Culture, Society, and Politics* (Boston: Da Capo Press, 2002). Schulman contends that by the 1970s, the conservative movement had coalesced around three primary ideas: national defense, anti-elitism, and a desire to protect and restore family values (199–201).

11. Dan Baum, *Smoke and Mirrors: The War on Drugs and the Politics of Failure* (New York: Little, Brown and Company, 1996), 6.

12. "The Vietnam Syndrome" symbolized a time of political passivity that had a profound impact on American identity and foreign policy after 1975. See George Herring, "America and Vietnam: The Unending War," *Foreign Affairs* 70, no. 5 (1991): 104–119; and Tom Engelhardt, *The End of Victory Culture: Cold War America and the Disillusioning of a Generation* (Amherst, Mass.: University of Massachusetts Press, 2007).

13. Tom Engelhardt, "What Trump Really Means When He Says He'll Make America Great Again," *The Nation*, April 26, 2016, https://www.thenation.com/article/what-trump-really-means-when-he-says-hell-make-america-great-again/.

14. Ronald Reagan, "Remarks at a Forum for State Government Officials and Business Leaders in Somerset, New Jersey," Public Papers of Ronald Reagan from the Reagan Library, October 13, 1987.

15. Lisa McGirr, *Suburban Warriors: The Origins of the New American Right* (Princeton, N.J.: Princeton University Press, 2002), 10.

16. Kevin P. Phillips, *The Emerging Republican Majority* (New Rochelle, N.Y.: Arlington House, 1969), 26.

17. Kim Phillips-Fein, "Conservatism: A State of the Field," *Journal of American History* 98, no. 3 (2011): 727.

18. Barry Goldwater, *Conscience of a Conservative* (Radford, Va.: Wilder Publications, 2009).

19. Steven F. Hayward, "Why Ronald Reagan's 'A Time for Choosing' Endures After All This Time," *Washington Post*, October 23, 2014, accessed March 14, 2018, https://www.washingtonpost.com/opinions/why-ronald-reagans-a-time-for-choosing-endures-after-all-this-time/2014/10/23/d833c49e-587a-11e4-bd61-346aee66ba29_story.html.

20. Craig Shirley, *Reagan's Revolution: The Untold Story of the Campaign that Started It All* (Nashville, Tenn.: Thomas Nelson, 2010), 8.

21. Jeffery Kahn, "Ronald Reagan Launched Political Career Using the Berkeley Campus as a Target," *UC Berkeley News*, June 8, 2004, http://www.berkeley.edu/news/media/releases/2004/06/08_reagan.shtml; Michelle Reeves, "'Obey the Rules or Get Out': Ronald Reagan's 1966 Gubernatorial Campaign and the 'Trouble in Berkeley,'" *Southern California Quarterly* 92, no. 3 (2010): 275–305.

22. Rick Perlstein, *The Invisible Bridge: The Fall of Nixon and the Rise of Reagan* (New York: Simon and Schuster, 2015), 82–83.

23. "Reagan the Berkeley Basher," *LATimes.com*, May 18, 2013, accessed March 14, 2018, http://articles.latimes.com/2013/may/18/opinion/la-le-0518-reagan-uc-rosenfeld-postscript-20130518.

24. Michael Oriard, *Bowled Over: Big-Time College Football from the Sixties to the BCS Era* (Chapel Hill: University of North Carolina Press, 2009), 3–4.

25. Oriard, *Bowled Over*, 8.

26. Sweeney and Babbidge quoted in Oriard, *Bowled Over*, 3–4.

27. Suzanne Clark, *Cold Warriors: Manliness on Trial in the Rhetoric of the West* (Carbondale: Southern Illinois University Press, 2000). See also Simon Henderson, *Sidelined: How American Sports Challenged the Black Freedom Struggle* (Lexington: University of Kentucky Press, 2013).

28. Montez de Oca, *Discipline and Indulgence*, 6–11; Kurt Edward Kemper, *College Football and American Culture in the Cold War Era* (Champaign, IL: University of Illinois Press, 2009).

29. Susan Jeffords, *Hard Bodies: Hollywood Masculinity in the Reagan Era* (New Brunswick, N.J.: Rutgers University Press, 1993), 123.

30. Daniel Marcus, *Happy Days and Wonder Years: The Fifties and Sixties in Contemporary Cultural Politics* (New Brunswick, N.J.: Rutgers University Press, 2004), 4.

31. "Reagan Gets Idea from 'Rambo' for Next Time," *Los Angeles Times*, July 1, 1985, accessed March 14, 2018, http://articles.latimes.com/1985-07-01/news/mn-10009_1_hostage-crisis.

32. Jeffords, *Hard Bodies*, 11.

33. On March 30, 1981, Ronald Reagan was shot in the chest by 25-year-old John W. Hinckley Jr. Reagan was struck in the seventh rib by a bullet that eventually penetrated and collapsed the left lung. The president, who had been in office only two months, was not "in any serious danger" but was taken into surgery and hospitalized. Three other people in his detail were also wounded in the attack. Howell Raines, "Reagan Wounded in Chest by Gunman; Outlook 'Good' After 2-Hour Surgery; Aide and 2 Guards Shot; Suspect Held," *New York Times*, May 30, 1981.

34. Steve Neal, "Reagan Cheered by 12,500 'Irish,'" *Chicago Tribune*, May 18, 1981, 1.

35. "A ND Diploma for the Gipper," *Chicago Tribune*, May 18, 1981, C12.

36. George de Lama, "Notre Dame Cheers Return of 'Gipper' Reagan," *Chicago Tribune*, March 10, 1988, accessed March 14, 2018, http://articles.chicagotribune.com/1988-03-10/news/8804060309_1_gipper-reagan-knute-rockne-football-star-george-gipp.

37. Neal, "Reagan Cheered by 12,500 'Irish.'"

38. "University of Notre Dame Football," accessed May 5, 2015, http://www.und.com/sports/m-footbl/archive/nd-m-footbl-archive.html; Jon Gilbert, "Notre Dame Football: The 51 Greatest Players in the School's History," *Bleacher Report*, February 1, 2011, accessed May 8, 2018, http://bleacherreport.com/articles/593324-the-50-greatest-players-in-the-history-of-notre-dame-football.

39. Ronald Reagan, "Address at Commencement Exercises at the University of Notre Dame," Public Papers of Ronald Reagan from the Ronald Reagan Library, May 17, 1981, accessed June 12, 2018 https://www.reaganlibrary.gov/research/speeches/51781a.

40. Reagan, "Address at Commencement Exercises at the University of Notre Dame."

41. Paul Kengor, "Reagan at Notre Dame," May 16, 2011, accessed March 14, 2018, http://www.nationalreview.com/article/267290/reagan-notre-dame-paul-kengor.

42. Montez de Oca, *Discipline and Indulgence*, 18.

43. Bradley J. Birzer, "Ronald Reagan's Ten Words that Changed the World," *The Imaginative Conservative*, May 16, 2016, accessed March 14, 2018, http://www.theimaginativeconservative.org/2016/05/ten-words-changed-world-ronald-reagan.html.

44. Ronald Reagan, "PEACE: Restoring the Margins of Safety," speech at the Veterans of Foreign Wars Convention, Chicago, Illinois, August 18, 1980, accessed March 14, 2018, https://www.reaganlibrary.gov/sites/default/files/archives/reference/8.18.80.html.

45. Tom Bowman, "Reagan Guided Huge Buildup in Arms Race," *Baltimore Sun*, June 8, 2004, accessed March 14, 2018, http://www.baltimoresun.com/news/bal-te.pentagon08jun08-story.html.

46. George H. Nash, "Ronald Reagan's Legacy and American Conservatism," in *The Enduring Reagan*, edited by Charles W. Dunn (Lexington: University Press of Kentucky, 2009), 64–65.

47. Peter Schweizer, *Reagan's War: The Epic Story of His Forty-Year Struggle and Final Triumph over Communism* (New York: Doubleday, 2002), 15.

48. Paul Kengor, *The Crusader: Ronald Reagan and the Fall of Communism* (New York: Regan Books, 2006), 190–199.

49. Nash, "Ronald Reagan's Legacy and American Conservatism," 64.

50. Ronald Reagan, "How to Stay Fit," *Parade Magazine*, December 4, 1983, 4–6.

51. "Public Papers of the President," Ronald Reagan Library and Museum, https://reaganlibrary.gov/archives/speeches.

52. "The American Presidency Project," UC Santa Barbara, accessed on March 15, 2015, HYPERLINK "https://urldefense.proofpoint.com/v2/url?u=http-3A__www.presidency.ucsb.edu_&d=DwMFaQ&c=GlhIK-Z7Itify6iax27XCf9KYFXDgbS2ET58kP-Ckgw&r=qIkjy-XqYl7XvXNzsqEzc6wukMfIQlbCOUtrgCeYIFw&m=ozu51m5TsGjdhZo__nyfSYTs89rFoBNqkqIqAnRRGKs&s=ZqxF_AWa5G5i_j7MLTGPeBkbGQXiwbUTRhCVw2gAGtY&e=" http://www.presidency.ucsb.edu/. This word search of the Presidency project revealed that Nixon mentioned football 75 times in presidential speeches, from August 8, 1968 to May 11, 1974. Ronald Reagan more than doubled Nixon's remarks on football, mentioning it 189 times, from February 19, 1981 to January 18, 1989. Obama surpassed them both, mentioning football more than any other president to date, 206 times from February 1, 2009 to January 16, 2017.

53. Martin Nolan, "Governors Reject Campus Probe," *Boston Globe*, February 28, 1969, 1.

54. Chesly Manly, "Predict Fight for G.O.P. Bid: Rejects Rocky for Nomination," *Chicago Tribune*, March 3, 1968, 1.

55. Michael Reagan and Joe Hyams, *On the Outside Looking In* (New York: Zebra Books, 1988), 57. Throughout the work, Michael refers to himself as Ronald's adopted son to emphasize his perception that his father did not acknowledge him as his "real" son or a "real" man. He also says that the media was quick to note the differences between Ronald's biological children and himself.

56. Reagan, *An American Life*, 39–40.

57. Reagan, *An American Life*, 60–66.

58. Reagan, *An American Life*, 60–66.

59. Troy, *Morning in America*, 52.

60. Jeffords, *Hard Bodies*, 5.

61. Dan Rather, "Introduction," in Dan Rather and CBS News, *Ronald Reagan Remembered* (New York: Simon and Schuster, 2004), xii.

62. Johanna Neuman, "Ronald Wilson Reagan, 1911–2004," in *Ronald Reagan Remembered*, 7–9.

63. Jon Meacham et al., "American Dreamer," in *Ronald Reagan Remembered*, 119–120.

64. Richard E. Neustadt, Presidential Power and the Modern Presidents: The Politics of Leadership from Roosevelt to Reagan, rev. ed. (1960; repr., New York: The Free Press, 1991).

65. Michael Duffy and Michael Scherer, "The Role Model: What Obama Sees in Reagan," *Time*, January 27, 2011.

8. "An outstanding representative of America"

1. Mal Whitfield, *Beyond the Finish Line* (Washington, D.C.: Whitfield Foundation, 2002), 50.

2. Whitfield, *Beyond the Finish Line*; John C. Walter and Malina Iida, eds., *Better than the Best: Black Athletes Speak, 1920–2007* (Seattle: University of Washington Press, 2010), 23–37; Frank Litsky, "Whitfield Revisits Olympic Moments," *New York Times*, February 24, 2002, 11.

3. Damion L. Thomas, *Globetrotting: African American Athletes and Cold War Politics* (Urbana: University of Illinois, 2012), 103–132; Whitfield, *Beyond the Finish Line*, vii–27.

4. See John Hoberman, *The Olympic Crisis: Sport, Politics, and the Moral Order* (New Rochelle, N.Y.: Caratzas, 1986); Mark Dyreson, *Making the American Team: Sport, Culture, and the Olympic Experience* (Urbana: University of Illinois Press, 1998); David Maraniss, *Rome 1960: The Olympics that Changed the World* (New York: Simon and Schuster, 2008); Nicholas Evan Sarantakes, *Dropping the Torch: Jimmy Carter, the Olympic Boycott, and the Cold War* (New York: Cambridge University Press, 2011); and Kevin Witherspoon, *Before the Eyes of the World: Mexico and the 1968 Olympic Games* (DeKalb: Northern Illinois Press, 2008).

5. See Russ Crawford, *The Use of Sports to Promote the American Way of Life during the Cold War: Cultural Propaganda, 1945–1963* (Lewiston, N.Y.: Edwin

Mellen Press, 2003); Heather L. Dichter and Andrew L. Johns, eds., *Diplomatic Games: Sport, Statecraft, and International Relations since 1945* (Lexington: University of Kentucky, 2014); Thomas M. Domer, "Sport in Cold War America, 1953–1963: The Diplomatic and Political Use of Sport in the Eisenhower and Kennedy Administrations" (PhD diss., Marquette University, 1976); Thomas M. Hunt, "American Sport Policy and the Cultural Cold War: The Lyndon B. Johnson Presidential Years," *Journal of Sport History* 33, no. 3 (2006): 273–97; Toby C. Rider, *Cold War Games: Propaganda, the Olympics, and US Foreign Policy* (Urbana: University of Illinois Press, 2016); and Stephen Wagg and David L. Andrews, eds., *East Plays West: Sport and the Cold War* (New York: Routledge, 2007).

6. The most thorough discussion of these exchanges is Thomas, *Globetrotting*. See also Ashley Brown, "Swinging for the State Department: American Women Tennis Players in Diplomatic Goodwill Tours, 1941–59," *Journal of Sport History* 42, no. 3 (2015): 289–309; J. M. Turrini, "'It Was Communism Versus the Free World': The USA-USSR Dual Track Meet Series and the Development of Track and Field in the United States," *Journal of Sport History* 28, no. 3 (2001): 427–471; Kevin B. Witherspoon, "'Fuzz Kids' and 'Musclemen': The US-Soviet Basketball Rivalry, 1958–1975," in *Diplomatic Games: Sport, Statecraft, and International Relations since 1945*, edited by Heather L. Dichter and Andrew L. Johns (Lexington: University Press of Kentucky, 2014), 297–326; Kevin B. Witherspoon, "Going 'to the Fountainhead': Black Athletes as Cultural Ambassadors in Africa, 1970–1971," *International Journal of the History of Sport* 30, no. 13 (2013): 1508–1522.

7. Thomas, *Globetrotting*, 122.

8. Whitfield, *Beyond the Finish Line*, 42–43.

9. R. H. W. Batchelor to Department of State, December 18, 1957, Box 130, Folder "032 White Eagle," Central Decimal File 1955–1959, Record Group 59, Department of State Central Files (hereafter RG 59), National Archives and Records Administration (hereafter NARA), College Park, Maryland.

10. Acheson quoted in Thomas, *Globetrotting*, 47.

11. Thomas, *Globetrotting*, 41–74.

12. "A Study of the Impact of Sports on the Achievement of US Foreign Policy Objectives," 5, November 5, 1965, Group 2, Series 3, Box 92, Folder 7, "Special Study on Sports Exchanges, 1960s–1970s," Bureau of Educational and Cultural Affairs Historical Collection, University of Arkansas, Fayetteville, Arkansas (hereafter BECAHC).

13. Memo from AmEmbassy Lagos to Department of State, June 26, 1971, Group 2, Series 3, Box 89, Folder 28, BECAHC.

14. Department of State, Transcript of Press, Radio, and Television News Briefing, June 3, 1971, Group 2, Series 3, Box 89, Folder 28, BECAHC.

15. "Three US Track Teams on Foreign Tours," *Amateur Athlete*, August 1947, 15.

16. Whitfield quoted in Walter and Iiad, *Better than the Best*, 24.

17. Frank Litsky, "Mal Whitfield, Olympic Gold Medalist and Tuskegee Airman, Dies at 91," *New York Times*, November 20, 2015, B14.

18. Litsky, "Mal Whitfield."

19. Whitfield, *Beyond the Finish Line*, 54.

20. See, for instance, Arthur Daley, "Sports of the Times: Man in a Rut," *New York Times*, February 5, 1953, 31; Joseph M. Sheehan, "Whitfield Lowers World 500

Record to 0:56.6 Indoors," *New York Times*, February 8, 1953, S1; Joseph M. Sheehan, "Whitfield Lowers 2 World Records in 600-Yard Race," *New York Times*, March 1, 1953, S1; and "Whitfield Lowers World Record for 880-Yard Run to 1:48.6 in Finnish Meet," *New York Times*, July 18, 1953, 9.

21. Arthur Daley, "Sports of the Times: In Search of Variety," *New York Times*, February 16, 1954, 32; Arthur Daley, "Sports of the Times: Picking Up Speed," *New York Times*, June 23, 1955, 36.

22. Joseph M. Sheehan, "Whitfield Is First Negro to Gain the Sullivan Trophy in Amateur Athletics," *New York Times*, December 31, 1954, 19; "Sullivan Memorial Trophy Winner," *New York Times*, February 21, 1955, 26.

23. Whitfield, *Beyond the Finish Line*, 55.

24. See Jules Tygiel, *Baseball's Great Experiment: Jackie Robinson and His Legacy* (New York: Oxford University Press, 2008); John C. Chalberg, *Rickey & Robinson: The Preacher, the Player, and America's Game* (Wheeling, Ill.: Harlan Davidson, 2000); and Arnold Rampersad, *Jackie Robinson: A Biography* (New York: Ballantine Books, 1997).

25. Dave Albritton to Dr. Olds, September 15, 1953, Box 1, Folder "AAU General, 1952–58," Avery Brundage Collection, University of Illinois Archives, University of Illinois Urbana-Champaign.

26. Derek Erskine to John A. Noon, April 14, 1955, Group 2, Series 3, Box 93, Folder 93-8: "MC 468, Whitfield, Malvin, Track & Field, 1954–1967," BECAHC.

27. Foreign Service Despatch from AMEmbassy, Tehran, December 22, 1954, Group 2, Series 3, Box 93, Folder 93-8: "MC 468, Whitfield, Malvin, Track & Field, 1954–1967," BECAHC.

28. Foreign Service Despatch from USIS Belgrade, January 18, 1955, Group 2, Series 3, Box 93, Folder 93-8: "MC 468, Whitfield, Malvin, Track & Field, 1954–1967," BECAHC.

29. Foreign Service Despatch from AmEmbassy Monrovia, October 4, 1957, Box 130, Folder "032 White Eagle," Central Decimal Files 1955–1959, RG 59, NARA.

30. Thomas, *Globetrotting*, 109.

31. Whitfield quoted in Walter and Iiad, *Better than the Best*, 30.

32. "Athlete to Aid G.O.P.," *New York Times*, August 3, 1956, 8.

33. Whitfield, *Beyond the Finish Line*, 56–58; "Mal Whitfield—US Ambassador of Sports," *Ebony* 16, no. 12 (1961): 82–85.

34. Whitfield, *Beyond the Finish Line*, xviii.

35. John C. Stoddard, AmEmbassy Vientiane, July 6, 1963, Group 2, Series 3, Box 93, Folder 93-8: "MC 468, Whitfield, Malvin, Track & Field, 1954–1967," BECAHC.

36. Whitfield, *Beyond the Finish Line*, 58–60.

37. "Whitfield Faces Charge," *New York Times*, December 15, 1953, 60; "Whitfield Draws Official's Support," *New York Times*, December 16, 1953, 52; Joseph M. Sheehan, "A.A.U. Disciplines Four Track Aces," *New York Times*, February 22, 1954, 23; "Athletes' Tours Hit by Brundage," *New York Times*, March 16, 1955, 44.

38. Whitfield, *Beyond the Finish Line*, 26.

39. Whitfield quoted in Walter and Iiad, *Better than the Best*, 32.

40. Rudolph quoted in Michael Davis, *Black American Women in Olympic Track & Field* (Jefferson, N.C.: McFarland, 1992), 127–128.

41. For more on African American athletes and Black Power, see Simon Henderson, *Sidelined: How American Sports Challenged the Black Freedom Struggle* (Lexington: University Press of Kentucky, 2013); Amy Bass, *Not the Triumph but the Struggle: The 1968 Olympics and the Making of the Black Athlete* (Minneapolis: University of Minnesota Press, 2002); Harry Edwards, *The Revolt of the Black Athlete* (New York: Free Press, 1969); and Thomas, *Globetrotting*, 133–170.
42. Witherspoon, "Going 'to the Fountainhead.'"
43. Mal Whitfield, "Let's Boycott the Olympics," *Ebony* 19, no. 5 (1964): 95.
44. Whitfield, "Let's Boycott the Olympics," 95.
45. Whitfield, *Beyond the Finish Line*, 40.
46. Whitfield quoted in Walter and Iiad, *Better than the Best*, 33.
47. "2 Sprinters Said to Charge Bias," *New York Times*, August 3, 1973, 65.
48. Whitfield quoted in Walter and Iiad, *Better than the Best*, 33.
49. Edwards, *Revolt of the Black Athlete*, 16–17. As Edwards and others have described, by the late 1960s, many black athletes had grown frustrated with an athletic system that offered few real benefits to them. Along with suffering overt racist attacks from some white coaches, spectators, and competitors, black athletes confronted many other challenges: limited endorsement opportunities, the "stacking" of multiple black players at a single position on a team, ostracism and social discrimination on college campuses, few if any black coaches, and others. For more on the "Revolt of the Black Athlete," see Bass, *Not the Triumph but the Struggle*; Henderson, *Sidelined*; and Kevin Witherspoon, *Before the Eyes of the World: Mexico and the 1968 Olympic Games* (DeKalb: Northern Illinois University Press, 2008).
50. Thomas, *Globetrotting*, 72–74.
51. See Edwards, *Revolt of the Black Athlete*.

9. "One of the greatest ambassadors that the United States has ever sent abroad"

1. "Wilma Rudolph Gets Sullivan Sportsmanship Award," *New York Times*, February 26, 1962, 34.
2. For perspectives on the United States' use of sport during the Cold War, see Thomas Domer, "Sport in Cold War America, 1953–1963: The Diplomatic and Political Use of Sport in the Eisenhower and Kennedy Administrations" (PhD diss., Marquette University, 1976); Russell Crawford, "Consensus All-American: Sport and the Promotion of the American Way of Life During the Cold War, 1946–1965" (PhD diss., University of Nebraska—Lincoln, 2004); Thomas Hunt, "American Sport Policy and the Cultural Cold War: The Lyndon B. Johnson Presidential Years," *Journal of Sport History* 33, no. 3 (2006): 273–297; Damion Thomas, *Globetrotting: African American Athletes and Cold War Politics* (Urbana: University of Illinois Press, 2012); and Toby Rider, *Cold War Games: Propaganda, the Olympics, and US Foreign Policy* (Urbana: University of Illinois Press, 2016).
3. Laura Belmonte, *Selling the American Way: US Propaganda and the Cold War* (Philadelphia: University of Pennsylvania Press, 2010), 3.
4. Belmonte, *Selling the American Way*, 95–115, 136–159.
5. While scholars have discovered omissions and inconsistencies, Wilma

Rudolph's 1977 autobiography remains the prevailing source for her childhood experiences; see Wilma Rudolph with Bud Greenspan, *Wilma* (New York: Signet, 1977). Numerous scholars have also analyzed Rudolph in accounts that determine her significance in terms of race and/or gender. See Cindy Himes Gissendanner, "African American Women Olympians: The Impact of Race, Gender, and Class Ideologies, 1932–1968," *Research Quarterly for Exercise and Sport* 67, no. 2 (1996): 172–182; Wayne Wilson, "The Making of an Olympic Icon," in *Out of the Shadows: A Biographical History of African American Athletes*, edited by David Wiggins (Fayetteville: University of Arkansas Press, 2006); Aram Goudsouzian, "Wilma Rudolph: Running for Freedom," in *Tennessee Women: Their Lives and Times*, edited by Sarah Wilkerson Freeman (Athens: University of Georgia Press, 2009); Jennifer Lansbury, *A Spectacular Leap: Black Women Athletes in Twentieth-Century America* (Fayetteville: University of Arkansas Press, 2014); Rita Liberti and Maureen M. Smith, *(Re)Presenting Wilma Rudolph* (Syracuse, N.Y.: Syracuse University Press, 2015).

6. For a thorough account of the Tennessee State women's track program, see Tracey M. Salisbury, "First to the Finish Line: The Tennessee State Tigerbelles 1944–1994" (PhD diss., The University of North Carolina at Greensboro, 2009).

7. "Mae Faggs Excels in 3 Track Events," *New York Times*, August 19, 1956, 171; Claude E. Harrison Jr., "Tennessee State Univ. Retains Jr. and Sr. AAU Track Titles," *Philadelphia Tribune*, August 21, 1956, 8; "Mrs. Brown Betters Two Track Records," *New York Times*, August 26, 1956, S1; "'My Dream Team,' Says Tennessee State Coach," *Afro-American*, September 1, 1956, 15; "Six Tenn. Girls, Matron Win Olympic Team Berths," *Afro-American*, September 1, 1956, 15.

8. Fay Young, "The Brown Girls," *Chicago Defender*, December 15, 1956, 17; Mabel Crooks, "Gala Welcomed Tendered Tennessee's 'Fabulous Six,'" *Afro-American*, December 22, 1956, 14.

9. Ed Temple interviewed by Cat Ariail, June 9, 2014, University Library, Tennessee State University (hereafter Temple interview).

10. Temple interview.

11. "US Leads Russia after First Day of Dual Track and Field Meet in Moscow," *New York Times*, July 28, 1958, 17; "US Captures Summit Meet from Russians," *Chicago Defender*, July 29, 1958, 24.

12. Pincus Sober, "US Track and Field Teams Compete in Moscow, Warsaw, Budapest, Athens," *Amateur Athlete*, September 1958, 5.

13. Robert Musel, "US Track Stars Upset Russians," *Chicago Defender*, July 29, 1958, 23.

14. Edward Temple with B'Lou Carter, *Only the Pure in Heart Survive* (Nashville: Broadman Press, 1980), 47. I invoke Evelyn Brooks Higginbotham's conceptualization of the politics of respectability, which describes how groups of African Americans historically have asserted their claim to citizenship through well-mannered, traditionally gendered comportment and presentation. See Evelyn Brooks Higginbotham, *Righteous Discontent: The Women's Movement in the Black Baptist Church, 1880–1920* (Cambridge, Mass.: Harvard University Press, 1994).

15. For a perspective on the gendered politics of the Civil Rights Movement, see Taylor Branch, *Parting the Waters: America in the King Years* (New York: Simon

and Schuster, 1989); Mary Dudziak, *Cold War Civil Rights: Race and the Image of American Democracy* (Princeton, N.J.: Princeton University Press, 2000); and Harvard Sitkoff, *The Struggle for Black Equality* (New York: Hill & Wang, 2008).

16. For a detailed discussion of Temple's policies, see Temple, *Only the Pure in Heart Survive*, 46–51; and Salisbury, "'First to the Finish Line.'" For broader discussions on the operation of ideologies of race and sexuality in women's sport, see Susan Cahn, *Coming on Strong: Gender and Sexuality in Twentieth-Century Women's Sport* (New York: The Free Press, 1994).

17. For analysis of the role of black athletes and other cultural figures in the Cold War, see Melinda Schwenk, "'Negro Stars' and the USIA's Portrait of Democracy," *Race, Gender & Class* 8, no. 4 (2001): 116–139; Penny Von Eschen, *Satchmo Blows Up the World: Jazz Ambassadors Play the Cold War* (Cambridge, Mass.: Harvard University Press, 2004); and Thomas, *Globetrotting*.

18. Rudolph, *Wilma*, 133.

19. Alex Haley, "The Queen Her Earned Her Crown," *The Rotarian*, May 1961, 38.

20. Rudolph, *Wilma*, 136.

21. Temple, *Only the Pure in Heart Survive*, 63.

22. "Olympian Quintessence: A Girl's Triple Win, A Caper in the Colosseum, A Russian Victory," *Life*, September 19, 1960, 115.

23. "Double Sprint Champion Hurries Only on Track," *New York Times*, September 6, 1960.

24. Barbara Heilman, "Like Nothing Else in Tennessee," *Sports Illustrated*, November 14, 1960, 48.

25. Melissa Harris-Perry, *Sister Citizen: Shame, Stereotypes, and Black Women in America* (New Haven, Conn.: Yale University Press, 2011).

26. Lula Garrett, "60's Top Ten," *Afro-American*, December 31, 1960, 12.

27. "Words of the Week," *Jet*, August 10, 1961, 30.

28. "Wilma Rudolph among 10 Top Young Women of '60," *New York Amsterdam News*, December 31, 1960, 9.

29. "Feminine Front," *Afro-American*, April 29, 1961, 4.

30. Heilman, "Like Nothing Else in Tennessee."

31. *London Daily Express* quoted in Eslonda Robeson, "London Raves Over the Olympic Games," *Afro-American*, October 1, 1960, A4.

32. "Europe Salutes Wilma Rudolph," *Chicago Defender*, February 4, 1961, 23.

33. Heilman, "Like Nothing Else in Tennessee."

34. "Australian Tour in Making for Miss Wilma Rudolph," *Philadelphia Tribune*, October 1, 1960, 12.

35. Amateur Athletic Union of the United States 73rd Annual Convention Meeting Minutes, Box 4, 73rd Annual Meeting Las Vegas, NV, November 30–December 4, 1960, Avery Brundage Collection, University of Illinois Archives, University Library, University of Illinois, Champaign-Urbana (hereafter Brundage Collection).

36. "New York Beat," *Jet*, February 16, 1961, 63.

37. "Wilma Named World 'Athlete of Year,'" *Jet*, December 29, 1960, 56.

38. "The Frozen Face of Fame," *Sports Illustrated*, June 26, 1961.

39. For a critical analysis of this film, see Schwenk, "'Negro Stars' and the USIA's Portrait of Democracy."

40. "Wilma Rudolph to Tour India during July," *Atlanta Daily World*, April 6, 1961, 5; "Wilma Sets Exhibitions on India Goodwill Tour," *Afro-American*, April 15, 1961, 14.

41. For examinations of State Department goodwill efforts featuring African Americans, see Von Eschen, *Satchmo Blows Up the World*; and Thomas, *Globetrotting*.

42. For analysis of Gibson's tour, see Ashley Brown, "Swinging for the State Department: American Women Tennis Players in Diplomatic Goodwill Tours, 1941–59," *Journal of Sport History* 42, no. 3 (2017): 289–309.

43. "Crack Athletes to Tour Three African Countries," *Chicago Defender*, March 31, 1956, 18; "US Track Athletes Hailed in Africa," *Amateur Athlete*, June 1956, 15.

44. "Wilma Looking Forward to First Visit to Russia," *Afro-American*, July 15, 1961, 14.

45. "2 Relay Marks Set," *New York Times*, July 16, 1961, S1.

46. Roy Terrell, "The High Meet the Mighty," *Sports Illustrated*, July 24, 1961.

47. Terrell, "The High Meet the Mighty."

48. Robert Daley, "US Trackmen Rout West Germany; Miss Rudolph Sets Record," *New York Times*, July 20, 1961, 20.

49. Robert Daley, "US Leads Poles in Track, 68–49," *New York Times*, July 30, 1961.

50. "Wilma Sets World Record in '100,'" *Afro-American*, July 29, 1961, 14.

51. "Wilma Rudolph Gets Sullivan."

52. Undated brochure on James E. Sullivan, Box 10, Sullivan, James E. Award 1904, 1930–31, 1935, 1946–50, Brundage Collection.

53. Joseph M. Sheehan, "Whitfield Is First Negro to Gain the Sullivan Trophy," *New York Times*, December 31, 1954, 19; Joseph M. Sheehan, "Sullivan Award Goes to Dillard," *New York Times*, January 1, 1956, S1.

54. For detailed perspectives on the cooperation between the AAU and other private sport organizations and the US government for Cold War propaganda, see Domer, "Sport in Cold War America, 1953–1963"; and Rider, *Cold War Games*.

55. James F. Simms to Members of the Tribunal for Award of the James E. Sullivan Memorial, December 7, 1959, Box 10, Sullivan, James E. Award 1951–60, Brundage Collection.

56. "Johnson Gains Sullivan Award," *New York Times*, January 1, 1961, S1.

57. Joseph M. Sheehan, "World Mark Set," *New York Times*, July 22, 1962, 123.

58. Sheehan, "World Mark Set."

59. Joseph M. Sheehan, "127–108 Triumph Paced by Oerter," *New York Times*, July 23, 1962, 24.

60. Tex Maule, "Whirling Success for the US," *Sports Illustrated*, July 30, 1962, 14.

61. "Atterberry Victor in 2 Swedish Races," *New York Times*, August 21, 1962, 40; "Hayes, Wilma Score for US," *Afro-American*, August 25, 1962, 9; "8 Firsts Go to US in Swedish Track," *New York Times*, August 31, 1962, 15; "Wilma Wins in Oslo," *Philadelphia Tribune*, September 8, 1962, 12.

62. "Wilma, Back from Latest Triumphs Abroad, Ready to Resume Studies," *Afro-American*, September 22, 1962, 9.

63. "Good Will Ambassador," *Philadelphia Tribune*, May 7, 1963, 13.

64. "Officers Guide: Division for Americans Abroad," Group 4, Series 1, Box 138, Folder 1, Bureau of Educational and Cultural Affairs Historical Collection, Special Collections, University of Arkansas Library, Fayetteville (hereafter BECAHC).

65. "American Specialists Program 1963: Introductory Remarks," Group 4, Series 1, Box 138, Folder 25: "US Specialists, 1962–1965," BECAHC.

66. Thomas Borstelmann, *The Cold War and the Color Line: American Race Relations in the Global Arena* (Cambridge, Mass.: Harvard University Press, 2009), 135–221.

67. "A Study of the Impact of Sports on the Achievement of US Foreign Policy Objectives," Group 2, Series 3, Box 92, Folder 7, "Special Study on Sports Exchanges, 1960s–1970s," BECAHC.

68. In *Globetrotting*, Damion Thomas discusses State Department officials' understanding of the symbolic power of black athletes. In his research on black Peace Corps volunteers, Johnathan Zimmerman discovered Peace Corps officials held a similar perspective; see Jonathan Zimmerman, "Beyond Double Consciousness: Black Peace Corps Volunteers in Africa, 19611971," *Journal of American History* 82, no. 3 (1995): 999–1028.

69. "Senegal in Salute to Wilma Rudolph," *New York Times*, April 14, 1963, 168.

70. "American Specialists Program 1963"; "Wilma Rudolph to Attend African Friendship Meet," *Chicago Defender*, April 4, 1963, 26; "Wilma Rudolph Off to Senegal," *New York Times*, April 13, 1963, 33.

71. "Senegal in Salute."

72. "Senegal in Salute"; "Rudolph Says She's 'Itchy' to Run Again," *Afro-American*, August 24, 1963, 10.

73. "Rudolph Says She's 'Itchy.'"

74. "Rudolph Says She's 'Itchy.'"

75. "Wilma Rudolph to Tour Ghana," *New York Times*, April 24, 1963, 55.

76. Wilma Rudolph interviewed by Tony Merrill, 8/13/1963, Group 19, Series 2, Subseries 1, Box 351, Tape 2, BECAHC.

77. Kwaku Adjisan, "Wilma Would Help Train Ghana Track Prospect," *Afro-American*, May 18, 1963, 7.

78. Adjisan, "Wilma Would Help Train Ghana Track Prospect."

79. Wilma Rudolph interviewed by Tony Merrill; "Rudolph Says She's 'Itchy.'"

80. "American Specialists Program 1963."

81. "American Specialists Program 1963."

82. Wilma Rudolph interviewed by Tony Merrill; "Wilma Rudolph in Upper Volta," *New York Times*, May 6, 1963, 40; "Rudolph Says She's 'Itchy.'"

83. "Wilma Rudolph Cited on Trip for 'Goodwill,'" *Chicago Defender*, May 6, 1963, 24.

84. Wilma Rudolph interviewed by Tony Merrill.

85. Nicholas Rodis, "The State Department's Athletes Give a New Look to Foreign Policy," *Amateur Athlete*, August 1964, 18, 36. Rodis misidentifies the African Friendship Games as the Pan-African Games.

86. "Rudolph Say She's 'Itchy.'"

87. "Rudolph Say She's 'Itchy.'"

88. It is important to realize that Africans did not necessarily absorb the message the State Department intended, despite their embrace of Rudolph. For a complementary perspective see Jonathan Zimmerman, "Beyond Double Consciousness: Black Peace Corps Volunteers in Africa, 1961–1971," *Journal of American History* 82, no. 3 (1995): 999–1028. Zimmerman explains that Africans separated their fondness for Peace Corps volunteers from their opinions of the

United States. His findings suggest that the Africans Rudolph met likely interpreted her in similar ways.

89. Wilma Rudolph interviewed by Tony Merrill.

90. Temple interview.

91. Rudolph, *Wilma*, 10.

10. Defying the Cultural Boycott

1. Arthur Ashe and Neil Amdur, *Off the Court* (New York: New American Library, 1981), 158.

2. Over the last decade, scholars have begun to analyze Arthur Ashe's important social contributions. Here are some of the most important recent works: Eric Allen Hall, *Arthur Ashe: Tennis and Justice in the Civil Rights Era* (Baltimore: Johns Hopkins University Press, 2014); Eric Allen Hall, "'I Guess I'm Becoming More and More Militant': Arthur Ashe and the Black Freedom Movement, 1961–1968," *Journal of African American History* 94, no. 4 (2011): 474–502; Damion Thomas, "The Quiet Militant: Arthur Ashe and Black Athletic Activism," in *Outside the Shadows: A Biographical History of the Black Athlete*, edited by David Wiggins (Fayetteville: University of Arkansas Press, 2006), 279–296; Damion Thomas, "'Don't Tell Me How to Think': Arthur Ashe and the Burden of 'Being Black,'" *International Journal of the History of Sport* 27, no. 8 (2010): 1313–1329; Eric Morgan, "Black and White at Center Court: Arthur Ashe and the Confrontation of Apartheid in South Africa," *Diplomatic History* 36, no. 5 (2012): 815–841; Kevin Witherspoon, "Going 'to the Fountainhead': Black American Athletes as Cultural Ambassadors in Africa, 1970–1971," *International Journal of the History of Sport* 30, no. 13 (2013): 1508–1522.

3. Thomas, Borstelmann, *Apartheid's Reluctant Uncle: The United States and Southern Africa in the Early Cold War* (New York: Oxford, 1993), 75–82; Damion Thomas, *Globetrotting: African American Athletes and Cold War Politics* (Champaign: University of Illinois Press, 2012), 5–15; Penny Von Eschen, *Satchmo Blows Up the World: Jazz Ambassadors Play the Cold War* (Cambridge: Harvard University Press, 2006), 2–6.

4. Borstelmann, *Apartheid's Reluctant Uncle*, 81.

5. Donald Culverson, *Contesting Apartheid: US Activism, 1960–1987* (New York: Westview, 1999), 35; Thomas, *Globetrotting*, 13; Von Eschen, *Race Against Empire*, 125.

6. Borstelmann, *Apartheid's Reluctant Uncle*, 75–77.

7. Leonard Thompson, *A History of South Africa* (New Haven, Conn.: Yale University Press, 2014), 186.

8. On the international implications of Eisenhower's decision to facilitate integration in Little Rock, see Cary Fisher, "Crossing the Color Line in Little Rock: The Eisenhower Administration and the Dilemma of Race for US Foreign Policy," *Diplomatic History* 24, no. 2 (2000): 233–264.

9. Thomas, *Globetrotting*, 4–6; Paul Gordon Lauren, *Power and Prejudice: The Politics and Diplomacy of Racial Discrimination* (Boulder, Colo.: Westview Press, 1988), 90, 192–193, 228; Borstelmann, *Apartheid's Reluctant Uncle*, 81.

10. Michael Krenn, *Black Diplomacy: African Americans and the State Department, 1945–1969* (London: M. E. Sharpe, 1999), 76; Thomas, *Globetrotting*, 5–9; Walter L. Hixson, *Parting the Curtain: Propaganda, Culture, and the Cold War,*

1945–1961 (New York: St. Martin's Press, 1997), 121; David Southern, *Gunnar Myrdal and Black-White Relations: The Use and Abuse of "An American Dilemma," 1944–1969* (Baton Rouge: Louisiana State University Press, 1987), 102.

11. Thomas, *Globetrotting*, 4–9; Krenn, *Black Diplomacy*, 30–31, 33; Mary Dudziak, *Cold War Civil Rights: Race and the Image of American Democracy* (Princeton, N.J.: Princeton University Press, 2000), 80.

12. For more on the connections between the civil rights movement, the anti-colonial movement, and the Cold War see Thomas Borstelmann, *The Cold War and the Color Line: American Race Relations in the Global Arena* (Cambridge, Mass.: Harvard University Press, 2001); Dudziak, *Cold War Civil Rights*; Penny M. Von Eschen, *Race against Empire: Black Americans and Anticolonialism, 1937–1957* (Ithaca, N.Y.: Cornell University Press, 1997); and Brenda Gayle Plummer, *Rising Wind: Black Americans and US Foreign Affairs, 1935–1960* (Chapel Hill: University of North Carolina Press, 1996).

13. Culverson, *Contesting Apartheid*, 200–201.

14. Håkan Thörn, *Anti-Apartheid and the Emergence of a Global Civil Society* (New York: Palgrave, 2009).

15. Morgan, "Black and White at Center Court," 825.

16. Hall, *Arthur Ashe*, 108–109.

17. Hall, *Arthur Ashe*, 109–113; Damion Thomas, *Globetrotting*, 128, 223–232; Morgan, "Black and White at Center Court," 827.

18. Morgan, "Black and White at Center Court," 832; "Hearings of Mr. Arthur Ashe," *Notes and Documents*, no. 11/70, April 1970, Unit on Apartheid Papers, United Nations Special Committee on Apartheid, Box 201, Folder 16: SA—Arthur Ashe, Charles Coles Diggs Papers, Moorland-Spingarn Research Center, Howard University, Washington, D.C. For more on sports and the global anti-apartheid movement, see Richard Lapchick, *The Politics of Race and International Sport: The Case of South Africa* (Westport, Conn.: Greenwood Press, 1975); Douglas Booth, *The Race Game: Sport and Politics in South Africa* (London: Cass, 1998); Malcolm MacLean, "Revisiting (and Revising?) Sports Boycotts: From Rugby against South Africa to Soccer in Israel," *International Journal of the History of Sport* 31, no. 15 (2014): 1832–1851; Douglas Hartmann, *Race, Culture, and the Revolt of the Black Athlete: The 1968 Olympic Protests and Their Aftermath* (Chicago: University of Chicago Press, 2003); Amy Bass, *Not the Triumph but the Struggle: 1968 Olympics and the Making of the Black Athlete* (Minneapolis: University of Minnesota Press, 2002).

19. Hall, *Arthur Ashe*, 139, 145–147; Morgan, "Black and White at Center Court," 829–830; "Ashe Denies Intent to Play Politics," *New York Times*, December 6, 1969, 11. For a fuller discussion of Ashe's 1970 goodwill tour, see Kevin Witherspoon, "Going 'to the Fountainhead,'" 1508–1522.

20. Hall, *Arthur Ashe*, 139, 145–149; Morgan, "Black and White at Center Court," 829–830.

21. "So. Africa Woos Miss Goolagong," *New York Times*, January 12, 1971, 41; "Miss Goolagong S. Africa Bound," *New York Times*, January 13, 1971, 31.

22. Hall, *Arthur Ashe*, 147; Grant Jarvie and Irene Reid, "Sport in South Africa" in *The International Politics of Sport in the Twentieth Century*, edited by James Riordan and Arnd Kruger (London: Routledge, 1999), 235.

23. Hall, *Arthur Ashe*, 143–148.

24. Borstelmann, *Apartheid's Reluctant Uncle*, 98–102.

25. Culverson, *Contesting Apartheid*, 36–41, 102; Donald R. Culverson, "From Cold War to Global Interdependence: The Political Economy of African American Antiapartheid Activism, 1968–1988," in *Window on Freedom: Race, Civil Rights, and Foreign Affairs, 1945–1988*, edited by Brenda Gayle Plummer (Chapel Hill: University of North Carolina Press, 2003), 232; Borstelmann, *Apartheid's Reluctant Uncle*, 98.

26. Borstelmann, *Apartheid's Reluctant Uncle*, 44, 92, 130, 23, 192.

27. Ashe and Amdur, *Off the Court*, 144–145; Borstelmann, *Apartheid's Reluctant Uncle*, 178.

28. Culverson, *Contesting Apartheid*, 136–142.

29. Thomas, "'Don't Tell Me How to Think,'" 1320–1329.

30. Arthur Ashe and Clifford Gewecke, *Advantage Ashe* (New York: Coward-McCann, 1967), 90; John McPhee, *Levels of the Game* (New York: Farrar, Straus and Giroux), 143.

31. Ashe and Amdur, *Off the Court*, 88–89.

32. McPhee, *Levels of the Game*, 145; Arthur Ashe and Frank Deford, *Portrait in Motion* (New York: Houghton Mifflin, 1975), 16–18.

33. Paul Fein, *Tennis Confidential: Today's Greatest Players, Matches, and Controversies* (Dulles, Va.: Potomac Books, 2003), 123.

34. Hall, *Arthur Ashe*, 170–172.

35. Hall, *Arthur Ashe*, 170–172.

36. Ashe and Deford, *Portrait in Motion*, 121–124; Morgan, "Black and White at Center Court," 820–827.

37. Ashe and Amdur, *Off the Court*, 155; Arthur Ashe and Arnold Rampersad, *Days of Grace* (New York: Random House, 1993), 105; Ashe and Deford, *Portrait in Motion*, 136.

38. Ashe and Rampersad, *Days of Grace*, 105; Ashe and Deford, *Portrait in Motion*, 121.

39. Hall, *Arthur Ashe*, 161, 195.

40. Hall, *Arthur Ashe*, 204.

41. Hall, *Arthur Ashe*, 200–205.

42. "The Black Scholar Interviews: Arthur Ashe," *The Black Scholar* 7, no. 3 (1975): 40–47.

43. "Should Famous Blacks Entertain in South Africa?" *Jet* 68, no. 11 (1985): 52–55. For an analysis of Artists and Athletes against Apartheid, see Jonathan Freeman, "Sun City and the Sounds of Liberation: Cultural Resistance for Social Justice in Apartheid South Africa" (master's thesis, University of California, Los Angeles, 2014).

11. Sport Is Not So Separate from Politics

The author would like to thank Toby Rider, Kevin Witherspoon, and the anonymous reviewers for their valuable feedback on this article. Lena Ånimmer at the Riksarkivet (National Archives of Sweden) located the image included in this chapter.

1. Dennis L. Bark and David R. Gress, *A History of West Germany*, 2nd ed., vol. 1, *From Shadow to Substance, 1945–1963* (Oxford: Basil Blackwell, Ltd., 1993), 23–29.

2. Heather Dichter, "'Strict measures must be taken': Wartime Planning and the Allied Control of Sport in Occupied Germany," *Stadion* 34, no. 2 (2008): 193–217.

3. Rebecca Boehling, *A Question of Priorities: Democratic Reform and Economic Recovery in Postwar Germany* (Providence, R.I.: Berghahn Books, 1996); Michael R. Hayse, *Recasting West German Elites: Higher Civil Servants, Business Leaders, and Physicians in Hesse between Nazism and Democracy, 1945–1955* (New York: Berghahn Books, 2003); Konrad H. Jarausch, *After Hitler: Recivilizing Germans, 1945–1955* (Oxford: Oxford University Press, 2006), 46–55.

4. Wanda Ellen Wakefield, "Out in the Cold: Sliding Sports and the Amateur Sports Act of 1978," *International Journal of the History of Sport* 24, no. 6 (2007): 776–795; Thomas M. Hunt, "Countering the Soviet Threat in the Olympic Medals Race: The Amateur Sports Act of 1978 and American Athletics Policy Reform," *International Journal of the History of Sport* 24, no. 6 (2007): 796–818.

5. Arnd Krüger, "United States of America: The Crucial Battle," in *The Nazi Olympics: Sport, Politics, and Appeasement in the 1930s*, edited by Arnd Krüger and William Murray (Urbana: University of Illinois Press, 2003), 44–69.

6. Walter Borgers, Jürgen Buschmann, and Karl Lennartz, *Olympischer Neubeginn: Gründung des Nationalen Olympischen Komitees, 24 September 1949 in Bonn* (Cologne: Carl und Liselott Diem-Archiv, 1999), 93.

7. The two French members were Marquis Melchior de Polignac and François Piétri. According to the British ambassador in France, Piétri had "remained in Madrid ever since Pétain sent him there as Ambassador and has never dared return to France for trial. Melchior de Polignac, on the other hand, after being in prison with his wife, who is a poisonous American, Nina de Polignac, somehow got himself white-washed to the extent that he is not at present suffering imprisonment or national indignity; although no decent French person will meet either him or his wife." Sir O. Harvey to Sir Orme Sargent, June 30, 1948, Foreign Office (hereafter FO) 371/73009, The National Archives, London, England (hereafter TNA).

8. Bark and Gress, *A History of West Germany*, 74–89; Ian Turner, "Denazification in the British Zone," in *Reconstruction in Post-War Germany: British Occupation Policy and the Western Zones, 1944–1955*, edited by Ian D. Turner (Oxford: Berg, 1989), 239–267.

9. Borgers, Buschmann, and Lennartz, *Olympischer Neubeginn*.

10. Heather L. Dichter, "Sporting Democracy: The Western Allies' Reconstruction of Germany Through Sport, 1944–1952" (PhD diss., University of Toronto, 2008), 191–205.

11. Ansprache des Buindspräsidenten Professor Dr. Theodor Heuss bei der Feier der Sportjugend in Bonn, September 25, 1949, Mappe 87, Carl Diem Papers, Carl und Liselott Diem-Archiv, Deutsche Sporthochschule, Cologne, Germany (hereafter CLDA).

12. Nationales Olympisches Komitee, Gründungsfeier in der Bundeshauptstadt Bonn am Rhein, September 24, 1949, Mappe 87, CLDA.

13. Bark and Gress, *A History of West Germany*, 74–75.

14. L. E. Norrie to OMGUS (Office of the Military Government of the United States) Education and Cultural Division Director, October 31, 1949, Entry 610, Records of the Education and Cultural Relations Division—Records of the Community Education Branch—Records of Mr. E. L. Norrie, Branch Chief, Record

Group (hereafter RG) 260, Military Agency Records, National Archives and Records Administration, College Park, Maryland (hereafter NARA).

15. Minutes, 5th Congress, International Amateur Handball Federation, July 9, 1938, International Amateur Athletic Federation 1938–39, Box 207, Avery Brundage Collection, University of Illinois Archives, University Library, University of Illinois at Urbana-Champaign; Horst Ueberhorst, "The Importance of the Historians' Quarrel and the Problem of Continuity for the German History of Sport," *Journal of Sport History* 17, no. 2 (1990): 241–2.

16. Georg von Rauch, *The Baltic States: The Years of Independence: Estonia, Latvia, Lithuania, 1917–1940*, translated by Gerald Onn (London: C. Hurst, 1974), 48; Werner Pade, "Zwitschen Wissenschaft, Abenteurertum und Kolonialpolitik Adolf Friedrich Herog zu Mecklenburg," in *Mecklenburger im Ausland: Historische Skizzen zum Leben und Wirken von Mecklenburgern in ihrer Heimat und in der Ferne*, edited by Martin Guntau (Bremen: Edition Temmen, 2001), 201–12; Rudolf Junack, *Adolf Friedrich Herzog zu Mecklenburg: Leben und Werken* (Hamburg: Verlag Krüger & Nienstedt, 1963), 213–4.

17. The initial claims in POL(50)39 regarding Mecklenburg's positions under the Nazis were later cleared, but any dismissals on the grounds of his close connections to royalty are presumably valid. Borgers, Buschmann, and Lennartz, *Olympischer Neubeginn*, 62; POL/P(50)39, June 29, 1950, FO 1005/1309, TNA.

18. Heather L. Dichter, "Game Plan for Democracy: Sport and Youth in Occupied Germany," in *Transforming Occupation in the Western Zones of Germany: Politics, Everyday Life and Social Interactions, 1945-55* , edited by Christopher Knowles and Camilo Erlichman (London: Bloomsbury Academic Press, 2018), 133-150.

19. Konrad Adenauer to John J. McCloy included in John J. McCloy to Secretary of State, April 29, 1950, Box 5252, 862A.453, Department of State Central Decimal Files 1950–54, Record Group 59, Department of State Central Files (hereafter RG 59), NARA.

20. "German International Relations," October 11, 1949, Box 5, Bureau of European Affairs—Office of German Affairs—Subject Files of the Officer in Charge of German Political Affairs, 1949–1956–Miscellaneous, RG 59, NARA.

21. Avery Brundage to John McCloy, October 14, 1950, Box 5252, 862A.453, Central Decimal Files 1950–54, RG 59, NARA. Although Germany had participated in the 1952 Winter Olympics, albeit after much controversy in Norway, all of these discussions about Germany's return to the Olympic movement focused on the 1952 Summer Games.

22. Auszüge aus dem Protokoll der Sitzung des IOC, Copenhagen, May 15, 1950, Heft 709, Deutscher Olympischer Sportbund, Frankfurt, Germany (hereafter DOSB).

23. POL/M(50)15, May 12, 1950, FO 371/85207, TNA.

24. POL/P(50)39, June 29, 1950, FO 1005/1309, TNA. The document does not make clear which British IOC member spoke with the government.

25. POL/P(50)39/2, August 7, 1950, FO 1005/1309, TNA.

26. POL/P(50)39/2, August 7, 1950, FO 1005/1309, TNA; POL/M(50)26, August 9, 1950, FO 1005/1305, TNA.

27. Verbatim Minutes, Thirty-Seventh Meeting of the Council of the Allied High Commission, August 17, 1950, FO 1023/319, TNA.

28. Brief for British Member on Item 4 of Agenda, German Participation in International Olympic Committee, prepared by Chancery, August 17, 1950, FO 1023/319, TNA.

29. Verbatim Minutes, Thirty-Seventh Meeting, AHC Council, August 17, 1950, FO 1023/319, TNA; HICOM/M(50)27, August 17, 1950, FO 1023/19, TNA.

30. Konrad Adenauer, *Memoirs 1945–53*, translated by Beate Ruhm von Oppen (London: Weidenfeld and Nicolson, 1966), 274–278.

31. HICOM/FED/M(50)10, August 17, 1950, FO 1023/3, TNA.

32. Konrad Adenauer to John J. McCloy, August 24, 1950, Box 47, Office of the Executive Secretary–General Records, 1947–1952, Record Group 466, Records of the High Commissioner for Germany (hereafter RG 466), NARA; John J. McCloy to Secretary of State, August 25, 1950, Box 5252, 862A.453, Central Decimal Files 1950–54, RG 59, NARA.

33. Bauwens, the only member from the initial delegation, was cleared, as he was able to prove that his membership in the Nazi Party from 1933 to 1934 was not only unbeknownst to him but also impossible. Konrad Adenauer to John J. McCloy, August 24, 1950, Box 47, Office of the Executive Secretary–General Records, 1947–1952, RG 466, NARA.

34. John J. McCloy to Secretary of State, August 25, 1950, Box 5252, 862A.453, Central Decimal Files 1950–54, RG 59, NARA.

35. The IOC delegation was J. Sigfrid Edström (Sweden), Avery Brundage (United States), Lord Aberdare (Great Britain), Comte Bonacossa (Italy), Col. P. W. Scharroo (Netherlands), Armand Massard (France), Angelo Bolanaki (Greece), and Albert Mayer (Switzerland). Protokoll der Sitzung des Exekutiv-Komitees des Internationalen Olympischen Komitees mit der Delegation des Deutschen Olympischen Komitees, August 29, 1950, Heft 709, DOSB.

36. Whereas Adenauer's letter to the Allied High Commission stated that Bauwens, Kolb, and Lingnau would comprise the German delegation, Georg Dietrich, another member of the NOC, was listed in the minutes in place of Lingnau. Protokoll der Sitzung des Exekutiv-Komitees des Internationalen Olympischen Komitees mit der Delegation des Deutschen Olympischen Komitees, August 29, 1950, Heft 709, DOSB.

37. Anthony Th. Bijkerk, "Pieter Wilhelmus Scharroo," unpublished biography in author's possession.

38. J. Sigfrid Edström to Carl Diem, June 13, 1950, Heft 709, DOSB.

39. Protokoll der Sitzung des Exekutiv-Komitees des Internationalen Olympischen Komitees mit der Delegation des Deutschen Olympischen Komitees, August 29, 1950, Heft 709, DOSB.

40. J. Sigfrid Edström to Otto Mayer, March 16, 1951, Presidents/J. Sigfrid Edström/Correspondence: 1951, Olympic Studies Centre, Lausanne, Switzerland (hereafter OSC).

41. Otto Mayer to J. Sigfrid Edström, March 19, 1951, Presidents/J. Sigfrid Edström/Correspondence: 1951, OSC.

42. J. Sigfrid Edström to R. W. Seeldrayers, April 13, 1951, Rodolphe William Seeldrayers/Correspondence: 1946, OSC.

43. J. Sigfrid Edström to Lord Burghley, April 9, 1951, David George Burghley/Correspondence: 1933–1969, OSC.

44. Protokoll der Sitzung des Präsidiums, Nationales Olympisches Komitee, May 16, 1951, Mappe 89, CLDA.

45. Avery Brundage to John J. McCloy, October 14, 1950, Box 5252, 862A.453, Central Decimal Files 1950–54, RG 59, NARA.

46. George A. Selke to Department of State, July 3, 1951, Box 5252, 862A.453, Central Decimal Files 1950–54, RG 59, NARA.

47. Heather L. Dichter, "'We have allowed our decisions to be determined by political considerations': The Cold War in the International Ski Federation," *Sport in History* 37, no. 3 (2017): 290–308.

48. E. M. Kraemer to Joseph Kolarek, December 12, 1951, Box 5116, 857.453, Central Decimal Files 1950–54, RG 59, NARA; Otto Mayer to J. Brooks B. Parker, May 25, 1950, Parker, James Brooks B., Correspondence, 1950–1952, OSC.

49. "Parker, J. Brooks B.," in *Who's Who in Pennsylvania*, vol. 1 (Chicago: A. N. Marquis, 1939), 670; "J. Brooks Parker, Olympic Official," *New York Times*, December 1, 1951, 9; "J. Brooks B. Parker," *Bulletin du Comité International Olympique*, no. 31 (January 1952), 24.

50. Telegram 2557, Donnelly, Vienna to Secretary of State, May 4, 1951, Box 4371, 800.4531, Central Decimal Files 1950–54, RG 59, NARA; Despatch 1232, E. Wilder Spaulding, Vienna, to Department of State, May 16, 1951, Box 4371, 800.4531, Central Decimal Files 1950–54, RG 59, NARA.

51. Telegram 946, Ward, Geneva, to Secretary of State, May 23, 1951, Box 4371, 800.4531, Central Decimal Files 1950–54, RG 59, NARA; Elwood Williams, memorandum to Miss Schukraft, August 23, 1951, Box 4371, 800.4531, Central Decimal Files 1950–54, RG 59, NARA.

52. Avery Brundage to Secretary of State, August 1, 1951, Box 509, 120.1/8-151, Central Decimal Files 1950–1954, RG 59, NARA.

53. Elwood Williams III to Byroade, August 30, 1951, Box 4371, 800.4531, Central Decimal Files 1950–54, RG 59, NARA.

54. J. Brooks B. Parker to Dr. W. C. Johnstone Jr., November 13, 1951, Box 5116, 857.453, Central Decimal Files 1950–54, RG 59, NARA; Joseph C. Kolarek to J. Brooks B. Parker, December 8, 1951, Box 5116, 857.453, Central Decimal Files 1950–54, RG 59, NARA.

55. J. Brooks B. Parker to W. C. Johnstone Jr., October 2, 1951, Box 4371, 800.4531, Central Decimal Files 1950–54, RG 59, NARA.

56. For more on German Cold War problems, see Uta Balbier, *Kalter Krieg auf der Aschenbahn: der deutsch-deutsche Sport, 1950–1972: Eine politische Geschichte* (Paderborn: F. Schöning, 2007); Heather L. Dichter, "'A game of political ice hockey': NATO Restrictions on East German Sport Travel in the Aftermath of the Berlin Wall," in *Diplomatic Games: Sport, Statecraft and International Relations since 1945*, edited by Heather L. Dichter and Andrew L. Johns (Lexington: University Press of Kentucky, 2014), 19–51.

57. Despatch 2333, D. Eugene Delgado-Arias, Mexico to Department of State, April 7, 1953, Box 4372, 800.4531; Telegram 499, Pearson, Munich, to Secretary of State, April 2, 1953, 800.4531, Box 4372; Circular Airgram, Dulles to Certain American Diplomatic and Consular Offices, April 7, 1953, Box 4372, 800.4531. All in Central Decimal Files 1950–54, RG 59, NARA.

58. Fernschreiben 51, Krekeler, Washington to Auswärtig Bonn, January 14, 1956, B 94/633B, Politisches Archiv des Auswärtiges Amt, Berlin, Germany;

Memorandum of Conversation, Richard Balken and Robert Creel, January 18, 1956, 800.4531, Box 4062, Central Decimal Files 1955-59, RG 59, NARA.

59. Dichter, "'We have allowed our decisions to be determined by political considerations.'"

12. Sport and American Foreign Policy during the 1960s

This chapter is a revised version of Thomas M. Hunt, "American Sport Policy and the Cultural Cold War: The Lyndon Johnson Presidential Years," *Journal of Sport History* 33, no. 3 (Fall 2006): 273–297.

1. Robert Kennedy, telephone conversation with Lyndon B. Johnson, May 28, 1964, Tape WH6405.11, Program No. 9, Citation No. 3539, Lyndon Baines Johnson Library and Museum, Austin, Texas (hereafter LBJL).

2. Robert F. Kennedy, "A Bold Proposal for American Sport," *Sports Illustrated*, July 27, 1964, 13–14.

3. Hubert H. Humphrey, untitled document, n.d., Box 92, Folder 14, Series 3, Group II, Bureau of Educational and Cultural Affairs Historical Collection, University of Arkansas, Fayetteville, Arkansas (hereafter BECAHC).

4. Hubert H. Humphrey to Lyndon B. Johnson, January 14, 1964, Box 4, File RE 13 11/22/63–9/30/64, Gen. RE 10, Subject File, White House Central File, LBJL (hereafter White House Central File).

5. Kenneth Wilson to Nicholas Rodis, April 30, 1964, Box 90, Folder 12, Series 3, Group II, BECAHC.

6. Louis [C.] Wyman to President [Lyndon B.] Johnson, February 8, 1964, Box 5, File RE 13 Olympic Games 11/22/63–3/31/64, Gen RE 10, Subject File, White House Central File, LBJL.

7. The committee was created on August 13, 1963, by Executive Order 11117; Executive Order no. 11117, August 13, 1963, *Federal Register* 28, 8397–8398.

8. The meeting is mentioned in Warren S. Berg [an Arthur D. Little employee] to [Assistant to the President] Kenneth P. O'Donnell, February 11, 1964, Box 5, File RE 13 Olympic Games 11/22/63–3/31/64, Gen RE 10, Subject File, White House Central File, LBJL.

9. Allison Danzig, "Olympic Group Opens a Drive to Restore Supremacy of US," *New York Times*, May 5, 1964, 1, 58.

10. Robert F. Kennedy and James Gavin, office conversation with President Johnson, June 12, 1964, Tape: WH6406.07, Program No. 16, Citation No. 3717, LBJL.

11. Lyndon B. Johnson to James Gavin, July 15, 1964, Box 60, Folder "Gavin, James M.," Name File, White House Central File, LBJL.

12. William P. Bundy, memorandum to Lucius D. Battle, April 10, 1964, Box 90, Folder 12, Series 3, Group II, BECAHC. My italics.

13. Rowan, message to all USIA posts, June 8, 1964, Box 90, Folder 12, Series 3, Group II, BECAHC.

14. Martin M. McLaughlin, memorandum to Nicholas Rodis, May 27, 1964, Box 90, Folder 12, Series 3, Group II, BECAHC.

15. Nicholas Rodis, memorandum to Martin M. McLaughlin, June 2, 1964, Box 90, Folder 12, BECAHC.

16. James D. O'Connell, memorandum to Johnson, May 18, 1964, Box 250, Folder Japan Memos [1 of 2] vol. 2 5/64–11/64, Country File, National Security File, LBJL.

17. Memorandum, O'Brien to the president, May 27, 1964, Box 4, Folder RE 13 11/22/63-9/30/64, Gen. RE 10, Subject File, WHCF, LBJL. Johnson decided that the effort was not worthwhile in a meeting with McGeorge Bundy on May 19, 1964. See Memorandum, Kermit Gordon to the President, June 5, 1964, Box 250, File Japan memos [1 of 2] vol. 2 5/64–11/64, Country File, National Security File, LBJL. This document also describes Karth's position while arguing against the expenditure.

18. Horace Busby, memorandum to the President, June 2, 1964, Box 4, Folder RE 13 11/22/63–9/30/64, Gen. RE 10, Subject File, White House Central File, LBJL. Italics underlined in original.

19. Recorded Statement Marking the Inauguration of Television by Communication Satellite between the United States and Japan, October 7, 1964, in *Public Papers of the Presidents of the United States: Lyndon B. Johnson, 1963–1964: Containing the Public Messages, Speeches, and Statements of the President*, 2 vols. (Washington, D.C.: US Government Printing Office, 1965), 2:1226–1227.

20. See John E. Findling and Kimberly D. Pelle, eds., *Encyclopedia of the Modern Olympic Movement* (Westport, Conn.: Greenwood Press, 2004), 168–169.

21. Seoul Embassy airgram to Department of State, September 4, 1964, Box 360, Folder Edu. 15-1, Record Group 59, Department of State Central Files (hereafter RG 59), National Archives and Records Administration, College Park, Maryland (hereafter NARA).

22. [Samuel D.] Berger, telegram to [Dean] Rusk, May 12, 1964, Box 90, Folder 12, Series 3, Group II, BECAHC.

23. [Dean] Rusk to US Mission Geneva, May 15, 1964, Box 90, Folder 12, Series 3, Group II, BECAHC.

24. See Findling and Pelle, *Encyclopedia of the Modern Olympic Movement*, 169. The Department of State was informed of the North Koreans' departure in American Embassy in Tokyo to Ruehcr/SecState, October 9, 1964, Box 366, Folder Edu 15-1 (10/6/64), RG 59, NARA.

25. Richard Espy, *The Politics of the Olympic Games* (Berkeley: University of California Press, 1979), 82–83.

26. Nicholas Rodis to Louis [C.] Wyman, October 22, 1964, Box 90, Folder 8, Series 3, Group II, BECAHC.

27. Robert H. Michel to Lyndon B. Johnson, June 17, 1965, Box 5, Folder RE 21 (6/25/65–), Gen RE 13, Subject File, White House Central File, LBJL.

28. See "President Appoints MacArthur Arbitrator," *Washington Post*, December 25, 1962, B10.

29. Lee C. White, memorandum to Bill Moyer, January 13, 1967, Box 60, Folder "Gavin, James M.," Name File, White House Central File, LBJL.

30. James M. Gavin to Lee C. White, July 8, 1964, Box 4, Folder RE 13 11/22/63–9/30/64, Gen RE 10, Subject File, White House Central File, LBJL.

31. Arthur D. Little, Inc., *Toward a More Effective United States Olympic Effort* (Cambridge, Mass.: Arthur D. Little, Inc., 1965).

32. Lyndon B. Johnson to James M. Gavin, May 7, 1965, Box 4, Folder RE 13 "10/1/64–," Gen RE 10, Subject File, White House Central File, LBJL.

33. The president's request that the report remain confidential is found in a note in his handwriting on a memorandum dated May 8, 1965, from Clifford L. Alexander Jr. to Jack Valenti. This document outlines the report's distribution to the United States Olympic Committee (USOC) Board of Directors and Gavin's plans with regard to *Sports Illustrated.* Box 5, Folder RE 13 "Olympic Games 11/1/64–8/23/66," Gen RE 10, Subject File, White House Central File, LBJL.

34. Jack Valenti to James M. Gavin, April 1, 1966, Box 4, Folder RE 13 "10/1/64," Gen RE 10, Subject File, White House Central File, LBJL.

35. Harry C. McPherson Jr., memorandum to Jack Valenti, June 21, 1965, Box 5, Folder RE 21 "6/25/65–," Gen RE 13, Subject File, White House Central File, LBJL.

36. See "Times Editorial: The Threat to Amateur Athletics," *Los Angeles Times,* July 19, 1965.

37. US, Congress, Senate, Committee on Commerce, *NCAA-AAU Dispute, Hearings Before the Committee on Commerce, United States Senate, Eighty-Ninth Congress, First Session, on the Controversy in Administration of Track and Field Events in the United States* (Washington D.C.: US Government Printing Office, 1965), 1.

38. US, Congress, Senate, Committee on Commerce, *NCAA-AAU Dispute.*

39. "NCAA, AAU Agree to Arbitration," *Washington Post,* August 26, 1965; "Truce Called by NCAA, AAU as Quiz Opens," *Los Angeles Times,* August 17, 1965.

40. White House Press Release, November 23, 1965, Box 168, Folder "11/23/65 Statement by the President in Response to Progress Report by the Council on Physical Fitness," Statements File, LBJL.

41. "President's Council on Physical Fitness and Sports Administrative History," 22–24, Administrative Histories File, LBJL. Results of the 1965 study are summarized in Paul A. Hunsicker and Guy G. Reiff, "A Survey and Comparison of Youth Fitness, 1958–1965," *Journal of Health, Physical Education and Recreation* 37 (January 1966): 23–25.

42. White House Press Release, "Statement by the President on Physical Fitness Awards Program," December 11, 1965, Box 168, Folder "12/11/65 Statement by the President Upon Announcing the Creation of the Physical Fitness Awards Program," Statements File, LBJL.

43. Nicholas Katzenbach to Stan Musial, January 10, 1966, Box 91, Folder 15, Series 3, Group II, BECAHC.

44. Miller's plan is articulated in Stan Ross, memorandum to Joe Califano, November 17, 1967, Box 31, Folder 165-11 "President's Council on Physical Fitness," Confidential File, White House Central File, LBJL.

45. President's Council on Physical Fitness and Sports, Executive Order 11398, March 4, 1968, published in *Weekly Compilation of Presidential Documents,* vol. 4 (Washington, D.C.: US Government Printing Office, 1968), 435–436. See also "President's Council on Physical Fitness and Sports Administrative History," 12, Administrative Histories File, LBJL.

46. Special Message to Congress: "Health in America," March 4, 1968, Lyndon B. Johnson, in *Public Papers of the Presidents of the United States: Lyndon B. Johnson, 1968–1969: Containing the Public Messages, Speeches, and Statements of the President,* 2 vols. (Washington D.C.: US Government Printing Office, 1970), 1:331.

47. President's Council on Physical Fitness and Sports Press Release, n.d., Box 91, Folder 15, Series 3, Group II, BECAHC.

48. Humphrey and Lentz quoted in President's Council on Physical Fitness and Sports Press Release.

49. "A Study of the Impact of Sports on the Achievement of US Foreign Policy Objectives," n.d. [ca. September 1965], Box 89, Folder 17, Series 3, Group II, BECAHC.

50. Administrative History of the Department of State, vol. 1, chap. 12, p. 52, Box 4, LBJL.

51. Nicholas Rodis, "The State Department's Athletes Give a New Look to Foreign Policy," *Amateur Athlete*, August 1964, 18.

52. See, for example, American Embassy in Panama to Department of State, August 31, 1965, Box 87, Folder 21, Series 3, Group II, BECAHC.

53. Quoted in "A Study of the Impact of Sports."

54. American Legation in Budapest to Department of State, August 29, 1965. See also American Legation in Budapest to Department of State, September 2, 1965. Both in Box 93, Folder 11, Series 3, Group II, BECAHC.

55. For a review of US coaches under the program from 1963 through 1969, see J. Manuel Espinosa, memorandum to Jerrold B. Speers, December 18, 1969, Folder 25, Box 88, Series 3, Group II, BECAHC.

56. Review of Advisory Panel for International Athletics meeting, January 16, 1967, by US Department of State Bureau of Educational and Cultural Affairs Athletic Exchanges Staff, Box 89, Folder 17, Series 3, Group II, BECAHC.

57. American Embassy in Bamako, Mali, to Department of State, September 19, 1966, Box 88, Folder 25, Series 3, Group II, BECAHC.

58. For a review of US coaches under the program from 1963 through 1969, see J. Manuel Espinosa, memorandum to Jerrold B. Speers, December 18, 1969, Box 88, Folder 25, Series 3, Group II, BECAHC.

59. American Embassy in Tehran to Department of State, January 9, 1968, Box 88, Folder 24, Series 3, Group II, BECAHC.

60. For a succinct analysis of the issues relating to the appropriations, see "Memorandum Concerning Appropriations for Mutual Educational and Cultural Exchange Activities," Box 8, Folder "Cultural Exchanges," Subject File, National Security File, LBJL.

61. Senator Fulbright to President Johnson, May 26, 1964, Box 8, Folder "Cultural Exchanges," Subject File, National Security File, LBJL.

62. Lyndon B. Johnson to John McClellan, June 12, 1964, Box 8, Folder "Cultural Exchanges," Subject File, National Security File, LBJL.

63. US Congress, House of Representatives, House Committee on Appropriations, *Departments of State, Justice, and Commerce, the Judiciary, and Related Agencies Appropriation Bill, Fiscal Year 1969. Report to Accompany H.R. 17522* (Washington, D.C.: US Government Printing Office, 1968), 8.

64. Republican Coordinating Committee Task Force on the Conduct of Foreign Relations, "The American Image Abroad," Revised Draft as of December 11, 1967, 2, 13, 6, 19–20, Box 33, Folder "FG 296 US Information Agency (196–)," Confidential File, White House Central File, LBJL.

65. For attempts to avert Republican criticisms, see Memorandum for the President through White House official Charles Maguire, January 31, 1968, Box 33, Folder "FG 296 US Information Agency (1967–)," Confidential File, White House

Central File, LBJL. Budget figures from Administrative History of the Department of State, 52.

66. See Administrative History of the Department of State, 51.

67. Jacob Canter to Glenn Ferguson, February 12, 1968, Box 92, Folder 37, Series 3, Group II, BECAHC.

68. "Review of International Educational and Cultural Exchange Programs and Their Relevance to US Foreign Policy Objectives: FY 1970 Budget," quoted in Administrative History of the Department of State, 64–65.

69. *Mexico '68 News Bulletin* 10 (February 27, 1967), Box 90, Folder 17, Series 3, Group II, BECAHC.

70. Memorandum of Conversation, June 28, 1967, Box 90, Folder 19, Series 3, Group II, BECAHC.

71. American Embassy in Mexico to Department of State, January 30, 1968, Box 90, Folder 20, Series 3, Group II, BECAHC.

72. American Embassy in Mexico to Department of State, March 7, 1967, Box 90, Folder 19, Series 3, Group II, BECAHC. See also memorandum for the files regarding "CU Assistance to Mexican Olympic Preparations," February 23, 1967, Box 90, Folder 15, Series 3, Group II, BECAHC.

73. White House Press Release, July 8, 1968, Box 4, Folder "RE 13 10/1/64–," Gen RE 10, Subject File, White House Central File, LBJL.

74. J. Manuel Espinosa, memorandum to Jean Joyce, October 28, 1968, Box 90, Folder 19, Series 3, Group II, BECAHC.

75. Proceedings of Meeting of the Board of Directors of the United States Olympic Committee, September 7–8, 1968, in Minutes of Meetings held March 23, 1968–Dec. 1, 1968 for the XIXth Olympiad (USOC Minutes, 7–8 September 1968–1 December 1968), 137, 141, United States Olympic Committee Library, Colorado Springs, Colorado.

76. On the American displays, see J. Manuel Espinosa, memorandum to Jean Joyce, October 28, 1968.

77. American Embassy in Mexico to Department of State, November 18, 1968, Box 90, Folder 19, Series 3, Group II, BECAHC. For the effort the Bureau of Educational and Cultural Affairs made on behalf of the Cultural Olympics, see also Administrative History of the Department of State, 51–52, 71.

78. A brief description of the effort is outlined in "Post *Scripts* . . . US Coaches for Mexicans," *Washington Post*, May 27, 1968.

79. American Embassy in Mexico to Department of State, May 21, 1966, Box 90, Folder 21, Series 3, Group II, BECAHC. The estimated number of Eastern-bloc coaches had grown to twenty by July 1966. See American Embassy in Mexico, D.F., memorandum of conversation, July 1, 1966, Folder 21, Box 90, Series 3, Group II, BECAHC.

80. American Embassy in Mexico to Department of State, November 18, 1968, Box 90, Folder 19, Series 3, Group II, BECAHC.

81. John W. Leslie, memorandum to George Reedy, July 27, 1964, Box 5, Folder RE 21 "Track & Field Meets," Gen RE 13, Subject File, White House Central File, LBJL.

82. A useful work on Ali is Elliott J. Gorn, ed., *Muhammad Ali: The People's Champ* (Urbana: University of Illinois Press, 1995).

83. Ali quoted in "The Thoughts of Muhammad Ali in Exile, c. 1967," in *Major*

Problems in American Sport History: Documents and Essays, edited by Steven A. Riess (Boston: Houghton Mifflin, 1997), 377.

84. See Harry Edwards, "The Olympic Project for Human Rights: An Assessment Ten Years Later," *Black Scholar* 10 (1979): 2–7.

85. See Edwards, "The Olympic Project for Human Rights," 2–7.

86. See Paul Zimmerman, "Negro Demands and Olympics," *Los Angeles Times*, December 24, 1967, G2.

87. Edwards quoted in Jeff Prugh, "Negro Group Votes to Boycott '68 Olympics," *Los Angeles Times*, November 24, 1967, 8.

88. Roby quoted in Proceedings of Meeting of the Board of Directors of the United States Olympic Committee, December 16–17, 1967 (USOC Minutes 16–17 December 16–17 1967), 8, United States Olympic Committee Library.

89. Coward's actions are discussed in Charles Frankel to Nicholas Katzenbach, December 14, 1967, Box 89, Folder 30, Series 3, Group II, BECAHC.

90. Dave Brady, "Humphrey Uses Council to Boost Negroes' Role," *Washington Post*, March 29, 1968, D1.

91. Roby quoted in Proceedings of Meeting of the Board of Directors of the United States Olympic Committee, December 16–17, 1967, 10.

92. "Olympic Boycotts," *Christian Science Monitor*, February 29, 1968, 16, Box 90, Folder 20, Series 3, Group II, BECAHC.

93. Edwards quoted in Pete Axthelm, "Boycott Now—Boycott Later," *Sports Illustrated*, February 26, 1968, 25.

94. Edwards quoted in Espy, *Politics of the Olympic Games*, 101.

95. Smith quoted in "Cause for Alarm," *Sports Illustrated*, September 25, 1967, 11.

96. Soviet Olympic Committee quoted in "Soviets Say Brundage Aids Racists," *Washington Post*, April 13, 1968, D4.

97. Thomas Hamilton, "South Africa's Ban from Olympics Confirmed," *New York Times*, April 25, 1968, 59; "Mexico Asks for an Emergency Session of International Olympic Committee," *New York Times*, March 10, 1968, S13.

98. USOC President Roby stated, "I asked [the IOC] what they would do if we would not take action. They said they might be forced to pull the entire United States team out of the Olympics." "Suspend 2 Negro Olympians," *Chicago Tribune*, October 19, 1968, A1.

99. These decisions were related in American Embassy in Mexico to Secretary of State, October 18, 1968, Box 90, Folder 18, Series 3, Group II, BECAHC.

100. "Negro Airs Possibility of Pullout," *Washington Post*, October 19, 1968, C2.

101. See Maher, "US Expels Smith, Carlos from Olympic Team."

102. See "Reaction to Expulsion Runs Gamut," *Washington Post*, October 19, 1968, C2.

103. American Embassy in Mexico to Secretary of State, October 18, 1968, Box 90, Folder 18, Series 3, Group II, BECAHC.

104. Benjamin H. Read, memorandum to Walt W. Rostow, October 18, 1968, Box 85, Folder "RE 13 Olympic Games (Pan American Games)," Confidential File, White House Central File, LBJL.

105. Torregrosa and Korobkov quoted in "Reaction to Expulsion Runs Gamut."

106. Bill Kelly to Lyndon B. Johnson, October 29, 1968, Box 4, Folder "RE 13 10/1/64–," Gen RE 10, Subject File, White House Central File, LBJL.

13. In Defense of a Neoliberal America

1. Ronald Reagan, *An American Life: The Autobiography* (New York: Simon & Schuster, 1990), 582–584.

2. "Jus" to Ronald Reagan, September 2, 1983, Box 8, Folder "OA 16248," Anne Higgins Files, Ronald Reagan Presidential Library and Museum, Simi Valley, California (hereafter RRPL).

3. Jean Pierre and Eva Bigotte to Ronald Reagan, n.d., Box 8, Folder "OA 16248," Anne Higgins Files, RRPL.

4. John Noble to Ronald Reagan, n.d., Box 8, Folder "OA 16248," Anne Higgins Files, RRPL.

5. Douglas Martin, "John Noble, Gulag Survivor, Dies at 84," *New York Times*, November 26, 2007, A21.

6. Noble to Reagan, n.d.

7. Stuart Young to Ronald Reagan, September 1, 1983, Box 8, Folder "OA 16248," Anne Higgins Files, RRPL.

8. Mr. and Mrs. Wilford W. Chapman to Ronald Reagan, September 1, 1983, Box 8, Folder "OA 16248," Anne Higgins Files, RRPL.

9. Douglas and Cathy Albrecht to Ronald Reagan, September 2, 1983, Box 8, Folder "OA 16248," Anne Higgins Files, RRPL.

10. Presidential Television Address: Flight 007, September 5, 1983, Box 28, Folder "KAL (2)," Jack Matlock Files, RRPL.

11. "Text of Reagan Letter to C.A.B. Chairman," *New York Times*, September 9, 1983.

12. "US Halts Aeroflot Business," *Milwaukee Sentinel*, September 9, 1983.

13. Richard Levine to Robert C. McFarlane, December 9, 1983, Box 30, Folder "Olympics 1984–USSR (2)," John F. Matlock Files, RRPL.

14. George Ramos, "Soviet Ship Focus of L.A. Harbor Protest," *Los Angeles Times*, September 7, 1983, 9.

15. Steven R. Churm and Steve Eddy, "Korea Sympathizers Protest Arrival of Soviet Freighter," *The Register*, September 7, 1983, Box "OA 11518," Folder "KAL Massacre I (1) - (3)," Linas Kojelis Files, RRPL.

16. Avo Piirisild, newsletter to Baltic American Freedom League membership, September 1985, The Baltic American Freedom League Records, Immigration History Research Center, University of Minnesota.

17. Alfred E. Senn, *Power, Politics, and the Olympic Games: A History of the Power Brokers, Events, and Controversies that Shaped the Games* (Champaign, Ill.: Human Kinetics, 1999), 197. In an autobiographical sketch, Balsiger referred to himself as an "investigative researcher and author of 18 non-fiction books." David W. "Dave" Balsiger Biographical Sketch, n.d., Folder "192867," WHORM Subject Files: CO165, RRPL.

18. Alfred Senn, "The Soviet Boycott of the 1984 Olympics: The Baltic Dimension," *Baltic Forum* 2, no. 1 (1985): 90.

19. Senator Doolittle Joins Ban the Soviets Coalition: Takes Off for New York and Washington To Promote Olympics Ban, October 19, 1983, Box 1, Folder "Ban the Soviets Coalition," John Kenneth Hill Files, RRPL.

20. John Hoberman, *The Olympic Crisis: Sport, Politics, and the Moral Order* (New Rochelle, N.Y.: Caratzas Publishing Company, 1986), 128–129.

21. Coalition Opposes New California Resolution Inviting Soviets to Olympics; Registers Protest with White House on Aeroflot Landing Request, n.d., Box 1, Folder "Ban The Soviets Coalition," John Kenneth Hill Files, RRPL.

22. Coalition Opposes New California Resolution Inviting Soviets to Olympics; Registers Protest with White House on Aeroflot Landing Request, n.d., Box 1, Folder "Ban the Soviets Coalition," John Kenneth Hill Files, RRPL.

23. David Balsiger to Michael K. Deaver, December 16, 1983, Box 6, Folder "Soviet Requests for Olympics (2)," John Kenneth Hill Files, RRPL.

24. Peter Ueberroth, Richard Levin, and Amy Quinn, *Made in America* (New York: William Morrow and Company, 1985), 236.

25. Maura Dolan, "Drive to Ban the Soviets from Olympics off to a Slow Start," *Los Angeles Times*, November 2, 1983.

26. Robert McFarlane, memorandum to Ronald Reagan, January 31, 1984, Box 9, Folder "LAOG Counter Intelligence & Security," Executive Secretariat, NSC: Subject Files, RRPL. Strikethroughs and italics indicate Reagan's edits.

27. McFarlane to Reagan, January 31, 1984.

28. National Security Decision Directive Number 135, "Los Angeles Olympic Games Counterintelligence and Security Precautions," March 27, 1984, Folder "NSDD 135," Executive Secretariat, National Security Council, NSDD112–35, RRPL.

29. Michael K. Deaver to Peter Ueberroth, March 14, 1984, Executive Secretariat, National Security Council Records, Folder "Olympics, Vol. 1," Box 23, RRPL.

30. Robert Edelman, "The Russians Are Not Coming: The Soviet Withdrawal from the Games of the XXIII Olympiad," *International Journal of the History of Sport* 32, no. 1 (2015): 5. For more about the history of the 1984 Olympic boycott, see Allen Guttmann, "The Cold War and the Olympics," *International Journal* 43, no. 4 (1988): 554–556; Nicholas Evan Sarantakes, *Dropping the Torch: Jimmy Carter, The Olympic Boycott, and the Cold War* (New York: Cambridge University Press, 2011), 244–261; Senn, "The Soviet Boycott of the 1984 Olympics," 88–104; Christopher Hill, *Olympic Politics* (Manchester: Manchester University Press, 1996); Philip D'Agati, *The Cold War and the 1984 Olympic Games: A Soviet-American Surrogate War* (New York: Springer Publishing, 2013).

31. For an outstanding account of the politics associated with the 1936 Berlin Olympics, see Barbara Keys, *Globalizing Sport: National Rivalry and International Community in the 1930s* (Cambridge, Mass.: Harvard University Press, 2006).

32. Rick Gruneau and Robert Neubauer, "A Gold Medal for the Market: The 1984 Los Angeles Olympics, the Reagan Era, and the Politics of Neoliberalism," in *The Palgrave Handbook of Olympic Studies*, edited by Helen Lenskyj and Stephen Wagg (London: Palgrave Macmillan, 2012), 134–162. Gruneau and Neubauer provide an outstanding history of the transition to neoliberal policies in the United States and an outline of how the Los Angeles Olympics benefited and advanced US neoliberal policies.

33. Peter Ueberroth, Rich Levin, and Amy Quinn, *Made in America: His Own Story* (New York: William Morrow and Company, 1985), 369.

34. Gruneau and Neubauer, "A Gold Medal for the Market," 145.

35. Mark Dyreson and Matthew Llewellyn, "Los Angeles is *the* Olympic City:

Legacies of the 1932 and 1984 Olympic Games," *International Journal of the History of Sport* 25, no. 14 (2008): 1991–2018.

36. Ronald Reagan, "Radio Address to the Nation on Administration Policies," August 18, 1984, accessed March 14, 2018, https://www.reaganlibrary.archives.gov/archives/speeches/1984/81884a.htm.

37. Lindsay Parks Pieper, *Sex Testing: Gender Policing in Women's Sports* (Champaign, Illinois: University of Illinois Press, 2016), 126.

38. Ronald Reagan, "Remarks at a Reagan-Bush Rally in Hackensack, New Jersey," October 26, 1984, accessed March 14, 2018, https://www.reaganlibrary.archives.gov/archives/speeches/1984/102684c.htm.

39. Ronald Reagan, "Remarks to Employees of Westinghouse Furniture Systems in Grand Rapids, Michigan," September 20, 1984, accessed March 14, 2018, https://www.reaganlibrary.archives.gov/archives/speeches/1984/92084g.htm.

40. David Winston and John Horne, "Underestimated Costs and Overestimated Benefits? Comparing Outcomes of Sport Mega-Events in Canada and Japan," *Sociological Review* 54, no. 2 (2006): 71–89.

Conclusion

1. Fort McHenry National Monument and Shrine, accessed July 4, 2017, https://www.nps.gov/fomc/index.htm.

2. Marc Leepson, *What So Proudly We Hailed: Francis Scott Key, A Life* (New York: Palgrave Macmillan, 2014); Marc Leepson, *Flag: An American Biography* (New York: Thomas Dunne Books/St. Martin's Press, 2005); Marc Ferris, *Star-Spangled Banner: The Unlikely Story of America's National Anthem* (Baltimore: Johns Hopkins University Press, 2014); George J. Svejda, *History of the Star Spangled Banner from 1814 to the Present* (Honolulu, Hawaii: University Press of the Pacific, 2005).

3. Leepson, *What So Proudly We Hailed.*

4. "The Star Spangled Banner," Smithsonian Museum of American History website, accessed March 14, 2018, http://amhistory.si.edu/starspangledbanner/.

5. A Google search of National Park Service monuments revealed that only Fort McHenry is designated as a national shrine. Search terms "National Park Service" + "Historic Shrine," search date August 10, 2017.

6. Douglas Hartmann, *Race, Culture, and the Revolt of the Black Athlete* (Chicago: University of Chicago Press, 2003); Amy Bass, *Not the Triumph but the Struggle: The 1968 Olympics and the Making of the Black Athlete* (Minneapolis: University of Minnesota Press, 2002).

7. Among the better artifacts that "Miracle" produced are the popular paperback produced in the immediate aftermath (Gerald Eskenazi and Dave Anderson, *Miracle on Ice* [New York: Bantam, 1980]) and an excellent made-for-television movie, *Miracle on Ice*, directed by David H. Stern, DVD (Burbank, Calif.: Moonlight/ABC 1981). See also the big-budget film made more than twenty years later (*Miracle*, directed by Gavin O'Connor, DVD [Burbank, Calif.: Buena Vista Home Entertainment, 2004]); and Wayne Coffey, *The Boys of Winter: The Untold Story of a Coach, a Dream, and the 1980 US Olympic Hockey Team* (New York: Crown, 2005). For an excellent analysis of the "Miracle on Ice," see Donald E. Abelson, "Politics

on Ice: The United States, the Soviet Union, and a Hockey Game in Lake Placid," *Canadian Review of American Studies* 40, no. 1 (2010): 63–94.

8. Photographs of the Fort McHenry "Stars and Stripes" timeline taken by McClane Dyreson, March 11, 2016, digital copies in author's possession.

9. Stephen J. Whitfield, *The Culture of the Cold War* (Baltimore: Johns Hopkins University Press, 1991); Douglas Field, *American Cold War Culture* (Edinburgh: Edinburgh University Press, 2005); Tom Engelhardt, *The End of Victory Culture: Cold War America and the Disillusioning of a Generation* (Amherst: University of Massachusetts Press, 2007); David C. Engerman, *Staging Growth: Modernization, Development, and the Global Cold War* (Amherst: University of Massachusetts Press, 2003); Robert A. Jacobs, *The Dragon's Tail: Americans Face the Atomic Age* (Amherst: University of Massachusetts Press, 2010); Andrea Friedman, *Citizenship in Cold War America: The National Security State and the Possibilities of Dissent* (Amherst: University of Massachusetts Press, 2014).

10. Damion L. Thomas, *Globetrotting: African American Athletes and Cold War Politics* (Urbana: University of Illinois Press, 2017); Thomas M. Hunt, *Drug Games: The International Olympic Committee and the Politics of Doping, 1960/2008* (Austin: University of Texas Press, 2011); Kevin B. Witherspoon, *Before the Eyes of the World: Mexico and the 1968 Olympics* (DeKalb: Northern Illinois University Press, 2008); Toby C. Rider, *Cold War Games: Propaganda, the Olympics, and US Foreign Policy* (Urbana: University of Illinois Press, 2016).

These four books are the tip of the iceberg. The recent focus over the past two decades on sport and the Cold War owes a debt to the scholarship of James Riordan, the pioneering polymath who during the Cold War provided extensive analysis of developments from the Soviet sphere. James Riordan, *Sport under Communism: The USS.R., Czechoslovakia, the G.D.R., China, Cuba* (Canberra: Australian National University Press, 1978); James Riordan, *Soviet Sport: Background to the Olympics* (Oxford: Blackwell, 1980); James Riordan, *Sport in Soviet Society: Development of Sport and Physical Education in Russia and the USSR* (Cambridge: Cambridge University Press, 1980); James Riordan, *Sport, Politics, and Communism* (Manchester: Manchester University Press, 1991). The work of Robert Edelman, especially *Serious Fun: A History of Spectator Sports in the USSR* (New York: Oxford University Press, 1993), has also been significant. Among the works that explore various aspects of the subject are Steven Ungerleider, *Faust's Gold: Inside the East German Doping Machine* (New York: Thomas Dunne Books/St. Martin's Press, 2001); Amy Bass, *Not the Triumph but the Struggle: The 1968 Olympics and the Making of the Black Athlete* (Minneapolis: University of Minnesota Press, 2002); Douglas Hartmann, *Race, Culture, and the Revolt of the Black Athlete: The 1968 Olympic Protests and Their Aftermath* (Chicago: University of Chicago Press, 2003); Susan Brownell, *Beijing's Games: What the Olympics Mean to China* (Lanham, Md.: Rowman & Littlefield, 2008); Guoqui Xu, *Olympic Dreams: China and Sports, 1895–2008* (Cambridge, Mass: Harvard University Press, 2008); Victor D. Cha, *Beyond the Final Score: The Politics of Sport in Asia* (New York: Columbia University Press, 2009); Kurt Edward Kemper, *College Football and American Culture in the Cold War Era* (Urbana: University of Illinois Press, 2009); Kay Schiller and Christopher Young, *The 1972 Munich Olympics and the Making of Modern Germany* (Berkeley: University of California Press, 2010);

Russ Crawford, *The Use of Sports to Promote the American Way of Life during the Cold War: Cultural Propaganda*, 1945–1963 (Lewiston, N.Y.: Edwin Mellen Press, 2010); Joseph M. Turrini, *The End of Amateurism in American Track and Field* (Urbana: University of Illinois Press, 2010); Nicholas Evan Sarantakes, *Dropping the Torch: Jimmy Carter, the Olympic Boycott, and the Cold War* (New York: Cambridge University Press, 2011); Mike Dennis and Jonathan Grix, *Sport under Communism: Behind the East German "Miracle"* (New York: Palgrave Macmillan, 2012); Stephen Wagg and David Andrews, eds., *East Plays West: Sport and the Cold War* (London: Taylor and Francis, 2012); Jeffrey Montez de Oca, *Discipline and Indulgence: College Football, Media, and the American Way of Life during the Cold War* (New Brunswick, N.J.: Rutgers University Press, 2013); Philip A. D'Agati, *The Cold War and the 1984 Olympic Games: A Soviet-American Surrogate War* (New York: Palgrave Macmillan, 2013); Heather Dichter and Andrew L. Johns, eds., *Diplomatic Games: Sport, Statecraft, and International Relations since 1945* (Lexington: University Press of Kentucky, 2014); Lindsay Parks Pieper, *Sex Testing: Gender Policing in Women's Sports* (Urbana: University of Illinois Press, 2016); Jenifer Parks, *The Olympic Games, the Soviet Sports Bureaucracy, and the Cold War: Red Sport, Red Tape* (Lanham, Md.: Lexington Books, 2017); Erin Elizabeth Redihan, *The Olympics and the Cold War, 1948–1968: Sport as Battleground in the US-Soviet Rivalry* (Jefferson, N.C.: McFarland, 2017); Stephen Wagg and David Andrews, eds., *East Plays West : Sport and the Cold War* (London: Taylor and Francis, 2012); Jules Boykoff, *Power Games: A Political History of the Olympics* (London: Verso, 2016); and John Peter Sugden, *Watching the Olympics: Politics, Power and Representation* (London: Routledge, 2012).

11. See "The Global History of Sport in the Cold War," Wilson Center, accessed March 14, 2018, https://www.wilsoncenter.org/article/the-global-history-sport-the-cold-war. See also the center's Sport in the Cold War podcast, available at http://digitalarchive.wilsoncenter.org/theme/sport-in-the-cold-war.

12. Henry R. Luce, "The American Century," *Life*, February 17, 1941, 61–65, quote on 65. Luce's editorial had a vibrant republication history and appeared in a number of widely read publications, including Henry R. Luce, *The American Century* (New York: Farrar and Rinehart, 1941). It appeared in a full-length version in the nation's leading newspaper: "The American Century," *New York Times*, March 4, 1941, 14–15. A condensed version of "The American Century," popped up in *Reader's Digest*, April 1941, 45–49. The US Congress included "The American Century" in its official record in 1914: US Congress, House, 77th Cong., 1st sess., *Congressional Record* 87, March 5, 1941, 1828–1831.

13. Luce quoted in Alan Brinkley, *The Publisher: Henry Luce and His American Century* (New York: Alfred A. Knopf, 2010), 401.

14. Donald J. Mrozek, *Sport and American Mentality, 1880–1910* (Knoxville: University of Tennessee Press, 1983); Mark Dyreson, *Making the American Team: Sport, Culture and the Olympic Experience* (Urbana: University of Illinois Press, 1998).

15. E. J. Hobsbawm, *Nations and Nationalism since 1780: Programme, Myth, Reality*, 2nd ed. (Cambridge: Cambridge University Press, 1992). On sport as a global arena for nationalism in the first half of the twentieth century, see Barbara Keys, *Globalizing Sport: National Rivalry and International Community in the 1930s* (Cambridge, Mass.: Harvard University Press, 2006); Richard Mandell, *The Nazi*

Olympics (New York: Macmillan, 1971); David Clay Large, *Nazi Games: The Olympics of 1936* (New York: W. W. Norton, 2007); Sandra Collins, *The 1940 Tokyo Games: The Missing Olympics—Japan, the Asian Olympics and the Olympic Movement* (London: Routledge, 2008); Alexander Kitroeff, *Wrestling with the Ancients: Modern Greek Identity and the Olympics* (New York: Greekworks.com, 2004); David Young, *The Modern Olympics: A Struggle for Revival* (Baltimore: Johns Hopkins University Press, 1996); Konstantinos Georgiadis, *Olympic Revival: The Revival of the Olympic Games in Modern Times* (Athens: Ekdotike Athenon, 2003); Daryl Adair and Wray Vamplew, *Sport in Australian History* (New York: Oxford University Press, 1997); Richard Cashman, *Sport in the National Imagination: Australian Sport in the Federation Decades* (Sydney: Walla Walla Press/Centre for Olympic Studies, the University of New South Wales, 2002); Peter Beck, *Scoring for Britain: International Football and International Politics* (London, Frank Cass, 1999); Matthew Llewellyn, *Rule Britannia: Nationalism, Identity, and the Modern Olympic Games* (London: Routledge, 2012); and Mark Dyreson, *Crafting Patriotism for Global Domination: America at the Olympic Games* (London: Routledge, 2009). For broad analyses of the Olympics and nationalism, see Maurice Roche, *Mega-Events and Modernity: Olympics and Expos in the Growth of Global Culture* (London: Routledge, 2000) and David Goldblatt, *The Games: A Global History of the Olympics* (New York: W. W. Norton, 2016).

16. The two finest comprehensive histories of the Olympics appeared as the Cold War ended. See Allen Guttmann, *The Olympics: A History of the Modern Games* (Urbana: University of Illinois Press, 1992); and Alfred Erich Senn, *Power, Politics, and the Olympic Games* (Champaign, Ill: Human Kinetics, 1999). Each provides an excellent view of Cold War Olympic intrigue while also showcasing the uncertainty of what might happen after the collapse of the Soviet empire. Goldblatt, *The Games: A Global History*, offers a fascinating post–Cold War perspective on recent developments. On the Seoul Olympics, see Brian Bridges, "The Seoul Olympics: Economic Miracle Meets the World," *International Journal of the History of Sport* 25, no. 14 (2008): 1939–1952; Gwang Ok, *The Transformation of Modern Korean Sport: Imperialism, Nationalism, Globalization* (Seoul: Hollym, 2007); Brian Bridges, *The Two Koreas and the Politics of Global Sport* (Boston: Brill, 2012); Victor D. Cha, *Beyond the Final Score: The Politics of Sport in Asia* (New York: Columbia University Press, 2009); and J.A. Mangan, Sandra S. Collins, and Gwang Ok, eds., The *Triple Asian Olympics—Asia Rising: The Pursuit of National Identity, International Recognition and Global Esteem* (London: Routledge, 2013). For medals counts in Seoul, see "1988 Summer Olympics Medal Table," accessed July 20, 2017, https://en.wikipedia.org/wiki/1988_Summer_Olympics_medal_table.

17. "1992 Summer Olympics Medal Table," https://en.wikipedia.org/wiki/1992_Summer_Olympics_medal_table; "1992 Winter Olympics Medal Table," https://en.wikipedia.org/wiki/1992_Winter_Olympics_medal_table. Both accessed July 20, 2017.

18. "1996 Summer Olympics Medal Table," accessed July 20, 2017, https://en.wikipedia.org/wiki/1996_Summer_Olympics_medal_table. Russia managed to stay on top in the 1994 Lillehammer winter games gold medal count, besting host Norway by eleven gold medals to Norway's ten; reunified Germany garnered nine medals. Norway won the overall count, with twenty-six, while Germany had twenty-four

and Russia twenty-three. "1994 Winter Olympics Medal Table," accessed July 20, 2017, https://en.wikipedia.org/wiki/1994_Winter_Olympics_medal_table.

19. Interestingly, after Russia the next highest of the former Soviet republics in the gold medal count were Ukraine, Kazakhstan, and Belarus, tied with three each. That put them in the same group with Canada, Spain, Turkey, and Iran. "1996 Summer Olympics Medal Table."

20. "2000 Summer Olympics Medal Table," accessed July 20, 2017, https://en.wikipedia.org/wiki/2000_Summer_Olympics_medal_table.

21. "2004 Summer Olympics Medal Table," https://en.wikipedia.org/wiki/2004_Summer_Olympics_medal_table; "2008 Summer Olympics Medal Table," https://en.wikipedia.org/wiki/2008_Summer_Olympics_medal_table; "2012 Summer Olympics Medal Table," https://en.wikipedia.org/wiki/2012_Summer_Olympics_medal_table; "2016 Summer Olympics Medal Table," https://en.wikipedia.org/wiki/2016_Summer_Olympics_medal_table. All accessed July 20, 2017.

22. "East Germany at the Olympics," https://en.wikipedia.org/wiki/East_Germany_at_the_Olympics; "Germany at the Olympics," https://en.wikipedia.org/wiki/Germany_at_the_Olympics. Both accessed July 20, 2017. See also Schiller and Young, *The 1972 Munich Olympics and the Making of Modern Germany*; Ungerleider, *Faust's Gold*; Riordan, *Sport under Communism*; Riordan, *Sport, Politics, and Communism*; and Alan McDougall, *The People's Game: Football, State and Society in East Germany* (Cambridge: Cambridge University Press, 2016).

23. In 1992, the Unified Team finished first, the United States was second, Germany third, and China fourth; "1992 Summer Olympics Medal Table." In 1996, the United States dominated the medal count, Russia was second, Germany third, China fourth, and France fifth; "1996 Summer Olympics Medal Table." In 2000, the United States again won, Russia came in second, China placed third, and Australia finished fourth; "2000 Summer Olympics Medal Table." In 2004, the United States triumphed, China was second, Russia third, and Australia fourth; "2004 Summer Olympics Medal Table." In 2008, China won the gold medal count while the United States won the overall count. Russia came in a distant third and Great Britain was fourth; "2008 Summer Olympics Medal Table." In 2012, the United States won handily, China came in second, and Great Britain was third; "2012 Summer Olympics Medal Table." In 2016, the United States again won by a substantial margin, Great Britain was second, and China slipped to third; "2016 Summer Olympics Medal Table," accessed July 21, 2017, https://en.wikipedia.org/wiki/2016_Summer_Olympics_medal_table.

24. "List of Countries by Projected GDP," Statistics Times, accessed March 14, 2018, http://statisticstimes.com/economy/countries-by-projected-gdp.php. Interestingly, the one nation for which rankings of gross domestic product (GDP) and Olympic medal production does not correlate is India. While India ranks sixth in the world in the 2017 GDP standings, it ranked 67th in the 2016 summer Olympic standings. Indeed, in the seven post–Cold War games, India has won only one gold medal, four silver medals, and nine bronze medals. If you subtract field hockey from the equation, where India has been a historic power with eight gold medals, one silver medal, and two bronze medals, India has managed only seventeen Olympic medals since it first debuted at the 1900 Paris games. "India at the Olympics," accessed July 22, 2017, https://en.wikipedia.org/wiki/India_at

_the_Olympics. India has grand plans to improve its Olympic output; see Manu Balachandran, "Great Expectations: India has Won Just 28 Olympic Medals in over a Century: It Now Aims to Win 50 in Just 8 Years," *Quartz*, September 22, 2016, accessed July 22, 2017, https://qz.com/787153/india-has-won-just-28-olympic-medals-over-a-century-it-now-aims-to-win-50-in-just-8-years/. For a fascinating historical perspective, see, Boria Majumdar and Nalin Mehta, *India and the Olympics* (London: Routledge, 2009).

25. "Cuba at the Olympics," accessed July 22, 2017, https://en.wikipedia.org/wiki/Cuba_at_the_Olympics.

26. Andrew D. Morris, "'I Can Compete!' China in the Olympic Games, 1932 and 1936," *Journal of Sport History* 26, no. 3 (1999): 545–566; and Andrew D. Morris, *Marrow of the Nation: A History of Sport and Physical Culture in Republican China* (Berkeley: University of California Press, 2004).

27. "China at the Olympics," July 22, 2017, https://en.wikipedia.org/wiki/China_at_the_Olympics; "2008 Summer Olympics," accessed July 22, 2017, https://en.wikipedia.org/wiki/2008_Summer_Olympics. The Chinese totals were later reduced to forty-eight golds and ninety-eight overall medals after three champion weightlifters lost gold medals due to positive tests for performance-enhancing substances. "List of Stripped Olympic Medals," accessed July 22, 2017, https://en.wikipedia.org/wiki/List_of_stripped_Olympic_medals#Medals_stripped_by_country. On China's ideas about the Olympics, see Susan Brownell, *Training the Body for China: Sports in the Moral Order of the Peoples Republic* (Chicago: University of Chicago Press, 1995); Brownell, *Beijing's Games*; and Xu, *Olympic Dreams*.

28. "2012 Summer Olympics Medal Table"; "2016 Summer Olympics Medal Table."

29. Mark Kiszla, "China, US Golden Rivals," *Denver Post*, August 1, 2012, B1.

30. Mark Dyreson, "Reading American Readings of the Beijing Olympics: US Interpretations of the China 'Threat,'" *International Journal of the History of Sport* 27, no. 14–15 (2010): 2510–2519; Mark Dyreson, "World Harmony or an Athletic 'Clash of Civilizations'? Nationalism versus Transnationalism in Olympic Spectacles," *International Journal of the History of Sport* 29, no. 9 (2012): 1231–1242; Mark Dyreson, "Preparing to Take Credit for China's Glory: American Perspectives on the Beijing Olympic Games," *International Journal of the History of Sport* 25, no. 7 (2008): 915–934.

31. Critics make these claims despite considerable success by the Chinese women's volleyball team, which includes three gold medals (1984, 2004, 2016) one silver medal, and two bronze medals since 1984. "China Women's National Volleyball Team," https://en.wikipedia.org/wiki/China_women%27s_national_volleyball_team. China's women's soccer team has won a silver medal and China's women's basketball team has won silver and bronze medals. "China Women's National Football Team," https://en.wikipedia.org/wiki/China_women%27s_national_football_team; "China Women's National Basketball Team," https://en.wikipedia.org/wiki/China_women%27s_national_basketball_team. All accessed July 21, 2017.

32. "Beach Volleyball at the Summer Olympics," accessed July 21, 2017, https://en.wikipedia.org/wiki/Beach_volleyball_at_the_Summer_Olympics.

33. Mark Dyreson, *Crafting Patriotism for Global Domination*; Mark Dyreson, "The

Republic of Consumption at the Olympic Games: Globalization, Americanization, and Californization," *Journal of Global History* 8, no. 2 (2013): 256–278; Mark Dyreson, "Johnny Weissmuller and the Old Global Capitalism: The Origins of the Federal Blueprint for Selling American Culture to the World," *International Journal of the History of Sport* 25, no. 2 (2008): 268–283; Mark Dyreson, "Marketing Weissmuller to the World: Hollywood's Olympics and Federal Schemes for Americanization through Sport," *International Journal of the History of Sport* 25, no. 2 (2008): 284–306; Mark Dyreson, "Crafting Patriotism–Meditations on 'Californication' and Other Trends," *International Journal of the History of Sport* 25, no. 2 (2008): 307–311; Mark Dyreson, "Globalizing American Sporting Culture: The US Government Plan to Conquer the World Sports Market in the 1930s," *Sportwissenschaft: The German Journal of Sport Science* 34, no. 2 (2004): 145–151; Dyreson, "Reading American Readings of the Beijing Olympics"; and Dyreson, "World Harmony or an Athletic 'Clash of Civilizations'?"

34. Dyreson, "Reading American Readings of the Beijing Olympics"; Dyreson, "World Harmony or an Athletic 'Clash of Civilizations'?"; Dyreson, "Preparing to Take Credit for China's Glory."

35. "Total Medal Count: Summer and Winter Olympics, [USA and USSR]," Great-Sports-Rivalries.com, accessed July 23, 2017, http://www.great-sports-rivalries.com/usa-ussr.html; Matt Ford, "The Geopolitics of Winter Olympic Medal Counts: Can Russia Reclaim Its Former Olympic Glory?" *Atlantic Monthly*, February 2014, accessed July 23, 2017, https://www.theatlantic.com/international/archive/2014/02/the-geopolitics-of-winter-olympic-medal-counts/283552/.

36. "China at the Olympics."

37. "United States at the Olympics," accessed July 23, 2017, https://en.wikipedia.org/wiki/United_States_at_the_Olympics.

38. Photographs of the Fort McHenry "Stars and Stripes" timeline.

39. The semi-autobiographical hagiography that Phelps and his chroniclers have developed revels in his transformation from an awkward working-class teenager into a world-beating American hero, the epitome of the gospel of neoliberalism. Through sheer willpower, he apparently transformed himself from a scrawny and troubled adolescent born into the sinking working class into an unbeatable titan and a global brand. See, particularly, the many editions of these two gems (latest versions cited): Alan Abrahamson and Michael Phelps, *No Limits: The Will to Succeed* (New York: Free Press, 2014); and Michael Phelps and Brian Cazeneuve, *Beneath the Surface: My Story* (New York: Sports Publishing, 2016). Indeed, had Walter LaFeber, the doyen of American foreign policy historians during the Cold War, not already fixed on Michael Jordan to illustrate the rise of neoliberalism in the post–Cold War universe in *Michael Jordan and the New Global Capitalism* (New York: Norton, 1999) and waited a few years, he would have been hard pressed not to substitute Phelps for Jordan. Given Phelps's adoration for Jordan in his semi-autobiographies and his oft-stated desire to be included next to Jordan atop the pantheon of this era's über-competitors, perhaps an edition of *Michael Phelps and the New Global Capitalism* is not an impossibility.

40. David Johnson, "Michael Phelps Has Won More Gold Medals than These 66 Countries," *Time*, August 12, 2016, accessed May 11, 2017, http://time.com/4446971/rio-2016-olympics-michael-phelps-gold-medals/; Erika Espinoza, "What if Michael

Phelps Was His Own Country?" *Chicago Tribune*, August 17, 2016, accessed July 5, 2017, http://www.chicagotribune.com/sports/international/; Greg Myre, "If Michael Phelps Were A Country, Where Would His Gold Medal Tally Rank?" *National Public Radio*, August 14, 2016, accessed June 22, 2017, http://www.npr.org/sections/thetorch/2016/08/14/489832779/if-michael-phelps-were-a-country-where-would-his-gold-medal-tally-rank; Chris Chase, "28 Incredible Facts about Michael Phelps' 28 Olympic Medals," *Fox Sports*, October 20, 2016, accessed March 14, 2018, http://www.foxsports.com/olympics/gallery/28-incredible-facts-about-michael-phelps-28-olympic-medals-23-golds-count-how-many-081316; Cork Gaines, "Only 12 Countries Have Won More Gold Medals than Michael Phelps in the Last 4 Summer Olympics, *Business In*sider, August 9, 2016, accessed May 10, 2017, http://www.businessinsider.com/michael-phelps-summer-olympics-gold-gold-more-gold-2016-8; "Rio 2016: Where Michael Phelps Rates Compared to Other Nations at Olympics," *Fox Sports*, August 13, 2016, accessed June 10, 2017, https://www.foxsports.com.au/olympics/rio-2016-where-michael-phelps-rates-compared-to-other-nations-at-olympics/news-story/e493456031284ad4e15b2218532dddd5; Tim Layden, "The Gold Standard," *Sports Illustrated*, December 26, 2016, 30–37.

41. Johnson, "Michael Phelps Has Won More Gold Medals than These 66 Countries."

42. "Michael Phelps Raced a Great White Shark and Lived to Tell about It," SBNation July 23, 2017, accessed July 30, 2017, https://www.sbnation.com/lookit/2017/7/23/16017978/michael-phelps-raced-a-great-white-shark-video; "Michael Phelps Didn't Actually Race a Real Shark on TV, and Viewers Aren't Happy," *Washington Post*, July 24, 2017, accessed July 30, 2017, https://www.washingtonpost.com/news/arts-and-entertainment/wp/2017/07/24/michael-phelps-didnt-actually-race-a-real-shark-on-tv-and-viewers-arent-happy/; "Michael Phelps vs. a Great White Shark: Here's What Happened," *Hollywood Reporter*, July 23, 2017, accessed July 30, 2017, www.hollywoodreporter.com/.../michael-phelps-a-great-white-shark-heres-what-happ; "Watch: Michael Phelps Loses to a Shark in an Epic Race," *Sports Illustrated*, July 23, 2017, accessed July 30, 2017, https://www.si.com/olympics/2017/07/23/michael-phelps-races-great-white-shark-video.

43. "Michael Phelps," accessed July 27, 2017, https://en.wikipedia.org/wiki/Michael_Phelps.

44. Mark Dyreson, "Region and Race: The Legacies of the St. Louis Olympics," *International Journal of the History of Sport* 32, no. 14 (2015): 1697–1707; Mark Dyreson, "Crafting Patriotism–America at the Olympic Games," *International Journal of the History of Sport* 25 (2008): 135–141; Mark Dyreson, "Return to the Melting Pot: An Old American Olympic Story," *Olympika: The International Journal of Olympic Studies* 12 (2003): 122; Mark Dyreson, "Olympic Games and Historical Imagination: Notes from the Fault Line of Tradition and Modernity," *Olympika: The International Journal of Olympic Studies* 7 (1998): 25–41; Mark Dyreson, "Scripting the American Olympic Story-Telling Formula: The 1924 Paris Olympic Games and the American Media," *Olympika: The International Journal of Olympic Studies* 5 (1996): 45–80; Dyreson, "The Republic of Consumption at the Olympic Games"; Dyreson, Making the American Team."

Contributors

Toby C. Rider is associate professor of kinesiology at California State University, Fullerton. He is the author of *Cold War Games: Propaganda, the Olympics, and US Foreign Policy* (2016), and the co-director of the Center for Sociocultural Sport and Olympic Research.

Kevin B. Witherspoon is professor of history at Lander University, where he was named distinguished professor in 2014. His book *Before the Eyes of the World: Mexico and the 1968 Olympics* won the 2009 North American Society for Sport History annual book award. His current research focuses on the US-Soviet sports rivalry during the Cold War.

Kate Aguilar is a PhD candidate in history at the University of Connecticut, where she studies racial formation, gender, sport, and political culture in the United States after 1945. Her dissertation, which focuses on the University of Miami's football team, the Hurricanes, analyzes the central place of football in the development of the New Right in the 1980s and the significance of transnational histories of South Florida and the Caribbean to Ronald Reagan's particular brand of conservatism and the masculine national identity it fostered.

Cat Ariail received her PhD in history from the University of Miami. Her dissertation, "Sprints of Citizenship: Black Women Track Stars and the Making of Modern Citizenship in the United States and Jamaica, 1946–1964," analyzes how the experiences of black women track athletes illuminate the rethinking of the raced and gendered boundaries of citizenship in the postwar era.

Robert K. Barney is professor emeritus at Western University in London, Ontario. He is founder of the International Centre for Olympic Studies and the scholarly journal *Olympika: The International Journal of Olympic Studies*. He is the senior author of the award-winning book *Selling the Five Rings: The International Olympic Committee and the Rise of Olympic Commercialism*.

Nevada Cooke is a PhD student in the Department of Kinesiology at the University of Western Ontario. His current research focuses on US participation in the Olympics during the Ford administration and amateur sport and late Cold War sport policy in America.

Brad Congelio is assistant professor and director of the Sport Leadership and Management Graduate Program at Keystone College. He was the 2013 recipient of the Ian Buchanan Memorial Scholarship from the International Society of Olympic Historians.

Heather L. Dichter is associate professor of sport management in the Leicester Castle Business School at De Montfort University and a member of the International Centre for Sports History and Culture. She co-edited *Diplomatic Games: Sport, Statecraft, and International Relations since 1945* and *Olympic Reform: Ten Years Later* and has published several journal articles on sport in occupied and Cold War Germany.

Mark Dyreson is professor of kinesiology and history at Pennsylvania State University. He is the author of several books and numerous articles on the history of modern sport, a fellow of the US National Academy of Kinesiology, managing editor of the *International Journal of the History of Sport*, and co-editor of the Sport in Global Society: Historical Perspectives book series published by Routledge.

Dennis Gildea, a professor of communications at Springfield College (the birthplace of basketball), is the author of *Hoop Crazy: The Lives of Clair Bee and Chip Hilton* (2013). He has published in *Aethlon: Journal of Sports Literature, American Journalism, Colby Quarterly, International Ski History Bulletin, and Journal of Intercollegiate Sport* and has published chapters in several sport history books. Prior to earning a PhD in mass communication at Penn State, he was a sportswriter and news reporter for thirteen years.

John Gleaves is associate professor in the Department of Kinesiology at California State University, Fullerton. His research focuses on ethical and historical issues relating to performance-enhancing drugs in sports. He is the editor of two books and the author of numerous peer-reviewed articles. He is currently the co-director of the International Network of Humanistic Doping Research and the co-director of the Center for Sociocultural Sport and Olympic Research. He is the coauthor, with Matthew Llewellyn, of *The Rise and Fall of Olympic Amateurism* (2016).

Thomas M. Hunt is associate professor in the Department of Kinesiology and Health Education at the University of Texas at Austin. Hunt is the author of *Drug Games: The International Olympic Committee and the Politics of Doping, 1960–2008* (2011) and the assistant director for academic affairs at the H. J. Lutcher Stark Center for Physical Culture and Sports.

Matthew P. Llewellyn is a professor in the Department of Kinesiology at California State University, Fullerton. He is the author of over thirty articles in refereed journals and the coauthor of *The Rise and Fall of Olympic Amateurism* (2016). He is the co-director of the Center for Sociocultural Sport and Olympic Research.

Lindsay Parks Pieper is associate professor of sport management at the University of Lynchburg in Virginia. She is the author of *Sex Testing: Gender Policing in Women's Sports* (2016).

Damion Thomas is the museum curator of sports for the Smithsonian National Museum of African American History and Culture. He is the author of *Globetrotting: African American Athletes and Cold War Politics* (2012).

Index

P

www.ingramcontent.com/pod-product-compliance
Lightning Source LLC
LaVergne TN
LVHW091106080826
845145LV00008B/1829